TO BE LOVED

BERRY GORDY

TO BE LOVED

THE MUSIC, THE MAGIC, THE MEMORIES OF MOTOWN

AN AUTOBIOGRAPHY

WARNER BOOKS

A Time Warner Company

Copyright acknowledgments appear on pages 423–426.

Copyright © 1994 by Berry Gordy

Warner Books, Inc., 1271 Avenue of the Americas, New York, NY 10020

W A Time Warner Company

Printed in the United States of America
First Printing: October 1994
10 9 8 7 6 5 4 3 2 1

Library of Congress Cataloging-in-Publication Data

Gordy, Berry.
  To be loved : the music, the magic, the memories of Motown : an
autobiography / Berry Gordy.
      p.   cm.
  ISBN 0-446-51523-X
  1. Gordy, Berry. 2. Sound recording executives and producers—
United States—Biography. 3. Motown Record Corporation.
I. Title.
ML429.G67A3 1994
781.644'092—dc20
[B]
                                                                94-29067
                                                                CIP
                                                                MN

Book design by Giorgetta Bell McRee

to my sisters Gwen and Anna,
who think they own me—
and they do

CONTENTS

CONTENTS

ACKNOWLEDGMENTS

When I started writing this book I thought it was no different from any other creative project that I attacked: a song, a screenplay, a stage play, a TV special or a live show. I figured that as long as I was honest and put everything down as it happened in a creative way that was all there was to it. Not so. I ended up having to put a team together just as I did to run my company.

Over the years, whether it was making records or movies or developing business policies, I've worked with some of the best. This has never been more true than of those who supported me in writing this book.

Like me, many of the people working on the book had never been involved with writing one before. Lucky for me the first person I want to thank was one who had. Thank you, Mim Eichler, for teaching me so much about structure, design and generally just putting a book together. Also for your dedication, attitude, and oh yes, your resilience.

I want to thank three longtime Motown employees for their continued loyal dedication: Brenda M. Boyce—among other things for doing a superhuman job of research, interviews, fact finding and document checking. Rebecca Jiles-Davidson—for transcribing and organizing hours and hours of audio- and videotapes to near perfection and without complaint. Fay Janet Hale—for transcribing twenty- to thirty-year-old meeting tapes and for helping to select and document photographs taken throughout the years. Brenda, Rebecca, and Fay, not only was your loyalty the lifeblood of Motown, but for the book as well.

Martina Gruber, for helping to organize my ideas, focusing on concepts that were turning points in my life, and for challenging me to answer tough questions.

Marianne Partridge, journalistic veteran, for overseeing the organization and selection of photographs, and for bringing your great editorial sensibilities and literary experience to the project.

To my friend and adviser Ewart Abner, thank you for your passionate storytelling about the past that inspired me so much.

To Linda Palmer, busy professional writer and longtime friend, who came in as an editorial assistant for the last six months of the project and worked practically around the clock proofreading and copyediting my constantly changing manuscript. You were that breath of fresh air we needed at such a critical time.

And Christie Burton. When I first met you I was amazed at how much you knew about Motown music. You've continued to amaze me as you've risen to every challenge I've thrown your way. During the years of this book's development I discovered you are a natural-born writer and editor. You took on the job of book manager, handling everybody's problems, keeping the team together and keeping me together. And being my biggest critic, you made sure my writing stayed true to me. I would have to write another chapter to list all the ways you've contributed to this project. I love you. I am so fortunate to have you in my life.

SPECIAL THANKS TO:

Edna Anderson, for lending your keen insights, keeping the rest of the business running smoothly at the same time, and for conducting some of the first interviews.

Suzanne de Passe, who encouraged me to write this book in the first place. Your ideas and thoughts were so invaluable, it's hard to imagine what the book would've been without you. You never let me take the easy way out of telling the real story.

Mario Escobar, for doing a brilliant job behind the camera and in the darkroom and, as part of my permanent staff, for so many other things important to the book. Video librarian Donna Merchant, for pinch-hitting on transcription and research. To Randy Robbins for overseeing the numerous video interviews shot at my home, for your technological expertise in every aspect of this book, including interfacing a computer system with this project in ways everyone else had told me couldn't be done.

To the current staffs at Jobete Music and the Gordy Company, for your prompt attention to our research questions.

My niece Iris Gordy for sharing documents, memories and helping in so many ways. And Susan Hendler for jumping into the project wherever you were needed. David Ritz whose original outline gave me a place to start and made the blank page less ominous. Billie Jean Brown for helping to prod my memory with your recollections.

To Ron Fauntleroy for doing such a great job handling so many corporate and family matters for me during the writing of the book.

I am most grateful to Nanscy Neiman, Warner Books Vice President, publisher and the editor who guided this project from beginning to end, and for going along with my "crazy" ideas that made this project seem like a bottomless pit. And to the phenomenal team at Warner Books who took this project very seriously in every detail.

MORE SPECIAL THANKS:

To those who gave interviews, whether on the phone, on camera, or in person, you not only enriched the book but touched me deeply in recalling so many of the wonderful experiences we shared: Al Abrams, Barney Ales, Gil Askey, Danny Bakewell, Robert Bateman, Shelly Berger, Paul Bloch, Angelo Bond, Thomas "Beans" Bowles, Janie Bradford-Hobbs, Elaine Brown, Chris Clark, Dick Clark, Rob Cohen, Guy Costa, Hal Davis, Roquel Billy Davis, Ann Dozier, Harvey Fuqua, Sidney Furie, Junius Griffin, Calvin Harris, Frances

Heard-Maclin, Brian Holland, Janet Hubbard-Luck, Willie Hutch, Jermaine Jackson, Jesse Jackson, Marv Johnson, Bob Jones, Phil Jones, Maurice King, Gladys Knight, Nancy Leiviska, Miller London, Magnificent Montague, Jerry Moss, Tom Noonan, Harold Noveck, Sidney Noveck, Martha Reeves, Deke Richards, Paul Riser, Smokey Robinson, Michael Roshkind, Diana Ross, George Schiffer, George Schlatter, Dick Scott, Ralph Seltzer, Raynoma Singleton, Daniel Skouras, Gary Smith, Armin Steiner, William "Mickey" Stevenson, Barrett Strong, Russ Terrana, Jean Terrell, Marjorie Wallace, Georgia Ward, Mira Waters, Norman Whitfield, Billy Dee Williams, Stevie Wonder. And to Harry Balk who did a wonderful job running A&R in Detroit when I left for California and, among other things, developed the group Rare Earth.

And thanks to all the people who supported Motown in the early years, including: George Albert and the folks at *Cash Box* magazine; John H. Johnson and Bob Johnson of *Jet* and *Ebony* magazines; the DJs, the retailers, the rackjobbers and the independent distributors who made it possible for us to get our records out to the public in the first place.

THANKS TO ANOTHER GREAT TEAM:

Roger Campbell, when I met you at the Century Plaza Hotel almost thirty years ago you were a limo driver. What I saw in you never changed—your goodness, your qualities of character, your dedication. Now my longtime chief of staff and close friend, I thank you for your loyalty throughout the years. To Les Peterson for working so hard with me and making it all look easy, for your dedication and calm, even in the eyes of so many storms. To Andrew Davis, protective, smart, funny and the most clever Dirty Hearts player I've ever seen, for serving me and Motown well for many years. And Tony Greene, who is so special, one of a kind, always worried about things being just right.

A very special thank-you to Angelo Fernando, my wonderful chef, for keeping not only me but the entire book staff healthy and strong during our dramatic ordeal.

THANKS TO FAMILY AND FRIENDS:

Robert Gordy for always caring so much about me. George Gordy, my older brother, whom I always admired and looked up to. Even today you are one of the few people who can soothe me when I'm troubled. Esther Gordy Edwards for your memory, your great record-keeping and your attention to detail. My cousins, Gwen Joyce Fuller, who's always been a sister to me, and my dear, dear Evelyn Turk-Johnson.

And to my beloved kids—Hazel, Berry IV, Terry, Kerry, Sherry, Kennedy, Rhonda and Stefan—our relationships are more precious to me than any words I could say here. And to my grandchildren. I love you all.

Loving gratitude goes to my ex-wife Grace Gordy. Though our paths have taken different turns, thank you for being there during some of the difficult times I've written about and for urging me to stay with the writing.

To Sy Weintraub, Gary Judis, Sidney Poitier, Hugh Hefner—just thanks.

To Suzee Ikeda—when you started as a singer I never expected that you'd turn into the great protégé and assistant to me that you became. Your integrity and constant support are qualities I have always appreciated. And to Melvin Franklin, a loyal and rare man whose loving ways have never changed.

To the very, very special Ron Garnett. I shall never forget you.

Also in memory of my oldest brother, Fuller, for being the first in so many ways—the firstborn, the first boxer, the first songwriter and the first clown, entertaining us with all your different characters, including "Mr. Koochenheimer," that hunched-over little man with the German accent who always made us laugh. Mr. Koochenheimer, we miss you.

AUTHOR'S NOTE

Even with extensive research, interviews, audio- and videotapes, meeting notes, memos and all the other sources of information to jog my memory, there are still some important unsung heroes I am bound to not mention. I apologize. I never intended to write a documentary. I wrote everything from memory, pulling from all this documented material, aiming for truth and accuracy in depicting the spirit and intent of what was said and done at the time.

PREFACE

I am not your average writer. I've never written a book before. In fact, I haven't even read that many. I never had time.

I had learned a long time ago it was much more comfortable staying out of the public eye. But after thirty years the misconceptions about me and Motown became so great I finally had to deal with them.

Those closest to me had been after me for years to set the record straight, but the time was never right—now it is. I thought about so many people I've admired who had not had (or taken) the time to tell their own stories in their own words. I could see that history was judging them not by their truth but by what was being written in books by others. It was then I realized how fortunate I was to be able to put down on paper my own life story—not only for me and my family, but for those many unsung heroes without whom there would not have been a Motown.

When I started this book I had no idea what I was in for. My wonderful agent, Norman Brokaw, of the William Morris Agency, put me together with Larry Kirshbaum and Nanscy Neiman of Warner Books. I liked them. Nanscy, becoming my editor, told me I could do the book in "about a year." What a liar! But she paid for it by chasing after me for the manuscript over the next five. And she gave me such brilliant input along the way I had no choice but to forgive her.

I knew I had to devote a lot of time to reliving history. When I began to look back and unravel the past thirty years of Motown I realized I first had to unravel me, Berry Gordy—who I was, how I did what I did, and who I became.

Many people believe that dreams like Motown just don't come true. Well, *To Be Loved* is the story of one that did.

PART ONE

YOU ARE YOU

YOU ARE YOU

You are you—
That's all that matters to me.

You are you—
And only you can be the one I love and yearn for,
the one that my heart burns for.

Yes, you are you—
And that makes you best of all.

Never wished that you were more beautiful
More lovely or a star
For God made all your features
I love you as you are

Yes, you are you—
And that makes you best of all.

BERRY GORDY, JR.

1

SUCCESS IS A MF

THAT PERIOD OF TIME before the selling of my company was probably the most confusing of my life.

It was about a month before I would surrender my title as chairman of the board of Motown Records. As I made my way through the heavy wooden doors of our eighteenth-floor corporate offices I could feel the panic. It was everywhere—a quiet panic. Negotiations with MCA were supposed to be secret, but the daily leaks to the press were so accurate they seemed phony.

Fay Hale, a black woman in her fifties, one of the many unsung heroes of Motown, greeted me in the lobby with a cheerful "Good Morning," and her everyday beaming smile. But her eyes gave her away. She was petrified. For almost thirty years she, like so many others, had been loyal to *me*. For almost thirty years she had fought every president of the record company, including me, to keep us from overshipping and overpaying. I knew she loved me and she knew I

3

loved her. I also knew she knew she was about to lose her job—her life. Yet, she and I chatted as if nothing was happening.

The impending doom was felt by everyone. Especially by my son, Berry IV, who had hoped someday to run the company. But he had been through this before.

A year and a half earlier I had come close to selling. But the day before I was to sign the papers, I changed my mind. I couldn't go through with it. MCA had offered me more money than I could spend in a lifetime, but I just didn't want to give it up at that time. All those restrictions they put in the contract didn't help either: "Refrain from the record business for five years," "refrain from using your name," "refrain," "forbid," "shall not engage." *Yeah? Well, shall not sign. How's that?*

MCA was shocked and so was I. But it seems the fighter inside me had taken over. That night, December 30, 1986, I passed on the deal even though my company was losing millions.

When the news broke that I had refused to sell, people were overjoyed. Calls and letters came from all over the world telling me how much Motown was loved, respected, and how our music had touched their lives. This outpouring of love and admiration was overwhelming. It made me feel like a hero or something just because I didn't sell.

I got psyched. I would answer the bell one more time and come out fighting, creating new hits just like the old days.

Get everybody together! Get inspired, perspired, fired up, go for the throat! We need hits. No. Smashes! That's the only way—smash product.

There had always been a standing debate in our company as to which was more important—Creative or Marketing. Creative had always won. Our slogan, "It's what's in the grooves that counts," was proven right over and over again. Great records had always solved any and all problems for me. But gung ho as I was—marshaling forces, reshuffling and bringing in manpower, digging in at the studio—that had not been enough. Times had changed.

Now, some seventeen months later, as I gazed from my office window across the forest of corporate buildings to the Capitol Records tower, I realized many of them, too, were in the process of being taken over. Everybody was either buying or selling.

Technology was moving faster than the speed of light. Global communications, cable, satellite dishes, computerization and digitalization were the new order of the day. A video of a song could now be played once for 200 million people and if 1 percent bought the record you had a two million seller, a super hit by any standard.

Conglomerates were taking over. These multicorporate entities, with their dominating distribution capabilities and their powerful foothold in a radically changing world economy, had the edge. A big edge.

For years we had shown the world what we could do with talent and ingenuity as our base. And now these new corporate entities were showing me what they could do with money and power as theirs. I, who had prided myself on always being ahead of the game, had fallen behind. My company was in no position to take advantage of these new developments. We had too much overhead and had to gross $40 million a year just to break even.

Selling wasn't just the right thing to do, it was the only thing to do.

I shifted my eyes from the window to the gleaming baby grand in my office. It seemed to be saying "Come let me soothe you." I went over, sat down and started running over some chord changes that had formed the foundation of many songs I had written. As I pounded away at those simple chords, humming and singing anything that came to mind, I was back to basics—and comfortable.

The realization of what I had accomplished first brought pride, then sadness. Sadness because now I understood the real reason I was in trouble. It wasn't the conglomerates. It wasn't the technology and the changing world. The world had been changing since the day I was born. The real reason was, I was just tired. I didn't want to do it anymore. It had long stopped being fun for me.

When I started out I was doing about 90 percent Creative and 10 percent Business. As the years went on the percentages more than switched; and now, doing about 98 percent Business and 2 percent Creative, I was stuck and I hated it.

The explosion of so many things at the same time, the industry, the artists, the music, together with the normal internal and external problems that growth presents, had finally caught up with me. On top of all that were over two decades of rumors, gossip and misinformation that I had never taken time to deal with. "Let others say and write what they want. We'll take the high road—stay on course," I used to say.

Though I tried to be strong and take it all in stride, the rumors about my cheating the artists always bothered me the most. I knew someday I would definitely have to clear that one up.

Thoughts of the past were bombarding me, but they couldn't overcome the problems of the present. "What do they mean I can't sell my own company?" I had yelled at my secretary, Edna Anderson, a few days before. Edna knew everything there was to know about the street. Her black militancy had not mellowed much in the sixteen years she had been my right arm.

"They say Motown is too important. It means too much to too many people to sell," she said. "It's an institution. How can you sell a way of life?"

"They say! Who in the fuck is they? Do they know I'm losing millions?" My voice had jumped into high C. She knew when that happened it was time to back off. She said nothing. "How in the hell can anybody tell me I can't sell something I created, nurtured and built from nothing?"

Edna watched me for a moment, then came over and put her hand on my shoulder and said in her all too familiar sarcastic, Southern drawl, "Success is a MF, ain't it?" If she had said "motherfucker" I would have probably laughed out loud.

But as it was I smiled, knowing she knew I knew very well who they were. They were the people who had grown up with Motown and loved it the same as I did. They were the people who believed in me and Motown no matter what they had heard or read in the newspapers. They were the people who believed—and rightly so—that Motown was a dream that happened to have come true. They were the fans who collected every record we made from day one. They were employees, the dedicated people who I knew would go down on any ship I was commanding. They were the white people

6

around the world whose main connection to black culture had been through our music. *They* were the black people around the world who felt their heritage was being sold down the drain. Yes, I knew who *they* were.

My anger just as quickly turned to gratitude for all those who were letting me know that after almost thirty years the legend of my company and the music we made was now even bigger than ever. I knew I had to protect that legacy.

Still banging on the piano I started reflecting back to the early sixties, to a house at 2648 West Grand Boulevard in Detroit. A place we called "Hitsville U.S.A." There was no way our purpose was vague.

The "Hitsville" sign over the door let it be known that if you set foot inside you were expected to sing, dance, write, produce, sell or manage. That name kept our mission in focus. I knew something very dynamic was taking place. This thing was becoming a force to be reckoned with and I was its leader. The successes, the challenges and our determination were meshing together into something tangible. It was turning me into a real boss. I said and others did. I complained and they strained to do better. I was pushing and driving people beyond their sense of what was possible. I expected more— they gave more. Our work was producing results that gave me confidence, even more confidence than I already had.

The mixing of our respective talents inside those walls gave me my first taste of something that I would grow quite used to—power. The irony was that it would slowly transfer from me to the artists, the people I used it for. I had never realized there was such a thin line between their having to laugh at my jokes and my having to laugh at theirs. One day you wake up and the stars you polished so hard to shine are not only shining but in orbit—out of control of themselves and *in* control of you.

Power—its uses and misuses—is something that has fascinated me over the years. My first encounter with it came when I was very young.

2

WHERE I CAME FROM

DETROIT 1938

POWER

THAT NIGHT THE HOUSE erupted with joy. The whole family exploded out the front door, down the steps, into the streets, jumping and hollering like a bunch of crazy folks! Echoes of the announcer's voice were still ringing in my ears: "Left to the body, right to the head, left, right, left—a smashing right to the chin. He's down. He's down. Schmeling is down! Three . . . Four . . . Five . . . Six . . . Seven . . . Eight . . . Nine . . . He's out . . . Max Schmeling is knocked out! . . . The winner and still heavyweight champion of the world, the brown bomber, Joe Louis!" Euphoria everywhere. Horns honking, streets filled with madness! Everybody was reacting the same as we were: Joy—Pride—Ecstasy!!!

"How could I ever do anything in my life that could make this many people happy," I thought to myself.

This was not just a fight, this was tradition. Whenever Joe Louis fought it was a holiday for black folks. Before, as a toddler, I had always been swept up in the euphoria of the moment, feeling what everyone else was feeling—yet not knowing exactly why. But this time it was different. A lot different. This fight had been perceived by everyone as a superpower contest between America, the land of the free, and Nazi Germany.

I was only eight at the time, but I knew Joe Louis was a hero, a hero of *all* the people, but he was black like me. I knew what that meant. Even at eight years old I had gotten a taste of the world— the real world—the white world.

That same night I watched my brothers and sisters running off to roam the neighborhood with their friends while I sat down on the street curb remembering back to when I was almost five and thought the world was all black except for Santa Claus. I thought the few white people who came to our neighborhood were accidents of nature. But then around the time I started kindergarten, I was jolted into reality, not once but twice.

Christmas had always been the most magical day of the year for me. The night before was never one when Mother had to make me go to bed on time. As quick as it seemed my eyes had closed, they were open again. Rushing downstairs into wonderland, I always found things I wanted.

If I didn't get exactly what I asked for, I knew it was because I hadn't been good enough. Santa was the one person I could never fool. And one Christmas I found out why.

Pushing down the sidewalk on my brand-new bright red scooter I shouted to a kid from the neighborhood, "Look what Santa brought me!"

"Junior. You know it ain't no Santa Claus, don't you?" he yelled.

"Oh yes there is!" I replied. "And he knows when you are bad, too."

He laughed, motioning to some other kids, "Junior still believes in Santa Claus."

"Then where do all these presents come from?"

"Your father put 'em there, stupid."

I rushed home and told my sister Gwen what had just happened. When she said he was right I was devastated, but acted like it was no big deal. I told her I really knew it all the time. I was dying inside, realizing the wonderment I had known on that special morning would never be again. A fraud. I had been betrayed. Betrayed by—of all people—my own parents. Why?

I didn't understand how my parents could carry on such a lie and hurt me like that. I must have been real smart at that young age because after a week or so it became clear: because they loved me, and wanted to see me thrilled and happy. That was the good news. The bad news was, I would now automatically question everything anybody told me—including my own parents.

Only in retrospect would I fully recognize the irony of my having felt betrayed by Mother and Pop. After all, this was during the Great Depression and to be able to create that vision of wonderland for us, to be able to give each of the children something special on Christmas Day, Mother and Pop had to sacrifice and save all year long, with Pop sometimes working four jobs at a time. Not only that, they didn't even take the credit for it. They gave it to Santa Claus.

I thought there could be nothing worse than no Santa Claus. I was wrong.

A short time later, I discovered the world was not all black. Worse, it was all white except for a few "other" people. And we were considered the lowest class of those "other" people—"Niggers." I didn't know exactly what that word meant but I knew it was real bad.

I remember rushing home from school one day telling my mother a white boy had called me one.

"Sticks and stones may break my bones but names will never hurt me," is all she said.

Though her words were strong and gave me comfort at the time, I still felt bad.

At school most of the kids were black—we called ourselves colored then—but all the teachers were white. They were the bosses and had all the right answers. They had us read stories. There was *Snow White and the Seven Dwarfs*, *Little Red Riding Hood*, *Cinderella* and *Prince Charming*. And then there was *Little Black Sambo*.

At the movies I also found the heroes were all white: Shirley Temple, Clark Gable, Errol Flynn, Tarzan, the Cowboys, the President! And then there was Stepin Fetchit. Negroes were caricatures who made up the comedy relief: bulging eyes and bobbing heads—that they were always scratching. They had a "buck and shuffle" walk, and were scared of *everything*.

Though my parents tried to protect us from the outside world of

10

racism by giving us lots of love and strengthening us through philoso-phy and religion, I could see how they sometimes covered their own pain with laughter. Some of the older kids in the neighborhood even made fun of themselves with chants like: "If you're white, you're all right; if you're yellow, you're mellow; if you're brown, you can stick around; but if you're black—get back." Even in jest, nobody wanted to be black.

But now in 1938, three years later, all of a sudden it wasn't so bad to be black. A black man, Joe Louis, was the greatest hero in the universe—at least for the moment. But in that moment a fire started deep inside me; a burning desire to be special, to win, to be somebody.

I stood up from the curb and headed back into the house, a new certainty to my eight-year-old stride.

When I settled into bed that night and began to drift into sleep, it was with a haunting mix of glorious, inspired, yet confused feelings.

I didn't know it then, but that fire inside me started a conflict between me and the family work ethic, built into my system by the man I most admired, most loved and most wanted to be like, my father. He was a hero, too. But not like Joe Louis. Joe Louis didn't have to labor from sunup to sundown to be great, to be respected, to be loved. Pop did.

Pop had made us all believe that a hard, honest day's labor was the only way. That was not just his personal credo, it was our family history.

THE ROCK

I DON'T KNOW MUCH about the South at all but over the years I've heard many stories about our family history, not only from Pop but from my grandmother and my aunts and uncles. There's one story they all seemed to tell, each in their own way.

A nine-year-old mulatto boy watched outside a small wooden slave

11

cabin on a Georgia plantation in 1862. He saw a gray-haired old man pleading intensely with his grown son, who lay writhing in pain on the dirt.

"Goddamn it, boy you gon' get yo self killed talkin' back to dat boss man while you gettin' whipped," cautioned the old man, holding back tears. "It never would'da happened if you had done did what you was told."

"Ah wish ah could kill 'em all," his son cried out, clenching his arms tightly around his body. "And you too! You care mo' 'bout dat white man than you do me."

"Shut yo mouth boy. You don' know what you sayin'. If dey tells you to do som'n you does it and you don' say nothin'. You hear?"

The nine-year-old could see that the father was trying to protect his son. He watched as the old man knelt down, softly whispering, "Jes hold on son, I know dere gon' be a better day. I jes know it is."

The very next year, the old man's prayers were answered. Slavery was abolished and they were freed.

The son of Esther Johnson, a slave woman, and her white plantation owner, that little mulatto boy was Pop's father, my grandfather—the first Berry Gordy.

Once freed, Esther Johnson left the plantation taking her young son, Berry, with her. Though he was no longer a slave, he continued to work like one for many years. He acquired 168 acres of his own land, married Lucy Hellum and together they had twenty-three children. Only nine lived. One of them was my father, Pop—the second Berry Gordy.

Pop loved to tell us his own stories about our origins. He said that he and Mother were as different as you could get. He was a country boy who had learned practically everything on the farm. She was a scholar whose life was dedicated to gaining more knowledge through education. He was simple, carefree and popular with the girls; she was complex, serious and more interested in her work than boys.

Light-skinned, Pop had a slender frame about five foot nine and muscles of steel. A normal handshake to him was slightly less than bone-crushing to anybody else. He was funny, too. He had wit and great timing. When his punch line came—you laughed.

One day in 1916, at twenty-eight, Pop walked into a small schoolhouse in Sandersville, Georgia, took one look at Mother, the sixteen-year-old girl in charge of the third-grade class, and said, "There is my wife."

Of direct African descent on her father's side, African and Indian blood on her mother's, Bertha Ida Fuller had coffee brown skin, a round face, deep reflective eyes and a full figure. She looked just like the girl Pop had always imagined he would marry—cute, intelligent, a Christian woman who loved children and would raise them just like his mother did.

But during the courtship she told Pop that while she wanted to be a good wife and mother, she was a scholar and an educator and would not give that up.

Pop, who had never been challenged like that by a woman, didn't know what to think. But he liked her spunk, and soon realized that while they were of different backgrounds, their basic values were the same. He was in love. She agreed to marry him only after he reluctantly accepted the fact that she wanted a partner in life, not a boss.

Two years later, when he returned from service in World War I, they married. They planned to have six children, and by 1922, three had arrived.

That year, Pop sold some timber stumps for $2,600. It was more money than he had ever seen. Worried that some white people wanted to beat him out of it, he went all the way to Detroit, where his brother was, to cash the check. Once there he stayed and sent for his wife and family.

Like so many other black people who migrated from the South in the twenties, Pop was filled with hope and dreams. He was thrilled to bring his family to this new world, leaving bigotry and hatred behind. There was a real competitive spirit among the people in Detroit, a determination that came from the need just to survive. Even getting to work during those hot, hot sticky summers, or those brutally cold winters could be a full-time job. The automobile plants attracted people from everywhere, particularly Negroes from the South. But Pop didn't want to make cars. He wanted his own business.

Though he had been real smart as a country boy, when it came to city living he had a lot to learn. The first thing he learned was that it was not a new world at all, but the same old one with a different accent. Prejudice existed in Detroit just as it did in the South, and in some cases more insidiously. There were many areas where he was not allowed to live.

After a few years of living in different parts of town, with his family continuing to grow, he decided the Westside was the best place for colored people to raise a family. He found exactly what he was looking for—a nice residential neighborhood with decent, churchgoing folks.

"Why rent when you can buy?" A white real estate salesman told him about a house at 5419 Roosevelt Street. Compared to the two-room house Pop had built down South, this looked like a palace. Pop loved what he saw but knew he couldn't afford it. The man told him he would loan him some of the money and work out a special payment plan for the rest. Pop liked the idea, making the worst deal of his life.

The house was sinking into the ground, walls rotting under the wallpaper and the plumbing soon to be condemned. He was left with no choice except to fix it up himself.

By now it was 1929. Pop had a big house note to pay, seven mouths to feed: a wife, six kids and another on the way—ME!

As the Depression hit, the thought of my arrival was less than thrilling.

Nevertheless, on Thanksgiving Day, November 28 of that same year, at Harper Hospital in Detroit, I was born. I didn't know what time it was, how much I weighed or how bad times were. I was just happy to be here.

A year and a half later my brother Robert came along. The Depression deepened and so did our troubles. Although Mother had been a schoolteacher down South she couldn't get a job because her Southern teaching credentials were not accepted up North. It was all on Pop. He had to hustle every odd job he could find, for instance, renting an empty lot across the street from where we lived selling ice, coal, wood, Christmas trees, watermelons, old car parts. He would do anything.

Though he saved every dime he could to make ends meet, they never did. By 1931, we'd lost the house and had to go on welfare. Pop made a deal with Mother's brother, Uncle B.A., to fix up a small two-story shacklike house he owned a few doors down the same street in exchange for low rent.

We were a close family. We had to be, always bumping into each other just moving from room to room in our new home, where eight kids, four girls and four boys, had to scramble for a place to sleep. Crowding was a way of life. I loved it. I didn't know any better.

Three of my sisters—Esther, Anna and Loucye—slept in one bed. My brothers—Fuller, George and Robert—had to bunch together in another. Gwen and I slept together. We had no crowding problem at all—we wet the bed.

A short time later she stopped. I then had the bed all to myself.

The new house was even more run-down than the old one but Pop had always taught us, "Your home is your castle"—and you protect it no matter what. And we knew he would.

Once or twice a week when we heard banging on the pipes and knocking on the walls at night in the kitchen, we knew it was show time. We'd all pile in there to watch him kill rats. Big rats. He could step on them and squeeze them to death with his foot. I wanted to be a man someday like Pop, but if this was part of the test I knew I could never make it. He was fearless—stomping on one while beating another with the broom.

I was always afraid for him because it seemed whenever he stirred them up they would all come out on attack. I remember one night he was searching inside the oven and a rat jumped down on his head. When Pop jerked his head out, we all saw blood running down his face. Instead of responding to our cries of concern, he grabbed a broom and started chasing that big rat around the room. The rest of the family was scrambling like mad trying to get out of the way. I was standing on a chair. I was always on a chair. I do not like rats. Never did, never will. (And it would surprise no one in the family when one day I'd be called the Chairman.)

Pop didn't like being on welfare, but he believed that if you worked hard, paid your taxes, did all you could and then you fell on hard times and just couldn't make ends meet, there was nothing wrong with getting help. As a taxpayer you had put money into the pot

15

that was to be used by anybody who truly needed it. Then as soon as you got back on your feet you got off. "In the meantime," he told us, "hold your head high and don't look down on poor people. To be poor is not a crime."

As the Depression continued, Pop remembered what his father told him many times: "People have to eat." This gave him an idea for a new business. He found a small failing grocery store across town on the Eastside, took over the rent payments and ran the store, turning it into a profit-making venture.

Though Pop was now making money on the Eastside, he kept his family on the Westside where things were good. It's hard to imagine how good that was when nowadays in any large city you can't even go to the street corner without worrying about your life.

I was fortunate to spend the first six years of my life in the down-home, warm, friendly atmosphere of Detroit's Westside. It was a place that gave me a sense of right and wrong, a sense of safety in the family, a sense of love and kinship in a community where being good was actually a good thing to be.

Later I came to understand that Pop's bringing us to the Westside was a major factor in who I became.

Race, religion, education, competition, family, money, ego, fame, upbringing seem like random words, but are some of the things that shape our lives. They fit loosely—very loosely—into a category I call "crosscurrents." Other things included in that category might be politics, age and environment. Unnoticed as they may be they are always there. And being at the right place at the right time is a major factor in all of our lives. Luck plays a big part in everything.

One of the luckiest things that could happen to anybody was being born into the Gordy family.

Within our family there were two teams, the males and the females. Me, my brothers and Pop—full of foolishness—provided the comedy. Mother and my four sisters—naturally more serious—provided the culture.

Even as young children we had different personalities, but as a family we were taught to operate as one. "There is strength in unity" Mother always used to say.

Everyone had his own part to play and Pop was considered the

16

leader. I say "considered" because Mother was the support, anchor and keeper of the kitchen. I think that made her the boss. In fact, somehow the women always had the control. I never quite figured out how they got it. But it stayed that way throughout the years.

The kitchen was the place we hung out most. Whether it was a holiday or just coming in from school, there was always something going on there.

No one could cook like Mother. Today we call it soul food. Back then it was just called cheap and good. Every meal was delicious but the feast of the year was always Thanksgiving dinner.

Since my birthday, November 28, was always around Thanksgiving and sometimes fell on that day, I grew up feeling that somehow Thanksgiving dinner was a special party for me. I always tried not to eat that whole day so I would have room for everything: chitterlings, corn bread, turnip and collard greens, black-eyed peas, ham hocks, buttermilk biscuits, candied yams, sweet potato pie and, of course, turkey—all sitting on that overcrowded table with more coming.

By the time we sat down, my hunger pains were unbearable. Seeing all that great food, and knowing Pop still had to bless the table, was real torture. Pop blessed the table all the time but nothing like on Thanksgiving. It took forever. He thanked the Lord for everything under the sun. When he got to "Amen," everybody repeated it quickly. They were just as anxious as I was to dig in. The wait was always worth it.

The family would gather together most nights in our small living room and listen to the radio, me usually curled up on the floor. *Ghost Stories, Amos 'n' Andy, The Lone Ranger*, we listened to them all. Rochester, on *The Jack Benny Show*, became part of the family. My only problem was staying awake. There was something about lying there, listening to that little radio, the family around me, that always put me to sleep.

"Junior, get up and go to bed," I'd hear Mother's voice as I dozed.

"I'm not sleeping," I'd always say, struggling to keep my eyes open, hoping I wouldn't be sent away from that warm, safe, comfortable spot. I guess it was that sense of security we all feel when surrounded by people we know love us.

Aside from a radio, no matter how poor, I think every black family had a little upright piano. Ours sat in the hallway leading to the kitchen.

The only person who could play it was Uncle B.A. But he wouldn't be caught dead playing ours. It was old and out of tune. A somewhat elegant gentleman with a pompous manner, Uncle B.A. had once been a concert pianist but was now teaching piano. Nobody seemed to really like him but me. He used to let me come to his house because I liked hearing him play the classics. He started giving me free lessons and afterward he would take over the keyboard. "Clair de Lune" and "Prelude in C# Minor" were my favorites. I was frantic to play that real stuff, and kept begging him to show me.

But Uncle B.A. was of the old rigid school and forced me to study music theory and practice boring scales and arpeggios endlessly. I was just too impatient for that. But in the process I made a discovery: the arpeggios he made me play were made up of chords played one note at a time in rapid succession. Playing three of the different notes at the same time made a chord that brought little melodies into my head. Once I started playing and singing those melodies, there was no way I could concentrate on studying theory. I quit my lessons after a year.

Messing around with the only chords I knew—C, F and G—I began to put some of my thoughts to music. Before long I was learning to play everything by ear, especially the different types of Boogie Woogie I was hearing on the radio. My favorite was "Hazel Scott's Boogie Woogie." I eventually created my own Boogie Woogie.

"Berry's Boogie" had a bouncy, uptempo walking bass line that my stretching fingers had trouble playing. But I soon got good at it and became a star on that little upright.

Mother and Pop did everything they could to keep us on the straight and narrow, including giving us a good religious foundation. They were serious about their Christian faith. Three times a week and all day Sunday, they would herd us off to one of the storefront churches in our neighborhood. The preachers were the stars; dynamic, moving and emotional, they wielded great power and influence. Their words were strong, solid, repetitious and infectious. They could send the congregation into a frenzy.

It was in that atmosphere that I first saw someone getting the Holy Ghost—shouting, jumping up and down, shaking, even speaking in tongues—locked into the spell of the spirit. It was shocking and amusing at the same time.

As I sat there watching, I felt embarrassed for the people. But when I was told they had the Spirit and were possessed by God, I wondered why I didn't have it. I kept sitting there waiting for lightning to strike and it didn't.

Did that mean that I wasn't a God-fearing person? Did that mean I wasn't holy enough? I didn't see Mother and Pop do it either, and I knew how holy they were. That made me feel better.

All the people in church seemed strong and fearless. I guess that's how Pop could carry on after losing his home and going on welfare. He had God.

Pop was forever telling us how hard he'd worked for just two dollars a day to learn plastering. He wanted us to appreciate the value of learning a trade, so he made us all work hard for little or nothing. Fuller and George got the little and Bobby and I got the nothing.

Whenever any of us complained, Pop would launch into stories we'd heard over and over again about how rough times had been in the South.

"Shuck, boy," he'd chuckle, "y'all chillin' don't know what real work is. Not only did Papa work for somebody else, he was owned by somebody else. What could be worse than that?"

I could never fully comprehend the idea of being owned by somebody else.

I remember Pop telling us one day that he thought his father was the meanest man in the world, making him work so hard. But on May 31, 1913, he saw his father struck down by lightning. "It all come to me then, as I watched him layin' there, why Papa had prepared me so well." Whenever Pop got to this part of the story he always slowed a bit and the expression in his eyes told us how much love and respect he had for his father. "Mama had told me if anything was to happen to him, I was the one to step into his shoes. And

19

now that it had, I wasn't even ready to shine his shoes let alone wear 'em. Nobody could do that."

Once Pop got to talking about the South we all knew he might go on forever. But we didn't mind because we knew as long as he talked we didn't have to work.

He told us white folks wanted their land. The same land his father had worked so hard to keep in the family was now in jeopardy. Bank debt and taxes were owed. Even people they'd never heard of were making claims. Pop had worked close with his father and knew many of those claims were lies. "Most all the family felt we gon' lose that land if we don't get a white administrator to handle it for us in court. But not Mama Lucy. She didn't trust none o' them white lawyers in town to protect our land. She said they was some of the very ones who wanted to steal it."

Pop would beam with pride when he talked about how smart his mother was. He had learned a lot from Mama Lucy. She was a great believer in the Golden Rule: "Do unto others as you would have them do unto you." But she also believed that if you're right—fight. She told him he had to represent the family in court.

Pop told us how scared he was when he went into that courtroom. "But I just told 'em the truth and we won. It was simple as that," he said. "All the family was jumping for joy, so happy they didn't know what to do. But I told 'em all, not to be doin' no braggin' and stuff like that. Wasn't no need for us to do nothin' but be quiet. We had done won our case."

Pop seemed to always end his stories with something profound. There was always a message there somewhere.

Mother and Pop were forever giving us messages, one way or another. I can never remember them ever disagreeing with each other on anything concerning us. They were quick to praise us for good deeds and just as quick to punish us for bad ones.

I got more punishments than rewards. If it was something minor, it might be Mother who would take a switch to us. But if it was major, it would be Pop and the ironing cord. Once you felt a good whuppin' from Pop, you didn't forget it. My worst experience with that ironing cord came all because of a stupid little rock.

20

Gwen had the unfortunate luck of having her birthday fall on November 26—two days before mine. I would always get her a really good gift because I knew she would get me something twice as good on my birthday two days later. This particular year her birthday was just a few days away and I had no money. I just happened to be in Fuller's room that day and just happened to see in one of his drawers all these coins—nickels, dimes, quarters—big money! I figured he wouldn't mind me "borrowing" some. I knew this wasn't exactly right, but what I was taking was so little compared to what he had that there was no way it could hurt him. And besides, I knew God wouldn't punish me because he would recognize that I was gonna keep track of everything I took and pay it all back as soon as I got the chance.

Two days later Mother and Pop got us all together. They wanted to see who had saved the most money. We all wanted them to be proud of us so everyone brought out every cent they could find. I felt bad because I had nothing to show. I had just bought Gwen a birthday gift with the money I took, and had loaned her the rest in case there was something *she* might have wanted to buy.

After Mother and Pop had counted everybody's money, Pop asked Gwen where she'd gotten hers.

"I don't know," she said.

"Well you better know because Fuller marked his money and some was taken from his drawer and you got it."

Everything went silent. We all looked at Gwen (yeah, including me). Glancing over at me with a suspicious look, Gwen swore up and down she didn't take it. She was so convincing that Mother said, "Well, I don't know who did, but the *Spirit* will."

That scared me.

She had us all stand in a straight line. Pointing to a rock in Pop's hand, she said, "Your father's going to throw that rock and it's going to hit the one who stole that money."

"Stole," what does she mean "stole"? I just borrowed it.

Pop pulled his hand way back. Pretending to throw the rock, he threw his arm toward us with a mighty swing. I was terrified! Jumping back and protecting my face, I almost fell down. No one else had moved.

Pop pointed his finger at me, motioning for me to get into my room while he went to get the ironing cord.

I didn't look at anyone's face as I arrogantly walked to my room. I didn't want them to think I thought it was a big deal. Then I heard Pop coming and the sound of that ominous cord swinging back and forth. I was so scared I didn't know what to do. I imagined him turning into a madman. And when I saw his face as he entered the room, I knew I was right.

The next thing I knew he was slashing me from one end of the room to the other.

I wasn't tough anymore. I no longer cared what the rest of the family thought. I was doing all kinds of contortions with my body, trying to keep him from hitting the same spot twice, hollering, and begging for mercy, promising to never ever do it again.

"Hush up boy or I'm really gon' give you somethin' to cry about," he threatened.

What?! What could be worse than this? And expecting me to shut up while I'm getting killed?

The more he hit me the more I hushed up. Pain from the last lick and fear of the next one made me suck up all my screaming and crying to a mere whimper. He hit me a few more times and I did not make a sound. Then he stopped.

The lesson Pop taught me was something much deeper than it appeared to me at the time. He never explained it but I knew he loved me and if it made him that mad it had to be something more than just the money. I figured out later it was the principle. If I stole a dime I was a thief. Why not stop me right then, rather than wait until I stole a thousand dollars and on my way to jail?

I was six and a half when we moved to the Eastside. It was an important turning point for the family. Pop had finally seen his struggles pay off. During those Depression years, he had not only survived—hustling his way up from being an apprentice plasterer to getting his contractor's license and hiring men to work for him—but had saved enough to make a down payment on our very own two-story commercial building at the corner of Farnsworth and St. Antoine Streets, not far from that first little grocery store he had been running. (So much would happen to me at this new home I would later buy the actual pole on top of which are those two street sign markers—one reading "Farnsworth" and the other "St. Antoine"—and plant it in a corner of my backyard in California.)

On the top floor of our building there were two flats where the family lived. And on the street level were four storefronts. The biggest was on the corner and had become our new grocery store, which Mother had named after the famous black educator, Booker T. Washington.

I had always heard that the Eastside was where all the bad people lived. The two worst places there were Hastings Street, where you could easily be killed by drunk people, and Black Bottom, a place near the Detroit River, where you would just disappear and never be heard from again.

Suddenly, I found myself living there, one block from Hastings Street. I was scared. There were the dirtiest rat-infested alleys you ever saw running behind our house. Strange old white men with black hats and long white beards came down them on horse-driven carts—searching through trash and garbage, picking up stuff that had been thrown out. I wondered why in the world would anyone want to be a junkman. I would soon find out. In fact, I would soon find out a lot of things.

The infamous Hastings Street turned out to be exciting and colorful, changing my fear into awe. There were bars and pawn shops, five-and-ten-cent stores, the little Warfield Theater and greasy spoons that made the most delicious chili hot dogs in the world. When I'd gone exploring for the first time and stepped over a wino sitting on the sidewalk drinking out of a paper bag, I remember feeling a strange desire to talk to him and find out why he was there.

At night Hastings lit up like a Christmas tree. You could always hear shouting Blues songs blasting out of the bars, and exciting women standing out front with nothing to do. I liked it.

Coming to the Eastside was like moving from the country to the city—there was action all the time. There were so many different kinds of people—all hustlers in their own way. There was the street kind: pimps, gamblers and numbers men. Most of them were smart, hip people who wanted to be somebody the only way they knew how.

Then there was the Pop kind: religious, hardworking, buying and selling everything. And there was the Mother kind: homemakers, educators, pushing to learn and teach. Yes, all hustlers.

Besides being an additional source of income, as well as a cheaper method of feeding our large family, Mother and Pop used the corner grocery store to teach us daily lessons about business.

We were the only colored people in the neighborhood who owned a commercial building, and for the first time people looked up to us. But Pop was smart. He remained humble. He loved serving people. He sold for the lowest prices he could and was forever telling us "The customer is always right." That made no sense to me. How could all those people be so much smarter than we were?

"We in business to satisfy them," Pop would say. "They're spendin' their money. That makes them right."

I didn't get it.

Frequently, he'd take me with him to the Eastern Market, a place where farmers came and sold their produce for lower than wholesale. We would get there even before the farmers had set up their stands. I loved the 5:30-in-the-morning smell of the fresh fruits and vegetables. No one seemed to mind me testing a juicy apple every now and then as we walked along. It was great. I could easily see what Pop meant when he said, "The early bird gets the worm." They sold everything. And it seemed Pop tried to buy everything at the cheapest prices he could. He loved to negotiate.

I remember one day we came home with a truckload of vegetables. Mother was so exasperated. "We can never sell all this stuff before it spoils."

"But I got a great bargain!" he said.

Even the kids at school had their own way of hustling. On my first day at Balch Elementary, I was standing out on the playground with four or five other kids, excited just to be a part of the group.

One asked me if I knew what time the milkman came to my house every day. I said I didn't.

"Ask yo' mama," he said, "she knows."

I had no idea what he meant, but everybody laughed. I tried to laugh along with them, but I only made it about halfway.

I later found out I was right not to laugh. In fact, I should've beat him up. He was putting my mother down. He was playing "the Dozens."

"How's yo' mama?" Another kid half my size asked me a few days later amid the protection of larger boys who seemed to think he was real funny.

"Look man," I said adamantly, "I don't play the Dozens!"

"Oh? Well, just pat cho' foot while *I* play 'em then," he said, reaching his nose up almost touching my bottom lip.

During their outburst of laughter, I knew I had two choices: Fight or cry. I did neither. A wimpy smile appeared on my face. Something told me it wasn't too wise to be beating up on people—especially a group.

I decided I'd better learn to play the Dozens. But no matter how hard I tried to be funny, there was always somebody who would out-Dozen me. My mother took a real beating. The Eastside kids were just hipper, sharper and funnier. They probably knew about Santa at two.

Then, in class, there were these little whiz kids with the thick glasses who sat right up front and always had the correct answers. Most of the time I couldn't even understand the question, let alone the answer. I was always so far behind the rest of the class, I just knew I had to be dumb.

Mother, more than anything else, tried to make us good students. Before I even started school I'd heard her say, "Speak up in class. Whatever you say, say it loud, strong. It'll give you confidence."

My answers were always loud—too loud. At first, I sounded like I knew what I was talking about. But, soon, my shouting out the wrong answers became funnier and funnier. That's when I decided to take class disruption to an art form. My rule of thumb became: No gag too big, no laugh too small. Sometimes I was so funny I actually made the teacher laugh.

Every now and then in her desperate attempt to keep order, the teacher would make me sergeant-at-arms. I had to sit in front of the class and identify troublemakers. I didn't learn very much but I must have been great at my job because whenever I was up there the class always ran smoother.

A year behind me in school, my brother Bobby always got As and Bs. I got Ds and Es. (In those days E did not mean "excellent.") When he came home with a C, he was a bum. If I got a C, I was a hero. The better he was the worse I got. I figured if I acted like I wasn't trying so hard I wouldn't look so dumb. I knew that C meant average and I resented that I was getting applauded for it. Still I couldn't seem to do any better.

I wanted to impress people somehow, especially Mother and Pop. So I learned my ABCs backwards. They didn't think too much of it, but Mr. and Mrs. Delaney did.

On the ground floor of our building in addition to the grocery store on the corner, there was a beauty shop, which would one day become the 3D Record Mart, my first venture into the music business. There was a barbershop, whose space would later be filled by the Gordy Print Shop owned by Fuller, Esther and George. To the right of the front door as you came out of the building was a big plate glass window on which was clearly painted the name "Delaney's Cleaners." It was always a thrill whenever I'd be passing by to hear Mr. Delaney bragging to his friends how smart I was and motioning for me to come inside.

"Junior," he'd say, "do the alphabet backward."

"Oh, sure," I'd respond and quickly rattle off "zyxwvutsrqponmlk-jihgfedcba."

"Hey, hey, slow down, slow down," he'd tell me. "I'm not sure you're doing it right."

That was sort of our little routine. I would start off real speedy to show my dexterity, he'd stop me and then I'd redo them very slowly . . . and very accurately. I loved the proud, smug look he'd give to his awed friends.

They thought I was the smartest kid around. I could rattle off my ABCs backwards perfectly! But what they didn't know was I had trouble saying them frontwards.

The minute you'd step outside our building, the mouth-watering aroma of smoldering ribs would hit you in the face. Directly across the street from our front door was CT's, a busy little storefront barbecue joint where all day long a steady stream of people were coming

26

and going, including the police. I quickly learned that more than just ribs were cooking. CT's was headquarters for the numbers, the illegal lottery, a way of life in our neighborhood. Everybody played them. Everybody's biggest dream was to hit the number. It was the best way to get quick cash without risking jail. The only people who ever got busted were the pickup men or women; and most of them were protected by the police.

A number was any three digits. You could play it straight, say, 2-4-7, or box it, which would be any combination: 742, 427, etc.

Some people were known to play the same number day in, day out and whenever that number came up everybody in town knew that person was rich. At least for a few days.

Pickup runners would go all over the Eastside, to poolrooms, barber shops, private houses—anywhere. Each pickup person would have their established route and would come by every afternoon around one o'clock to take the numbers you wanted to bet that day. You could play for as little as a nickel, or as much as you wanted.

Some of those pickup people were mathematical geniuses who could tell everybody what numbers they had played and when—from memory. I remember one day while getting my hair cut, my barber had an argument with a numbers guy.

"Yesterday," my barber argued, "the number was 748 and I had 487 in the box for five dollars. Where's my money?"

The numbers guy was incensed. Never looking at a piece of paper he stuttered as he replied, "W-W-What the f-fuck you talkin' 'bout man, you b-boxed 481 and 369 and played 822 straight. And Harold, over th-there, b-boxed 213. W-What the f-f-f-fuck you tryin' to p-pull? D-do you want something f-for today or not?"

My barber, after checking his piece of paper, said, "Uh, yeah, you're right."

When the numbers guy left, my barber laughed. "He cain't talk a bit but the mothafucker sho' knows his shit, don't he?"

The fact that most of those guys were not even educated fascinated me. It did not teach me education was worth nothing. What it taught me was that just because I wasn't doing well in school didn't mean I *had* to be dumb. I began to realize that intelligence and education were two different things. If you had them both you had it made.

But if you could only have one—and wanted to survive in *my* neighborhood—it'd better be intelligence.

Compared to the cats where I lived, I was just average. But that really wasn't so bad because many of those "geniuses" were too smart for their own good and ended up dead or in jail.

"Junior!" The sound of Pop's Southern voice was soft and shattering. It was Saturday morning and I'd overslept again.

This was some six months or so after the historic Joe Louis victory. Since then, I'd spent most of my waking and sleeping hours fantasizing about becoming a boxing champion. Just this past night I was having exciting dreams of me and Joe doing all sorts of things like climbing trees, skipping school and him even turning into a squirrel.

Pop's voice put an abrupt halt to that. I could hear the cold, bristling wind outside my window while the rising steam from the inside radiators made me feel warm and cozy.

Wiping the sleep from my eyes, I realized I wasn't warm at all; I was wet, real wet. My nightmare, once again, had reared its ugly head. I had to think fast. To Pop everything was controllable, especially bed-wetting. If you had the desire to stop, you could. If you didn't, it was only because you didn't want to, or you were just too lazy to get up. I would forever disagree with this inflexible stance, but then was no time to debate.

"I'm up," I mumbled, pulling myself up into a crouch, my head in my hands, posing as though I were about to pray. In fact, I did pray; I prayed that Pop, a God-fearing man, would respect my privacy with the Lord. He did and left the room.

I quickly jumped out of bed, ripped off my wet underwear, slipped into another pair, some trousers, a shirt, socks, shoes, and cap, all in less than two minutes. I then walked calmly out to the small pickup truck that bore the name "Gordy Contractors" and joined my brothers. Fuller and George took their seats in the cab with Pop, while me and Bobby braced ourselves for the cold wind in the back. We were off to another plastering job.

By this time I had grown to really hate everything about plastering, especially the back of the truck. That Saturday, not only did I resent the bitter wind ripping my body, but my close call reminded me of the last time I got punished for wetting the bed. I resented that, too. The fear of getting found out by my friends also haunted me. I knew how kids in the neighborhood felt about bed-wetters and after all I was almost nine.

I tried everything I could to get myself to stop. Still, I would wake up wet more often than not. Just two nights before I had forced myself to stay awake all night to avoid the problem. I was so proud when around three o'clock in the morning I pulled myself up out of bed and rushed to the bathroom, stood over the toilet and let it go. What a relief! Then I woke up. Soaked again!

Just one block north of us on Frederick Street was our family's place of worship, Bethel AME, a Methodist church. Unlike the storefront churches on the Westside, it was a regular church building like the ones I had seen in books. But what was special about this church was the man in charge, Reverend William H. Peck.

He was a little guy, thin, with an angelic face. Soft-spoken and big-hearted, he never seemed in a hurry. He had time for everyone, including me. I would go visit him at his house next door to the church. It was obvious to me that how he acted away from church was what he preached in church. All the family loved and respected him the same as I did.

Then came awful news: Reverend Peck had gotten some sort of promotion and was leaving. Seeing me so depressed about it, everyone assured me that there would be a new pastor coming in and everything would be all right. Not so.

The new pastor never caught on with me. Totally different in his approach, he always gave me a threatened feeling. If I wasn't good I would burn in hell forever. His teachings weren't about being good for the sake of righteousness as Reverend Peck's were, but being good only so you wouldn't burn in hell for eternity. I found myself feeling bad when I'd leave church, not knowing why.

So I would avoid his services whenever I could. Since Mother and Pop were busy with official duties in the church I got away with it—for a while.

"Son, have you been to church lately?" Pop asked one day as I was tinkering around on the piano.

Trying to appear nonchalant, I stopped playing, thought about it for a moment and answered as truthfully as I could, "Yes, but not every Sunday. I don't always feel good when I go." I braced myself, expecting his wrath.

Instead, he calmly spoke. "Son," he said, "you don't have to go to church to find God. I know what kind of person you are and I know God is inside you. Whatever you do is between you and God and nobody else."

After that, going to church was not a problem for me. I could enjoy listening to anybody, including the new pastor, realizing their views were just their views—and I could either agree with them or not.

Pop telling me this at an early age gave me a good feeling about myself and would set a foundation for everything that was yet to come.

3

MUSIC VERSUS BOXING
1938–1951

HOW I GOT MY NAME

I DON'T CARE what anybody says, what a child is named helps shape his or her personality. A name is something we wear throughout our lives. It has its own power. The sound, the personality and the meaning all affect both our perception of ourselves and others' perception of us. I was lucky. I was named after Pop.

By thirteen I had become somewhat cocky. Even though I was considered the black sheep of the family—mischievous, terrible in school, always in trouble—I still had the notion that somehow I was the chosen one.

"I may be the black sheep but I'm the one they waited for to name after Pop," I bragged one day at the dinner table.

This was one of those days when Esther (who we called Sua, short for sister) was in charge of getting us to eat dinner together. Mother and Pop were away and a lady from church had helped with the cooking.

"Waited for?!" Sua shouted from her seat at the table right across from mine. "No one waited for you. You weren't even supposed to

31

be here!" Catching herself, she stopped quickly and started eating again.

Everybody looked at her like she had spoken the unspeakable. That is, everyone except Bobby and me. We looked at each other in confusion. I didn't know what she was talking about but it sure made me feel strange. Not supposed to be here? What did she mean by that?

Sua wasn't happy with me to start with because earlier, when she was trying to get me to come to the dinner table, I was jammin' in the living room to our new Grundig radio, locked in a trance. Sua's calling me sounded like a far-off dream. I was listening to a song by the Mills Brothers called "Paper Doll." "*I'm going to buy a paper doll that I can call my own, a doll that other fellows cannot steal.*" I was feeling sorry for the guy who was singing it, but I felt more sorry for myself because guys were stealing my girls even *before* I got them.

I loved songs that meant something to me, songs that I could relate to, mostly about sadness connected with girls. Another group I liked was the Ink Spots. Their lead singer, Bill Kenny, had the cleanest, purest falsetto voice I'd ever heard. I loved the way their hit song "We Three" expressed loneliness: "*We Three, we're all alone living in a memory, my echo, my shadow and me.*"

Over time those clear, simple, lyrical concepts would form the basis for my own approach to songwriting.

When I heard Sua's footsteps coming toward me, I jumped up and raced to my seat at the table. If I had known what I was in for from the family, I might have stayed in the living room with the Mills Brothers. I don't think anything could have prepared me for "You weren't even supposed to be here."

The moment Sua said it, I could see she was sorry. I looked to see if anybody else knew anything. Their faces said they did.

"Well it's sorta true," Gwen said. "See, Mother and Pop had planned to have only six kids." She paused and looked to the others for a little help.

Fuller said when he was born Pop would have named him Junior but Mother and Pop had made an agreement that each would have picks in naming us. When he was born, he said, it was Mother's pick. So she named him Fuller, her maiden name.

All of a sudden, everybody in the family was chiming in to tell me this horrible story. The next child, they told me, was a girl and Pop gave her the name Esther, after his grandmother.

It so happened that every time it was Pop's turn to name a child, it was a girl. Mother named the third child Anna Ruby after her mother, Anna, and her Aunt Ruby. Two girls in a row! Pop just knew the next child had to be a boy, but it wasn't. He named her Lucy after his mother, Mama Lucy. (Loucye changed the spelling when she got older.) George was named after Mother's brother and even though Pop didn't get to name him, he was so happy to have another boy that he put seven hundred dollars on his new son's chest at birth. (Don't ask me why, all I know is that he put it there.) The sixth and "last" child was a girl. Pop was not happy. He named her Gwendolyn—the first name that popped into his head.

Pop's frustration—and begging—convinced Mother to go for it one more time. Finally, a boy!! Pop was ecstatic. But again, it was not his pick. (I could never understand why Pop made such a stupid deal like that in the first place.)

But this time Mother gave him shocks of joy when she named the baby Berry Junior. When asked why, she said she was just tired. She knew he would never stop until he got a Junior. I was lucky. But how my younger brother, Bobby, got here I'll never know. He was even luckier.

I may have been living a lie for thirteen years thinking I was the chosen one, but the die had already been cast. It was too late to change my Junior status, too late to change who I thought I was.

People become what they think they are. For example, I didn't know much about astrology and didn't believe in it. But still, subconsciously, I accepted the good qualities about my sign and began emphasizing these traits in my personality.

I was born a Sagittarius and everybody told me that Sagittarians shot straight like an arrow, were honest and couldn't be contained easily. They also had a good sense of humor, were philosophical, competitive and adored women. Sounded good to me!

"IF"

I WAS A GAMBLER. Craps, blackjack, poker, anything. I loved it all.

My parents were very strict about gambling, but when I moved to the Eastside it became one of my favorite pastimes. I was about six when I learned my first card game, war. We would pitch pennies in the playground, and hiding in the school bathrooms, we matched nickels and dimes. By the time I was fourteen I had graduated to more sophisticated games.

"Daddy needs a new pair of shoes!" I remember screaming one day in a hot crap game in the backyard of Dewit Lavender's house. I meant that literally. I did need a new pair of shoes, but the dice didn't give a damn about my needs! As usual I lost everything.

I always wanted to hit that big one. Whenever I was ahead I knew with a little more luck I could make it. Getting over that hump was something I had to do. One last pass on the dice would do it. But the last pass was always the next one. I would play until I missed, no matter what. After I'd borrowed all the money I could, I'd go down on Hastings Street and pawn something: my watch, my suit, whatever it took to get me back in the game. When I'd lose, and I always did ultimately, I'd realize too late that if I'd just saved all the money I borrowed, I would have been way ahead of the game.

In my neighborhood, the cats were clean, sharp, especially when it came to our shoes. Once the soles became too thin we threw them away.

So, after the game that day, with nothing left to hock, I squeezed a little more money out of Gwen, promising her that I wouldn't gamble with it, and hit the shoe stores on Hastings to find a bargain. Having no luck and about to give up, I was leaving the last store when I saw an expensive-looking pair sitting in a bin. They were perfect and they were half price. I tried them on—my size and everything. What luck! I bought them quickly, making out like a bandit.

It wasn't until I got home that I realized they were my own shoes—the same pair I had thrown out three weeks before. They had been found by those junkmen, fixed up and put in that shop on Hastings Street, which they owned. I later found out most of the buildings in our neighborhood were also owned by some of these same guys.

The next time I went to a pawn shop to hock my valuables for a mere fraction of what they were worth, I found that it, too, was owned by—guess who? It was not difficult for me to clearly understand the laws of supply and demand.

I was fascinated by these junkmen as they went about their business in the alleys behind our house. "No job too big, no job too small," their creed, was the same as Pop's, except they didn't have to pay for their *material!* Probably what impressed me most was they weren't ashamed of going through our alleys picking up our trash. The more I talked to these little guys with their long beards, wisdom and wit— I later found out they were called Jews—the more I liked them. They liked me, too. They were always giving me advice. About everything! "Never buy anything that you can't afford," was big with them.

"Well, how will I know if I can afford it?" I asked one day.

"When you can pay cash for it."

A dollar down, a dollar a week was the way most of the people in my neighborhood bought things—clothes, hats, Cadillac cars! I didn't take their advice at the time, but I never forgot it.

We were at war. Ever since the bombing of Pearl Harbor, December 7, 1941, life had changed one way or another for everybody—food rationing and air-raid drills, war films, propaganda, fear. I had nightmares about airplanes coming over and bombing us and never getting to see my brothers again. First Fuller had been drafted into the army and shipped off to the Philippines; then George joined the navy, stationed at the Great Lakes naval base.

Meanwhile, there was another war raging inside of me: That little upright had taken on a major contender, boxing gloves. For a long time entertainers like Nat King Cole, Billy Eckstine and the Mills Brothers had shown us that music could lead to the good life. But Joe Louis, and now Sugar Ray Robinson, were also showing us that boxing was another way out of the slums to success, fame and fortune.

The upright versus the gloves—that was the beginning.

But whether I admitted it or not, there was already an ulterior motive for everything I did—girls. Romance and love were always on my mind. In fact, girls were always on everybody's mind. That's why we went to dances and wanted to excel at sports and music and anything else.

I knew so little about women and wanted to find out everything I could.

I had always been fascinated by those exciting older women with great bodies who hung around Hastings Street at night with not a lot to do. When I found out what they did, I was even more fascinated. I had heard they would let you "do it" to them for just a few dollars. Wow wee! Those sexy-looking women, who I would always have trouble calling whores, had style and class. At least enough not to accept money from a fourteen-year-old punk kid.

They just ignored me as I strolled past, money in my sweaty outstretched hand.

"Sorry, short shot," said one fine, honey-skinned beauty. "There's some things even we won't do."

I was thrilled to know I wasn't invisible. But I didn't know how to take that. Was I too young, or too ugly? I persisted, continuing to walk by another and another.

Finally, after parading up and down the two-block stretch for the third time, one who had given me a subtle smile my last time around whispered softly, "Hey, you wanna do some business?"

Rocketed off guard, heart in mouth, I stammered, "Uh, business? I mean . . . uh . . . business, like what?"

"Like fuck, that's what!" she said, staring right at me while I looked quickly to the stars off in the sky somewhere.

"Oh . . . well, I . . . uh . . ."

"Follow me, sweetie," she said in the softest, sexiest voice I'd ever heard, as she darted across the street.

And so I did—on wings! Going through a dark alley and up some back stairs was exciting, but scary. I passed two old men sitting in a dimly lit kitchen playing cards. This was new territory. But I was much more excited than frightened.

I followed her into a small, overused room with a small, overused bed that I couldn't get my clothes off fast enough to jump into.

"Baby, you got to pay me first," she said as I was scrambling to get out of the inside-out pants leg that was clutching my foot.

"Oh yeah, of course," I said, trying to find my pants pocket somewhere on the dark floor.

It was an exhausting night but so well worth it. Like riding wild horses and a magic carpet at the same time. Phenomenal! All two minutes of it!

The next morning I was in the back of Pop's pickup truck, wondering if I looked any different. We were arrowing down John R Street on the way to the day's first plastering job. I hated having to get up on those cold mornings, knocking out dirty ceilings, sucking in dust through every pore. And being tired all the time. I worked with Pop most weekends and sometimes during the summer.

He never came out and told me, but I knew he wanted me to take over his business one day. Maybe it was because I was the only son working with him at the time. Whatever it was, it made me proud, but Pop never changed. I had to do it his way. The "keeping busy" way.

When we ran out of material and had nothing to do, Pop would create something, anything. "Boy, don't just stand there," he'd say. "Get a move on ya. Do something. Sweep the floor, pick up nails— somethin'. Don't let me catch you loungin' around doin' nothin'."

I tried to convince him to let me plan more and work less. For instance, to let me figure in advance how much material we'd need for a job. Because if we ran out of material and four people were out of work for one hour, that's four hours we lost. Me picking up nails and sweeping the floor was not going to make that up. Pop paid no attention, thinking I was only trying to get out of physical work. And maybe I was. But I was sure we could save money.

One summer Pop had to make a trip down South and left me in charge of the two plasterers and a laborer. I was ecstatic. Oh boy! This was my chance to do it better. I planned everything ahead. When materials were low I rushed out and got more long before we ran out. I kept the men busy all the time. They loved it because they accomplished so much more without having to rush.

I was an executive!

The day that Pop was due back, we were way ahead of schedule. I couldn't wait for Pop to see that it was not necessary for my body to be abused when my mind could do the job.

I hustled around at top speed, making sure everything was in order: bags of material in a special lineup, floors clean, truck organized. When we saw him coming, we all quickened our pace. As he got closer we all slowed a bit in unison. It was as if the rest of the crew was reading my mind, my wanting him to see all the progress that was made under my direction so effortlessly. I was cool—real cool. My work spoke for itself.

Pop ambled in, happy to be back. He talked about the South a bit. Then noticed me being cool. "Junior," he said, "get busy."

I got busy. But glancing at him from time to time I could see that he'd begun to notice the work that had been done, inspecting the nicely plastered walls and the clean floor, noticing the organized way the materials were stacked and then casually looking over at me. Though he never verbalized it, his attitude toward me said, "You did a good job, son."

While he was away, the woman who owned the house told me she was paying the contractor $4,000 for the job so it'd better be good.

Four thousand dollars? I knew that as the subcontractors we were doing all the work and we were only getting $2,000. The guy who had hired us was cheating us! I was so mad I couldn't wait to tell Pop.

"Boy, don't never worry 'bout what somebody else is makin', as long as you get what you bargain for," he scolded. "We make a good livin'. And if we didn't have them to call us, where would we find work?"

They loved Pop, and who wouldn't? I was proud of Pop for believing in his own convictions and keeping us steadily employed. But on the other hand, I realized, what was right for Pop was not necessarily right for me.

When I wasn't working with Pop I tried other things to make money. I once built a homemade shoeshine stand with two buddies, Bud Johnson and Frank Griffin. It was nothing more than a chair with stirrups on top of a wooden box—an eyesore. But undaunted, we took it right into the heart of white downtown outside of Hudson's Department Store and got to work.

Popping my rag and singing, I was a real joy to my customers. But the downtown proprietors were anything but joyful. Not wanting a ragtag bunch of kids outside their premises, they ran us off every corner we tried to set up on. We spent more time running than shining.

From the shoe industry, I turned to journalism, selling the *Michigan Chronicle*, Detroit's top colored weekly newspaper. One weekend I packed up some papers and went to sell them in the white neighborhood. I figured white people there would probably love to buy them if they got the chance. After all, you could always find them hanging out at the black nightclubs—like the Flame Show Bar or those down in Paradise Valley. I felt that everyone in the world had a lot more in common than they realized.

Well, I was a big hit and sold more papers in less time than ever before. I decided I could afford to share the wealth and brought brother Bobby down with me the next week.

We did not do well. We both got a hard, fast lesson in race relations. It seemed one precocious little black kid was cute, but two were a threat to the neighborhood.

My next enterprise was the first time I tried to make money at something I loved—music.

Lloyd Sims, a kid about my age from the neighborhood, had one of the most beautiful voices I'd ever heard. He sounded just like Bill Kenny of the Ink Spots, but he was shy and didn't like singing for strangers. I convinced him that: 1) He had talent; 2) He could make people happy; and 3) We could make money!

I took him from door to door to sing for neighbors.

Everybody loved him, especially when he crooned out "Danny Boy." There wouldn't be a dry eye anywhere. His voice was as silky and smooth as I'd ever heard. We made money, about fifty cents a house. He was talented. I thought I was, too, but all I could play were some simple chords, one-finger stuff and Boogie Woogie. Nevertheless, I'd be right there trying to accompany him whenever I thought I could. But it seemed whenever I did, people's faces would quickly let me know that I should cool it on the piano. Some would motion to me with their hands or even say something out loud. I *hated* it when they did that. But I was cool. I would just sort of stop playing as if it was my own idea.

It was fun while it lasted but I think people finally convinced Lloyd I wasn't really needed.

As bad experiences often do, this one made me realize something— maybe I shouldn't have quit my piano lessons after only one year.

But that didn't stop me from refining "Berry's Boogie" into a musical masterpiece. When I heard that Frankie Carle—a big band leader from Hollywood—was coming to town looking for talented Boogie Woogie piano players for his amateur contest, I rushed downtown to the Michigan Theater where it was to be held and signed up immediately. My great chance for the big time.

I was sensational. I wowed both audience and judges with my unique, original composition and grinning smile, but still lost. The kid who stole the show was less than half my age, Sugar Chile Robinson. They called him a five-year-old prodigy, but when I went back to the neighborhood I told my friends he was a grown midget who won by playing with his knuckles.

It was a few months after my fifteenth birthday when Sua handed me a piece of paper, saying, "Here's something you should read."

She was always giving me something to read or study. I was not a reader and certainly not a studier so I had ignored most everything in the past. Probably it was the simple one word title, "If," that grabbed my attention. I started reading a poem by Rudyard Kipling. The first few lines were simple, too:

If you can keep your head when all about you
Are losing theirs and blaming it on you.
If you can trust yourself when all men doubt you,
But make allowance for their doubting too;

Hmmmm, interesting.

If you can wait and not be tired by waiting,
Or being lied about, don't deal in lies,

Or being hated, don't give way to hating,
And yet don't look too good, nor talk too wise.

Don't look too good nor talk too wise? Sounded like wisdom to me.
I read on. The more I read, the more fascinated I became with its
meanings.

If you can dream—and not make dreams your master;
If you can think—and not make thoughts your aim,
If you can meet with Triumph and Disaster
And treat those two impostors just the same;
If you can bear to hear the truth you've spoken
Twisted by knaves to make a trap for fools,
Or watch the things you gave your life to broken
And stoop and build 'em up with worn-out tools:

If you can make one heap of all your winnings
And risk it on one turn of pitch-and-toss,
And lose, and start again at your beginnings
And never breathe a word about your loss;
If you can force your heart and nerve and sinew
To serve your turn long after they are gone,
And so hold on when there is nothing in you
Except the Will which says to them "Hold on!"

If you can talk with crowds and keep your virtue,
Or walk with Kings—nor lose the common touch,
If neither foes nor loving friends can hurt you
If all men count with you, but none too much;

When I got to the end—

If you can fill the unforgiving minute
With sixty seconds worth of distance run,
Yours is the Earth and everything that's in it,
And—which is more—you'll be a man, my son!

—something happened to me.
A big question had been answered—what made a man a man? I

41

was told that when you turn twenty-one you were legally a man, but that didn't necessarily make you a man. You could be one at fifteen, or didn't have to be one even at fifty. I had always thought to be a real man I had to be like Pop, have muscles of steel, work from sunup to sundown—kill rats.

This was the first time anyone or anything had told me that emotional strength was just as important as physical strength. *"You'll be a man, my son!"* That stuck with me.

I learned "If" by heart, picking apart each verse and finding ways to apply its philosophies to my own life.

By this time, my friends and I were starting to go out to dance at places like the Club Sudan and the Graystone Ballroom and Gardens. Club Sudan had the younger crowd, around my age. We usually went there on the weekends. Graystone Ballroom and Gardens was where we went on Monday nights, the only night colored people could go. That was our big night. Everybody who was anybody would be there, dressed to kill. It was the place to go for all the pretty people, or people who thought they were pretty, or who wanted to be pretty, or who wanted to meet somebody pretty.

Yeah, that was our night—wall-to-wall people inside and out, not letting the hot, sticky summer weather keep them from wearing the finest clothes possible, moving and grooving to the live music of Duke Ellington, Count Basie or one of the other top colored bands.

I was plagued by the fact that girls I liked seldom liked me. I guess I didn't look good enough or dance well enough or maybe I just wasn't cool enough. Whenever I was around a girl I liked, I overreacted. My tongue played tricks on me. Nothing I said came out right.

Around the girls I liked I was being someone I thought would impress them, but around the girls I knew liked me I was just being myself.

So I started playing a little game. When I saw a girl I really liked I convinced myself that I didn't. She was no big deal. This was not easy but in time it started working. I began to come off more like a human being.

That helped some but not enough. The guys who got the girls first were the best dancers and I was not one of them. It was a long torturous walk back to my laughing friends from the middle of the large dance floor after being turned down abruptly or ignored by a pretty girl. But every now and then one would say yes. I then developed a theory I called two out of ten. If I asked ten girls to dance, the percentage was two would say yes. I usually got laughed at eight times and envied twice.

After school and whenever I wasn't working for Pop, I'd hang around the Brewster Center, a city-run recreation facility for inner-city kids, some five miles from my house and not far from Black Bottom.

The first day I stepped inside I was in another world—the smell, the feel, the action, the excitement. Kids of all ages were bouncing around shadow boxing, punching on the big bag and sparring with each other. I wanted in.

It must have been obvious because one of the trainers told me to go to the locker room, put on some trunks, and get into the ring. Harold Smith, a stocky kid about my size except slightly shorter and slightly wider, was already in the ring and needed a sparring partner. Despite a twinge of reluctance, I said okay. Although I had done my share of street fighting, and had learned about jabs, hooks and right crosses, once I got into the ring I realized how different things were inside that little area. Harold was tough and strong and immediately went for me. I tried to bounce back and forth like I had seen other fighters do but he was coming so fast I never had a chance to make it forth. Punching and chasing me around the ring, he hit me everywhere: the top of my head, my ears, my back. He even punched my butt. I never hit him once. I just kept ducking and running and covering up and hoping for the bell to ring. Three minutes felt like three hours.

I was so relieved when I finally heard the sound of that bell. Embarrassed and out of breath, I wondered whether this fight game was really for me. I stumbled out of the ring with a shit-eatin' grin, trying not to faint from fatigue.

"Thanks," I muttered to Harold as he bounced by. I was too tired even to remove those tight gloves.

As I sat down, I noticed one of the trainers coming toward me.

He was a handsome brown-skinned man about thirty-five, with a medium build and a kind expression.

"Let me help you," he said, unlacing my gloves. "Young man, you move very well. Or maybe I should say you run very well," he joked. I kept smiling but didn't think it was funny worth a damn. All I wanted to do was take off those gloves and get the hell out of there.

"There's one thing you should always remember," he said. "The best defense is a good offense."

"Yeah, I know. My father told me that one, too," I mumbled through swollen lips.

"That guy wasn't really that good. He just had nothing to think about but beating on you. You've got to put something on *his* mind—make him think. And you could start with a jab in his face."

That made some sense to me, but I didn't ever want to see Harold again, let alone try to put a jab in his face.

"But first," he said, "maybe I should show you how to do it."

He had decided to take me on. He told me he could see that I not only had great speed but heart as well. His name was Eddie Futch. (He would later go on to train many champions. In the heavyweight category alone he would have Joe Frazier, Ken Norton and Riddick Bowe.)

Mr. Futch told me I had to be serious. I was serious. After all, I had decided that this was to become my career. It took me weeks to get in shape—running five miles at 5:30 in the morning, sweating for hours in the hot gym every day, building muscles, no smoking, no drinking, no girls. The girls part really bothered me, but I wanted to be a champion.

After two or three months under Futch I was a star in my weight class, 112 pounds. I had outboxed every kid around my size. Well, not every. There was still Harold Smith, who had now grown ten pounds heavier than me. I had no intention of ever getting back in the ring with that guy.

"Berry," Futch said one day, "I want you in the ring with Harold Smith."

Oh shit.

Futch told me he knew I was worried but I needn't be. I was much better now and he wanted me to prove it to myself. I believed him, but was still scared to death. But this time we went three rounds and Harold hardly touched me. I touched him a lot.

The air inside the bus one autumn evening was thick with tension. It was my first amateur fight and the Brewster team was on its way to a small local arena. While other fighters were talking, roaming the aisle, I sat quietly alone in my seat, filled with emotion.

In the large locker room we shared with the opposing team, I saw the one kid I hoped I would not be fighting. He was the meanest, toughest-looking one there—puffy, defiant eyes, cheekbones like leather, and gashes all over his face. When I heard he was in my same weight class I felt sick.

Then Futch came over and pointed out the kid I would be fighting—a skinny-looking little guy with no scars, no bruises, no muscles, no nothing. I was bathed in relief. Thrilled. My fear turned to ecstasy.

Futch quickly set me straight. "Those the ones you gotta watch out for," he whispered. "If his face isn't battered that means he hasn't been hit much. Why do you think he hasn't been hit much?"

"He hasn't fought much?"

"Take it lightly if you want to," Futch said. "This kid could be good."

Futch was right again. Once in the ring, the kid was surprisingly quick with his hands and fast on his feet. It was only a three-rounder, but from the beginning I realized I was in big trouble.

I lost my first amateur fight and felt awful. Seeing my dejected state, I expected Futch to try to cheer me up. He didn't.

"You *should* feel bad. You underestimated your opponent, you got tired and made a lot of mistakes. You learn a lot more from losing than you do winning."

I knew there was something to that but I couldn't help wondering how Sugar Ray Robinson had learned so much. He had never lost—except once against Jake LaMotta.

I was now in the tenth grade and by that time a big fan of Sugar Ray's. He was king. Like Joe Louis, he was from Detroit. He had everything—finesse, flair, hand speed, style, elegance, showmanship and heart.

He wrote the book on how to hit without being hit. He could turn

45

his head in a split second to avoid a devastating right cross. Beautiful. He was just beautiful. His slicked-back, processed hair rarely got messed up. But if it did, we knew it bugged him and we'd take bets that he'd knock the guy out in the next round.

More than anything else he made me understand that boxing was a science.

But my inner battle was still raging—in one corner, boxing; in the other, music. Whenever I wasn't at the Brewster Center training I was somewhere writing songs—which no one wanted to hear. On one hand, I was frantic to be like Sugar Ray; on another, Nat King Cole, whose velvet voice and piano playing could romance a song like no one else.

I really wanted to sing just like him, but had a voice problem. I was sort of a mixture of him, Billy Eckstine and Donald Duck. My sound-alike percentage weighed heavily toward the latter. Yet, strangely enough, there was one part of my lower register that I *could* make sound a lot like Nat.

I'd also been bitten by the Jazz bug and was becoming an avid fan of many of the greats—Charlie Parker, Dizzy Gillespie, Miles Davis, Erroll Garner and the like.

I shared this passion with my friend, Billy Davis, who had been a part of my family since grammar school. He was a fast mover, hip. And he could dance. Boy, could he dance. A year younger in age and about five years older in experience, Billy was a man about town but he always wanted to hang around with me because, he said, he was sure I was going someplace. He didn't know where, but someplace.

I knew I needed to get a more solid musical training. So I applied for classes in school.

Unfortunately, the only music class with any openings left was clarinet. I hated clarinet, but grabbed it.

For two weeks I studied my butt off, trying to learn everything I could—theory, technique, everything. I had actually managed to learn to play the damn thing.

It so happened that I had also, over the years, built up a far-reaching reputation for making trouble in classrooms. It was to the point where I was expected to do something bad. About my third week in clarinet class, the teacher announced that she had put up with enough fooling around. She told us clearly that any troublemakers would be put out immediately. I knew she meant me and I wasn't opening my mouth for nothing.

One of my partners in crime told me something funny. I ignored him completely. Honest. But a couple of people around me snickered.

The teacher pointed directly at me with delighted viciousness. "Gordy, out!"

"But . . ."

"No buts! Out! And I mean now!"

I never got another chance. I had just gotten kicked out of the only class that really interested me. Walking down the hallway I started thinking and by the time I got outside I had made a major decision. Since my first amateur loss I had won all of my fights. Eddie Futch believed in me. I believed in me. I was going to quit school and turn pro.

From childhood, I had wanted to make my parents proud. I knew I hadn't done such a good job up to now, and quitting school didn't help. Of course I didn't come right out and announce it to them. Instead of going to school, I'd go off to the gym every day and work out. Lucky for me Mother was distracted with her work. But when she finally found out she was devastated. Maybe she felt she had failed in some way. Pop, whose education had come primarily from his own life experiences, was not as upset, though he acted so for Mother's sake.

But whenever I fought the whole family was there—in my corner—strong, cheering me on. I loved it! I was always a performer in that ring, and the larger the crowd, the better. With my number one fan there, my younger brother, Robert, I was even more of a show-off. Being able to be a star in front of my family gave me an instantaneous edge on my opponent.

Such was the night of November 19, 1948, when I was fighting on the same card with my hero, Joe Louis!, at the Olympia Stadium in Detroit. They all came out. Not just the family, but everybody.

My conscience was getting me because I knew I had broken a cardinal rule of boxing—abstinence. We were supposed to stay away from girls for ten days before a fight because sex drains your energy. Normally that wasn't a problem because I didn't have that much luck with girls anyway. But the more popular I got, the luckier I got. Not only had I broken the rule, but I'd done it the night before the most important fight of my life.

It was a four-rounder and by the end of the first I was already getting tired. My only chance was to knock my opponent out early. But by the second round, I felt like I was dragging last night's girlfriend around the ring with me. I had to pull out all stops.

In the third round I got lucky. I connected with a combination of solid punches that sent my opponent reeling. Hearing the roar of the crowd really turned me on. I got crazy trying to finish him off but he just wouldn't go down. Now my girlfriend had a tight choke hold around my chest and I could barely breathe.

Since I couldn't knock him out I wanted it to look like I wasn't really trying, so I pulled back, trying to catch my breath. Bouncing around, cocky and playful. Doing something Futch had always warned against—dropping my arms, slapping punches at him.

Next thing I knew I was down kissing the canvas. I never saw the right cross that floored me. Embarrassed, I jumped up just as the bell rang.

I was so tired I could hardly walk to my corner. But Futch's words of encouragement, along with a phrase from Kipling's poem gave me new life: *"If you can force your heart and nerve and sinew to serve your turn long after they are gone, And so hold on when there is nothing in you Except the Will which says to them 'Hold on!' "* And I did. I held on in the last round and won the fight by decision.

Though my family cheered me when I joined them later to watch Joe Louis fight, I knew in my heart I hadn't done my best.

It was the first time I'd seen my hero in person. Looking at him box with such courage and skill I realized that if I wanted to be a champion I would have to do a lot better than I was doing. That included taking strict control over the one thing I loved most in the world—being with women. That was the night I learned that when a fighter gets real tired in the ring it's not necessarily because he's out of shape.

After that I really worked hard, I put on weight and moved up to the featherweight division, but I was disappointed that I wasn't getting many matches and I didn't know why. Futch explained it was because I was really good, but didn't have a high ranking, so name fighters

1. On top of my world at nine years old.

2. My beautiful mother on her 16th birthday.

3. Mother and Pop around 1922.

4. The whole clan gathered to honor Mama Lucy (*holding gift*) on her 75th birthday in Detroit, 1935. I'm sitting on the floor holding my face.

5. In this 1938 school picture one thing is clear: my brother Robert (*right*) wa
well behaved and studious; I was trouble.

6. Thanksgiving, 1945. I always thought that Thanksgiving dinner at the Gordy household was a special party for me. I'm in the front on the right.

7. Pop was a strong task master. That's me on top hating the construction business. Robert didn't look too thrilled either.

.. OLYMPIA BOXING PROGRAM ..
Friday, Nov. 19, 8:30 p.m.

1ST BOUT—4 RDS.—128 LBS.	1	2	3	4	
BERRY GORDY DETROIT, MICH.					*Winner*
CIRO MONTALZO MEXICO CITY, MEXICO					

2ND BOUT—4 RDS.—152 LBS.	1	2	3	4
CECIL KRAFF DETROIT, MICH.				
CHUCK ROSS KALAMAZOO, MICH.				

3RD BOUT—4 RDS.—145 LBS.	1	2	3	4	
AL GRONIK LINCOLN PARK, MICH.					
~~SIDNEY MILLER~~ *Joe Henderson* DETROIT, MICH.					*Winner*

5TH BOUT—5 RDS.—137 LBS.	1	2	3	4	5
JAY WATKINS FLINT, MICH.					
~~TOMMY MATHEWS~~ *NATE Bridges* DETROIT, MICH.					

6TH BOUT—5 RDS.—155 LBS.	1	2	3	4	5	6
BILLY BORNE LINCOLN PARK, MICH.						
LEON WASHINGTON DETROIT, MICH.						

MAIN EVENT—10 RDS.—137 LBS.	1	2	3	4	5	6	7	8	9	10
LEROY WILLIS DETROIT, MICH.										
JOEY ANGELO PROVIDENCE, R. I.										

6 RDS.— HEAVYWEIGHTS— Exhibition	1	2	3	4	5	6
JOE LOUIS World's Heavyweight Champion DETROIT, MICH.						
VERN MITCHELL DETROIT, MICH.						

Berry Gordy Jr.
'Honorary Chairman'
Salute to the Champ

NATIONAL LEAGUE HOCKEY
Sunday, November 21, 1948
RED WINGS *vs.* CANADIENS
Prices: $3.00 - $2.40 - $1.80 - $1.25

8. One of my biggest thrills was appearing on the same fight card as my hero, Joe Louis. My photo was added years later when I chaired a committee honoring the Brown Bomber.

AMERICA'S MOST AMAZING FAMILY

The Famous Gordys Of Detroit Have What It Takes

IT IS really a tough job to try and name America's most talented family, because there are so many outstanding families which could be given that honor. Our intentions are not to deny credit to many of America's top families, but if there were a national contest to select the most gifted family in America, the editors of COLOR would nominate the Gordy family.

We invite you to examine the following story to find out for yourself why we would nominate the Gordys as America's most talented family.

In Detroit, Michigan, the internationally famous "Motor City," lives one of America's most interesting families—the talented, energetic, and the tireless Gordys. This unusual family, headed by Mr. and Mrs. Berry Gordy, Sr., is a big family in more than one way. Although there are eight children in the Gordy family, which naturally places it among America's big families, it has developed over a period of years into one of the most successful families in the nation. Under the expert guidance of their parents, the Gordy family, four boys and four girls, have all developed into healthy unusually gifted American men and women.

No matter how viewed, the achievements of the Gordys are exceptional and impressive. This is realized when one notes that the family boasts of top-rank business men, sportsmen, civic leaders, all of whom are leaders in their field.

Boxing is only one of the sports in which the Gordys indulge. Detroit's Number One sepia family has its own bowling team, composed of the four Gordy brothers, George, Robert, Berry, Jr., and Fuller and Berry, Sr. The father, always greatly interested in developing and expanding his family's athletic interests and ability organized his sons into a bowling team several years ago. Since then, the Gordy Bowling Team has been the recipient of many prizes and honors. Fuller Gordy, however, is the top bowler among the family members and Detroit's best. He has won a nation singles match, and has also won honors in the Pittsburgh Courier Bowling Classic in Motor City. The Gordy team, which has won the City Championship Class C Trophy and the Garfield Lounge prize trophy, often plays under its own name as the Gordy Contractor and Associated Builders. Most tournament play, however, has been under the sponsorship of either Airplane Sausage Company or Friars Ale.

Every member of the Gordy family is a veteran at horseback riding, but Loucye and Gwendolyn are the best at this sport and ride most frequently. They are enthusiastic members of The Bit and Spur Riding Club of which Loucye was a founder. Loucye is also a member of Boots and Saddle, and is an accomplished instructor in riding.

Berry Gordy, Jr., the musician in the family, won the semi-final competition in Frankie Carle's Boogie-Woogie contest at the Michigan Theater in Detroit. He also provides the music for frequent family song sessions in the Gordy home.

It is worth while to note that whenever a Gordy appears on a (CONTINUED ON PAGE

9. The 1949 *Color Magazine* article on the family really made us feel special. I'm on the piano.

OPPOSITE PAGE:
10. Me and my sidekick Billy Davis on the streets of L.A. in 1949 imitating the Nicholas Brothers.

11. The Gordy women were always in charge. *Left to right:* Esther, Anna, Mother, Gwen and Loucye.

12. In Korea I drove the chaplain to the front lines—and prayed a lot.

13. Halloween,1957, at the Gordy, Jr., household, with Thelma and our first two children, Hazel Joy and Berry IV. Working on the assembly line had done nothing to improve my looks.

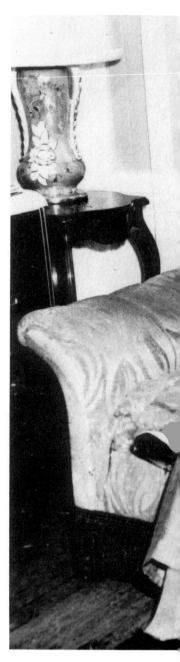

14. Music business night at the Flame Show Bar. Front row: Nat Tarnopol *(far left)*, DJ "Frantic" Ernie Durham *(fourth from left)* and me *(standing far right)*. Second row: Roquel Davis *(far left)*, Phil Jones *(sixth from left)*, DJ "Long Lean" Larry Dean *(third from right)* and DJ Larry Dixon *(far right)*. Back row: *(only female)* Rosemary Gordy, wife of my brother, George.

were less willing to fight me, having little to gain and a lot to lose. Even so, I managed to grind out fifteen fights—ten wins, four by knockouts, two draws and three losses, two of which I will always maintain were bad decisions. I trained rigorously, working harder than ever, hoping to one day get my shot at the title.

Then, one hot August day in 1950, a remarkable thing happened. The Woodward Avenue Gym was packed. I was training hard. Pitting myself against the big bag and feeling very much the victor, I decided my tired, profusely sweating body deserved a break. As I sat down on a bench, my eyes fell on two posters on one of the four square pillars that supported the gym's ceiling. I got up and walked closer.

The top poster announced a Battle of the Bands between Stan Kenton and Duke Ellington for that same night. The one below was advertising a bout between two young fighters, scheduled for the following Friday night. There it was again: Boxing versus Music. This time it was visual.

I stared at both posters for some time, realizing the fighters could fight once and maybe not fight again for three or four weeks, or months, or never. The bands were doing it every night, city after city, and not getting hurt. I then noticed the fighters were about twenty-three and looked fifty; the band leaders about fifty and looked twenty-three.

The war that had been raging inside me—music versus boxing—was finally over. I had my answer.

No more sweating in a hot gym every day, no more running those five miles around Belle Isle at 5:30 A.M. No more abstinence. No more abstinence!!

That day I took off my gloves—for good.

WHAT DO YOU DO, YOUNG MAN?

FOR THE NEXT FEW MONTHS all I could think about was songwriting. I wrote about everything, license plates, the sky, people, love, paper clips, you name it. I was a writing fool. Ideas were coming to me from everywhere. Even in my dreams I would hear songs and think to myself, "I wish I could have written something as beautiful as that." Then I'd wake up and realize I *had* written it. It was *my* dream. Amazing! But I could seldom remember the actual songs and arrangements. All I could remember was that I loved it. It was wonderful and the feeling stayed with me.

(Years later I began to keep a tape recorder next to my bed for these late-night inspirations. Saving ideas would become one of my greatest passions.)

I always wanted to try my new song ideas on somebody—anybody. But trying to get people to listen was tough.

Luckily, the Gordy Print Shop, in our building, owned and run by Fuller, Esther and George, was where I knew I could always find a captive audience. Their business was housed in two storefronts attached together. The first was used as an office, and straight through in the back, the second was where the printing presses and equipment were.

"Hey, I gotta great new song idea that you just gotta hear" is usually how I'd start off their day. They liked hearing all my little songs, at first.

But my ideas were coming much too fast. Many times after I'd left, I'd pop right back in before they knew it.

"By the way, I forgot to tell you about this other new idea . . ."

Pretty soon they, too, were no longer willing listeners. I became aware of that one day when I came in and saw all three of them in the back lounging around.

"Great," I thought. "They'll be glad to hear my new song." But as soon as they spotted me, they became the busiest little shop in town—moving papers, stacking supplies, starting the presses rolling. Well, a house didn't have to fall on me.

I stood there in the outer office for a moment wanting to sink through the floor.

"Hey," I said, waving as I backed out, speaking over the noise. "I had something for you to hear, but you're too busy now so I'll come back later."

They all nodded.

I was a little lost, but then I got to thinking how other people must have felt whenever I talked to them about my new song ideas. They were either preoccupied or waiting for an opportunity to jump in and start talking about themselves. Like me, everybody seemed to have a great urge to be heard.

It occurred to me that if I listened to what *they* had to say first, then maybe they'd be more receptive to hearing my ideas. So I became a good listener. It worked! But too well; I got hooked on people.

Listening to their problems, thoughts and feelings excited me because I connected with them. I learned that what they were interested in is what *I* was interested in—what everyone was interested in. I learned we all basically wanted and needed the same things.

As a songwriter that's what I wanted to write about—what people needed—whether it was love, a reason to dance, a reason to cry.

I had made that big discovery all because I was forced to listen.

One thing I knew the Gordy Print Shop needed was customers. And I had an idea to help them. When I went in to see them about it, as always, they got real busy and tried to avoid me. But I knew this was going to help them, so I hid behind a column and waited. Seeing no customers, I knew they couldn't fake it too long and the minute that they relaxed—voom! I jumped out.

"Fuller," I said, landing right behind him.

He screamed. They all jumped. I had never heard my oldest brother holler like that before. "Junior! What the heck are you doing?" he yelled.

"That's not funny," Esther said.

"I thought we were being robbed," George shouted.

I told them I was sorry but I was so excited about my idea to help their business. "I just wrote a great radio commercial for you. It's a song called 'Let Gordy Be Your Printer Too,' and it sounds just like Nat King Cole!"

"Who's singing it?" Fuller asked.

"I am."

"I know, but who's going to sing it on the radio commercial?"

"I am."

Interest was disappearing fast. But before they could say another word I began snapping my fingers and singing . . . *"Whether your job is large or small, Gordy Printing will do them all. Give us a try, we'll do it right and Gordy will be your printer for life. Let Gordy . . . da da da da . . . be your printer too!"*

They liked it and arranged for me to record it in the basement studio of a local disc jockey named Bristol Bryant. Soon it was playing on the station where he worked, WJLB. Some people really thought it *was* Nat King Cole. Even though it was just me singing and playing the piano on the one-minute commercial, I'd written and produced something meaningful. Their business picked up and my proud family started taking me a little more seriously.

Shortly after that Mother had some friends over. I was sitting in the living room and could hear voices from the dining room bragging about their sons and daughters who were in college studying to be doctors and lawyers.

"Yes, that's right," one of the guests was saying to Mother, "the two younger boys are at Wayne State. One's majoring in electronics. The other premed. Oh, and you know my oldest son, he's got his own manufacturing company. Yes, indeedy Bertha, they're doing so well."

It was time for me to leave the house. But I had to go through the dining room. Not good.

I, a twenty-year-old, was quietly making my way out, when I heard this same voice directed my way, "And what do *you* do, young man?"

I stopped. "I write songs!"

"I know," he said, "but what do you *do?*"

What could I say? How dare he dismiss my songwriting! This was just as much a profession as doctor or lawyer and it could make thousands of people happy.

"Uh, that's it. I write songs."

He looked at Mother. As happy as she had been at my doing that commercial, she hadn't exactly planned on that being my life's work. She was a scholar, an educator, a Daughter Ruler of the Elks Club, and the recipient of the Eleanor Roosevelt Mother of the Day Award. She smiled. I was proud of what I was doing; but I did feel a little sorry for Mother. These were her friends. And I knew parents had peer pressure, too.

I left the house that day knowing more than ever I had something to prove.

From all those people that I'd been listening to, I'd been hearing the theme of a common fear that they wouldn't be loved if they exposed who they really were. This was something I thought a lot about. My belief was if someone didn't love you for yourself, but for who you were trying to be, the relationship wouldn't last too long anyway. But if you're just you, you'll eventually be loved by the right person.

So "You Are You" was how I titled my next song. I wrote about individuality—being yourself—the magic inside:

You are you—
That's all that matters to me.

You are you—
And only you can be the one I love and yearn for,
the one that my heart burns for.

Yes, you are you—
And that makes you best of all . . .

After I finished it, I saw an ad in a magazine where for twenty-five dollars you could send off a coupon with a recording of a song and get sheet music written. I jumped on it right away.

A few weeks later I received this beautiful piece of sheet music— my first complete song all professionally written. I was legit.

Thinking of general audiences even then, I had written this song with Doris Day in mind. She was America's girl next door. I knew when she heard it she would feel about it the same as I did and would die to record it.

Excited, I sent it off with a little note saying, "Dear Doris, here's a song I've written for you." I addressed it to: "Doris Day, Hollywood, California." Return address: "Berry Gordy Jr., 5139 St. Antoine,

Detroit, Michigan." I was on top of the world with anticipation. I waited. And waited. And waited.

Finally! After about three months a letter came, but it was not from Doris Day. It started with "Greetings" and ended with "Please report to Fort Custer." I had been drafted.

4

FACING THE REAL WORLD
1951–1957

PRIVATE GORDY

THE KOREAN WAR. Not only was this a total disruption to my focus and goals, it was something I didn't understand. I didn't want to go. I purposely answered all the questions wrong on the IQ test at the induction center but they passed me anyway. (On an up note it was one of the few tests I had passed in recent years.)

From June through September of 1951 I was stationed at Camp Chaffee, Arkansas, for basic training. Wanting to make the best of a bad situation, I tried to get into Special Services, a branch of the army that entertained the troops. I heard they had it made. I was an entertainer—a comedian since grade school. But when I applied they told me I didn't have enough experience. Determined to show them I was good, I did whatever job they gave me in the most entertaining way I could think of, hoping to get discovered.

When I was assigned to call out the marching drills for our platoon, I would sing out those commands and create all sorts of new cadence calls. As flag bearer of our platoon I'd be clutching that pole, holding my head and that flag up high—strutting like mad. I also became something of a boot camp star at company boxing matches, knocking out all my opponents.

Nothing worked. I did, however, pick up my high school diploma through the GED test. I hadn't realized how proud I'd feel, being a high school graduate.

Shortly after, I was selected for leadership school right on the base where I learned a lot about discipline and organization. Boy, were they strict. We had to make our beds so tight that if you dropped a quarter on the sheets, it had to bounce back up. We had to be extremely clean to pass the dirt patrols that would all too often surprise us.

My high ratings in passing these inspections gained me a lot of respect. I was outstanding. Proud.

Then one night it happened. I awoke in mortified shock to find that after all these years, my childhood problem had not disappeared. I had wet the bed!

This school was like West Point. We were the cream of the crop— and I had wet the bed. It was a replay of my days with Pop when I had to think fast. Balling up my sheets tightly, I hustled into the fast-moving line at the laundry, tossing my bedding to one of the guys behind the counter. As I moved on down, from the corner of my eye, I saw that same guy looking up the line to see who had turned in the smelly sheets. But sheets were coming at him so fast he had to let it go.

What a relief! I could never let that happen again and made sure it didn't. I never drank any liquids later than 4:00 P.M.

I liked leadership school but how to get out of going to Korea and back home to my music was the only thing on my mind. I knew some other guys were getting out but I couldn't find out how.

By the time I did, I was already on a troop ship in the middle of the Pacific. That's where I heard some of the saddest news of my life.

Out on the deck, I was listening to some of my buddies talking about two guys who had both gotten out with no trouble.

I jumped in. "How, how'd they do it? Murder? Sabotage? Insanity?"

"No," one of them said. "They wet the bed."

!?#!@?!

TO BE LOVED

* * *

The minute I arrived in Korea, I was impressed by its people, especially the children—amazing little baby salesmen who greeted us on the docks hawking gold watches, rings, radios, everything.

After that, all I can remember is riding in trucks further and further into the jungle and further away from home and hope. I was frightened numb. So numb I started trying to think positive.

"What a wonderful experience," I told myself, trying to appreciate things around me: a new environment, new country, new language, new people, new culture. Didn't work. Well, maybe a little, but my fear and longing to be back on American soil were greater than ever.

I was assigned to the Third Division. Once we got settled in at our camp near Panmunjom, I slowly got used to the routine, mainly because of the warm connection I had with the Korean people who worked on the base. Most of them looked like fourteen- or fifteen-year-olds—not too much older than those baby salesmen. They mostly worked as kitchen help and could barely speak our language. Many GIs treated them like they were ignorant children, pushing them around and making fun of them.

We all learned some great cuss words and phrases in Korean. But watching the faces of the locals I could see that while they might laugh with us, they didn't like it. Some seemed hurt.

It dawned on me that the same Koreans being kicked around in our mess halls during the day could easily be sniping at us at night. Who could tell the difference? We were fighting alongside the South against the North. But the North and the South were the same people.

I was interested in how they felt, what they thought. So I learned the language, starting with simple verbs like *come, go, like,* especially *like—I like you.*

The Koreans were so happy I was trying to learn their language the right way, to communicate with them, not insult them. Not able to pronounce Berry, they called me something that came out sounding like Bad-du-die. Before long I was even being used as an interpreter, straightening out little problems.

57

This added to my ongoing fascination with communication. At home there were language barriers, too, known as semantics. Words can mean different things to different people. Wherever I was, I was always more concerned with what people *meant* rather than what they *said* or what words they used. In Korea, for my own self-preservation, this was vital.

The nights were most fearful. Especially guard duty. Walking through the jungle alone for three hours, hoping not to see anything move and knowing you're a sitting duck, was no fun. I hated the times I had to pull it.

Other nights, when I wasn't on guard duty, listening to my little battery-operated radio, weren't as bad. Most of the music I heard was Korean or other foreign stuff I couldn't understand. But once in a while they would play something in English. The only American song I can remember hearing became my favorite—"Mom and Dad's Waltz," a country song by Lefty Frizzell. Yeah—Lefty Frizzell. So what! I was scared and lonely and this simple music spoke to my homesick heart.

I had been assigned to the Third Division artillery unit, stationed behind the front-line infantry battalion as backup. From time to time soldiers from our unit were transferred to those units at the front line. That was the last place any of us wanted to be.

An opening was announced for a chaplain's assistant to play the organ and drive his jeep. This was a job everybody wanted. It was not exactly Special Services but definitely the next best thing.

I was not the first person in line, but lucky for me I still knew my chords and one-finger stuff and was familiar with some of the hymns from church. My ear did the rest. I got the job.

What was my job? Driving the chaplain to the front lines to give services to the troops fighting there.

!?#!@?!

Horrified as I was, as soon as the chaplain and I arrived at our destination, bombs going off around us, I'd jump out of the jeep, open a suitcase that became an instant organ and start to play. I knew the quicker we got started the quicker we could get out of there.

Driving back we'd usually pass foot soldiers moving toward the front line. I will never forget the terrified look on those young faces walking into the unknown while I was driving away.

As crazy as these times were, there was always an unbelievably warm response and appreciation we'd get from those men. While I know we affected them, they probably affected me more, because after seeing what they went through day after day, I was not fearful for myself anymore.

GETTING THE BLUES TOO LATE

IN 1953 I HAPPILY RETURNED HOME. I wanted to go into business on my own doing something I loved and I decided to open up a Jazz record store. To me, Jazz was the only pure art form. No matter how complex the rhythms and the melodies, I loved it just because it was Jazz. All the hip young people were into it, and I was sure the people in my neighborhood would love it as much as I did.

My plan was to open the store with my buddy, Billy Davis. Inducted into the army on the very same day, the two of us had run into each other overseas and had talked about investing our severance pay in a business when we got out.

But once we were discharged and had gotten home, he claimed his severance pay never arrived. Seeing him every day, dressed "sharper than a dog," I became suspicious. He finally confessed he loved clothes more than he loved being in business with me.

Even though Pop was somewhat disappointed that I didn't want to take over his plastering business, he borrowed money from the church credit union and loaned it to me. My brother George invested some of his own money, becoming a partner. Before we even opened our doors my new partner and I had a major disagreement.

Because three-dimension was the technology of the times, I wanted to call our store the 3D Record Mart with the subtitle, The House That Jams Built.

George agreed with me on the first part but had different ideas for the subtitle. "No, it should be House of Jazz," he insisted.

I didn't dislike House of Jazz, but I wanted something hipper, more catchy. Since the greatest records were called "jams" and the best musicians were always somewhere "jammin'," I wanted that name bad.

George said no. He loved House of Jazz.

I reminded him he came into business with me. The store was my idea, and most of the money was mine. "So I should run the business."

"Well, you *can* run it but all I'm saying is I want House of Jazz," he said, not budging.

At wits' end, I went to Pop, hoping he would help persuade George to my way of thinking. Instead, he gave me words of wisdom I would always remember: "Whenever they pay they have a say."

We called our shop the 3D Record Mart—House of Jazz.

I could see right then partnership was not for me but still I was determined to have the best record store in town.

We created a heavy Jazz atmosphere that you could feel the moment you walked in. Using the album covers, we decorated the walls with the hottest Jazz musicians of the time. Constantly playing was the cool Jazz of Miles Davis, the fluid chords of George Shearing, the dexterity and sensitivity of Oscar Peterson, the commercial groove of Erroll Garner, or the Bird—Charlie Parker—just blowing like mad, as only he could. I felt great.

That is, until my very first customer came in, a short heavyset guy who appeared to be a factory worker.

"Excuse me," he said. "Do you have any records by Muddy Waters?"

"Muddy who?"

"Waters."

"Never heard of him."

"John Lee Hooker? Jimmy Reed? B.B. King?"

"I'm sorry," I told him, "we don't sell that stuff here."

When he asked why, I explained, "Jazz is complex. Jazz is as different as each musician playing it. Those Blues records pretty much all say the same thing—'I love my baby, but my baby don't love me.' "

He looked at me like I was crazy and left.

I knew I had to educate my customers about the beauty of Jazz—right away. I would quickly launch into why Charlie Parker was the most brilliant genius of all time and how Miles Davis's horn could soothe you to death. But these people were hardheaded. They wanted what they wanted. And they wanted the Blues. I told them to try Hastings. They did.

Meanwhile, the Jazz lovers were few and far between. Most days it was only me hanging out with my sidekick Billy Davis, trying to look cool. Even though he hadn't invested with me he hung around, still convinced I was going someplace.

It dawned on me, one day, that I was losing the store. I started realizing this was a business, not a school, and in trying to educate my customers about great Jazz, we were going broke. I remembered what Pop had tried to get me to understand years before: "The customer is always right." It was time to change my ways. It was time to get the Blues.

Once word got out that we were stocking them, there was a significant pickup in business. During this period Blues artists had come into their heyday, especially in my neighborhood. I started paying more attention to the records, studying them. I began to enjoy and appreciate many of the artists. Among them was Louis Jordan. His music was a departure from the normal lowdown Blues, cleverly mixing lyrics with wit while usually varying from the normal chord structures.

One week the Midnighters, Fats Domino, Louis Jordan and Jimmy Reed were all hot at the same time and our store was jammed with people asking for their records. Some we couldn't get. Nobody had any, not even the distributors. That is, nobody except the Mad Russian.

After scrambling around everywhere trying to find them, I heard about him, a guy over on Hastings who always had the hottest records. The Mad Russian had a great nose for smelling a hit. He bought them all up as soon as they came out and then sold them out of his store, a one-stop, a place where record store owners could purchase all of the different distributors' merchandise at one place. He charged a nickel more than the distributors. So if you wanted the record first, you had to deal with him.

Walking into his store was like walking into a circus, with him playing all the characters. It was always packed with everyone trying to get his attention to buy records. He talked a mile a minute, mostly incoherent.

"Okay okay, you wanna buy five, you wanna buy ten, what d'ya want? what d'ya want? Oh, big deal, big deal. See the light shining in my head. It's cold outside. Open the door—get outta my store. Oh, open the door—get outta my store, ha."

Everybody called him crazy, and he *was*—but like a fox. The bottom line was, he wanted to sell quantity, but most of the dealers wanted to buy two or three of each record.

As soon as I was able to understand his game and was a little able to pick the hits myself, I would offer to buy a whole box of twenty-five of one selection, that is, when I got my turn to talk to him. The more I bought, the more chances I got. He really acted like his name, a Mad Russian, although I soon found out he was a Jew. At that time, I didn't know it was possible to be Russian and a Jew at the same time.

Becoming friendly with him, we were able to get the records early and business started to boom. But the store was too far in debt for us to turn things around.

The more I heard the Blues the more I liked it. I finally had to admit to myself Blues was in my soul, probably stemming from my early exposure to Gospel. There was an honesty about it; it was just as pure and real as Jazz. In fact, Jazz had its roots in the Blues. Ironically, that same simplicity I'd rejected in the Blues was the very thing that people related to.

This important lesson came too late to save the store, but would not be too late to make a difference in my songwriting.

Not only had I lost George's and my money, but I had lost the money Pop had borrowed from the church credit union.

Pop was a strange man, a beautiful, strange man. He knew how much I wanted to do my own thing and even though I was out of a job, he never even mentioned my coming back to work for him. On the outside he seemed tough and hard, but his actions showed me he was always coming from a deep sense of caring and love.

I was more than ever determined to make him proud.

My next job was as a salesman for Guardian Service Cookware. While I had sold things before, it was at Guardian Service that I really learned the techniques of it.

I remember how I almost didn't take the job when they told me I had to learn to cook, but Mother's words rang in my ears: "Nothing you learn is ever wasted."

At the end of the sales training we were so pumped up we felt we could sell anything to anybody. They had taught us all the right questions to ask, the right responses, all the tricks of the trade. But the most important knowledge to come from this was learning how to close.

We would prepare a whole meal with this cookware, using no water at all. People would give parties and invite guests over and I would cook for as many as twenty people, then make appointments with them at their homes to sell my pots.

But closing was the key. And that was easy for me because I believed so much in the product. I also believed it was worth the enormous prices we were asking. It didn't hurt that I was getting a good percentage of that. I did well, so well in fact, that I took Pop with me to show him how successful his son had become.

He stood quietly at my side as I knocked on the door of my first appointment that morning.

The man who opened the door recognized me from a cooking demonstration a few days before. He had loved the idea that my pots and pans would save the lives of his loved ones. That was then, when he was eating free. But now, a few days later, it was pay time.

"Good morning," I said brightly. He eyed Pop skeptically.

"Mr. Johnson, this is my father. He decided to come out with me this morning. Would you believe that my own father has never eaten food cooked in Guardian Service? I wanted him to hear how you thought it tasted. What about those carrots? Have you ever tasted carrots as sweet as that before?"

"Sure haven't," the man said. "They were so sweet."

"Of course. Most of the time carrots have a slight bitter taste to them. Those carrots were sweet because they were cooked in their own juices." I noticed Pop taking all this in. "The vitamins were all locked in—yummm," I added. "I can still taste them."

I sat down at a little table, pulling a chair over for Pop. I laid my sales forms on the table. At least three small half-naked kids darted around that little wartime prefabricated house with worn furniture.

"You have a wonderful family," I told him. "My father here had eight kids to feed." Looking at Pop I said, "I was telling Mr. Johnson and his friends the other night at the dinner about this woman at the funeral of her husband, just crying her eyes out after it was too late to do him any good. I wondered what had she done to keep him healthy while he was alive?"

That had been one of the stories I was taught in the sales meetings at Guardian Service. But then I added to it something that I truly believed. "You know," I said, not looking squarely at either of them, "you got to take care of people when they're still here, not cry for them after they're gone."

I could see they both agreed, the man nodding his head and Pop looking at me proudly.

Now it was time for the closing. I reminded the man that it was only $10 down and $10 a month. Certainly that was not too much to pay to keep a loving family healthy.

"So now, do you want the complete set of nine pieces of Guardian Service cookware for $272 or the cheaper four pots for $150?" I reminded him again, it was only $10 down and $10 a month.

"Well," the man said, "I do want the best for my family."

"I had a feeling you'd say that," I said, writing $272 on the form. Laying it down in front of him, I dropped the pen—just as I'd been taught. As he picked it up I said, "Press hard. There are three copies."

He pressed real hard. I had closed another deal.

Once outside, bubbling with pride, I was anxiously waiting for Pop's evaluation. He said nothing. Being as cool as I could, I said, "Well, what do you think?"

"I didn't like it. I didn't like it at all," he said.

Shocked and hurt, I couldn't believe what I was hearing. I had been brilliant.

"You sold that man somethin' he couldn't afford. That po' man with all them little babies to feed, and you sold him pots he didn't even need. Same thing he could do with all them, he could do with one or two."

My hurt turned to a little bit of anger. "Yeah, well, that man was grown and he had a choice. I didn't make him buy it."

"He loves his family and you took advantage of that. You did a good sales job. You reminded me of that white real estate man who sold me my first house on Roosevelt Street. I'm disappointed in you, son."

That really hurt. Pop's being disappointed in me affected me as much as that whuppin' he'd given me when I'd taken Fuller's money.

"Look into yourself, son. If you feel that was right, then it was. If you don't, then it wasn't."

Once again, that was a lesson about principle.

I never forgot it.

I never sold another pot.

THE TREADMILL

AFTER QUITTING GUARDIAN SERVICE, I took another turn at being a full-time songwriter. Pop let me live rent-free in an old apartment building he owned on Meldrum Street near the river. In return, I helped take care of the place.

By now I had my own family to support.

Shortly before my record store had closed my sidekick Billy Davis— apparently no longer sure I was going somewhere—had decided to go to work in a nightclub down South as a waiter. But before that, he had come into the store one day with two young ladies. One was the fast, hip type of girl he was usually attracted to. But the other, Thelma Coleman, wasn't. With her smooth, brown, flawless complexion, she was pretty but she was more than that. She seemed shy and sweet. Maybe the white nurse's uniform she was wearing had something to do with it, but she seemed to have the qualities of that supportive, helpful someone with whom I could have kids and carry on my strongly ingrained family tradition. But I thought it best not to say all this to her in those initial moments. In fact, I was a little nervous about what to say to her, period.

I didn't want to come on too strong so I waited quietly for an opening. Finally, when she said she worked at Harper Hospital, I seized the moment. I told her I was born there and that fate and destiny should never be ignored.

Within a week or two, we started going together. Now in my early twenties, the idea of settling down appealed to me.

I was ready to devote myself to being a family man. Having come from a large one, I probably had always subconsciously wanted kids. Thelma and I were married a few months later. It wasn't long before she was pregnant. When she announced it, I was ecstatic. More than anything in the world, I wanted a son.

August 1954. It was hot. I was corraled in a room with other expectant fathers, sweating with nervous anticipation. Other new fathers had come and gone but I was still pacing. By morning, when Thelma still hadn't delivered, I rushed home for a few minutes to change clothes and freshen up. The phone was ringing as I walked in the door. It was the nurse from the hospital.

Fear gripped me.

When she said, "You are the proud father of a baby . . ." my anxiety intensified as I waited for her to complete the seemingly hour-long phrase . . . "girl."

Sadly, I lowered the phone to its cradle, muttering, "Thanks." I rushed back to the hospital, my emotions in turmoil. I had wanted a son so badly, but when I looked at my baby girl I immediately felt so stupid. I was so in love with the little thing I didn't know what to do. She captivated me in that first minute and would continue to captivate me throughout my life. We named her Hazel Joy, after Thelma's mother.

That night I composed a little tune called "Joy." "*Even though we wanted a boy that's how it goes. We named her Joy and I know I'm happier by far with you baby exactly just as you are, a little bundle of joy . . .*"

And to this day, every time I sing it to her, she cries.

In October of 1955, I finally got my wish to have a son. We named him Berry IV. A year later, in August, we had another son, Terry James.

As a young father, I loved spending time with my children. Nothing inspired me more than those young, open minds. I was determined to make learning fun. I had fun, too, creating games, puzzles, riddles, contests, even flash cards for learning math and spelling. I'd be right in there competing with them, tussling and rolling on the floor. I started teaching them "If" as soon as they could talk.

One of our favorite games was when I'd line them up like little soldiers. "Okay, here we go, ready?"

Nodding, their bodies were poised to move as soon as they heard me yell out the commands in rapid succession, like my army cadence calls.

"On your knees, on your butt, on your back, stand up!"

All three scrambled to get into each position, breathlessly trying to be the first to finish, ready for the next command.

"On your front, on your back, on your knees, on your head, on your back!" And so on for several rounds until Hazel, Terry and I were all exhausted. But Berry IV was always ready for more.

Early on they began to show distinct personalities of their own. In lessons of morality, Hazel Joy was the walking and talking conscience of the family. As the oldest child, she kept her brothers in line, like a cop. Berry IV already had emerged as very athletic, later excelling at all sports.

Terry, more than the others, loved anything having to do with money. As soon as he learned to talk, he had a knack for facts and figures.

One night when Thelma and I had company over, the kids were upstairs making an awful racket. Nothing I'd said had managed to quiet them down. Not having forgotten the sting of those whuppin's of Pop's, I tended to spare the rod. Psychology usually got the job done for me.

Entering their room with a pillow fight in full force, I announced, "Whoever goes to sleep first gets some money."

They stopped.

Hazel shouted, "What? Some money?"

Berry followed, "Daddy! For real?"
Terry was snoring.

Thelma's parents helped us a lot with food and toys for the kids.
Wonderful grandparents, they thought the world of those kids. As
for their son-in-law? Not too much. And now that I was out of a
regular job, they thought even less.

Their helpful hands became very painful to my self-esteem. Soon
my songwriting endeavors became as much a joke to me as they were
to everyone else. I had been called a bum for so long I thought maybe
I was.

I decided I was willing to take a real job, a nine-to-fiver.

The minute my mother-in-law heard I would work, she wasted no
time in using her union connections to get me a job in the Ford
foundry. She told me I was lucky because the job I was getting had
been a woman's job, and I should be able to handle that easily.
Sounded okay to me but I had no idea what I was in for.

That foundry was hell, a living nightmare. Hot, blowing furnaces,
loud clanging noises, dust, smoke and soot everywhere, red molten
metal pouring out of huge stoves on conveyor belts. When the bright
red liquid steel arrived at my station, it would be cooling down from
red hot to black hot. We had to wear large asbestos gloves to keep
our hands from burning, while we knocked the newly formed nuts
and bolts from their casings with big mallets. This place made Pop's
plastering job seem like a holiday picnic. After five minutes on the
first day, I was dead. Every fifty minutes when we got a ten-minute
break, I stumbled out of the foundry room. I could see people talking,
but couldn't hear a word they were saying. How was I possibly going
to make it through the whole day?

Lunchtime took forever to come but when it did, I couldn't eat.
I sat there coughing up black gook from my chest. I kept telling
myself I couldn't give up. I had to make it through this first day
even though there was no question in my mind that it would
definitely be my last. Finally the eight hours were over. I could
hardly walk. My wrists were swollen. My body was stiff. My head,
arms and ears, everything ached. I slowly made it to the car, a
crippled man.

Driving home, I was in a surreal nightmare. If someone blew their horn at me, I wouldn't hear it. I kept to a snail's pace, wondering whether I was going to hit or be hit by something. Finally, in a total vacuum of silence I made it home.

At the door, Thelma and little Hazel—Puddin' we called her—were proudly waiting for the working man to come home. In agony, I tried to tell her that I couldn't go back. If sound was coming out of my mouth, I couldn't hear it.

From what I could determine through lip reading, she was assuring me that this had just been a hard first day and that I would be just fine.

She had not understood that I was saying I would never go back to that job again. When she finally got it, she was adamant, shouting at me. "Think of all the trouble my mother went through. You can't embarrass me like this," I imagined she was saying to me.

"I can't do it. I just can't do it," I mouthed.

The next morning I rushed back to the Ford foundry to beg the supervisor for another job, enthusiastically expressing my sincere desire to work in some other capacity.

He reminded me that the job I was telling him I couldn't do had been a woman's job—an obvious attack on my manhood.

But thanks to "If" that didn't bother me. I laughed and said, "If it's a woman's job then she's a much better woman than I am a man. I still can't do it."

"There is no other job," he told me. "If you don't take this one, you're fired."

"I guess I'll just have to be fired then."

Thelma's mother was furious. But three weeks later she had me on my way to another nine-to-fiver. If my mother-in-law's plan was to set me up to love this new job, she sure succeeded.

The minute I walked into the Lincoln-Mercury assembly plant and saw how cool it was—no furnaces, fire or hot metal—I knew this was going to be my home for a while. Little did I know when I started how important to my future that assembly line was going to be. All I knew was those slow-moving car frames were the loveliest sight I'd ever seen. There was a pleasing simplicity to how everyone did the same thing over and over again.

For $86.40 a week, I fastened upholstery and chrome strips to those frames being pulled down the line on conveyor belts. It was a snap. I learned it so fast I could jump into each car as it arrived, do my job, get out and have time to spare. Before long that extra time was devoted to singing and writing songs.

Since I had no piano I had to devise another method of writing. I used "Mary Had A Little Lamb," the simplest song I could think of, to form the basis to remember song ideas in my head. I gave each note or tone of the scale a number from one to seven. "Mary Had A Little Lamb" turned out to be 3212333-222-355-32123333-22321. I practiced other simple songs putting numbers to them as well. Once I could identify each tone with a number of the scale, I had it made. As I began to create interesting melodies in my head, I would associate each note with a number. This allowed me to remember my new musical ideas.

Working fast up the slow-moving line, getting ahead of myself, I had time to rush back to my station and write down the numbers that corresponded with my new ideas. How wonderful—getting paid for a real job and composing songs at the same time!

On top of that I hustled every way I could to make extra money: working overtime, Saturdays and Sundays, and joining a poker club, playing every weekend at a different person's home.

The poker club was fun, but not too profitable. It didn't take me long to see that the house made the most money by getting a cut out of each pot. The house, that's what I wanted to be. At first they said no, I was too new. But they eventually agreed to let me have it at my house every fifth week. Playing poker, sometimes I'd win, sometimes I'd lose. But when it was at my house, I'd always make money.

Things went well for a few months. But after one such party, two numbers guys showed up at my house with a lot of cash, wanting me to play some blackjack. With the main party over and still a few people hanging out, I thought I'd give it a try. They played their game real good, first losing badly to me and all the while acting drunk and silly, like they were having fun doing it. Then the rhythm changed. By the time the sun came up they had won not only the money I'd made earlier, but also my savings. Nobody could be that lucky!

I suspected something. But what? The cards we were playing with were mine . . . or were they? If the cards were marked they had switched decks on me and would have to switch them back before leaving. I took three cards out of the deck we were playing with.

They finally left, taking three thousand of my hard-earned dollars with them. Meanwhile, I took the three cards into my bathroom and sat under the light, staring at the diamond patterns on the back, examining every one. After a while my eyes started playing tricks on me, but I kept staring and comparing. Finally I saw that the thickness of some of the diamond patterns was different on the sides. I had found it! The cards were marked after all. Those crooks had ripped me off.

Unable to contain my anger I went to my brother George's house, looking for a gun to go find them and take my money back. I was more furious than I had ever been in my whole life. But George's street wisdom forced me to cool down.

"First," he said, "anything that happened in your house is your fault. You're responsible for making sure no one's bringing in marked cards. Secondly, if you handle it your way two things can happen. You kill them; they kill you. And if you kill *them* you go to jail."

Never one to ignore clear logic and common sense, I knew I had to find a smarter way. I decided to try to outhustle the hustlers— that is, if they ever came back.

The next time the poker party was held at my house, I made my usual profit but kept looking at the front door, hoping the next knock would be theirs. Eventually it was.

There they were hoping to again reap the benefits of the house spoils, the same two guys, acting silly and high like before. They had come again to play blackjack. They were great actors. But not great enough.

After a few hands of them playing crazy and winning, I played out my scene.

"You guys are so damn lucky. I don't understand it," I said, squinting my eyes and staring at the cards. "Something must be wrong with these cards."

The two pickup men laughed nervously.

"If you think the cards are marked," one said, "why don't you just cover 'em up."

"Okay, I will." After dealing them their cards I covered the top of the deck. Now I could see what was coming and they couldn't.

I eventually won all my money back, plus another three thousand. They had baited me with other people's money. I had beaten them at their own game. This time, they did not leave happy.

I put a down payment on a two-story house at 414 Melbourne, which had two kitchenette apartments upstairs that I rented out for $15 a week. With that extra $120 a month, less my monthly house note payment of $80, I was living rent free and making a $40 profit.

I had been at the factory now for about two years, hustling like mad and still writing my songs. I was happy until one day, sitting around during the lunch break, I heard one of the older guys bragging that he had only three more years before retirement. Another said he had about eight years. A third guy was not as happy. He said he had twelve before he could really start living.

Then it hit me. I had thirty-three years left before I could live. What?!

I was on a treadmill, moving fast, but not really going anywhere. It was time to get off. I had money saved and a backlog of song ideas. It was now time to pursue my dream.

The news I was quitting my job at Lincoln-Mercury to write songs was not greeted with a retirement party by Thelma or my in-laws.

In retrospect, I can see how difficult it must have been to be married to me, a creative person. I was a dreamer, my wife was a worrier. I probably made her that way, always coming home with new thoughts, new ideas, new moods.

Soon after quitting my job, I bought me a silk suit and got my hair processed, losing any resemblance to a factory worker. People seemed to like me more. But to Thelma and her parents I was back to being a bum. And maybe I was—but I was a happy one.

THE SCENE

TIMING, IN MORE WAYS THAN ONE, was about to work in my favor. In early 1957 music was literally everywhere—people were singing on street corners, in barber shops, nightclubs, the churches, the movies, on the radio, everywhere. Now that music was my business, I wanted to be a part of all of it.

During the day I worked on my songs, and at night I made the scene, hanging out with people who worked in and around music, listening and learning.

All the beautiful people came to life at night—the sharpest-dressed black and white people I had ever seen—jewelry flashing, beautiful furs—something else. When Sugar Ray Robinson or Billy Eckstine came to town, they became part of the scene. John R Street was jumping with clubs like Sonny Wilson's Garfield Lounge, the Chesterfield Lounge and, nearby, the Frolic Show Bar.

But where you'd usually find me was down the street on the corner of John R and Canfield at the most popular of all, the Flame Show Bar. The top club acts performed on a stage built right into the bar. One night it might be Dinah Washington, on another Sarah Vaughan or Billie Holiday. They were my favorites.

Dinah had her own style. Shoutin' the Blues, she'd walk the bar, shakin' her behind, working it from end to end, (both the bar and her behind). During her lifetime, she had about eight husbands, and would sing about all of them. She was the original spokeswoman for women who had anything against men. Then she could switch to a standard like "What A Diff'rence A Day Makes." Great.

Sarah's voice was an incredible instrument. From the low lows to the highest highs her voice quality was strong and pure.

And then there was Billie Holiday, Lady Day. My fascination with her was total. She sang from her soul, about her troubled life, coming from a place of both pain and purity.

One of the great things about the Flame was that my sister Gwen

73

owned the photo concession there. Anna worked for her. The two of them were camera girls, taking pictures of the clientele, while Robert and George worked in the darkroom.

Gwen and Anna—beautiful, glamorous, with business in their blood and love in their hearts—turned heads when they came through the room. Everyone adored them and seemed pleased to meet me, their brother, the songwriter.

The night Gwen introduced me to Al Green was a big one for me. Besides owning the club, he managed a few singers—Johnnie Ray, LaVern Baker and a guy he had just signed by the name of Jackie Wilson.

Al told me he also owned a music publishing company and was always looking for new material and told me to stop by his office with some of my songs.

The following day I rushed over to Pearl Music Company, a four-office suite on Alexandrine Street. The only person there was a slender, youngish black guy with a thin mustache on a kind face. His name was Roquel Billy Davis. When he told me how good my songs were, my hopes lifted, then sank just as quickly when he said he wasn't the publisher, but just a writer like me.

We spent hours talking about the music business. I was impressed by his knowledge of it. Even though he hadn't gotten any big hits, he told me he had songs recorded by some good artists and had connections with people like the Chess brothers, who owned Chess Records in Chicago. He suggested we write together.

"I don't know," I said, "my sister Gwen's helped me on some songs and I intend to give her a piece of them."

"That's no problem," he said. "I write with others, too, so however many writers there are we'll split it that many ways."

Why not? I liked him and he liked me. He also liked my sister Gwen and before long, they were going together.

Roquel and I made a solid writing team. I was the active go-getter, the extrovert. He was more passive and had a patient way about him. I'd watch how business and creative people seemed to feel comfortable dealing with him.

We were writing for all of Al Green's artists, especially Jackie Wilson. Just hearing them try the songs out was exciting. It was my first experience of having professionals interpret my song ideas. The winds were blowing my way.

But by late spring, those same winds brought on the rain. It was on such a drizzly day that I found myself entangled in a major argument with Thelma over Hazel Joy.

Puddin' was now almost four years old. This day I wanted to take her to my friend Cecil Alleyne's house. Thelma said no, the baby had a cold and I could not take her outside in this wet weather. Made sense. I didn't like it but I understood.

A few minutes later Thelma's mother called and I heard Thelma agree to let her come pick up my little girl.

I called out to Thelma while she was still talking on the phone, "If I'm not good enough to take her out, nobody is."

Glancing at me she just continued talking. After hanging up the phone she starting getting the baby dressed to go out.

"That baby ain't goin' nowhere," I shouted. "It's wet outside, remember."

We stared at each other for a moment, then looked away.

When Thelma's mother arrived I was very strong. I repeated to her that the baby had a cold and couldn't go out. My mother-in-law shot a puzzled look over to Thelma, who waved back a pay-no-attention-to-him gesture.

Still cool, I just waited, more determined than ever. For whatever reason, I knew this time I had to prevail. Maybe it was being called a bum one too many times.

I watched as they got Puddin' all dressed up in her cute furry little coat, boots and pretty little white mittens. There was no question about what I had to do. Grabbing the baby's wrist, I looked at Thelma and said, "I told you she's not going nowhere."

A tug-of-war erupted in full force among us—me, my mother-in-law, my wife—and the baby, who by this time was crying her lungs out. I stared both women directly in the eye. They knew for the first time I was determined to win decisively. But then my pride and joy did something I would never forget. She reared her head back, crying and snarling at me as if I were the worst villain in the world.

My best little friend in the world had turned against me. I was not prepared for this. She was pulling and twisting her arm away from me as hard as her little muscles would let her. Relaxing my hold on her, I was devastated as her soft little hand slipped from my grasp.

Leaving the room I walked down a narrow hallway and into a small broom closet, closing the door behind me. I have no idea why, but I stood in the little dark area for about an hour. I thought about my life, I thought about my kids, I thought about my future. I was lost.

For the next couple of days I tried to zero in on where and who I was. Could I make this marriage work? Did I want to? Thelma seemed much nicer, as if she was sorry for what had happened, which made me feel better. I was just beginning to feel more hopeful about things when the doorbell rang.

"Are you Berry Gordy?" the man on my doorstep asked.

When I told him I was, he handed me an official-looking letter and left. The last time I had gotten such a letter I had been drafted. This time I was being divorced.

I never mentioned that letter to Thelma. I did very little talking that day, but a lot of thinking. As reality sank in there was a subconscious sense of relief, while consciously I was back to what I was feeling in that dark little closet. Except now it was worse—I knew I had to leave my home and family. But was this really my home?

I had heard once that "home" is a place where when you *have* to go there they have to take you in. So I grabbed some things and headed for home—Gwen's house. It was that same flat she'd once shared with Anna, across the hall from where Mother and Pop still lived in the family building on St. Antoine and Farnsworth.

When I arrived at Gwen's I was a wreck. I felt I had lost my kids forever. I told her that I was being divorced.

"So what!" she said. "That's not the worst thing in the world."

"But my kids," I told her. "What about my kids?"

"What about them?" she said. "You will always be the only father they will ever have. And they will always love you the same as we do."

It's funny how tears come at the strangest moments. I couldn't hold them back. I hugged her quickly so she couldn't see me crying. The emotions I felt that night are still hard to explain. All I know is at that moment I loved Gwen more than anything in the world.

Still depressed and scared, but happy because I felt so loved, I sat down at her piano. The words came easily: *"Someone to care, someone to share, lonely hours and moments of despair, to be loved, to be loved, oh what a feeling, to be loved."* I had written a song. I had written a beautiful love song.

At that time I thought I was writing "To Be Loved" strictly about the love of my children. Later I realized that I was writing about more, a lot more, my family, my friends—anybody.

And though I didn't know it then, I had found the key to who I was and all that I ever wanted—to be loved.

PART TWO

I'LL TRY SOMETHING NEW

I'LL TRY SOMETHING NEW

*I will build you a castle with a tower so high
it reaches the moon.
I'll gather melodies from birdies that fly
and compose you a tune.
Give you lovin' warm as Mama's oven
and if that don't do,
Then I'll try somethin' new.*

*I will take you away with me as far as I can
to Venus or Mars.
There we will walk with your hand in my hand
you'll be Queen of the stars.
And every day we can play on the Milky Way
and if that don't do,
Then I'll try somethin' new.*

*I will bring you a flower
from the floor of the sea to wear in your hair.
I'll do anything and everything to keep you happy girl
to show you that I care.
I'll pretend I'm jealous of all the fellows
and if that don't do,
Then I'll try somethin' new.*

*I'll take the stars and count them and move a mountain
and if that don't do,
Then I'll try somethin' new.*

© 1961 Jobete Music Co., Inc.
WILLIAM "SMOKEY" ROBINSON, JR.

EDNA BURST INTO MY OFFICE. "What's wrong with you," she shouted, "banging on that damn piano, disturbing everybody? We're trying to get some work done here."

I stopped.

"I've been buzzing you for the last ten minutes. I need answers," she said. "Plus your piano playing ain't that good."

I didn't laugh.

"C'mon boss, you're the one who's always pumping everybody else up. We can't have you bein' down."

She was right. The last thing anyone needed was to see me discouraged. "All right, what d'ya want?"

She told me I had a phone call from the head of my negotiating team, Harold Noveck, Motown's tax attorney. Harold and his brother, Sidney, a CPA, had watched over me and my money like careful parents for more than twenty-five years.

I listened as Harold updated me on the talks he and Lee Young,

81

Jr., head of our legal division, had had earlier that day with Irving Azoff, the head of MCA's record division. The negotiations were not going well. Their offer was too low—only slightly better than before—and still too many unresolved points. But before, I had reserve cash. This time I didn't.

MCA was still my first choice because they were already distributing us and knew the value of our catalogue. But they also knew we were in trouble. I had long admired their operation and for years had been a friend of their chairman, Lew Wasserman. But that didn't matter. This was business and I understood that. Sid Sheinberg, also a friend and second only to Wasserman in the MCA hierarchy, had put the fear of God into their lawyers and accountants. If they paid me one penny more than they had to, he'd have their heads.

Azoff, who had been responsible for getting our distribution there in the first place, was frustrated. He seemed to want to make a deal as badly as we did, but said his hands were tied.

The interest from Europe and Japan had been much greater than in this country, but when they reviewed our financial statements their offers were not only unacceptable but insulting. They were estimating the value of Motown based on its current income, while its true value reached far beyond what could ever be interpreted from a profit-and-loss statement. My task was to somehow make everyone understand the real value of the company—the worldwide recognition of the Motown name, the valuable artists' contracts and the vast catalogue of master recordings.

I was aware, however, that anything is only worth what somebody else is willing to pay for it. That bothered me.

My big fear was not only Motown going down the drain but taking Jobete, our valuable music publishing arm, with it.

When the question came up about Jobete being part of the package, I was so anxious to sell I made it known that I would consider it. The offers then increased, to around the $40 million range. I was insulted. Jobete by itself was worth much more than that. I wasn't used to this. I had always been a buyer, not a seller. This was new to me.

"Berry," Harold had told me, "they're not even coming close to the price we want."

"Well, then, raise it," I said.

"What?"

"And not only that, take Jobete out of the deal altogether. Now, I want more money for less assets. The ceiling has now become the floor."

I knew that was a big gamble but if others were not going to put a real value on my companies, I was.

When we're young we take major risks. We're fearless. And that's okay because we have little or nothing to lose. Now, the clock was ticking, and it was attached to a time bomb. I had gambled since childhood but nothing like this. All of a sudden everything I had worked for was at stake. I was playing the biggest poker hand of my life. I kept promising myself that if I made it through this, it would be the last big hand I'd ever play.

When I ended my phone call with Harold, Edna reminded me I had a meeting that next morning with Danny Bakewell, a black leader from South Central L.A. I had agreed to the meeting, not knowing exactly what he had in mind. But I knew it was something to do with the sale. That's all I needed now—somebody else to come along and try to pressure me not to sell.

Daniel Skouras, VP and head of operations, joined Edna and me in the office. He had not been involved with the negotiations, but was well aware of what was going on, especially with the traumas of running the company. At the time he was a permanent house guest of mine. He told me how amazed he was at my being so cool with everything that was going on. I told him I wasn't as cool as he thought, but that was part of the game—fooling myself into believing I couldn't lose.

When I was younger it never occurred to me that I *could* lose. Now I kept wondering—what if I did? What would happen to all the people who depended on me?

Going to sleep that night was tough. I kept thinking about when I was younger. I thought about 1957.

5

THE SONGWRITING YEARS

1957–1959

JACKIE WILSON

I was surprised by the white man I saw through the double glass windows standing in the middle of the studio floor, directing the band. Eyes closed, he was gesturing to the musicians to slow the tempo while finding a real groove. He was good. A white man with that much rhythm? I was impressed. His name was George Goldner.

Roquel had gotten a tip that George was in town doing a session at United Sound Studios. He was the colorful owner of Gone and End Records out of New York, one of the many small independent record companies that sprang up in the early fifties.

The independent scene had been developing for over a decade. Early on some of the major record companies had established special labels on which they recorded black music, then called Race records—colored Blues singers expressing their own personal attitudes and feelings. Later it was the young Doo-Woppers on street corners—reflecting a changing culture. The majors paid little attention. But street-smart businessmen recognized the commercial potential of these new sounds, and independent labels came into being, opening doors for people like me.

"I heard you were a good writer," was the first thing George Goldner said when Roquel introduced us in the lobby of the studio.

"I am," I said, smiling.

After looking over a couple of my songs, he told me, "Not bad." He then asked what I thought made a great record.

"Many things," I said.

"Like what?"

"Well, first of all, the song should be honest and have a good concept. The performance is important but the song's got to be sayin' something."

"Oh, is that so?"

"Probably the first thing people relate to is the melody, which includes hooks—phrases of repetition," I went on. "If that hook is infectious it's usually a hit. If it's monotonous, usually not."

George nodded slowly. He was impressed. "Got any money?"

"What's that?"

He pulled out a hundred dollar bill and gave it to me.

"What's this for?"

"It's like a down payment in case we ever do any business together." Then he left.

Wow! My ideas had translated into quick cash, ideas I felt I had a limitless supply of. I left that day in high spirits. It was more than just the hundred dollars. Here was a perfect stranger who saw value in my creative ideas.

While we were waiting for Al Green's artists to record some of our songs we intensified our writing efforts—developing material for other artists we were beginning to meet.

We were even "writers for hire." George Kelly, a local businessman, paid us fifty dollars a day to work with Frances Burnett, a singer he was managing. We also sought out new young artists to teach songs to. Among them were Erma Franklin, whose younger sister Aretha at the time was singing Gospel, and a teenage Freda Payne, who I hoped would become my first big female star.

Besides our in at Pearl Music Company and some local labels, other companies were becoming aware of us. LaVern Baker at Atlantic Records was hot with a record called "Jim Dandy." We wrote an answer to it that she recorded, "Jim Dandy Got Married." She also recorded our "It's So Fine." Both did okay, nothing great. But the song we wrote for Etta James on Chess Records called "All I Could Do Was Cry" *was* a hit and went to the top of the R&B charts. More artists and local groups were beginning to seek us out, looking for songs.

Though I would go on to have many exciting times in my life, the release of our first record on Jackie Wilson ranks among the top. Jackie took "Reet Petite," a so-so song, and turned it into a classic.

By then I had moved in with my sister Loucye and our cousin Evelyn Turk on Hague Street. That had been a great opportunity for me because since they worked during the day, I had the whole house to myself.

This particular day when I heard Joltin' Joe Howard from WCHB say, "And now folks, the hottest new record in the land—'Reet Petite' by Jackie Wilson," I was thrilled.

Turning the volume up as loud as I could, I danced around the room. Passing the TV set, I turned on *American Bandstand.*

Shock! There it was *again!* Jackie's big booming voice blasting for millions all over the country, and all those white kids dancing up a storm to my song. It was playing on local radio *and* national TV at the same time. At the same time!

"Reet Petite" was a smash, not just in Detroit but all over the country—Wow!

The excitement gave me a headache. My dream had come true. I was a hit songwriter. My troubles were over forever. I'd be rich! All the girls I ever wanted would now want me!

Then a feeling of anger started coming over me. All those people who said I'd "never be nothing" would now have to eat their words. Getting madder by the minute I started thinking how I was going to get even with everybody who had ever doubted me or treated me bad.

Wait a minute! What are you doing? You'd just better be happy and thankful for your own good fortune and not try to get back at anybody. After all, you're a star now and you better act like one.

I had given myself some good advice. I must admit though, that moment of anger felt pretty good.

I hadn't yet named it as such, but my *Cycle of Success* had just begun. Through the years, I would come to recognize and probe this most powerful pattern. When someone—anyone—becomes a star, his or her life goes through multiple changes brought on by fame, fortune and power.

Very few can survive this vicious Cycle. People treat you differently. You treat people differently. You have newfound friends, newfound relatives, newfound business deals, newfound everything. You're expected to pay for things you've never had to pay for before— bills, commissions, taxes. Taxes by far are the most dangerous. The government doesn't care what you *have*, they only care what you *made*.

Since others treat you like a king you expect more respect from your family and close friends. But those who really know and love you see you as the same person you were—and are. Herein lies an insidious trap, avoidable only by knowing that your accomplishments are only your accomplishments—they're not you. Only you are you.

The Cycle has many aspects. When you feel like a star, you act and spend like one, racking up bills you can't afford.

In my case I had to keep up a front—that of a hot and happening songwriter. I had no clue how much money I was going to make, I just felt with a big hit I'd automatically be rich. Whenever I went out to bars or clubs, others would expect me to pick up the tab. I did.

The Cycle has some good sides, too. I was so inspired that the sky became not the limit but just the first goal. That same day I called Jackie, burning with desire to show him our ballad, a slower song that meant the world to me, "To Be Loved."

With his own Cycle of Success having begun some time ago, Jackie was hard to get to. By now, Al Green had died and his assistant, Nat Tarnopol, had taken over Jackie's management. And even he had a hard time finding Jackie.

Though it took Jackie about three days to return my call, I counted myself lucky that he was willing to carve out some time for me. Not very much, but some. I was still in the clouds about "Reet Petite" when I opened my front door a couple days later and there he was with his pretty-boy face and pretty-boy hair, a doo with an upswept pompadour in front, and a tight-fitting tailored suit. He walked in giving me a hug, but I could see he wanted to get right down to business.

" 'Reet Petite' is a smash everywhere," I shouted.

"I know," he said, "people love it. What cha got?"

Since he was already a star the song's success wasn't as big a deal to him as it was to me. Jackie really liked me but he just wanted to hear the new song and get out. He always made up his mind fast. Too fast for me. He had hastily rejected some of our other songs almost before we got started, so I had to nail him quickly.

I jumped into it, playing my usual simple chords on the piano, but singing with great soul and conviction. Even in my squeaky voice, it was easy to hear the deep passion I had for this song, singing for all I was worth hoping he wouldn't stop me before the first hook. He didn't. I made it through the whole first verse. Great. But just as I was getting ready to start the second he said, "Okay, Okay, hold it! That's enough."

I *hated* it when he did that. One of my greatest performances— thwarted. Never opening my eyes, I stopped, frustrated.

"Gimme that paper," he said, grabbing the lyric sheet off the piano. "I got it, I got it!" Circling his pointed finger at me, "Play, play," he said.

My emotions jumped from the square root of one to a hundred to the tenth power. Jackie had fallen in love with the song. And I fell in love with his dynamic golden voice all over again the minute he sang the first few words: "*Someone to care, someone to share, lonely hours and moments of despair, to be loved, to be loved, oh what a feeling, to be loved.*"

I had never heard him do a ballad before. His voice was strong and deep and sincere. It was as if he had written it for himself. He brought up the entire range of emotions I had felt the night I wrote it. My tears came again and everything.

Jackie Wilson was the epitome of natural greatness. Unfortunately for some he set the standard I would be looking for in artists forever. I heard him sing many, many times and never a bad note. A bad song maybe, but never a bad note. Watching this man perform "To Be Loved" was always a thrill.

One night I had gone with him to Flint, Michigan, where he was appearing at the Armory. I had never seen anything like that in my life. Crowds pushing and shoving to get into the sold-out house. I had heard Jackie was known as Mr. Excitement. When he hit the stage I could see why. It was like a lightning bolt. Strutting and dancing with his coat slung over his shoulder singing "Reet Petite," spinning and turning, he jumped off one level of the stage to another, landing in a perfect split. I was worried like many others that he had to have hurt something. But without stopping he squeezed his legs together and propelled himself up into a standing position just in time to do another twirl, drop to his knees and finish the song.

Jackie had worked himself and the audience into a frenzy. He was sexy and knew it. I could tell by the way he winked his eye at the front-seated women right on beat. I had never seen women throw panties on stage before.

He *was* Mr. Excitement! Even at the end of the show, his energy was still flowing like electricity, body pouring with sweat, his shirt hanging open—and me helping him off stage as women were trying to jump all over him.

Fantastic! If only I could be Jackie, just for a night.

I thought about that more than once. Then, another night the strangest thing happened to me when one of the many girls who always seemed to be waiting for him asked me, "Berry, why can't Jackie be more like you?"

"What?!? What do you mean like me?"

"You're so patient, understanding and easy to talk to. Jackie's not."

"Oh really. You think so? Maybe you'd like to go out with me?"

Of course she said no.

Another time I was at a show of Jackie's and found myself seated next to the sweetest girl I'd seen in a long time. She had no eyes for me, but I kept doing everything I could to get her attention. After a while, she softened—just enough to tell me she was not "that kind of girl."

The more I persisted, the more she resisted. "At least give me your phone number."

"I don't give my number out to nobody unless I know them really well."

We were having so much fun together watching the show before Jackie came on, I tried to kiss her.

"Oh, no," she said, "it wouldn't be proper."

"Not even on the cheek?"

"Not even on the cheek."

I was impressed. She wasn't just a good girl, she was the perfect girl. Marriage was not out of the question.

Needing to see Jackie before he went on stage I had to leave quickly. She agreed to meet me at that same spot right after the show.

I returned breathlessly once the show was over and—nothing. Couldn't find her anywhere. Giving up, I headed back to the dressing room where, as usual, I saw a crowd of women around Jackie. And, as usual there was one in the middle, clutching him for dear life, her tongue down his throat, her skirt pulled up around her waist. There she was in all her glory—my ex-future wife.

SMOKEY

As important as my association was with Jackie Wilson, an even greater one began in late '57. I was in Nat Tarnopol's office working on some lyrics when a group calling themselves the Matadors—four young guys and a pretty teenage girl in a military uniform—came in to audition for him. I watched from an obscure corner while the group, singing their hearts out, tried hard to impress Nat with their little dance steps. I could see they had something, but Nat didn't think so. He stopped them midway through their third song, and sent them off with the advice that they should sing more like the Platters.

I related to that lead singer. Disappointment was hanging on him like his oversized pants. As they left the office and started down the hallway, I followed—as cool but as fast as I could, almost catching up with the lead singer, a light-skinned teenager with greenish eyes and boyish charm.

"Hey, I liked you guys a lot!" I called out.

They all stopped. "You did?" the lead singer said, looking at me doubtfully.

"Oh yeah, I thought you all were really good."

Thanking me, they introduced themselves as Ronnie White, Pete Moore, Bobby Rogers and Bobby's cousin Claudette.

"I'm William Robinson," the lead singer said, "but they call me Smokey. Who are you?"

"My name is Berry Gordy."

"Berry Gordy! You write for Jackie Wilson. You wrote 'To Be Loved' and 'Reet Petite.' "

"I know." Delighted he knew me, I asked him who had written their songs.

"I did."

"Got any more?"

"Right here," he said, showing me a school notebook full of song lyrics written in pencil.

"Follow me," I said, walking into a small room. They did. When I told Smokey to sing the song he liked best, he started singing the first song in the book. Reading along, I stopped him about halfway.

"These lyrics," I said, "what do they mean?"

"The song is about a boy and girl in love," Smokey explained.

"Yes, but so what? Everybody's in love. What's different about your song? And you're rambling all over the place." I told him to sing the next song he liked best. He turned the page and enthusiastically started singing the second song. This made me nervous. I noticed he had about a hundred songs in that notebook and at the rate we were going I'd be there for days.

He reminded me of me—so excited and passionate about his music.

The second song, too, had a lot wrong with it—and I told him so. Again, with the third. But instead of being upset, he got more excited with each criticism, asking me if I had time for another—and another—and another. His enthusiasm after each rejection really impressed me. Anybody who could take that much criticism and keep coming back for more had to be either crazy or one of the most special people I'd ever meet.

We finally got through his whole notebook and I had turned down every single song. But at the end I assured him that he had a wonderful talent for expressing his feelings with poetic, catchy lyrics. As for the songs, I told him that some had clever concepts but missed the point; others had good hooks, but no real story. And when there *were* good stories, they weren't unique enough.

"Other than that, I liked 'em." I laughed.

He laughed louder.

That's how it all started between Smokey and me. Our relationship was simple. I wanted to teach, he wanted to learn. He started bringing me songs on a regular basis. I continued to turn them down just as regularly, but I knew it was only a matter of time before he'd come to me with something I'd really like.

That day arrived in January of 1958 when he found me in a Pearl Music office with Roquel. Smokey burst into the room bubbling with excitement.

"Berry," he said, "man, I got to see you now. Can we go somewhere?"

For him to break into my meeting like that, I knew it was something. I had never seen him so excited.

Once out in the hallway Smokey started frantically looking for someplace to go.

"In there," I said, pointing to an empty room nearby.

Rushing in, quickly closing the door behind us, he looked around to make sure we were alone, like a person who had stolen something.

Then he whispered, "I got it, man! I really got it this time!"

Staring at him suspiciously I nodded okay.

Then, closing his eyes, and in a slow, melodic tone, he started singing, *"Walked all day 'til my feet were tired. I was low, I just couldn't get hired."* In the quietness of that room his voice sounded clearer and purer than ever—almost like a prayer. *"Saw a sign in a grocery store, help is slight and we need some more. I got a job! sha da da da, sha da da da da da da."*

Smokey was singing all the parts. Coming from that high tenorish voice to singing the low, low, bass on *"I got a job,"* then picking up the tempo to a heavy, faster rhythm, singing the group's part, *"sha da da da, sha da da da da da . . .*" He had finally come through—an answer song to the #1 record in the country, the Silhouettes' "Get A Job."

"Stop, stop, I love it!" I shouted.

Stopping he said, "Wait, there's a lot more."

"Oh, I know that, but I love it now," I said, "and I got to tell you now, because I may not love it when you get to the end."

Beaming, he continued—and continued—and continued—for about ten minutes.

I was glad I had stopped him up front. "Well, I still love it," I told him, "but it's way too long, needs work but it's definitely a hit."

For the next couple of weeks I worked on the song with Smokey, editing it down to a little over three minutes. Making a deal with George Goldner to put it out on his End label, I hustled the group into Loucye's basement where we rehearsed with local piano player Joe Hunter and his small band. We learned it so well that when we went into United Sound Studios to record it, Joe Syracuse, the engineer, had no trouble capturing the sound and feeling of the band and the group. We recorded two tunes that day—"Got A Job" and "My Mama Done Told Me," one of the songs I had liked the first time I saw them in Nat's office.

I suggested they change the name from the Matadors to something different since they had a girl in the group. They all placed names in a hat and Smokey's choice—the Miracles—was pulled. To make things even more special for Smokey, their record was released on his eighteenth birthday, February 19, 1958.

PROTECTING MY LOVE

SINGERS WERE BEGINNING to come to me and Roquel from everywhere, hoping to find the same kind of hits we had given Jackie. The young singer I used to make some of my demo tapes for Jackie

93

Wilson was a kid named Eddie Holland. He introduced me to his younger brother, Brian. The Holland brothers were both talented, good-looking guys. Eddie's tenor voice was so powerful and clear, I felt he could be a solo star on his own. His look-alike brother had the same type of voice, but mellower. With his feel for music and sensitivity in the studio, Brian had great instincts for producing and quickly became a protégé of mine. I recognized in him the same kind of potential I saw in Smokey.

Roquel and I were putting together a stable of artists to do our songs. Brian was in one of our groups called the Satintones. Robert Bateman, another future writer/producer, was also a member. The Five Stars and the Voicemasters were other groups I worked with. Among these groups and single artists, some of the individual names at varying times included Walter Gaines, Henry Dixon, Crathman Spencer, Ty Hunter, Lamont Dozier, David Ruffin and Melvin Franklin—names that would later be part of the Originals, Holland-Dozier-Holland and the Temptations. In addition to the groups, I had been working with Singin' Sammy Ward, a phenomenal talent who could really belt the Blues, and Mable John, the sister of Blues singer Little Willie John. Mable not only had a big voice but a big heart. She hung with us a lot, often driving me around when I didn't have a car of my own.

Whenever I could scrape the money together, I'd book studio time at United Sound. I always had to work fast. One particular night Smokey, Singin' Sammy Ward and Mable were all there with material to record. For weeks I'd promised my brother Robert I'd record a song he'd written called "Everyone Was There," a catchy tune with clever lyrics that incorporated titles and lyrics from the biggest Pop songs of the day.

I told him that if time allowed I would have one of the artists cut his song. At the end of the session we had about twenty minutes left. Nobody wanted to cut his "white-sounding" song. I told him he had twenty minutes to do what he wanted. In a panic he got the band together, got behind the mike and sang his heart out:

I thought those "Yakkety Yak'ing" "Western Movies"
made a "Hard-headed Woman" out of you—hoo—hoo.
You—hoo—hoo—hoo—hoo—hoo

94

Elvis was "Secretly" on the scene.
His "Hound Dog" thought "Bony Maronie" was queen.
Everyone was there, everyone but you.
Oh "Lonesome me," then I met The
Pretty "Peggy Sue"—hoo—hoo
Sue—Hoo—hoo—hoo—hoo—hoo.

As always, Robert proved himself to be a "natural" in the studio, as he was at anything he undertook. Just walking down the street one day he noticed a place where they were having a bridge contest, walked in, sat down, and won first place—and a brand-new car. I never even knew he could play bridge. Later, as more and more of us got into playing golf, Robert was so good he had to play below his ability in order to find someone to play with.

We got a deal to release "Everyone Was There" on Carlton Records. Robert chose Bob Kayli as his stage name. The record was a smash. Then the company sent him out to promote it through live performances. He rehearsed and rehearsed before leaving, and I thought he was pretty good. But after he performed in two or three cities, the record dropped off in those cities only.

"Bobby," I told him, "you've got to work on your act. You must be dying out there."

"No," he said, "my act is great."

A week later when he appeared on the big Dick Clark Saturday night TV show, I got a chance to check him out for myself. And Bobby was right—he was great. But after the broadcast the record died altogether. The problem then became clear: people were shocked. This white-sounding record did not go with his black face. Bob Kayli was history.

When that happened I realized this was not just about good or bad records, this was about race.

In the music business there had long been the distinction between black and white music, the assumption being that R&B was black and Pop was white. But with Rock 'n' Roll and the explosion of Elvis those clear distinctions began to get fuzzy. Elvis was a white artist who sang black music. What was it? (a) R&B, (b) Country, (c) Pop, (d) Rock 'n' Roll or (e) none of the above.

If you picked C you were right, that is, if the record sold a million copies. "Pop" means popular and if that ain't, I don't know what is. I never gave a damn what else it was called.

When I started writing another song for Jackie, I decided to do something different. Convinced he could do anything, I created a story about a guy crying, begging a lost love to come back. I started with *"My eyes are crying lonely teardrops . . ."* I liked it but not exactly. Too common. I changed *"My eyes are crying . . ."* to *"My heart is crying . . ."* I liked it.

Jackie's producer, Dick Jacobs, a respected New York arranger, heard the demo and sent for me. He wanted to be sure to capture that same feeling. I was being called to New York to help Dick Jacobs—wow!

A few days later I was in the Big Apple, New York City! It was my first trip there. I remember lying in my hotel room bed thinking how wonderful it was to be a songwriter.

The next morning I found myself standing in the middle of this huge, modern studio with Dick and all the musicians. The give-and-take between Dick and me was wonderful. Together, we worked out the tempo to his great calypso-type arrangement without losing the feel and drama. Everybody in sync: the horns, the strings, the flutes, the bells. And a harp. All this music over the speakers surrounding me felt like I was in a concert hall. Hearing the background voices on "Shoo-be-do-bop, bop, bop . . ." and then the sound of Jackie's powerful voice clean as a whistle made it sound like a finished record right there in the studio.

I knew that was the way great records should be made and I became a fanatic about getting that kind of sound quality—an experience that would come back to haunt me.

Though Jackie went on to get more hits on several of our songs, "Lonely Teardrops" was the biggest. But despite the success of these songs, Roquel, Gwen and I had little to show for it financially. They paid us all right. But only for the A side of the record, our song, the song that people heard on the radio and asked for in the stores. By the time we split our money three ways we had trouble surviving. We noticed on the other side of the record, the B side, our tunes were never used. Instead, Nat would use songs written by others—usually his aunt—who would get a free ride, making the same amount of money we did.

We agreed that Roquel, the businessman, would be the one to talk to Nat about us getting the B side on some of the records. But Nat was elusive. Roquel could never seem to pin him down.

One day when Nat and I were alone in the office it just jumped out of me.

Nat was shocked. "You want the B side, is that what you're saying to me?"

"Well, uh, yeah."

"Or . . . or what?" he said in a taunting way.

"Or we can't write for Jackie anymore," I heard myself blurt out.

"Jackie is a star. You need him—he doesn't need you," Nat said, dismissing me completely.

A dilemma. On the one hand, Jackie *was* the star; I *did* need him. But, then again, I felt he needed our songs, too. I had sometimes felt like Cyrano de Bergerac, knowing that my words and feelings had gone into the love songs that Jackie sang to seduce all those women who wouldn't give me a second thought.

I turned around at his door before leaving.

"I just want you to know, we really won't be writing for Jackie anymore," I said.

"That's up to you," Nat said as I left to tell Jackie about it, hoping he might be able to alter the situation.

His bottom line, he told me, was although he loved me and my songs, he couldn't go against his manager.

And so, after five consecutive hits we and Jackie parted ways.

Gwen and Roquel were not at all happy about the results of my meeting with Nat, but in a matter of days they had rebounded, buzzing over Gwen's idea that we should start a record company of our own. She even had a name—Anna Records—after our sister.

Another dilemma. I loved Gwen and didn't want to turn her down. But partnership in a business? No way. I had learned a lesson back in the record store with George. My only problem was telling them. Each day, with my not saying anything, it got worse. They had now made a deal with Chess to distribute Anna Records nationally. They were getting happier and happier that we'd be in business together for ourselves. At the same time I kept implying that I didn't want to be in business with anybody. Gwen knew I was reluctant but felt she could make me feel more comfortable.

"Berry, we want you to be president," she said one day, trying to tie up loose ends to their well-thought-out plans.

Unable to look directly at her, my eyes on the floor, I said, "President? Oh, wow, that's really wonderful but . . . you see, I'm . . . I just want to write and think and kind of be by myself and try . . . I have some other ideas and thoughts and I want to perfect my writing . . ." I was stumbling like mad, trying to find the right words— anything other than, "I don't want partners."

After a period of silence and disbelief Roquel spoke. "This is a chance of a lifetime. Chess is going to distribute our records. We can only win with this situation. Our own record company. Don't you understand? It's great!"

Finally, the only thing I could think to say was the truth; "I really would be happier just being by myself. I wouldn't be happy with partners." Thinking the deal they made with Chess might have hinged on my being part of it, I promised that I would help in any way I could—including writing and producing for them. And I told them they could let Chess know that.

"Baby," Gwen said, "we understand. You've got to do what makes you happy."

"Thanks."

We had taken separate paths and for the first time I was really, really on my own and really, really happy.

Like many artists who'd been referred to me, two sisters came to audition one day at Loucye's, hoping to get a shot at recording. Raynoma Liles, an exciting, light-skinned, fast-talking ninety-eight-pounder, and her younger sister, Alice, were a nice-looking duo. Sensing their singing hadn't knocked me out, Raynoma was quick to shift my attention to her other qualities. She told me she could arrange and write sheet music.

"Oh," she added, "and I have perfect pitch."

"Perfect pitch! You got perfect pitch?"

"Oh, of course," she said.

I had never met anyone with perfect pitch before. I knew a lot of people with relative pitch. I was one of them. Relative pitch is when you hear a note on a piano, tuning fork or whatever. And you can, using that note as a base, identify other notes. Perfect pitch, however, is when you don't have to hear anything for reference and you can pick the note right out of the air.

I immediately started banging a lot of notes on the piano to throw off any sound references she might have had. Walking to the other side of the room I said, "Uh, Raynoma, would you sing me a C please?"

"High or low?" she asked.

That tickled me. "High will be fine, thank you."

She put her hand on her forehead, closed her eyes, bit her lip, all the while slightly bobbing her head as if counting intervals or something. Everything was silent. The pain of anticipation on Alice's face added to the tension. Ray—as I called her from that day on—then came out with a soft, but shrill very high-pitched sound.

I slowly walked back over to the piano looking at their faces. Alice was nervous, Ray confident. I stabbed a high C with my finger. Amazing. Both sounds were exactly the same. "Incredible! That's incredible."

Now I had a problem. I didn't like their singing voices well enough to record, but I liked them. I particularly liked Ray's attitude and energy. When I told them I couldn't record them "at this time," Ray said she understood and asked if they could visit our rehearsals sometime. I said okay.

The very next day Ray was back at Loucye's, bouncing around, helping me in every way she could. She figured out what I needed and got it for me, even before I asked. Soon she was writing out little lead sheets, chord arrangements and helping with background singing. She made life easier for me. I liked it, and before long I was used to it.

I later had Ray put together a backup vocal group using some of our singers who were around. When it came to a name, since I loved contractions, I decided to call them the Rayber Voices—standing for Ray and Berry. The singers were Ray, Brian Holland, Robert Bateman, Sonny Sanders and, later, Gwendolyn Murray.

Once Anna Records got going, Gwen and Roquel rented the space downstairs that used to be my record store, and I moved my operation back over to Gwen's.

By this time I had fallen into the role of an artists' manager. It really began with the release of "Got A Job." Though it didn't chart high nationally, within a few weeks it had become one of the hottest records in Detroit and everyone was asking for the Miracles. They became local stars overnight. Preparing for that first live appearance we began rehearsing like crazy.

Their first show was at the Gold Coast Theater on 12th Street, where most of the top local acts played. Some were killer performers like Andre Williams, Gino Parks, Johnnie Mae Mathews, and Nolan Strong and the Diablos. Andre had had a big local hit called "Bacon Fat" and was the headliner that week.

Figuring we now had the hottest new record in town, and rehearsing as hard as we had, I knew the Miracles would jump on that show and tear it up.

It's funny how wrong you can be. They got killed. Or better stated, they killed themselves. They couldn't even get on or off the stage without bumping and stumbling over each other, let alone know what to say and do between songs. After the show it was major depression time for all of us.

I told them as long as they had hit records people would come to see them anyway. And if I kept throwing them on stage they would have to get better eventually. I took my management role seriously, taking them everywhere to perform. It didn't matter to me how much money we made, I knew the more they worked the more they would learn.

One night at a small, dingy club in Pontiac, Michigan, the Miracles were up on top of the bar lip-synching along with their record, "Got A Job," when suddenly a brawl broke out. All around us bottles were crashing and chairs flying. They were trapped. I ran to the end of the bar, motioning them toward some narrow steps. We made a mad dash for Smokey's car.

There was a lot of nervous talking as we drove off. Sitting in the front with Smokey and Claudette I heard voices in the back say, "Why were we booked into a joint like that anyway? We could have been killed. It's not worth it."

"Besides," another said, "we ain't got no uniforms, and we supposed to be stars. Isn't that what a manager is for?"

Saying nothing, I glanced over at Smokey, who was always reassuring me that he understood what I was doing, but this time he didn't say anything.

Finally, Smokey, still nervous from what had happened, glanced back. "Yeah man, you guys are right. It's not worth it."

That hurt. I knew they were right, but still it hurt. Probably more because Smokey said it. Maybe I wasn't qualified to be a manager, maybe it wasn't worth it for me, either. I had to rethink this whole thing. Before I knew it, we were at the corner of Farnsworth and St. Antoine. Smokey had decided to drop me off first.

Caught somewhere between self-doubt and self-pity, I walked up the long stairs to Gwen's flat, went into my little room in the back and pondered my disappointment.

A short time later Gwen popped her head in my door. "Smokey's here," she said.

I was surprised but happy.

"I had to come back and talk to you," Smokey said as I came into the living room.

"About what?"

"About what happened in the car." He then told me the minute he had agreed with the others he felt bad. He had come back to talk about it. "I understand where they're coming from," he said. "They're like my family and I just felt I had to say somethin' to let them know I thought they were right. But taking them home we discussed it and they felt as bad as I did. We all know what you're trying to do for us. I'm sorry, man. We all are."

"I'm so happy you came back," I said as I sat down on the floor, leaning my back against a couch.

"So am I," he agreed, and joined me on the floor.

We stayed on that floor till around five o'clock in the morning talking about everything under the sun. I told him about my failed marriage and feeling like a bum and people telling me I would never be nothin' writing those songs. He told me about the time he told his father he wanted to drop out of college and be a singer, and how his father had surprised him by telling him that he had his whole life ahead of him and if that's what would make him happy, he should do it.

"And I did," Smokey said. "He had faith in me and I never wanted to let him down. And just as I was feeling that I had, I met you. I will always be grateful that you noticed something in us no one else did." Smokey was serious. Sentimental.

"You're right about that," I said, "but I got a confession to make. I did believe in you and I was happy with the singing and all, but that was not the first thing that caught my eye."

Smokey gave me a puzzled look.

"Claudette," I said. "It was Claudette, man, in that army uniform. She really looked good. But once I got into your music I forgot all about her—until three days later when I called her up and asked her for a date." Smokey was silent. I kept going. "But sweet and nice as she could be, she told me in no uncertain terms that she was *your* girl. All I could think was, out of all the cats in the whole world, why did she have to be *Smokey's* girl! I apologized to her and told her how lucky she was to have a great guy like you."

He looked at me with a little smile and said, "Yeah, I know. She told me all about it."

We both laughed.

"I was so happy you said what you did about me," Smokey said.

I went on to tell him about how bad I felt one time as a kid when my brother George's girl knew I liked her and hit on me to make him jealous. I fell for it.

"Though nothing really happened, I saw how a girl could come between not only friends, but brothers. I made up my mind back then to never get caught in that trap again. So when Claudette told me it was you, man, I had to pull back. What a drag!"

102

"Yeah," he smiled.

In those early-morning hours Smokey and I made a little pact to never let anything ever come between us. But what really developed that night was something more, much more—the beginning of a lifelong friendship.

Songwriting was my love, and protecting that love, in many ways, was the motivation for everything I did in the early years of my career. Producing the artists who sang my songs was the next logical step to making sure my songs were done the way I wanted. Protecting my songs was also the reason I got into publishing and eventually the record business.

Publishing came about when I couldn't get my songwriter's royalties from a New York publisher. I wanted to sue.

But a lawyer advised me, "Forget it. It's not worth it."

"What do you mean, it's not worth it? We're talkin' 'bout at least a thousand dollars."

He told me I would get perhaps two hundred to three hundred dollars in a settlement, but by that time the legal fees would be about six hundred.

That made no sense to me.

"How could a company stay in business that way and not pay writers?"

"Some companies don't intend to." He explained that the owners pay themselves big salaries and expenses, go out of business, collapse the corporation and start the whole game all over again. There were always new writers eager to write for their new corporation.

The more I understood this the madder I got. It was wrong, unfair. And on top of that—bad business. I knew there must be thousands of other writers out there just like me, and all they wanted to do was write songs—and get paid. If I set up a company that did that, I was sure all the writers would come to me.

So that's what I did. I called my company Jobete, a contraction of my children's names—JOy, BErry and TErry.

Smokey was my first writer.

I hadn't been in the publishing business long when I made the

103

other critical move. Frantically waiting for my producer's royalty check for "Got A Job," it finally arrived. Smokey happened to be with me that day. I couldn't wait to tear open the envelope.

When I did, we saw a check for $3.19!

We stood speechless.

"You might as well start your own record label," Smokey said. "I don't think you could do any worse than this."

I agreed.

The only problem was coming up with enough money to put out one record. That wouldn't take a lot of money, just enough to pay the recording, pressing and label costs.

I already knew what song I wanted to release—"Come To Me," which I had written with Marv Johnson, a young singer I'd recently discovered in a record store. Now all I needed was about a thousand dollars.

But hustling around town I soon discovered it was hard to find anyone to invest in my project. They either wanted too much for too little or had their own financial problems.

I turned to Fuller. Probably dating back to childhood, I had a hunch he might have that kind of money stashed somewhere.

"Hmmm," he began in his laid-back style and then asked me the same old question I'd been getting from everyone: "How are you planning to pay it back?"

My answer was always the same old answer: "No plan, just my word."

"Oh, I see. But do you have anything of *value?*"

I laughed, because I knew he was trying to make a joke, but he could see I was desperate.

"I'll think about it," he said.

"You don't have time to think about it!" I instinctively shouted. "I'm letting you in on something great! I have no time."

"Junior," he said. He hadn't called me that for fifteen years. I figured that meant he felt sorry for me. "Y'know, I think Ber-Berry might be a possibility. Why don't you try that?"

He was referring to our family savings fund owned by my parents, siblings and me. Started about two years before, it operated much like a credit union and had been named after Mother and Pop—

BERtha and BERRY. We all contributed ten dollars a month. It was easy to put money in, but impossible to get it out.

"Thanks anyway," I told Fuller as I headed downstairs into the freezing night air. Pulling my coat tighter around me, I thought about the even colder reception I might get if I tried to borrow the money from Ber-Berry. If you wanted to borrow from it you had to have a "good" reason. So far, no one had had one good enough. Everybody had to vote for you, not just a majority—everybody!

For a couple days I'd tried to think of other options. I had none.

D day. A week later, I found myself shivering on the corner of Farnsworth and St. Antoine, looking up at my family's building. It had been harder than I thought, just to arrange a special Ber-Berry meeting. Nearing the moment of truth, I spotted a familiar face rounding the corner. It was Bud Johnson, my childhood friend. "Bud," I called.

"Junior," he said, "what you doing standing here in the cold?"

He brought back memories of the days when we frequently found ourselves in fistfights for leadership of our little neighborhood gang. At one time I was the undisputed leader because I was the best fighter. Then Bud began to grow bigger and bigger and bigger.

He was the oversized mauler while I was the undersized boxer. Though I was scientific in my approach, quick with my hands and feet, there came a time when the growing weight difference made me realize I'd better make a deal. With bluffing and negotiating, I'd brought about an agreement for a friendly dual leadership. But those days were gone forever because now there was no question of superiority—he had money and I didn't.

Hope. He was my very last hope before facing the dragon of a Ber-Berry meeting. I told him about the great ideas I had and how he couldn't lose. All he had to do was invest a thousand dollars in my project and just sit back and reap the benefits.

"Benefits of what?" he laughed. "Junior, come on now, you still messin' with them songs an' stuff. Look man, I could probably letcha have a few dollars or so but I don't wanna invest no thousand dollars and stuff like that."

(A few years ago, about thirty years later, I ran into him on a trip back to Detroit and was amazed to see that he still carried in his pocket the actual bills he had three decades before. He said it was a reminder to himself of an investment that got away. Bud and I laugh about this each time I see him.)

That night of the meeting I was more apprehensive than ever. Sure, Gwen and Anna would vote for me, no matter what. Robert and George would probably go along, too, thinking they would be able to borrow later if I got my loan. The fact was, George had already tried to borrow money and failed. Fuller, always frugal, I could expect to start off noncommittal. But since it was on his advice that I came, I was pretty sure he would go with me in the end.

It was clear from the beginning that Esther was going to be my big problem. She had power and influence. Organizing the savings fund had been her idea in the first place. Like Loucye, she was a strong businesswoman, and very careful with money. The family depended on Esther to keep these kinds of things together. And I was uncomfortably aware that she knew if I got money easily, George would be next, then Robert, and so on.

We all sat around the dining room table as questions started flowing. By this time I was a little smarter in answering their "What is your plan?" question. I let them know I had no real plan as such, but then carefully wove into the most brilliant sales pitch imaginable—my real last shot.

I was in rare form that day, reminding them of the importance of independence and control, and just how badly I wanted to start my own record label. "And remember," I pointed out, "my songs have been big hits on Jackie Wilson, and this new artist, Marv Johnson, has the makings of a star. Who's to say he won't do twice as good as Jackie?" Naturally, I topped everything off by promising to repay the loan with full interest.

By the time I finished, I was so confident with my presentation I almost blew it.

"Yeah," I joked, "when I get really big and famous, I might just let y'all be in my good graces."

The family did not think that was funny.

"Just joking," I said. "It was just a joke."

Still, no one laughed. It looked as if I had lost them.

Though Gwen and Anna both thought the ending of my performance somewhat ill-timed, they continued their support. I will always remember them getting up, walking around the table saying things like, "Give him the money. Give him a chance." They had some influence, too.

Loucye appeared to have softened slightly, and I could see she was leaning my way, but from Esther's face and rigid posture I could tell that she hadn't bought my pitch. Her favorite line to me since I was a kid was "If you're so smart, why ain't you rich?" But, of course, at such a serious meeting in which she needed to be proper and reserved, she would never ask such a question. As she began to raise her various objections, her tone somewhat heated, it all of a sudden slipped out—"Well, if you're so smart, why ain't you rich?"

The family looked at me for a response. There was none.

Esther continued. "You're twenty-nine years old and what have you done so far with your life?"

I was stunned for a moment because I hadn't realized how old I was. And she was right, I was twenty-nine years old and hadn't made any money yet. But I knew I was on the right track. Age was something I was never conscious of before. I had to regroup fast. I attacked. "So what if I'm twenty-nine. I could be thirty-nine, forty-nine or fifty-nine. So what! What's age got to do with it? So I haven't been a real success in my life. Big deal. Tomorrow could be a total turnaround. That's what's wrong with people; they give up their dreams too soon. I'm never going to give up mine." I was really serious when I said that, but at the same time I knew it would have an effect on them.

Esther stuck to her guns. "That's very nice, but how are you going to pay it back?"

I *hated* it when she said that! So I ignored it and looked at Mother and Pop. While they had been neutral before, their body language told me they were proud of my performance. Mother, in her resolved, quiet way, gave a tiny nod to Gwen and Anna letting them know she was on their side. Pop and my brothers followed next. Then Loucye and finally Esther gave in.

A loan of eight hundred dollars was voted for unanimously—but not before they made me sign an additional note pledging my future royalties as security. Esther had been tougher than I'd anticipated.

BER-BERRY CO-OP
5139 St. Antoine
Detroit, Michigan

SAVINGS SHARE LOAN NOTE

SHARE LOAN NUMBER_____

$ *800* —

DETROIT 2, MICHIGAN

FOR VALUE RECEIVED ON OR BEFORE ___*Jan. 12, 1959*___ I promise to pay
BER - BERRY Co-op
~~HOME FEDERAL SAVINGS AND LOAN ASSOCIATION~~ OF DETROIT, at its office in

the City of Detroit at ~~9100 Woodward Avenue;~~ the sum of _____

Eight Hundred + 00/100 ——————————— ($ *800* —)

with interest at the rate of _____*Six*_____ per cent (___)

per annum, payable ————————— Monthly, Yearly, ———————————.

I hereby transfer, assign and pledge my share account # *113*
of said Association owned by me and the Certificate evidencing the
same as security for the payment of said amount when due, and upon the
failure of full payment thereof when due, do authorize said Association to repurchase, in accordance with its charter and by-laws, suffi-
cient of said share account and to apply so much of the purchase price
therefor as may be necessary to pay and discharge the amount then due
including interest and I hereby appoint the Treasurer of said Association or in his absence the President, my Attorney-in-fact to execute
for me any papers and to take any other action necessary to carry out
this agreement.

AMOUNT OF NOTE_____*800.—*_____   DATE OF NOTE_____*Jan. 12 1959*_____

AMOUNT OF INTEREST___*48.—*___   DUE DATE OF NOTE_*Jan. 12 1961*_

TOTAL_____   _____*Berry M.*_____
                            SIGNATURE OF BORROWER

                            SIGNATURE OF BORROWER
                            1719 Gladstone
                            ADDRESS
                            TR 1-3340

*In addition
I also hereby assign
my future savings, the
amount necessary, at any
given date, to repay any
unpaid balance due at
this ~~same~~ note.*
Berry Gordy

But I knew right then—if I ever made money, she would be the one
I'd get to watch it for me.

6

MOTOWN
1959–1960

HITSVILLE USA

DAMN," I HEARD SMOKEY MUMBLE as my white, '57 Pontiac convertible spun out of control, skidding into a ditch. This was the second time it had happened but once again we were lucky enough to get a tow truck to pull us out. Smokey and I were on our way to get the newly pressed records of "Come To Me" from the plant in Owosso, Michigan, fifty miles away. It was the excitement of getting our hands on copies of that first Tamla release that had us creeping along through a blizzard in the dead of winter, sliding slowly over icy roads.

We had recorded the song just two days before at United Sound Studios. The air had been filled with energy, love, talent and panic. I supplied the panic. The musicians improvised off my little handwritten chord sheets. And there was Ray, slapping a tambourine on her hip and leading the Rayber Voices with the "Yeah, Yeahs" and "Bop Shee Bops."

It was a wonder Marv Johnson—who was singing his heart out on every rehearsal run-down—still had any voice left for the actual recording. Once I had the feeling I wanted down in the studio, I rushed up into the control room while they were still playing so I could hear what it sounded like. There I found the sound was totally different.

Joe Syracuse, the engineer, had balanced everything smoothly—too smoothly.

"Where is the bass?" I screamed. "My drum? What happened to that sound I had out there?"

He didn't know what I was talking about since he hadn't been out there.

"Pull up the bass. Pull up the drums. Pull up the group," I said. He did.

"Where's Marv? You've lost the lead singer," I shouted over the blaring music.

"Pulling everything else up, you buried him," he shouted back.

"Well, pull him up higher."

"I can't. Distortion. See those needles?" he said, pointing to the meters on the console, "they're all in the red."

"What do we do now?" I asked.

"Take something down," he said.

"Like what?"

"I don't know."

"Okay," I said, "take *everything* down. We'll start from the beginning."

He looked at me in frustration. "You have no idea what you're doing. Why am I listening to you?"

He was at his wits' end. I could see that.

"The customer is always right?" I smiled.

He stared at me for a moment, then he smiled back, pulling the faders all the way down, cutting off all the sound. We started again, first rebalancing the rhythm section—heavy on the bass and drums.

"Okay, that's good. Now bring in the background voices," I said. "Beautiful." The balance was coming along great.

I told Joe to put a separate mike on the tambourine. He did. I kept going. I had him move Robert Bateman, a member of the Rayber Voices who I thought was the best bass singer in the world at the time, to his own mike and turn it way up—over the drums, tambourine and the Voices. Then I reached for the fader that carried Marv's vocal and pulled it up over everything else. Yes! There it was. It took about ten takes but finally I got an even better sound than I had heard down in the studio.

With Marv's inspired performance and the great flute solo by Beans Bowles, one of Detroit's best Jazz musicians, I felt I had what I needed for a big hit.

Once Smokey and I made it through the storm and returned safely from Owosso, we quickly carried a carton with little boxes of the newly pressed records inside. We had controlled our excitement and not ripped open any boxes at the plant, or in the car. Pulling out the first box of twenty-five records, I told Smokey of the times I had opened up the same kind of boxes from other record companies for my record store. Now this was *my* box of twenty-five. Those shiny 45s with the Tamla name printed across the top looked so beautiful. The name for my label, Tamla, came by chance. One day looking through an old *Cash Box* magazine I noticed that "Tammy" by Debbie Reynolds had been the #1 Pop record in the country. I knew millions of people were already familiar with that name. I decided to use it.

But when I sent it to Washington to be registered, I found somebody had beaten me to it. By that time I had gotten so used to the name I wanted to at least keep the sound of it. So I dropped the last two letters of "Tammy" and added "la"—"Tamla."

I rushed the 45s of "Come To Me" to the DJs at WJLB and WCHB, the two radio stations in town that played black music.

My history with WJLB went back many years before when they had played my Gordy Print Shop commercial. Their DJs—Bristol Bryant and Frantic Ernie Durham—began to play my record immediately.

Their competition, the newer WCHB in Inkster, Michigan, owned by Dr. and Mrs. Haley Bell, was one of the few black-owned stations in the country. Though only a daytime station with a small signal, it quickly became the #1 black programming station for the time it was on the air. Joltin' Joe Howard, Long Lean Larry Dean and Larry Dixon, the DJs there, all started wailing on "Come To Me."

In just a few days I had cut a record, pressed it and got it on the air. "Come To Me" was a hit and people were calling and telling me so. But I had no time to revel in any glory. Now *I* was a man on the move just like Jackie was that day at Loucye's when I told him about "Reet Petite" being such a hit.

I had to quickly figure out what to do next. I had no money. I had originally figured since it only cost ten cents to press a record and it sold for almost a dollar in the stores, this was definitely the business for me. But I hadn't thought about the fact that the distributor only paid the record company (me) about thirty cents for the record, sold it to the stores for about sixty cents, who then sold it to the public for close to a dollar.

Then I got a call from Frantic Ernie Durham telling me United Artists wanted to buy the master and distribute it nationally. I hopped a plane to New York and made a deal, signing Marv to a long-term contract, with me producing the masters for them.

Because of the many soundtracks they had released from their films, United Artists was known as an album company. But when "Come To Me" took off nationally, they had their first big single hit. No longer considered just a hit songwriter, I was a hit producer as well.

Now, when I went to their headquarters in New York, I was greeted by smiling faces who buzzed me into the inner offices before I could close the lobby door behind me.

"Good afternoon, Mr. Gordy." "How are you, Mr. Gordy?" "Can I get you something, Mr. Gordy?" "Right this way, Mr. Gordy." I was king.

I loved the way the executives rushed me to the different departments to show me how well the record was doing in all parts of the country.

Soon I signed a second artist to UA, Eddie Holland, after writing and producing a song on him called "Merry-Go-Round." Now I had two acts on United Artists. I was on a roll.

Writing songs came easy to me, but in the case of Marv Johnson's second record for UA, "I'm Coming Home," maybe a little too easy. It didn't sell. Eddie's sales on "Merry-Go-Round" were also less than expected. But I wasn't worried. I knew I'd make up for them later.

Earlier, when Ray suggested I move my operation from Gwen's to her place, it seemed like a good idea. She had a three-year-old son and a three-room apartment on Blaine Street. It would be quiet, I could work around the clock. It would be strictly business—a platonic relationship.

I accepted.

There was one bed.

The first night we slept on opposite ends—with a lot of clothes on and a big space in the middle. As time went on that space got smaller and smaller. Soon it had vanished and so had our clothes.

With Ray at my side, helping me however she could, my operation continued to grow. Before long we needed more space and moved to a larger apartment on Gladstone Street. One day Smokey hurried in.

"I know you're really gonna like this one," he said, handing me a lyric sheet that read: *"She's not a bad girl, because she made me see how love could be, but she's a bad girl because she wants to be free. She's not a bad girl to look at, finer than fine. Said she was mine, but she's a bad girl because it was only a line."*

The minute he started singing it, I knew what I was hearing was in a class by itself. So simple, so clear, so pure, yet so clever. All I could think about was how happy I was that I had met this young genius.

Then, while singing the bridge, he stopped. "I'm having trouble with this part. I need your help."

Before when Smokey had come to me with songs, though I enjoyed working with him, it was still work. Now, all of a sudden, I felt honored.

Jumping on the piano bench I helped him with some chords and ideas in keeping with the simplicity and integrity of what he had written before. I was crazy about the melody of "Bad Girl," but I loved the lyrics and the concept even more. That was the first time I could feel his true brilliance as a poetic storyteller.

"What a great song we wrote," Smokey said.

"*We* wrote? *You* wrote. I just helped. It's your song."

"Oh no. We wrote it together," Smokey insisted.

Less than a week later I managed to get "Bad Girl" recorded at United Sound by working a special deal with Joe Syracuse. Not only the main engineer, he was also the owner's son and was able to let us record there in the middle of the night, when nobody else was using the studio. That gave me a chance to cut several songs at a lesser rate.

The record came out so great I decided to use it to launch another label. The Tamla name was commercial enough but had been more of a gimmick. Now I wanted something that meant more to me, something that would capture the feeling of my roots—my hometown.

Because of its thriving car industry, Detroit had long been known as the "Motor City." In tribute to what I had always felt was the down-home quality of warm, soulful country-hearted people I grew up around, I used "town" in place of "city." A contraction of "Motor Town" gave me the perfect name—Motown. I would later use that name to incorporate my company.

Now I had two labels. My original plan was to put out all the solo artists on the Tamla label and the groups on the new Motown label. Each label would have its own image and identity—solo artists versus groups. But this plan, like some others, turned out not to be practical.

After making test pressings of "Bad Girl," I found—once again— I could not afford to put it out myself. Too much money had gone into cutting songs and making the masters. My second attempt at going national had failed.

I took what little cash I had, bought a plane ticket, grabbed my best masters, and headed off to New York on what turned out to be a very fateful trip.

My sister Anna, always supportive, had driven me to the airport, but just as I was walking up the steps to board the plane, I heard my name. Turning around I saw her frantically running toward me, waving a newspaper.

"Wait a minute," she yelled, "don't get on that plane! Today and next Monday, bad days for Sagittarians to travel."

She's got to be kidding.

Here I am, about to go on possibly the most important trip of my life and she has to come to me with something like this. *But what if she's right?*

I knew if I didn't go I would be dead anyway. So I smiled and waved her good-bye.

That flight was probably not much rougher than any other but every bump had me in constant panic, much more than usual. When we finally landed I was a wreck and decided that day that touching down in that airplane was the second best feeling I'd ever had.

My first stop in New York, naturally, was to be United Artists.

Walking down Seventh Avenue near the UA building, I ran into some people from Detroit. I didn't even know them that well, but being alone in a strange town made anyone from home your instant friend. Before I knew it, I had invited them up to the company with me.

"Listen," I said, knowing how impressed they would be, "the executives at UA would be real hurt if they found out I was in town and hadn't given them first crack at my hot new product."

Most people in Detroit had heard that no matter how big you are, you hadn't really made it until you were big in New York. Well, I was big, and I couldn't wait to see their faces when they saw how big.

Once upstairs in the UA outer offices, however, there was no buzzing me in, no "Mr. Gordy this, Mr. Gordy that."

This must be a new receptionist who doesn't know who I am. Motioning for the others to have a seat in the lobby, I moved to her quickly. "I'm Berry Gordy, the producer for Marv Johnson."

No reaction.

"I produced 'Come To Me' and I'm—"

Before I could say anything more, I heard this nasal voice coming at me with "Could you spell that last name please?"

The knot in my stomach told me I was in trouble. "Gordy, G-O-R-D-Y," I said, glancing back at my friends sitting on the couch trying hard to act oblivious. I leaned forward to the young lady and whispered, "You're gonna be in real trouble if you don't call the Sales Department right now and let them know I'm here."

We locked eyes for a moment or so before she decided to make the call. While talking to someone, I saw her expression go from fear and concern to confidence and arrogance as she put the phone down. "I'm sorry, sir, they're all busy now. You'll just have to be patient. Why don't you have a seat, Mr. Gorney?"

I felt the full impact of the expression "you're only as good as your last hit." My friends and I headed for the elevator.

During the long ride down I knew I had learned something that would shape the way I would handle fame forever. Never again would I allow myself to get psyched out by the impostor of success.

Trudging up and down the streets of the big city—this time alone— I went everywhere, including the Brill Building, the place where most of the independent music companies had offices. I talked to anyone who would listen to my soon-to-be-smashes, asking cash up front. No takers.

One of my last meetings was with Sam Clark, head of ABC Paramount Records.

"Nah," commented Sam, after listening to "Bad Girl," "yours is not quite there but let me play you a real smash coming out next week." He then played "Personality" by Lloyd Price.

"I really like it," I said, trying to smile, "but mine is a hit, too. Don't sound like that one, but still it's a hit!"

He wished me luck.

Frustrated with that town, I jumped on a plane to Chicago—right in the middle of an electrical storm. Once in the air, it hit me. *This is Monday—the other day I wasn't supposed to fly.* That plane was jumping, bumping and turning sideways.

Loud crackling noises illuminating the sky with sharp, thin flashes of light were jarring the life out of the plane—and me. I was sure the astrologer was right this time. I'd finally pressed my luck too far.

Well, miraculously, we finally landed safely. This time touchdown jumped easily to the number one spot of the greatest feelings I had ever had.

Not only that, but Leonard and Phil Chess of Chess Records in Chicago took all six of my masters, including "Bad Girl." Not necessarily because they loved them so much but because they didn't want anybody else to have them. Of course, I didn't tell them that I had been turned down by everybody else.

A short while later, according to our contract, UA released my third record on Marv—"You Got What It Takes." It was one of the songs that Roquel had originated, with Gwen and me as co-writers. And again, the message of "You only have to be yourself for me to

116

love you" came through loud and clear: *"You don't drive a big fine car and you don't look like a movie star. And on your money we won't get far, but baby, you got what it takes."*

I had produced Marv's biggest hit and, once again, I was king and in great favor. Phones jumped off the hook. I was invited everywhere. But unless I really had to go, I stayed in Detroit—taking care of business. My business.

Meanwhile, with a hit on "Bad Girl," the Miracles were getting hotter than ever. Everybody wanted to book them, but Smokey wanted the Apollo—and he got it. It was Smokey's dream to play where all his idols had played. But in his case, it was "Be careful what you wish for, you just might get it."

I sent the group off to New York and stayed home where I needed to be, waiting anxiously to hear how the Miracles were doing. My first hint came when Frank Schiffman, the owner of the Apollo, called wanting his money back.

Smokey later filled in the gory details. First he told us they wouldn't have even made it through rehearsal had it not been for Ray Charles. Those basic little chord sheets we always used were a joke to the house band, who refused to play them. They had expected full arrangements.

Just as the management of the Apollo was about to cancel them, Ray stepped in. "Well, you know, they're just kids starting out. Let's give 'em a little help." In no time, Ray learned the songs from Smokey by ear and told the musicians how to play them.

In spite of Ray Charles's help their performance wasn't much better than their chord sheets; they were still bumping into each other. The audience laughed a lot, especially when Smokey tried to save the show by dancing.

Gwen and Anna were quick to tell me, as they often did, that this kind of thing wouldn't happen if we had an artist development department. But I gave them my usual response: "I don't give a damn about none of that stuff. All I care about is getting hit records."

My relationship with Ray continued to grow on many levels. I saw in her the ultimate mother, a quality she had illustrated with her

117

son, Cliff, and continued to show with our son, Kerry, who was born on June 25, 1959.

The divorce from my first wife was just now becoming final. I, not unlike the up-and-coming stars, was also enjoying the female attention I was getting. Although Ray seemed to understand, she didn't hesitate to bring up the topic of marriage every now and then. I was in no rush.

The thing I was thinking about most was the fact that the Gladstone Street apartment had become too crowded. I had sent everyone out looking for a larger place, but it was Ray who found the one I liked, a two-story house at 2648 West Grand Boulevard with a big picture window in the front and a photography studio in the back. Perfect for my growing operation. I put a down payment on it and we moved in.

A couple of weeks later, George Kelly, the local club owner who had earlier hired Roquel and me to work with his singer, Frances Burnett, came by to check things out. The two of us stood out on the sidewalk, looking back at the building.

"What are you going to call it?" he asked. This was something I'd been thinking hard about, wanting to come up with the perfect name. Standing there looking at that unique picture window, I came up with it.

"Hitsville," I proclaimed.

He laughed. "You're joking."

"No, I'm serious. That's the only name I can think of that expresses what I want it to be—a hip name for a factory where hits are going to be built. That's it, Hitsville."

Mother had always asked me if I wanted to be a big fish in a little pond or a little fish in a big pond. I didn't know. But it so happened that the very nature of what I had been doing locked me into the big fish, little pond concept. Over the past few years, my pond had grown—from Gwen's house, to Loucye's, to Ray's, to Gladstone and now Hitsville.

Thanks to my brief training in electronics school, where I had gone on the GI Bill, I was able to set up a two-track recorder that I bought from Bristol Bryant. Mother was right again—"Whatever you learn is never wasted." And again, my family was right there with me, pitching in. While I set up the microphones and strung wires to assemble my first mixing board, Pop and my brother George handled the plastering, sealing of cracks and installation of soundproofing material.

The house needed a major top-to-bottom scrubbing and repainting, and many of the artists and creative people I was working with came to help.

In no time at all that house at 2648 West Grand Boulevard took on a whole new life. From a photo studio, the garage was turned into a recording studio, the first floor became the lobby and the control room. Between the basement and first and second floors we had to cram everything in, including living quarters for me, Ray, Kerry, and Cliff.

Down in the studio, finishing up our work, surrounded by all this activity there was Pop, finding an opportunity to give me advice: "Well, just remember, son, a smart man profits from his mistakes."

Now that I was my own boss I could add my own variations to my father's philosophies. "But a *wise* man," I said, "also profits from the mistakes of others." I told him if I had to make all my own mistakes I would not live long enough to do half the things I wanted to do in my lifetime.

Pop chuckled just as Ray came buzzing in with her arms full of a heavy velvet material. "Will this kind of stuff do?" she asked.

"It definitely will," I told her.

Only that morning I mentioned that I needed something we could use for soundproofing and here she was—with pieces of theater curtains. A real busybody who never sat still, Ray had this wonderful ability to not only get things done but to also be right there ready to go when I needed anything.

The white lady who had sold me the house came around a few times making repairs—fixing little things, painting, trying to keep it up. She had gotten it back twice before in foreclosures. And with no credit rating and no visible means of support, and her seeing young black kids running in and out and making all that noise, she was certain it would soon be hers again.

119

I don't think she realized that we were there to stay until one day she came by and saw the place looking better than ever. And above the big picture window, stretching from door to door, were big beautiful letters spelling out "HITSVILLE USA."

MONEY

MY PRIVACY BEGAN to disappear as more people became drawn to what I was doing. Besides aspiring artists, writers and producers who had started hanging around, others who had business skills were also looking for ways to get involved.

Upstairs, in a bedroom-turned-bookkeeping-office, my sister Esther ran a tight ship handling the money matters, helped by her husband, George Edwards, a Michigan state representative and an accountant.

In another upstairs office my sister Loucye, who left her government job with the Army Reserves, set up her area. It wasn't much then, but would soon be what was loosely called the Manufacturing Department. She would handle everything from the pressing plants, shipping, billing and collections, to sales, graphics and liner notes for the album covers. A real dynamo!

Downstairs Ray had her own office area. Because of her knowledge of music and lead sheets, I put her in charge of the publishing operation, where she got tremendous help from her brother, Mike Ossman, and Janie Bradford, our first receptionist.

Janie Bradford was something else. While she was hardworking and capable, she never lost her demented sense of fun. One July day in '59 I was walking through the lobby on my way to the studio, studying a lyric sheet, when I felt someone pinching my butt.

One of her favorite things to do was sneak up behind me and do that. It never mattered to her who I was talking to at the time. As I'd jump and look around, there she'd be, smiling as if nothing happened. Then she'd whisper, "Just couldn't help it. You're sooo special."

I sort of bought that special line until later I found out Brian, Smokey and a few others were "special," too.

When she did it that day, I jumped a little but seeing who it was I kept walking. From my attitude, she could see I was in no mood for talking—or being pinched.

She caught up with me again. "Mr. Gordy," I heard her say cheerfully, "I'm sorry but I couldn't help it, you are just—"

"Unh, unh," I said, cutting her off. "I'm trying to finish a song."

Janie, a songwriter herself, was interested in any song I might be writing. "Oh yeah? That's great! What's it about?"

Magic words. I was always a sucker when someone really wanted to hear my new song ideas. It was a throwback to my youthful days when people saw me coming and would go the other way. "Well," I began, "it's a long story."

"Tell me about it," she said. "I got plenty of time."

"Okay. A couple days ago while walking down the street I decided to write a song. So I asked myself the same question I always do whenever I start a new song. What am I really feeling right now?" I told her I was having a mixed bag of emotions: anticipation, exhilaration, motivation. I was thinking about what most other hit songs were written about—love! "Yeah, love," I said, "the most beautiful thing in the world."

"You sho' ain't lying there, baby. That's great," she shouted.

"Yeah, I know, but I didn't want to write about that. Everybody writes about love. *I* wanted to write about something different. But what? Then it popped into my head, the most obvious thing of all, the thing I needed most—money. And I'm almost finished. Got one more verse to go."

"But won't people think that's all you care about?" Janie said.

"So what? Some will be shocked, some will think it's cute, some will think it's funny. I think I'll make money. What do you think?"

"How's it go?"

By this time we had reached the studio. Standing at the piano, I began to play some of the chords to my song, telling her how as a kid I'd heard people say, *"The best things in life are free,"* but knowing how much easier that was to say when you had money I sarcastically added, *"But you can give them to the birds and bees, I need money . . ."*

She laughed.

I loved the fact that she laughed so I rushed into the next verse singing the song as I played—*"Money don't get everything it's true, but what it don't get I can't use, I need money."*

She laughed again.

Then I really got into it, singing the chorus—*"Money, that's what I want. Yeah, yeah, that's what I want . . ."*

Janie was ecstatic. Still laughing, she offhandedly threw in her own line—*"Your love gives me such a thrill, but your love don't pay my bills, gimme some money, baby."*

"Great! That's great," I said, continuing to jam on the chorus line. "I'm gonna use that."

Barrett Strong, an artist I had started working with, who was writing a song in another room, ran into the studio and started jamming along with us. He slid next to me on the piano bench, playing away and joining me singing the chorus—uninvited. This was uncharacteristic of Barrett, who always seemed quiet, shy and a little in awe of me. But not this day. His voice was soulful and passionate. I didn't have to think twice about who I could get to sing my song. Barrett was it.

Janie didn't realize I was serious about using the line she had just blurted out spontaneously in a moment of fun. She was more convinced when she saw the songwriter's contract. Thinking her verse was the best of all, I gave her fifty percent.

"Money (That's What I Want)" was one of the first records cut at our own little studio. It was less like any record session I can remember. More like an in-house rehearsal—a party. One long party. It lasted a few days. We took take after take. Fun. I no longer had to worry about the cost of the studio. I owned it.

Being one of the earlier sessions, we recorded everything together, the singer, the band and the background voices. That gave it a raw, earthy feel.

Early into rehearsals I was in the middle of the room, jumping up and down, a directing fool, arranging as I went along. I had Barrett kick it off with that funky piano riff. And before I had a chance to point to anybody, I believe it was Brian Holland who jumped in, picking up the beat with a groovy tambourine.

Right before the first verse came in, I remember jerking my hands wide cutting off the piano and tambourine and pointing to the drummer, a guy by the name of Benny Benjamin. Wanting something different, I settled for a vision of Indians dancing around a teepee and had him do a heavy tom-tom beat.

By the time we got to some of those last takes, I had worked everybody into a frenzy—me gesturing wildly, Benny's sticks flying, Barrett screaming, *"The best things in life are free, but you can give them to the birds and bees . . ."* and the Rayber Voices jumping in on the chorus with *"Money, that's what I want."*

It felt good. It felt real good.

This time *nothing* was going to stop me from having a national release on my own label. "Money" became Tamla 54027. I purposely used a large number so people would not know how young my label was.

After I put the record out in Detroit, I sent it to the Washington-Baltimore and the Cleveland-Cincinnati areas. I had planned on spreading it from there. But orders came in so fast from Schwartz Brothers in Washington, D.C., and Cosnat distributors in Cleveland, there was no way I could afford to press enough records to send them around the rest of the country.

Gwen had a suggestion. Since Anna Records had national distribution through Chess, why not put "Money" on her label?

I liked the idea—a good opportunity to fulfill my promise to her and Roquel to help them in any way I could. A win-win situation I thought.

But by early 1960, I discovered that I had made more money from those three areas where I was working directly with the independent distributors than I did from the entire rest of the country. The distributors had to pay Chess, Chess had to pay Anna Records, and then Anna paid me. I was the furthest away from the money. By the time it trickled down, I got less from the whole country than I got from the three areas that were paying me directly.

On my next record I knew I had to go for it by myself—national all the way.

RATS, ROACHES, SOUL, GUTS AND LOVE

WILLIAM "MICKEY" STEVENSON showed up at Hitsville for an audition one day with an official-looking briefcase and a big, easy grin.

Sharply dressed, hip, fast-talking, Mickey was street, much more street than I was. I could see he was definitely an Eastside graduate while I was still sort of that Westside boy at heart. I liked him a lot. Then he sang a song. I liked him less.

"Your singing is okay," I said, "but I just don't need another singer right now. What I really need is an A&R director. Can you do that?"

"Do a bear shit in the woods?" he said.

I didn't think he knew what an A&R man was—I wasn't so sure *myself*—but I knew he could do it. All I knew was it stood for Artists and Repertoire and that every record company had one. And I could see Mickey was a guy with a kind of talent that I wanted. He was a throwback to my childhood—that numbers guy—that hustler—that kid who was the best at playing the Dozens, all rolled up into one. He had the job. Now he had to figure out what the job was.

It turned out that while A&R director might mean something different at other record companies, at ours it meant somebody in charge of all the creative activities of producing a record.

It was really with Mickey that I began something that was unique to my management style, building the structure around the person rather than fitting the person into the structure. People over structure would continue to dominate throughout the years.

Right at the start, he went on the lookout for great musicians, combing even the seediest of bars and hangouts. If they could play, Mickey would bring 'em in, putting together the greatest house band that anyone could ever want. They called themselves the Funk Brothers.

Probably the two musicians who were the key for me in this loosely organized group were Benny Benjamin on drums and James Jamerson on bass. The other two members that made up the core of the Funk Brothers were Earl Van Dyke (on piano) and Robert White (on guitar). Others included from time to time Joe Hunter (piano), Eddie

Willis (guitar), Johnny Griffith (piano), Joe Messina and David Hamilton (guitar), drummers Uriel Jones and Richard "Pistol" Allen, and percussionists Eddie "Bongo" Brown, Jack Ashford, and Jack Brokensha. Our saxophonist/flute player extraordinaire was Thomas "Beans" Bowles—nicknamed "Beans" for being tall and thin like a stringbean. I had first spotted him at the Flame Show Bar, playing in Maurice King's band, and used him on the "Come To Me" session. Maurice King also joined Motown, where he wore many hats.

Whenever a new player came into the group the sound would change slightly, based on his style.

Artists sang background on each other's sessions, or played the tambourine or clapped their hands; any employee who could carry a tune or keep a beat was used.

Each person—whether directly in the creative process or behind the scenes—somehow affected the mix.

The love we felt for each other when we were playing is the most undisputed truth about our music. I sometimes referred to our sound as a combination of rats, roaches, soul, guts and love.

On my sessions we'd work from handwritten chord sheets. The "feel" was usually the first thing I'd go for. After locking in the drumbeat, I'd hum a line for each musician to start. Once we got going, we'd usually ad lib all over the place until we got the groove I wanted. Many of these guys came from a Jazz background. I understood their instincts to turn things around to their liking, but I also knew what I wanted to hear—commercially. So when they went too far, I'd stop them and stress, "We gotta get back to the funk—stay in that groove." Then I'd make it as plain as possible: I would extend my arms a certain distance apart, saying, "I want to stay between here and there. Do whatever you want but stay in this range—in the pocket." But between "here and there" they did all kinds of stuff—always pushing me to the limit and beyond. Especially Jamerson.

James Jamerson was a genius on the bass. He was an incredible improviser in the studio and someone I always wanted on my sessions. He'd get a simple chord sheet and build his own bass line so intricately it was hard to duplicate. Even he had trouble. That was great for the record, but when he stayed in Detroit and other musicians went out on the road to play the song live, they'd go crazy trying to play his lines. Some of the stuff he did on the bass, people are still trying to figure out today.

Another musician I had to have on all my sessions was Benny Benjamin. He was so good on the drums and had a feel no one could match. He had a distinctive knack for executing various rhythms all at the same time. He had a pulse, a steadiness that kept the tempo better than a metronome. Benny was my man.

Sometimes when Benny didn't show, Mickey would have to find him, root him out of some dive or somebody's house, and get him to the session, even propping him up if he wasn't sober. But once Benny had those sticks in his hands, drunk or sober, he was the best.

At the beginning we did our sound engineering with the existing equipment—the little two-track I had bought from Bristol Bryant. Then I hired a young technical genius named Mike McLean. He slowly rebuilt our equipment, creating as he went along. Very worried about how "his" equipment was going to be used, he made all the producers and engineers take classes from him on how to operate it—including me.

I was never really happy with our studio sound. But as it turned out, its many limitations forced us to be innovative. For example, having no room in the studio for a vocal booth, we made one out of the hallway that led from the control room to the stairs that took you into the studio. Since there were no windows we couldn't see the singer, so we communicated only over the microphones. But the end result was a good, clean vocal.

Our first echo chamber was the downstairs bathroom. We had to post a guard outside the door to make sure no one flushed the toilet while we were recording.

Later we also adapted an attic area as an echo chamber. That worked very well, except for an occasional car horn, rain, thunder or any other outside sounds that came in through the roof. Eventually we started recording the songs dry and adding echo afterward. Echoes gave the recording a bigger sound and made the voice sound fatter with a lingering feel to it. We bought a German electronic echo chamber, called an EMT, which we installed in the basement. That worked the best of all.

We put partitions around the different instruments to keep the horn sounds from bleeding into the bass, or the drums into the piano, and so on.

To get a clean, clear sound on the guitars, without any hum or feedback from the amps, we started feeding the guitars directly into the control room. (Several years later we brought in Armin Steiner from the West Coast to rebuild and modernize our studio.)

Long before there were electronic synthesizers, I was looking for new ways to create different sound effects. We would try anything to get a unique percussion sound: two blocks of wood slapped together, striking little mallets on glass ashtrays, shaking jars of dried peas— anything. I might see a producer dragging in big bike chains or getting a whole group of people stomping on the floor.

Never having forgotten that big orchestral sound from the Jackie Wilson "Lonely Teardrops" session, I tried to re-create it in our own studio, often bringing in string players from the Detroit Symphony. At first they had no idea what to make of me or how their music would fit into ours. But in time they became an integral part of the Motown family and our sound.

Another regular aspect of our early productions was the background voices of the Andantes—Judith Barrow, Louvain Demps, Jacqueline Hicks—another backup group.

Since many producers, myself included, lacked a lot of formal music education, when it came time to merge all these different elements, we sometimes looked for help from some of our arrangers. In the process, the talents of such people as Johnny Allen, Willie Shorter, Paul Riser and Hank Cosby would also leave a distinctive mark on our music.

Mixing was so important to me that it seemed I spent half my life at the mixing board. To get just the right sound, just the right blend, I would mix and mix and then remix. Smokey and I had a running joke over what a mix maniac I was.

Often the differences between the various mixes were subtle; but those subtleties, I felt, could make or break a record.

Whether I was cutting a record, mixing it or listening to someone else's, I was open to just about anything.

I may not have always known what I was looking for exactly, but when I found it I knew it. While open to a broad range of influences—

Gospel, Pop, Rhythm & Blues, Jazz, Doo-Wop, Country—I always emphasized simple, clear communication.

And that's exactly what I got one day as I was heading into the studio to record a follow-up record on Barrett Strong. Ray walked up behind me and in her regular, peppy, high-pitched enthusiastic way, she communicated to me very simply: "Oh, Berry, we're getting married next week on Thursday."

"Terrific, yeah sure," I mumbled, knowing she could not be serious.

The next day Ray mentioned "it" again. We were walking into a small room where Brian Holland was banging away on an upright, when she whispered, "Don't forget, next Thursday."

That bothered me. After that the days shot by like rockets. "Don't forget we're getting married in three days." "Two days, I just want to remind you."

The next thing I knew Robert Bateman was driving us to Toledo, Ohio, around sixty miles from Detroit. We were crammed in the car with both sets of parents. Hers were smiling all over the place. Mother and Pop were happy, too. I felt more pressured than I could remember.

On the way Ray talked constantly, fast, keeping everyone excited, and trying to keep my mind off what she knew I was thinking. Going nonstop for eighteen, twenty hours a day for months, I hadn't had time to stop and listen to my feelings.

Looking up I saw a sign: Toledo 30 miles. My heart was pounding, my stomach aching. *I don't want to go through with this, but I should have said something when we were fifty miles out.*

I was quiet on the outside, but inside, voices were screaming at me: "Are you a man or a mouse? Speak now, or forever hold your peace! You're on the move, why get tied down now? There's always tomorrow." And another voice: "She's such a devoted woman. Marriage would mean so much to her. You have a son together—and you do love her."

Off in the distance I saw a sign moving toward me at breakneck speed: Toledo 15 miles.

"This is your life and you only have one. You better be true to yourself." As we got to the edge of the city limits one of the voices drowning out all the others kept repeating: "I'm not getting married, I'm not getting married, I'm not getting married."

Finally I said, in what I thought was a quiet mumble amidst the chatter around me, "I'm not getting married," only to hear it resound through that car as if it had been blared through an amplifier.

Silence! Everybody seemed frozen. I was shocked as well, but happy I had broken the ice. Now I could talk about it. "I really don't think I should get married," I tried to explain. "I just don't think it's right. I only knew about this a week ago and it just doesn't feel right to me, and I think it's better I say it now. I know I should have said it before but . . . I wasn't too sure. I had no time to think. I mean . . ."

I waited for a response from somebody. Nothing. In a low voice I said, "Robert, you might as well turn the car around. I'm not getting married. Not right now. I've changed my mind."

Caught in the middle, Robert acted like he didn't hear me and continued driving. I was about to tell him a little louder when Ray spoke up.

"Robert, turn the car around," she said. He quickly made a U-turn at the outskirts of Toledo and we headed back.

Relieved, I tried to explain more, but it didn't seem to matter to anyone. We were all quiet for the rest of the trip.

Once back at Hitsville Ray was her old self again—cheerful, bouncing around and really nice to me. After three days of having time to think about it, that next morning I walked behind her in the bathroom as she was brushing her teeth and whispered, "Will you marry me?"

We were off again to Toledo. This time Robert Bateman drove us alone. When we returned we got back to doing what we loved most—work.

WAY OVER THERE

MY BIGGEST CHALLENGE was coming up with the right record to take us into the national picture. In the summer of '60 I had it. Smokey brought it to me.

"Way Over There" had great feeling, great melody and great lyrics. Smokey sang it as if his life depended on it, with passion and inspiration:

I've got a lover way over there on the mountain side
And I know that's where I should be . . .
They tell me that the river's too deep and it's much too wide,
Boy you can't get over to the other side . . .

"Way Over There" will always be a special song. For the guy in the song Smokey was singing about, it was where his lover was, but for me "way over there" was where my dreams were—for Motown, for happiness, for success. And with my first national release I felt I was moving closer to all of them.

Loucye started right away on the distribution, getting a master DJ list from Gwen and the names of all the Chess distributors. She organized everything for our first big shipping, recruiting anyone she could find—including me. We gathered around a long table to package the disc jockey copies in an assembly-line style. One person took the records out of the box, another put each one between two pieces of cardboard, sliding it into an envelope, and another sealed it with a sponge.

I was so confident about this record that I decided to advertise in *Cash Box* magazine like the big boys seemed to do so successfully. I wanted to do it "right." I wanted to say "Watch out world, here I come!"

Since we didn't have an advertising executive, I designed the ad myself based on an idea I remembered from an old Western movie ad. It started with "From Out of the West Comes . . ." and as it read down from the top, each line spread out wider and wider, forming a pyramid. It gave me feelings of action and excitement.

Here's the ad that ran in the July 23, 1960, issue of *Cash Box*:

When Esther saw it she said, "Don't you think that sounds a little arrogant?"

"Who's gonna know I wrote it?" I said.

With distribution and advertising in place, everything was riding on getting airplay. Thanks to Cleveland's Ken Hawkins and Cincinnati's Jockey Jack Gibson, "Way Over There" started happening fast in those cities, spreading through much of the Midwest.

I was told if I wanted the East Coast, the man I had to get was Georgie Woods at WDAS, the kingpin in Philadelphia.

Though I didn't know a thing about promotion, I was off to Philadelphia. I knew of the heavyweight promo guys from the other record companies, like Bunky Sheppard from Vee Jay, Granville "Granny" White from Columbia, Joe Medlin and Larry Maxwell from Atlantic, and Dave Clark from Duke-Peacock. I didn't know how they got their records played but I did know they were unconventional characters who had spent years perfecting their art, using every trick they knew to promote their records.

How to get mine played was what I was worried about as I walked

131

into station WDAS in Philly and first saw Georgie. Handsome, smooth, suave, with a large commanding voice and the size to match, he was holding court while playing records on the air.

Smiling, minding my manners, I waited patiently, hoping for a chance to be seen, heard, talked to, or even maybe think of something clever to say. But then I remembered something I heard as a kid. "It's better to be thought a fool than to open your mouth and remove all doubt." I waited.

Finally alone, I had outstayed everybody. Still paying no attention to me, Georgie kept doing his thing, talking fast, sexy and cool. I could see why they called him the king. When one of his assistants walked into the room the king said to her, "I want a hot dog."

"Hot dog? I'll get it," I volunteered, rushing out. I returned quickly to continue my wait.

At last he looked in my direction: "Whatcha got there?"

I jumped up. "Oh, I got a really great record here, 'Way Over—' "

"Give it here," he said, taking it from me. He turned back around in his chair, placed my record on a turntable, put his earphones on and touched down with the needle. Seconds later he pulled it back off the record, saying nothing.

My heart dropped.

As he started fading down the on-air record he said over the open mike: "Here is a brand-new record, a brand-new group, a brand-new smash . . . 'Way Over There' by the Miracles. It's hot, folks!"

And it was. Philadelphia ordered one thousand records about two days later.

But each time I heard the record, I thought how much better it could be if it only had strings on it. Finally I couldn't stand it anymore and found myself assembling the troops and flying to Universal Studio in Chicago. I wanted that big New York sound and, in my mind, there was no way I could get that in our little Hitsville studio, which produced a thin, somewhat distorted sound with a heavy bottom. On the flight over, I told everybody how the Chicago Symphony was going to play the strings on the new version and how the new record was going to be so much better, cleaner, fuller.

The Miracles were terrific—becoming inspired at hearing the difference in the sound quality. The session was by no means an easy one. But, at last, we got a great take. On the playback, I was convinced that we'd laid down the most beautiful strings I had ever heard. This new version sounded identical to the old one, except bigger and better.

Ecstatic about the great sound, we then switched the records and started shipping the one with the strings. A huge ordeal. We got the DJs to change from the old one to the new one. They loved it, too. In fact everybody loved it, that is except the public. I had lost the magic. We never sold more than the original sixty thousand copies.

The first version had an honesty and raw soul, the second was a copy. It was then I began to better appreciate the sound produced by our own little studio.

Even though my idea to recut hadn't turned out so well, "Way Over There" was a real victory. After many tries, I had finally done it. I had gone national. Motown had now entered the music scene.

BLACK RADIO

BLACK RADIO WAS EVERYTHING to people like me.

The Sutherland Hotel in Chicago was the site of my first-ever convention, the annual meeting of the black disc jockeys, NARA— the National Association of Radio Announcers. In my new role as independent record company owner, this was a big deal to me. It was the first time I could put faces with some of the reputations I'd heard so much about. It was the first time I heard manufacturers and disc jockeys referred to as "partners." And—it was the first time I met Ewart Abner.

Seeing so many important DJs under one roof was incredible. Everybody was partying like a dog—day and night. I wanted to be a part of it all, but only a few guys remembered me from my Jackie Wilson days and my writing and producing for Marv Johnson. So I had to be cool. Even though I was national with my own label, I was still just a little guy amongst these big independent companies who were wining and dining the DJs like mad.

Downstairs at the bar, I spotted Jockey Jack Gibson holding court with some other biggies—master rhymers and rappers like Eddie O'Jay from Cleveland, whose deep baritone voice sent people rushing to record stores. Next to him was the smooth-talking Tommy Smalls, known as Dr. Jive, a killer with the women, and the jockey you needed if you wanted New York.

Jockey Jack knew me because of Jackie and waved me over, introduced me to some of the guys and then jumped back into his conversation. With an intellectual, champagne-drinking style, Jockey Jack was one of the first really hip-talkin' DJs. He was an original rapper, in the days when rapping was how we talked to women to make them like us.

The convention was great fun for me until a meeting on the last night, when things got serious.

After a short opening announcement, one DJ after another walked up to the podium expressing their discontent as they addressed the ills of the industry. I sat and listened as they said: "We play your records, we make you rich, and we have nothing to show for it." And they told us that we should come up with ways to help them make more money.

Rushing to their support, representatives of the other record companies got up and presented all sorts of ideas, from giving them free records they could sell at their record hops to paying them as advisers.

Meanwhile I'm sitting there thinking, "What can I do? What am I supposed to say?" I knew I *had* to go up and say something in support of the people who were my life's blood. But what? How could I compete with those other companies?

Then, while I was sitting there dreading the inevitable, Ewart Abner, a distinguished-looking light-skinned black man, the president of Vee Jay Records, walked up to the podium. "Gentlemen," he said, "I've listened to all your suggestions and think we need to just stop for a second. We're going in the wrong direction."

Everything got real quiet. I was fearful for the man and didn't even know him.

After pausing for a second he said, "For you to ask us to do more than we are already doing is not the answer." The majors were not at this convention, he reminded them. "Most didn't even bother to have their representatives here. Yet you play *their* records. Sure we want to help and we have helped and we will continue to help. But we should not be your primary source of income. That you should get from the station you work for. You are the stars. You are the power. You are the forces in your communities that get that station high ratings and big money from their advertisers. It's because of your artistry and talent that they become number one. Negotiate a better deal with them. And remember, if your station won't pay you, their competitors will!"

Abner had electrified the audience with passion, conviction and guts. He said what I would have liked to have said. I knew I would always respect that man. He got a standing ovation, which ended the meeting.

Growing up with my ear plastered to our old Grundig, I was no stranger to the power of the disc jockey. These guys didn't just spin the records, they provided entertainment—jiving, preaching, teaching, each with his own style. They took us along the road of the incredible changes that were going on in music.

The Detroit area jocks at WCHB and WJLB were the first I got to know. WCHB was the home of Joltin' Joe Howard, this jolly big cat—always moving fast—his energy contagious. Also on this station were the Larrys—Dean and Dixon. Each was hot—Long Lean Larry Dean with his very cool delivery and deep voice, Larry Dixon using a bedroom, melodic style, introducing sex appeal with his every word.

Meanwhile, across town at WJLB, was one of the hottest guys around—Frantic Ernie Durham. Talking fifty miles a minute, creating a fever pitch of excitement, he wasn't called Frantic for nothing. But being frantic didn't keep him from being an excellent businessman— a smart self-promoter. He would hold the record hops at local clubs, showcasing artists and their new hits, meeting his listeners in person, promoting his radio show.

When heavy hitters like Georgie Woods in Philly thought a record was a hit, they would call powerful jocks in other cities. Georgie was a mover, not only of records but of the community as well. Another real activist was a top New York DJ, Hal Jackson, the nicest guy around, who worked especially well with the kids. He was always trying to help somebody. New York also had Jack Walker. Jack didn't seem to be a killer like some of the power DJs, but you didn't have to be to have the listeners love you.

In Baltimore Maurice "Hot Rod" Hulbert would burn up the airwaves with his supercharged raps and rhymes. Jocko Henderson in Philly hooked his audiences with phrases so witty they became part of the local slang.

In black radio women DJs were already part of the scene. Mary Dee in Pittsburgh, Dizzy Lizzy in Houston, Chattie Hattie in Charlotte, and Martha Jean "The Queen," first in Memphis, then in Detroit. Every one of these women were important DJs with good time slots and they all played my records.

To drive their stations to #1, DJs fought hard to get the hit records before anyone else.

Individually, each was a character, a promoter and a star who would go to any extreme to capture listeners.

Once, a guy who always treated me special, my friend the smooth-talking E. Rodney Jones, disappeared from a new station he was working at in Chicago, WVON, owned by the Chess brothers. Each day speculation grew that he had been kidnapped and possibly murdered. The other stations began carrying updates on their news programs. It seemed the whole town was worried sick about E. Rodney Jones. When he showed up a few weeks later everyone was thrilled, especially the Chess brothers. I never found out where he was and neither did anyone else to my knowledge. If it was a publicity stunt it worked because the station immediately jumped to #1.

They came up with any gimmick possible. John Bandy, known as Lord Fauntleroy, out of Washington, D.C., perfected an aristocratic British accent, while in Pittsburgh a monocled Sir Walter Raleigh spoke in a working-class dialect. I don't know if either of them had ever been to England.

Then, there was the Magnificent Montague. Once you heard his outrageous oratory, you couldn't forget it or him. "I want you to put your hand on the radio and I'll touch your heart. I will give you a feeling of love that others could never give you. I am the true lover, your truest friend and wherever you go I will be with you. Wherever you are within the sound of my voice, if you want to feel what I am saying, just touch the radio, touch the radio, touch the radio. Feel the heat I'm sending to your soul. Burn, baby, burn!"

He was known to play a song fifteen times in a row. Crazy! Irate fans would call the station, protesting vigorously. The owners, fearing a loss of listeners, demanded he stop.

He'd snap at them: "You fools. Why do you think I'm number one? As long as they're complaining, they're listening to our station."

I, as a manufacturer, was not too happy myself. That is, until my record was the one he played fifteen times. This habit, as well as others, got him fired from many stations. But usually not before he became #1.

When he'd get fired, he'd call his friends for help. I seemed to be at the top of that list. It was easy for him to get help from me because I knew wherever he went he'd become #1 before he'd be fired again.

When he lost a job at WVON in Chicago he called. I sent him money for his cross-country move to Los Angeles. Sometime later, I was shocked to find that other manufacturers had paid for that same move.

When I confronted him with this revelation, he just looked at me. "My dear man," he proudly smiled, "you wouldn't expect me to deprive anyone of the pleasure of helping the Magnificent One, would you?"

I always get a good feeling when I think back to how they, the jocks in black radio, many of whom I never met, took so much pride in helping me, a young black cat out of Detroit. My appreciation to this day has never diminished.

7

SURVIVAL OF THE FITTEST
1960–1964

STREET BUSINESS

Detroit's hottest nightclub, the 20 Grand, was packed. People were jammed into every corner of this unique entertainment complex, which had two separate showrooms on one level and a bowling alley downstairs.

The Miracles were getting ready to perform in the main room. Way on the other side of the building, I had just finished directing Marv Johnson at a record hop put on by DJ Frantic Ernie Durham from WJLB, who had been wailing all week on Marv's latest record, "I Love The Way You Love."

These appearances were great promotion for us and a source of revenue for the DJs. They would play the hell out of the record on the air and in return the artist would appear at the DJs' hops to sing over their records.

Lip-synching was an art to us. Our artists had to do it perfectly, and they knew it. I was always right there watching for mistakes. Marv was a smash that night. He didn't even miss a breath.

I was thrilled with the crowd's reaction but I had to get out of there fast to get to the other side of the building before the Miracles hit the stage. I wanted to check the sound before they went on and I was already late. Pushing my way through the crowd of noisy, excited people, with Robert Bateman and Ray leading the way, I heard this little voice: "Mr. Gordy, Mr. Gordy."

"Yeah?" I answered, looking back at a little brown-skinned girl with broad features and big eyes, running toward me.

"Mr. Gordy," she said, trying to catch her breath, "I've been trying to get to you all night. I got a song. It's great, it's great, it's really good. Can I have an appointment with you?"

I was walking fast, she faster. "I have no time for a meeting," I said.

Glued to my coat tail, she seemed to be lock-stepping in sync with all my moves. "Oh, please, Mr. Gordy . . ."

"Can you sing it?" I yelled, bobbing and weaving through openings in the crowd.

"Oh yeah—really good, I can sing it good."

"Well then sing it," I said.

"Sing it?"

"Yeah."

"Now?"

"Yeah, right now."

She jumped right into the song with vigor and desperation:

You know you took my heart
and you broke it apart.
Why did love baby have to ever start?
You know you took my love, threw it away.
You're gonna want my love someday.
Well, bye, bye, baby.

Over all the noise, confusion and everything, I loved that raspy, soulful sound. I slowed. All of a sudden I did have time.

"What's your name?"

"Mary . . . Mary Wells."

"Okay Mary, meet me at the studio tomorrow."

"But how will I get in?"

"Don't worry, you'll get in."

When I met with her the next day, she said she had written the song for Jackie Wilson, but when I told her she was the only perfect person to sing it, it seemed her wildest dream had come true.

I knew how Mary felt because my own dream for a hit factory was quickly taking form, a concept that had been shaped by principles I had learned on the Lincoln-Mercury assembly line. At the plant the cars started out as just a frame, pulled along on conveyor belts until they emerged at the end of the line—brand spanking new cars rolling off the line. I wanted the same concept for my company, only with artists and songs and records. I wanted a place where a kid off the street could walk in one door an unknown and come out another a recording artist—a star.

But I knew, unlike cars, each person was unique, with his or her own talents, dreams and ambitions.

I had never seen anything like what I had in mind and had no formal business training, so I had to figure out my own methods for building such a company.

I broke down my whole operation into three functions: Create, Make, Sell. I felt any business had to do that. Create something, Make something and then Sell it. Using this phrase as a slogan kept my thinking in focus.

The Create phase—writing, producing and recording—was really starting to come together as the Hitsville talent pool expanded on a regular basis.

The Make phase—manufacturing, pressing of the records—was the process that Loucye oversaw. It now required a growing support staff to deal with inventories, the plants, deliveries to distribution points and the billing to the distributors.

We were doing fine with the Create and Make phase but the Sell phase—placing records with distributors, getting airplay, marketing and advertising—was the area I needed to develop. Since our Sales Department at the time consisted of one guy—me—I knew I needed more help, somebody who could get to the broader market.

I knew a little about getting white airplay from having made friends with a local DJ named Tom Clay. When I had Marv Johnson's record on UA, "You Got What It Takes," he was at the #1 Pop station in town, WJBK. I was told I could never get the top Pop DJs in town to play records by local black artists.

Not so. Tom liked me and my record. Not only did he play it, but he introduced me to Barney Ales, telling me he would be a great local distributor. Barney knew the business and was aggressive. When I let him distribute both my labels, Tamla and Motown, I never suspected he would go on to become a major contributor to the success of the company.

In July of 1960 he was handling the Miracles' "Way Over There," still going strong on Tamla, and Mary Wells's "Bye Bye Baby," just out on Motown. Barney was getting airplay on both records through-out the whole state, but when "Bye Bye Baby" didn't take off in sales quite as fast as the Miracles had, I figured it wasn't getting enough promotion.

"You got two records with the same distributor," somebody told me. "They only have so many people to work both records. What you should do is split the lines. Take one of your labels and give it to another distributor. You'll have many more people working each record."

That sounded smart to me.

I moved the Motown line from Barney to one of his competitors. All of a sudden I wasn't hearing "Bye Bye Baby" on the radio at all.

I got the new distributor on the phone. "We're doing the best we can," came his weak reply.

Barney had the Motown line back the next day. I again started hearing Mary on the air.

Later, I asked Barney if he had anything to do with the slowdown.

"Absolutely not," he said. "All I did was call the DJs to let them know if they wanted to do something for me, they might want to play my new Shirelles record on Scepter. And oh yeah, I did tell them that Mary Wells was no longer my record."

It was then I decided maybe this guy should be on my team as more than just my distributor.

I invited Barney to hang out at Hitsville more and we became even better friends. He'd usually wind up in the back playing cards or Ping-Pong. Like the rest of us, he was a fierce competitor. He hated to lose.

Pheasant hunting wasn't exactly a regular activity in the neighborhood where I grew up, but Barney convinced me to try it.

It began on a nerve-wracking note. I had never been around that many people, that many white people . . . out in the woods . . . with guns. The shotgun Barney gave me was so heavy that when I fired it, it was like being kicked in the shoulder by a mule. I hated the hunting but there was something fun about being around Barney. What I learned most from that trip was why Barney was such a great salesman. It wasn't so much what he did, but the way he did it—warm, personal and familylike. If he could get me to enjoy hunting pheasants, I wondered what he could do with disc jockeys, program directors and distributors.

I began to think of ways to woo this master salesman to my company. What I didn't know was he wanted to be there, too. That's why he took me on that hunting trip in the first place.

Around that time, the fall of 1960, Smokey, who was always running in excited to see me about something, found me in the studio at the piano working on something of my own. This time he wanted help on a song he was writing called "Shop Around." As he sang the lyrics I forgot about whatever I was writing and told him what he was singing was going to be the Miracles' next big hit.

"Oh no, no, it's not for me," he argued. "I don't feel it for myself."

"What, are you crazy? You don't feel it?"

"Nope. I don't."

That was the first time I realized that artists don't necessarily always know what is best for them.

We argued back and forth as I helped him work on it. When it was finished he was still adamant that it was not for him.

"Maybe you're right, Smoke," I said, "but can you just do me a favor and try it? Try it for me?"

He stopped. "For you?"

"For me."

"Okay."

That was a lucky day for both of us.

Up until then Smokey and I had written everything together. But on each song I was doing less and less. Finally, on this record, I quietly took my name off the label so when it was released he would realize he had come into his own as a songwriter. He didn't need me or anybody else.

But when Smokey found out what I had done he was furious. And without telling me, he made Loucye's label copy people put it back on. When the record came out, I was the one surprised.

"Why," I asked him, "that don't make no sense. You come to me with a song that's almost finished. I give you a few ideas and you give me half the credit. Ridiculous. Giving input is my job. I do it with everybody."

Smokey argued that I may have been the key to the song's success and deserved a piece. I told him I didn't care what he thought and that unless I personally felt I deserved it, there was no way my name was going on any label copy from then on.

And in any event, every time I heard "Shop Around" on the radio I got sick. Too slow. Not enough life. I was mad at myself for ever letting it be released.

Finally, after four or five days I couldn't stand it anymore. I had to recut it.

I thought back to how disastrous my recutting "Way Over There" had been. But to let that mistake keep me from doing what I now thought was right would be an even bigger mistake.

I called Smokey.

"Man, we've got to cut the song again."

"Who is this?"

"Me, Berry. We got to do it again, man."

"Do what?"

"I just told you, the song, 'Shop Around.' "

"It's three o'clock in the morning!"

"You busy or somethin'?"

"Naw, man, I was just sittin' here waiting for your call."

"Every time I hear it it drives me crazy," I said. "It's too slow, and you've got to get everybody to the studio right away."

"And you've got to be kidding."

"No, Smoke, I wish I was."

An hour or so later he had the musicians and the other Miracles at the studio. The piano player didn't show up, so I played it myself. We recut the new version with more life and a faster beat.

Within a few months, the new "Shop Around" had gone to #2 on the Pop charts. Our first million seller!

But I was still not totally satisfied. I felt #1 and #2 were miles apart. I believed that if I had been able to put together a strong in-house Sales Department sooner, that record might have gone to #1.

Near the end of 1960 Barney Ales accepted my offer to come head up our Sales Department. *Create, Make* and *Sell* would now be in full force.

After the success of "Shop Around" I needed to be in about ten places at once. I might have Mary Wells at the Warfield Theater, Barrett Strong at the Royal Blue nightclub, Marv Johnson at the Armory in Flint, Michigan, and the Miracles off to Philadelphia to appear on Dick Clark's *American Bandstand*. And now that the artists' *own* Cycles of Success were kicking in, it brought on a whole new set of responsibilities for me.

They looked to me for advice not only from a creative standpoint, but a business and personal one as well. For me to not get too sidetracked by all the various problems developing around me, I created an artist management company, naming it International Talent Management Inc. The purpose of ITMI—as we called it—was to act as personal manager to the artists. They did everything from getting them gigs, providing career guidance and negotiating with booking agents to making sure they paid their taxes—something I would continue to stress over the years.

My sister Esther—part mother hen and part general—was the perfect person to run it.

Hitsville was jumping. It was December of 1960 and we were having our first annual Christmas party. Everybody was there. In the control room, where I was laughing it up with Mickey Stevenson and Smokey, Gwen found me.

"Berry, you've got to hear this guy," she said. "He's great."

Over the years my sisters were always promoting somebody.

"Not now," I said to Gwen, "not tonight. This is our Christmas party."

15. The great Lady Day at Detroit's Flame Show Bar surrounded by me, my brother Robert (*left*) and friends Mable John and Cecil Alleyne.

17. Early Miracles: I kept throwing them on stage hoping someday they'd get it right. *Left to right:* Smokey Robinson, Bobby Rogers, Claudette Robinson, Ronnie White and Pete Moore.

18. Out on the town, Anna and Gwen with their husbands, Marvin Gaye and Harvey Fuqua.

OPPOSITE PAGE:

6. At a BMI Award Dinner with Mother and Pop, Anna and Jackie Wilson: don't know what thrilled me more, winning the award for "Lonely Teardrops" or Mother and Pop beaming at me.

19. My second wife, Raynoma, assisted me, boosted morale, worked with musicians, managed the office and was the first person I ever knew who had perfect pitch.

20. Our first building at 2648 West Grand Boulevard, which housed our studio, was always under construction.

21. At the office (*left to right*), Rebecca Nichols, Esther Gordy Edwards, Barney Wright, Raynoma, Diana Ross, Fran Heard and Billie Jean Brown watch as Little Stevie Wonder "X's" his autograph.

22. Jammin' with Little Stevie Wonder. *Right to left:* Brenda Holloway, Georgeanna Tillman, Katherine Anderson, Mary Wilson, Florence Ballard, Diana Ross, Iris Gordy, Wanda Young, Bobby Rogers and me on piano.

23. After a club performance the Vandellas, Rosalind Ashfor͏ Martha Reeves and Annette Beard, join our copyright lawyer George Schiffer, me, Margaret Norton and Anna Gordy Gay͏

24. The very first Supremes were called the Primettes. *Left to right:* Betty McGlown, Mary Wilson, Diane Ross and Florence Ballard.

25. Down South with the Motortown Revue. *Left to right:* Stevie Wonder; the Temptations; Eddie Kendricks, Elbridge Bryant, drummer Uriel Jones behind Elbridge, Otis Williams, Paul Williams, Melvin Franklin; Diana Ross, Robert Bullock, Patrice Gordy, Florence Ballard and Mary Wilson.

26. The Motortown Revue first played the Apollo Theater in Harlem in 1962.

27. "Slapjack" with Smokey Robinson: We've never stopped competing. We've never stopped laughing. And I've never stopped beating him.

28. Two piano players: Marvin Gaye (he's the one with the shoes) and me finding a way to crack Smokey up.

29. Christmas at the Graystone Ballroom, 1963. A once-in-a-lifetime performance: *(left to right)* Diana Ross of the Supremes, Melvin Franklin of the Temptations, our A&R Director, Mickey Stevenson, Smokey Robinson of the Miracles and Wanda Young of the Marvelettes with three of the Four Tops on stage: *(left to right)* Renaldo "Obie" Benson, Abdul "Duke" Fakir and Lawrence Payton.

30. The mixing fanatic.

31. Pop was a father figure to many in the Motown family. Here, at a party Marvin's doing his best to make him laugh.

32. Barney Ales, the Master Salesman, was a tough negotiator—especially with me.

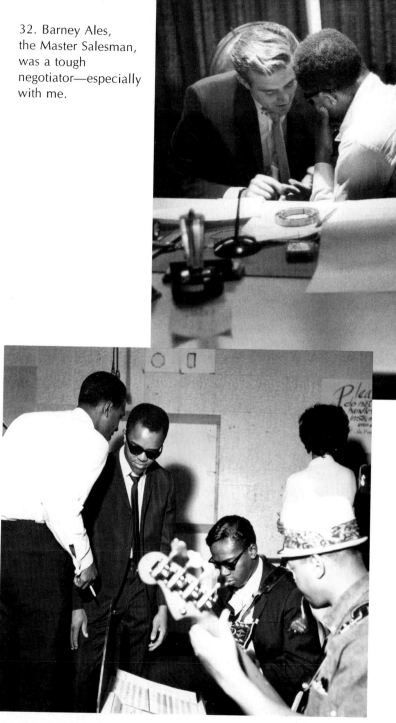

33. During this recording session with guitarist Marv Tarplin and bass player James Jamerson, Marvin Gaye gives me some creative input.

34. Harvey Fuqua directs a typical Artist Development session with the Temptations. Conductor and arranger, Maurice King *(center)*, works from behind perfecting harmonies. David Ruffin *(left)*, the lead singer on this song, watches intently.

36. Even back in 1965 I was fascinated with technology. We videotaped this rehearsal where choreographer Cholly Atkins tries to teach the wild Contours more polished steps. *Left to right:* Joe Green, Huey Davis, Joe Stubbs, Council Gay, Cholly, Dennis Edwards, Joe Billingslea and Sylvester Potts.

7. In later Motortown Revues, Gladys Knight showed off the polish that she and he Pips seemed to have been born with. *Left to right:* William Guest, Edward atten and Merald "Bubba" Knight.

OPPOSITE PAGE:

5. I bought the Graystone Ballroom in 1962, keeping a promise I made to myself s a kid. The Miracles are on stage.

38. I joined a meeting in Brian Holland's office. *Left to right:* Smokey, Lawrence Horn, Ralph Seltzer, Billie Jean Brown, Brian, me, Bette Ocha and Eddie Holland.

"But he's good, I'm tellin' you," she said, pointing through the thick glass window that separated the control room from the studio.

Looking out, I saw this rather boyish, slim, handsome guy. Sitting at the piano, gracefully stroking the keys in an almost melancholy fashion, he appeared to be deep in thought.

"That's Marvin Gaye," she said. "He's been singing with Harvey and the Moonglows, but wants to go solo."

"Why don't you put him on your label?"

"He wants to be with you."

There was something real special about the image this guy projected that made me want to hear what he was playing. I wandered into the studio, sitting down next to him on the piano bench.

He knew who I was, but he was cool. Real cool. He kept on playing without looking in my direction.

Over the party noise I could hear the soft, jazzy melodies he was weaving. There was a warmth and a sadness in the music that made me feel good.

"Berry Gordy," he said softly, "how you doin', man?"

"Fine. I heard that you're a really good singer."

"I'm okay."

"Well, how about doing something for me?"

"What do you want me to do?" he said, never lifting his eyes from the keys.

"I don't know, whatever you want," I said, expecting a bluesy kind of song more in the style of the Moonglows.

Instead, he continued playing those soft, jazzy chords and began to sing a warm, jazzy rendition of a standard, "Mr. Sandman."

His voice was pure, mellow, soulful and honest. I loved it, and now it was my turn to be cool. I knew right then that I wanted to work with this man. Not knowing what kind of person he was, my instincts told me not to get too excited. But at the same time I wanted to be honest with him.

"Not bad," I said. "I like that. I really do."

Although he quietly said, "Thank you," I could feel his excitement. Something about him was different—deep, intense.

A lot of things go through my mind when I first meet an artist. I don't always know what it is I love, but I can feel it. I've never been one to show my emotions by jumping up and down. But at that moment I wanted to. I told Marvin that he had something real special.

"You really think so?" he said.

"Definitely."

"What? What do you think it is?" he said.

I wanted to tell him something but I wasn't sure myself. It tickled me that here I was, the king of the party, and he had me on the defensive in our very first meeting.

"I can't talk about it now," I said, "but maybe I'll tell you later."

I'd meet artists in so many different ways. About six months before, I had been passing through the lobby when Robert Bateman was auditioning four girls singing an a cappella version of the Drifters' "There Goes My Baby." The whiny voice of the girl singing lead caught my attention. She was on the skinny side with great big eyes and a lot of self-confidence.

Just as they were finishing the song I stopped.

"Would you sing that again?" I asked, motioning to the lead singer with my hand.

"Okay," she smiled, in a bashful way.

As I turned away I heard her whisper to the others, "That's Berry Gordy."

The four of them—Diane Ross, Mary Wilson, Florence Ballard and Betty McGlown—started the song again. This time they seemed to be singing for dear life.

When they finished they could see I was highly impressed and wanted to know right away if I was going to sign them to a recording contract.

"What about school?" I asked.

The lead singer spoke up. "We're all seniors," she said.

I told them how important it was to finish high school and that I wasn't going to do anything that might interfere with that. "Come back and see me after you've graduated," I told them.

Despite their disappointment, almost every day after school they showed up at Hitsville. The girls were making friends with producers, trying to get gigs singing background for other artists.

Their determination paid off. In January of 1961 they were signed to Motown. They became a trio after Barbara Martin (who had replaced Betty McGlown) left.

Before then they had been singing under the name of the Primettes, a sister group to the Primes, who would later become the Temptations. When I told them I thought they needed a new name, they all came up with suggestions, but Florence had the name I liked best: *the Supremes.*

They were the sweethearts of Hitsville. Mary was probably the most popular with the guys. Flo was sarcastic from the start; her dry humor kept us laughing all the time. Diane had an innocent manner that let her get away with most anything.

Long before she was a star, there was a drive in her that could not be denied. Nor could her appeal—which she used to full advantage. I soon realized her name needed more sparkle. "Diane" seemed a little passive for what I saw in her. *Diana.* That was a star's name.

All three girls had qualities so unique I'd often think: "If they could make us feel the way we do, what could they do to the world at large?" My belief in them sustained my hopes during three years of flop after flop.

I might have seen Otis Williams, Melvin Franklin and Elbridge "Al" Bryant when they were with the Distants or Paul Williams and Eddie Kendricks in the Primes. But what I remember is seeing them together for the first time as the Temptations when they were auditioning for Mickey Stevenson at Hitsville. I loved their sound and told Mickey to sign them immediately. I loved the old raw songs they had, like "Oh, Mother Of Mine," which became their first record. Those songs didn't become big hits, but boy—did I love 'em.

The Tempts epitomized tall, dark and handsome, standing over six feet, each a distinctive personality. With Paul's emotionally charged, heart-stopping baritone, Melvin's warm, deep, rich bass, Otis's smooth, textured vocal blend, Eddie's lilting falsetto and the powerful, versatile tenor of David Ruffin, who replaced Al Bryant, they created some of the greatest sounds. Later they would also be known for their incredible showmanship, fancy footwork and dazzling wardrobe.

Each had his own job to do in the group. Otis let it be known right from the start that he was the leader and businessman. They looked to Paul Williams to create those soulful moves and routines, while Eddie Kendricks was the guy responsible for the look, the phenomenal uniforms.

Up on that stage were five stars, each of whom could have been a lead singer. David Ruffin oozed with artistry and talent but it was Melvin Franklin who showered everything and everybody with pure love.

Not too long after the Tempts were signed I was eating breakfast in my office when Mickey Stevenson burst in.

"BG, you got to come hear this little kid *now!*"

I hurried down to the studio and found a young blind kid that Ronnie White from the Miracles had brought in for us to hear.

He was singing, playing the bongos and blowing on a harmonica. His voice didn't knock me out, but his harmonica playing did. Something about him was infectious.

Signed as Stephen Hardaway Judkins, he was only eleven years old and people were already saying he could be another Ray Charles.

I don't really remember it, but Esther told me that one day in the studio, watching Stevie perform, I said, "Boy! That kid's a wonder," and the name stuck.

Stevie had a cute, mischievous personality and a great sense of humor. His blindness never seemed to bother him; instead he used it as an advantage. His list of stunts was endless. He'd do things like pretending to be reading something that he had learned by heart or trying to ride a bicycle or sitting behind the wheel of a car pretending he was about to drive off. He was also an amazing mimic. He could do all kinds of accents and voices, including mine.

Once I caught him out on the front lawn holding court, giving advice in my voice, an overexaggerated, drawling, cartoonish version of it. "If you make a mistake, I don't care, go with it. As far as I'm concerned, there are no mistakes. If the mike falls on the stage, you fall with it and you sing right there on the ground like it was planned like that."

148

As I walked up, everybody saw me but Stevie, who went on, "And another thing, that song you wrote is *gabbage*—na, na, na, na . . ."

"Yeah Stevie, and so is your imitation of me."

We all got a good laugh, especially Stevie. But this would not be the last time he would be caught impersonating me.

One of the acts I really wanted but had a hard time getting was the Four Tops. These four—Levi Stubbs, Lawrence Payton, Abdul "Duke" Fakir and Renaldo "Obie" Benson—had been around for almost a decade. Already seasoned performers, they had been on the road with Billy Eckstine, and had played Vegas clubs. Their vocal blend was phenomenal. Their Jazz-type harmony rang out in five parts even though there were only four voices. Smooth, classy and polished, they were big stuff. I wanted them bad. I could see how loyal they were to each other, and I knew they would be the same way to me and Motown.

"We'd like to sign with you," Levi said, "but we heard you won't let artists take the contracts away from the office."

"That's right," I said.

"Why not?"

"Because when I do they don't come back." They laughed as I went on. "I would rather have your attorney or whoever you want come here to the office, take as much time as you need, and go over them. This way we'll be right here to answer questions and explain what we do that other companies don't." I told them that most people don't really understand what we're about or what we're trying to do. It was not only hit records we were interested in, what we wanted to do was build careers.

They listened intently. Then they told me in essence that they were professionals and did understand the business. They assured me they could see what we were doing and thought it was great, but still wanted to take the contracts to their lawyers. Against my better judgment, I said okay. They took the contracts away.

They didn't come back.

Meanwhile, the success of "Shop Around" had sent shock waves of enthusiasm through the whole company. Up until now I had been the only hit producer. But just as I'd realized I couldn't manage all the artists myself, I knew I couldn't produce all of them, either.

I knew from my days of selling Guardian Service cookware that competition could be a very effective tool in getting results, so I made it clear that it was open season for anyone who felt creatively inclined to compete with me to get the next big hit. Smokey jumped on the challenge immediately, telling me what great ideas he had for Mary Wells. I had planned on continuing to produce her myself, but told him to take his best shot.

Over the next few months everybody started getting into the act. Clarence Paul, Mickey's A&R assistant, took Stevie Wonder under his wing. Mickey and my brother George were working on some ideas for Marvin Gaye. And I set out to get that first hit on both the Supremes and the Temptations.

In order to ensure top product, I set up Quality Control, a system I had heard about at Lincoln-Mercury. The producers would submit their final mixes into our Quality Control where Billie Jean Brown would listen to them. If they were up to par she would bring them into the Friday morning meetings. This gave her power. And she had the attitude to match.

Billie Jean Brown, a student at Cass Technical High School, had been hired by Loucye to help her out on a part-time basis, writing liner notes and being a general assistant.

During Billie Jean's first week I got a strong dose of her personality when I stopped by Loucye's office to read over a past-due payment letter being sent out. As I read it, I overheard the new assistant grumble loudly, "How are we going to get any work done if everybody keeps hanging out up here?"

Having seen me wandering around Hitsville with my young-looking face and processed hair she must have thought I was just another one of the aspiring youngsters trying to act important.

As soon as Billie Jean spoke, Loucye smiled apologetically and said, "Have you ever met Mr. Gordy? He owns the company."

"He owns what?" Billie Jean looked at me in disgust. She had thought it was Loucye's company all along.

I shrugged and smiled.

She walked away muttering something like, "They'll let just any-body own a company nowadays."

I was not crazy about her attitude, but Billie Jean, I was soon to discover, knew her music.

One day, seeing her listening to records on a small 45 player in her "office"—a little spot in the corner of the shipping room—I walked over.

"So," I said, "which one of these records do you like best?"

"You mean which one do I hate least, don't you?"

She proceeded to go over each song, telling me what she didn't like about them. She was strong, opinionated, honest, witty and had a good ear. That was good enough for me. I put her in charge of Quality Control.

The Friday morning product evaluation meetings were *my* meet-ings. They were exciting, the lifeblood of our operation. That was when we picked the records we would release. Careers depended on the choices made those Friday mornings. Everybody wanted to be there. The producers, whether or not they got their product on Billie Jean's "approved" list, wanted to be there to protect their own interests and to challenge each other and me.

Some of the employees who came to the meetings weren't creative people, but I felt their reactions to the songs would be like those of the average record buyer. A noncreative person's vote counted just as much as a creative person's. My three main rules for these meetings were: 1) No producer could vote on his own record; 2) Only I could overrule a majority vote; and 3) Anyone over five minutes late would be locked out.

There were many people locked out, but the funniest I remember was the day Smokey had no shame. We'd been into the meeting for about five minutes when we heard Smokey. He was crying and pound-ing on the door, begging to be let in. Being locked out of that meeting was like being locked out of your home. Of course I relented and let him in. After all, it was Smokey.

Another thing I was *very* serious about was people having the freedom to express their honest opinions openly at these meetings—without fear of reprisal. To me that was critical to the process. Everybody knew if I got a hint of a reprisal for something coming out of these meetings, the "reprisalor" would be in serious trouble.

This was the one place where everyone was not only free to speak their minds, they were expected to. They tested that freedom. Sometimes they jumped on me just because they could. That always bugged me, but I had to go along with it to make sure that everybody understood that they could say anything in any way. I liked it very much when they honestly criticized my work. When I had a product if people tried to compliment me and tell me it was good, I would always say, "Tell me what's wrong with it so I can make it better." Everybody in the room was fair game, even the sales executives who were sometimes attacked for not promoting the product well enough.

These product evaluation meetings became one of the key elements in our overall growth. Each time a record made it through one of these meetings and became a hit, we got a little bit bigger.

The house at 2648 West Grand Boulevard was becoming known as a place where dreams could be turned into realities. Local kids would line the sidewalk and the front lawn, trying to get discovered or just hoping to get a glimpse of one of the stars. They tried everything to get inside. Some succeeded, getting jobs as secretaries, office helpers, even janitors.

Now that "Shop Around" had peaked, I was about to learn another essential lesson in the record business: A big hit could put you out of business.

In those days it was common knowledge that the independent distributors would only pay for your last hit if you had another one coming up. We always had others coming up so they paid us, but only as much as necessary to keep getting our new ones.

My money was spread out all over the place. Not only was I owed for one hit record, I was owed money for many different records from many different distributors. And the bigger the hit, the more they owed me—and the more I owed the pressing plants and other suppliers. That was dangerous. That was how some other independent labels got into trouble. Without leverage of another hit to collect their money they couldn't pay their suppliers, who might then cut them off, putting them out of business.

That summer of 1961 I was nervous. Over the past year we had released about twenty records, many of which I thought should have been bigger hits than they were and I still hadn't gotten paid all the money for my big hit, "Shop Around." Loucye had pushed hard, but there was only so much she could do. We needed a new big hit.

At the next Friday meeting I found one. It was called "Please Mr. Postman," a cute, catchy little tune by a brand-new group called the Marvelettes—Gladys Horton, Georgeanna Tillman, Wanda Young, Katherine Anderson and Juanita Cowart. The record was produced by a new team, Brian Holland and Robert Bateman, under the name "Brianbert."

It was a bouncy track with a clever lyric that had Gladys begging the postman to: *"Deliver de letter de sooner de better . . ."*

After hearing "Please Mr. Postman" I was proud of my two protégés. I had seen that Brian had brilliant producing instincts, but this was the first tangible proof of what he could do. Both he and Robert had done some of our earlier engineering and now they were ready to take off.

Not too long before, Robert had come to me, asking, "Can Brian and I team up and produce something together?"

"I'm not sure you *can*," I had told him, "but you *may*." Robert was more used to me answering this kind of request with "You probably *can*, but you *may* not."

Leaving in 1962, Robert would not stay with the company long enough for me to know his full potential, but while he was with us he loved competing with me, especially when editing two-track tapes with razor blades. It may seem that we were using primitive methods back then, but it required exceptional precision and sensitivity. He was good. I was better. (To this day he swears it was the other way around.)

"Please Mr. Postman" became our second million seller and our first #1 Pop hit. All those distributors who hadn't had the money to pay us suddenly had it.

Within a short time after coming in to head sales, Barney Ales had gotten us our first #1 and proved to be that master salesman I always thought he was.

I learned quickly that when you have a master salesman, you have to deal with him in a masterful way. Barney was an extremely tough negotiator. Especially with me. Whenever he scheduled a personal meeting, I knew something was coming—a request for a raise, loan, bonus, advance—something. One moment of weakness could kill me.

Ours was a cat-and-mouse game that he played very well. But then so did I. Before a meeting with Barney I literally had to go into training: get lots of sleep, jog in the morning.

When I called a meeting with *him* it was different. I was usually getting on him about something. Like the time I called him in for selling to distributors that Loucye had put on hold for nonpayment of their bills.

Knowing Loucye had complained to me about the problem, Barney came into my office swinging.

"If we don't ship to those areas," he said, "that's gonna kill us. We'll lose chart positions. We'll lose momentum. We won't have hits and we'll be in more trouble."

"That's right," I said. "But if we don't get our money where will we be?"

It had become very clear to me that my *Create, Make and Sell* slogan had to be revised. We had to now focus more on one thing: getting our money—*collecting*.

Because I felt that *Create* and *Make* were pretty close to the same thing, I dropped the *Make* and changed the slogan to *Create, Sell* and *COLLECT*.

I knew that if Barney made his money only by selling, we would always have this same problem.

So I told him about my new focus on collections. "And," I added, "you're in charge of it."

Loucye was happy; Barney was not. Now Barney would have to do more than just sell, he would have to do the harder job of collecting the money.

He started right away calling distributors, letting them know of his dilemma: he couldn't ship them hot records if they didn't pay. And because of his relationship with them, things got easier. It was now in his interest not just to sell as many records as he could, but to collect the money for those records as well.

Collections rose dramatically. And, of course Barney asked me for more money—and got it.

THE MOTORTOWN REVUE

ON A COLD OCTOBER MORNING in the fall of '62, the members of the first Motortown Revue assembled outside to board the waiting bus and its convoy of several cars that were to become their home on wheels for the next two months.

When the Regal Theater in Chicago had booked its show the year before and all the acts were Motown's except one, we realized that we could put our own show on the road. Barney had mentioned something similar in the past but I hadn't thought the time was right. Now I thought it was. We had in-house everything: artists, producers, musicians, chaperones and road managers. It was a perfect opportunity not only to expose the artists who already had hits, but to break in lesser-known acts.

Esther had overseen all the planning and arranged the itineraries for the numerous cities. The Revue was to kick off with a one-week engagement at the Howard Theater in Washington, D.C., then continue with a series of one-nighters down South, ending with a ten-day engagement at the Apollo Theater in New York.

Most of the artists had never been out of the state. And as the clock ticked away, getting closer to departure, it was hard for them to avoid feelings of uncertainty about the unknown. It was also hard for them not to notice that someone was missing—me, their so-called fearless leader.

Unaware of the time, Fearless Leader was locked into a little dark dungeon—at the control board in the mixing room, where I had been for the past fourteen hours, frantically mixing the Supremes' next single, "Let Me Go The Right Way," which I had written and produced. I was fighting hard to be the first one to get them that hit they so badly needed. It was set for release in less than two weeks.

Smokey came in. "You're a madman. What mix is it now, one hundred?" he said, referring to my maddening need for perfection.

"No, one hundred and one," I responded. Actually that day it probably *was.*

"They're loading on the bus," he said. "Don't you want to say good-bye?"

Who? What? Of course! Tearing myself away from what I hoped would be the final mix, I rushed out and there they all were: The Miracles, Mary Wells, the Marvelettes, the Supremes, Marv Johnson, the Contours, Marvin Gaye, Martha and the Vandellas, Singin' Sammy Ward, Bill Murray—the high-energy emcee known professionally as Winehead Willie—our band led by Choker Campbell, and the chaperones.

Beans Bowles—who worked with Esther in management—would be serving double duty on the road: musician and tour manager. At his side was his assistant, Eddie McFarland.

Esther huddled with Beans and the three chaperones—Mrs. Ernestine Ross, Diana's mother, Bernice Morrison and Ardena Johnston—going over the strict rules and regulations of conduct.

As I was bidding them all my good-byes, Esther reminded the group that they would be out there representing us, the Motown Family, and to mind their manners.

Engines roared. They loaded in and were off. I was proud of them all. I waved as long as seemed appropriate, then rushed back to the mixing board.

So much had happened in the past year. During this time, Smokey and I intensified our ongoing competition in everything.

Aside from his Mary Wells stuff, earlier in the spring we had released the Miracles' "I'll Try Something New"—one of my favorite Smokey compositions. Then he wrote "You've Really Got A Hold On Me," a big hit right out of the box.

It was no contest—Smokey was killing me. But in June of that year I had a little victory. I wrote and produced "Do You Love Me."

Getting the concept for this song was easy. I just thought back to the days when I could never get girls I really liked because I couldn't dance.

You broke my heart, 'cause I couldn't dance
You didn't even want me around
And now I'm back to let you know
I can really shake 'em down.
Do you love me? (I can really move.)
Do you love me? (I'm in the groove.)
Now do you love me? (Do you love me?)
Now that I can dance? . . .

It took me about two hours to write it. But recording it was a little more complicated.

The session to lay the track down was moving smoothly until I had a run-in with my stubborn, outspoken bass player, James Jamerson. As that session ground on, I had decided that Jamerson—with his jazzy licks and upbeats—had gone way past the boundaries I'd set. Though I had warned him several times, he continued to do it so brazenly that I had had more than enough.

"Okay that's it! Hold it," I stormed furiously. "Stop the fuckin' music."

Dead silence. It was almost too quiet for me. Everyone eyed me with respect, waiting for instruction. Everyone except Jamerson. Staring me straight in the eye, he had this fire-me-if-you-want-to smirk on his face. The last thing I wanted to do was take him off the session. But I really had no choice because if I let him get away with it, I'd have no control over anybody else.

"Look man," I said. "I've told you over and over again this ain't no fuckin' Jazz session. You've got to stay on the fuckin' downbeat."

Jamerson said nothing, but gave a nod and a shrug, as if to say, "Okay, man, mess up your own session if you want to."

Everybody held their breath. They knew how much he loved to improvise and were waiting for the fireworks.

We started again, my eyes glued on Jamerson. I knew I'd have to kick him out if he deviated from my directions. I held my own breath, hoping he wouldn't. And he didn't—not until I got relaxed and comfortable. Dropping my guard, I had turned my attention to Benny Benjamin on the drums; he was grooving like a dog. In that split second, Jamerson hit four or five Jazz upbeats in rapid succession. Reeling around, I turned to let him have it. But before I could say anything he had jumped back on the downbeat so brilliantly I could only smile.

He glanced at me in impish defiance. He knew I loved what I'd just heard and everybody else knew it, too. They also knew he had gotten me.

When the musicians left the studio I put my voice on the track, making a demo record. I was singing so passionately that when people heard my growling gutty sound they told me it was a smash and I should release it just like that. For a moment I had thoughts of doing it, but I knew it would be better on a group. My first choice was the Temptations, but the day I was ready to record voices on the song, they were nowhere to be found. That's how the Contours got their shot. They were a local group that had been signed the previous year. Like so many artists, the members—Billy Gordon, Billy Hoggs, Joe Billingslea, Hubert Johnson, Sylvester Potts and Huey Davis—had been hanging around at the studio, hoping to get into something. Eager, boisterous guys, with dynamic, wild dance moves, they went crazy when I told them the Temptations couldn't be found and I wanted to use them.

My singing style was right up Billy Gordon's alley. His screaming lead vocals sounded just like me—but stronger, better. The rest of the group added soulful, uninhibited background vocals.

When the Motortown Revue buses pulled away from the curb that afternoon, the Contours were going strong and "Do You Love Me" was on its way to becoming our top song for 1962.

This same year had been big for Mary Wells, thanks to Smokey, who gave her "The One Who Really Loves You," "You Beat Me To The Punch" and "Two Lovers."

It hadn't taken Mary long to become a star. On stage, her attitude commanded attention. She wore long, glamorous gowns and stylish, trendy wigs—from black bouffants to blond ponytails. It looked like Mary would be that big female star I had always wanted.

Another attention-getter was Martha Reeves. She was Mickey

Stevenson's secretary and got her big break one day when Mary didn't show up for a recording session. To satisfy union rules, Mickey had to make sure there was a body behind the microphone. Martha turned out to be that body. All that was required of her was to stand there and do nothing. But when that music started, she took her shot—surprising everybody with her powerful, soulful voice, wailing like there was no tomorrow.

However, at the time the Revue was taking off, Martha and the newly formed Vandellas hadn't yet had a real hit. That meant they had no name value and had to work that much harder out on the road.

The Marvelettes, on the other hand, by now had developed a strong following. Though they had added two recent hits to their repertoire—"Playboy" and "Beechwood 4-5789"—it was "Please Mr. Postman," their first major smash, that continued to keep them hot.

Marvin Gaye, from the beginning, had been a challenge. After playing drums on "Please Mr. Postman" and some other early sessions, Marvin had gotten his big wish when we released an album of standards on him, *The Soulful Moods of Marvin Gaye*. It contained some beautiful, classy vocals, but it did not do well.

Still, he was sure he was destined to be a crooner like Frank Sinatra. Whenever we approached him about doing the more commercial stuff, he stubbornly refused. Marvin was the most stubborn guy around—about everything. That's exactly what Mickey and my brother George decided to write about. Marvin loved the idea so much, he even helped with the writing. Having turned from crooning to grooving, the aptly named song, "Stubborn Kind Of Fellow" catapulted him into hit status.

Now a second single, "Hitch Hike"—written by Marvin, Mickey and Clarence Paul—was moving up the charts.

Once Marvin got the taste of hit fever, it complicated things even more for him, because he never lost his belief that his true calling was as a Jazz balladeer.

Even with most of the main acts out on the road, Hitsville was as crowded as ever. There were many new faces. By now I had my very first real secretary—Rebecca Nichols.

Often working into the wee small hours with me, Rebecca seemed to fall easily into my work style without complaint. Today, after three decades, she can proudly claim title as the employee who has been with me the longest.

Some of the people who joined us in those early years were very important to the growth of the company. Fay Hale became our Processing Department head, Frances Heard our tape librarian, and Ann Dozier, Lamont's wife, came in as Loucye's assistant. Ann and Lamont had come to us from Anna Records.

From Harvey and Tri-Phi Records, owned by my sister Gwen and Harvey Fuqua, formerly of Harvey and the Moonglows, I inherited some of their roster: the Spinners, Jr. Walker and the All Stars, Shorty Long and writer/producer Johnny Bristol.

I also later acquired Golden World and Ric-Tic Records owned by Eddie Wingate and Joanne Jackson. Joanne was one of the most beautiful girls to grow up on the Westside. (I had a big crush on her when I was around five or six, but she was about the same age, which made me mentally too young.) She and her company had become our biggest local competitor. Despite the rivalry of our companies, we were friends and when she decided to get into a different business, she sold her record and publishing companies to me.

The Hitsville atmosphere lent itself to give-and-take. Employees and artists not only became involved in each other's work, but in each other's lives. Love affairs thrived and so did marriage. One of the first was Smokey and Claudette in '59. Since that time my sister Anna married Marvin Gaye, Gwen married Harvey Fuqua, who became our first promotion man, and Loucye married a saxophone player, Ron Wakefield. Mary Wells married singer Herman Griffin; the Marvelettes' Wanda Young married the Miracles' Bobby Rogers; the Marvelettes' Georgeanna Tillman married the Contours' Billy Gordon; my niece Iris married producer Johnny Bristol; and Mickey Stevenson married singer Kim Weston.

While others were getting married, Ray and I were about to be divorced.

I knew she really cared about me and though ours had started as more of a working relationship, I had grown to really love her. She was a tender and loving person and always there for me.

But there was something more I thought I wanted.

Women had been the inspiration of my life since childhood. They were what inspired me to do everything—create, make money, win. Now that I was winning, it was hard to turn down the opportunities with women I seemed to have been working for all my life. I didn't.

I guess I had always been in search of those elusive dream girls—the childhood fantasy that lingered. Well, I met one. Her name was Margaret Norton. I thought she was the most beautiful girl in Detroit. But soon I was caught in a paradox. The longer my affair with Margaret continued, the more I noticed how wonderful my own wife was.

Ray knew that running the business and creative aspects of the company had me going around the clock most of the time and never minded.

Not only had she not questioned my staying out but she came to me one day and said: "I never know when you're coming home. It's always at a different hour in the morning. I want you to be consistent. I'm going to give you a time to be in and I don't want you to be one minute later."

An ultimatum? All of a sudden I felt very scared. I realized then even more how much she meant to me and that I never wanted to lose her.

"What time?" I said.

"Six."

"Come on. Don't be ridiculous. I'm still at the office at six."

"A.M."

"Six o'clock in the morning?"

"Sure. You seem to have a lot to do at night. And remember, not one minute later."

I took her up on that immediately and started coming in every morning around 5:55, just to allow myself enough leeway. Never later than 6:00 A.M.

One night, very late at some party arguing with Margaret, I decided to go home. I had a great wife there and that's where I should be. *Was this a great woman or what! A 6:00 A.M. curfew. And I'm taking advantage of it and her. No more.* Telling Margaret the relationship wasn't good for either of us, I broke it off.

I left the party about 1:00 and headed home. When I arrived at

161

our little apartment on Lawton Street, where we had moved from upstairs at Hitsville, there was no Ray. Figuring she was still at the office, I got into bed, drifting quickly off to sleep. Four A.M. I woke up. Still no Ray. I tried to go back to sleep but couldn't. I called the studio. Not there. She had left around 11:00. Panic! I called two hospitals. No trace of her. That was good *and* bad news.

By 5:00 my heart was pounding. *Could she be cheating on me? No way.* Just the thought of it made me sick. I went outside and sat in my car parked in front of the house, debating whether or not I should drive around and look for her.

Five thirty. A car pulled up. It was Ray with her assistant, Sonny Sanders, at the wheel. She hopped out of the car and started into the house.

"Kind of late, isn't it?" I said, walking up behind her.

"Oh," Ray gasped, turning to me with a laugh. "You scared me."

"No shit."

When I asked where she had been, she explained: "Sonny, my nephew Dale and me were at the all-night movie theater."

"Oh?" I said as we both went into the house. "Why wasn't Dale in the car?"

"He was. He was asleep in the back," she said.

I was satisfied, but not completely. A few weeks later when I heard rumors she might be having an affair with a man in New York during her business trips there, I didn't ignore them. I confronted her.

Instead of denying anything, she refused to talk.

With rain pouring down that night I sat on the edge of the bed and confessed my affair with Margaret, hoping to provoke her into the truth. It worked. She told me everything. She started by saying she had known about Margaret all along. And not only was the New York rumor true but there was no all-night movie that night; and no nephew in the back of the car.

If she wanted to hurt me, she did. I left the house that night, walking and crying alone in the rain. Looking back I can see what a double standard I had and that I was the first to do wrong in the marriage. Ray only followed. But at the time I felt angry and abandoned. I had lost my devoted wife.

In the next few weeks my life was in total disarray. But at the same time I could see the company was at a critical point in its existence and I had to give it my full attention.

Both wanting the breakup to be quick and painless, we got a Mexican divorce by mail. Ray wanted to continue working for the company. She wanted to take Kerry, our son, and move to New York and open a Jobete office there. I said okay.

A short while later, I started going with Jeana Jackson, an attractive, outgoing friend of mine from Connecticut. Our love affair resulted in the birth of a beautiful baby girl we named Sherry. Jeana and I had a wonderful, but short, relationship.

Margaret kept coming in and out of my life. I couldn't get her out of my system. Before long we resumed our volatile relationship.

The Motortown Revue had been performing to sold-out houses at the Howard Theater in Washington, D.C., when I decided to show up for a surprise visit.

Everybody was happy to see me, hoping I would move them back later in the show, closer to the finale, the featured star spot. The only way they could get me to do that was if they left the stage so hot with applause and noise that the next performer's name couldn't be heard.

The show opened with the Supremes walking out to center stage, looking petrified. Without a hit, they were a little too refined to overcome the wild crowd, but that didn't bother me. Watching how much heart and soul they put into it, I knew one good record would change all that.

Then Martha Reeves and the Vandellas came out. They didn't have a hit either—but they sure acted like they did. Martha was soul personified. Her movements were understated, but soulful and sexy. I loved the way she could stand there, cool, feet planted and body pulsating to the music as she and the Vandellas, Rosalind Ashford and Annette Beard, captivated the audience.

The high-energy Contours were fearless as they jumped out on stage with splits, flips and wild gyrations to "Do You Love Me."

Marvin was a showstopper that night. Before he even opened his mouth the women in the audience went nuts. He left the stage so hot with his latest hit, "Stubborn Kind Of Fellow," we could barely hear the Marvelettes' name. It seemed that Marvin would definitely be moving back in the lineup.

But when the Marvelettes walked up to the mikes and Gladys Horton screamed, *"Wait!, oh yes, wait a minute Mr. Postman . . ."* it was all over.

I knew there would be no moving Marvin back now. The girls were sensational and the crowd let them know it.

And then, the entrance of our leading lady, Mary Wells. You could see right away she was experienced. She preached the intro to "Bye Bye Baby" and got the audience involved—"We-ee-ll, you know I feel a-a-all right. You over here and you over there—Do you feel all right?"

"Yeah!" the people screamed.

"I can't hear you. Do you feel all right?"

"Yeeeaahhhhh!!"

She went on from there doing all her hits, "The One Who Really Loves You," "You Beat Me To The Punch" and "Two Lovers," in classy fashion.

The show culminated with the Miracles, our biggest stars, who had their routines down pat by now. Moving through hits like "You Can Depend On Me" and "Shop Around," Smokey could really get the crowd going. He just stood there, and made love to the women. He could do that better than anybody. He fell to his knees and lay on the floor, singing up a storm. Closing with "You've Really Got A Hold On Me," he threw off his jacket, clutching his arms to his chest, closing his eyes, and begging, *"Hold me, hold me, hold me, hold meeeeee . . ."* Smokey was king.

I believed competition breeds champions and sitting there watching that show I could see our artists not only believed that, but were learning the true meaning of the phrase "survival of the fittest."

I joined up with Smokey to go out and grab a bite during their break before the next show. As soon as Smokey and I opened the backstage door, a mob of girls swarmed around and started fighting to get near him.

"Smokey!" "Oh, it's him, it's Smokey!" "We love you, Smokey!" "Over here, Smokey . . . !" "My leg, sign my leg, Smokey!" "No, mine!"

As they crowded tighter and tighter around him, I was squeezed further and further into the back. I was swallowed up by a sea of female bodies pressing against me, elbows, shoulders, behinds, hips and waving hands. (It wasn't the worst feeling in the world.)

Looking back over his shoulder for me he hollered, "Wait a minute!" raising his arms and gesturing to quiet them down. Everything stopped. To the silent crowd of worshippers, Smokey pointed toward me, announcing, "That's Berry Gordy back there, my manager. He's responsible for all of us. The Miracles, Mary Wells, Marvin Gaye, all the stars in the show."

"Hi, Berry Jerry," one girl said to me with a quick smile. But in the next instant out of her mouth came a monstrous scream as the pandemonium started all over again. She leaped forward, grabbing her leg, and shrieking, "Smokey, my leg! Smokey, mine, mine!! Sign my leg!!!!"

We laughed about it over a late lunch. I told him how much pleasure I got just watching how popular he was.

"Are you sure?" he asked.

"Smokey, don't ever worry about me," I told him. "I'm a behind-the-scenes person. You're the one out front and this is the way it's supposed to be. But thanks anyway."

This was not the first time I had seen that kind of mania. I remembered something like this happening with Jackie Wilson. But it was the first time it had happened for one of my artists, someone I had developed. And what was really special for me was how sensitive Smokey was to me, knowing that I might like attention from girls, too.

As the tour headed down South, I headed back to Detroit, riding high after seeing our success firsthand in Washington. I got back to work, caught up in the business at hand. Then came startling news. Shots had been fired at the Motortown Revue bus in Birmingham, Alabama. I was devastated. We were all aware of how tough the racial conditions could be—the motels, restaurants, filling stations and bathrooms where blacks were refused service. But my artists being shot at?

These were just kids out there, making music, making people happy and all of a sudden the real world had shown its ugly face. And I was responsible—I had sent them out there.

I remembered in 1955 how terrified I was when I'd heard about Emmett Till, a fourteen-year-old kid from Chicago who was visiting relatives in Mississippi. Dragged from his grandfather's home, he was beaten unmercifully, lynched and his body thrown in the Tallahatchie River. I couldn't believe it when I heard that his crime was "thinking" under a white woman's dress. *Thinking?!?* The two white men who had killed him were freed.

That had been the first time I clearly put myself in somebody else's shoes. If they could do that to him, they could do it to me. And now they were. They were shooting at my Motortown Revue bus. I wanted to cancel the tour but Esther, after conferring with Beans and the chaperones, convinced me that it was only an isolated incident.

Three weeks later there was more bad news.

I was jolted from sleep in the middle of the night with news that Beans Bowles and his assistant, Eddie McFarland, had been in an auto accident as the Motortown Revue traveled from Greenville, South Carolina, on the way to Tampa, Florida. Both were critically injured and not expected to live.

The next morning Eddie's mother, Alice, my sister Esther and I were on the first flight out. Once we got to the hospital, we could see that although Beans had suffered several broken bones, he was in good spirits. Unfortunately, Eddie's prognosis was not as encouraging.

Beans had lost $12,000 in gate receipts that he'd had on him. But when the Highway Patrol found the car, they also found the money and returned it to us. With relief, we realized that just because it was the South didn't mean all white people were bad.

Leaving Esther to handle things at the hospital, I went on the road to take over for Beans and Eddie. We had one-nighters for the next week: Tampa, Jacksonville, Macon, Daytona Beach, Miami, Orlando and Tallahassee. Though it was hard for us to keep our minds off the touch-and-go situation at the hospital, everybody gave their all every night.

That included me, who had no idea how much work went into handling these shows. I was struggling as hard as I could just to keep things together.

When the tour bus moved on to the next town, I would stay behind, clearing up business and flying in the following morning. One such night in Macon I checked out a local Blues club.

Walking in the joint, I was happy to hear some real down-home Blues. I saw in front of me a small stage where a little band was accompanying a singer who was wailing away. Not bad. Standing by the bar, I watched as another singer took his turn on stage. So-so.

It was some sort of amateur night. Anybody could go up. I was aching to. Not only did I want to hear the Blues, I wanted to sing 'em. When the emcee asked if anybody else wanted to come up, I raised my hand.

Within minutes he introduced me to the crowd, using the name I had given him—"Now put your hands together, ladies and gentleman, for Mr. Billy Jones!"

"Blues in F. As funky as you can get," I said to the piano player. And he did, low-down. I looked around at the faces of the people at nearby tables. Nobody knew me. Good.

I started, "*I love my baby, but my baby don't love me. Oh yeah, I said, I love my baby but my baby just don't love me . . .*" I went on to sing anything coming to mind with deep feeling. I had no idea what I sounded like but the crowd was with me. They felt whatever pain and whatever joy I was feeling. For those ten minutes up on stage I forgot about all my problems. It was just me and the crowd and the Blues.

As soon as I joined up with the tour the next morning, I called Esther at the hospital. Sounding optimistic, she told me to let everyone know things were looking good. That night all the artists went out with renewed vigor.

The next night, in the next town, right before the show, I was on the way to my seat when I got a phone call. It was Esther. Eddie had taken a turn for the worse in the night. He was dead.

All of a sudden my priorities changed. I canceled the rest of the engagement and we headed back to Detroit to bury him. A blood bank was established in Eddie's memory to be used for any Motown personnel or family member who might be in need. Almost everyone in the company lined up to donate.

* * *

We kept our mid-December engagement at the Apollo Theater in New York, adding Little Stevie Wonder to the lineup.

We knew that no audience in the world was tougher than the Apollo's but the emotion of what we had been through made that concern irrelevant. We sailed through thirty-one shows over ten days and nights. The response was so enthusiastic we recorded the show for a live album.

When I read the review in *Billboard* magazine, I could see we were definitely breaking ground:

> The Tamla-Motown rock and roll show opened New York's Apollo Theater last week and in its first few days appeared to be on its way to cracking box-office records. . . . This is not the first show ever sponsored by a label, but it is one of the most successful. It is understood that Gordy . . . who manages and books all talent on his two hot labels . . . will be presenting more shows of this type in the future.

I was big. I had made it in New York.

ASSEMBLY LINE

As OTHER INDEPENDENT record companies were failing, we were thriving. I am often asked, "How did you do it? How did you make it work at a time when so many barriers existed for black people and black music?" There are many answers to those questions but at the base of them is atmosphere. Hitsville had an atmosphere that allowed people to experiment creatively and gave them the courage not to be afraid to make mistakes. In fact, I sometimes encouraged mistakes. Everything starts as an idea and as far as I was concerned there were no stupid ones. "Stupid" ideas are what created the lightbulb, airplanes and the like. I never wanted people to feel how I felt in school—dumb. It was an atmosphere that made you feel no matter how high your goals, they were reachable, no matter who you were.

I had always figured that less than 1 percent of all the people in the world reach their full potential. Seeing that potential in others, I realized that by helping them reach theirs, maybe I could reach mine.

This atmosphere was captured in our company song. It was written when I decided that we should have a team song to express the pride we felt in what we were doing. I proposed a contest, a challenge to see who could write the best one. Smokey won:

Oh, we have a very swinging company,
working hard from day to day.
Nowhere will you find more unity,
than at Hitsville, U.S.A.

Our main purpose is to please the world
with songs the DJs are glad to play.
Our employees are the very best,
here at Hitsville, U.S.A.

Our employees must be neat and clean,
and really have something on the ball.
Honesty is our only policy,
we're all for one and one for all

We have a very swinging company,
working hard from day to day.
Nowhere will you find more unity
than at Hitsville . . . I said Hitsville . . . Than
at Hitsville, U.S.A.

Once a week we had a company meeting in the studio where everybody came. We sang the company song and we believed it. That unity was real.

Motown was a family, right from the beginning—living together, playing together, making music together, eating together.

When we weren't in the studio, the place most of us would be was in the kitchen—waiting to get a helping of whatever Lilly Hart was fixing up.

Affectionately known as Miss Lilly, she was an older, slow-talking, warmhearted woman who cooked the "family meals." Family was anyone who was in the building at one o'clock—lunchtime. There was always enough of her special chili to go around.

In many ways Hitsville was like growing up in the Gordy family— fierce closeness and fierce competition and constant collaboration.

That's why, no matter what would happen over the course of the next thirty years, I would always love every person who was a part of this story. They're all in my blood, and I in theirs. They cannot not love me; I cannot not love them. I know it. They know it. And there is nothing anybody can do about it.

Create, Sell and COLLECT had been effective in keeping our overall focus. So I decided to add three more words to complete the cycle: *Pay, Save* and *Reinvest.*

What I hoped to do was, *Pay* the bills, *Save* a little money, then *Reinvest* what's left back into the business. But at that time there was no way I could think of *Saving* or *Reinvesting*. Overloaded with bills, royalties and taxes, my focus had to be on *Paying*, and I needed someone new to handle it.

George Edwards, CPA, Esther's husband, had been doing a great job as General Manager and running my Finance Department part-time but he was overloaded, too. Especially since he had just been reelected to the Michigan State legislature for his fifth term. (In 1957 I had helped him get elected by persuading Jackie Wilson to record a campaign song I wrote and got played on the air, called "By George, Let George Do It.")

Up to now, I'd always had family members in charge of my money. Now I had to find an outsider I could trust.

One of the luckiest days in my life was when I met the Noveck brothers.

Sue Weisenfeld, a Detroit attorney who had done some work for us, set up a meeting between me and Harold Noveck.

I liked him a lot but when he told me he was a tax attorney, I

170

said I didn't need one of those at the moment. What I needed was someone to help keep track of the money transactions.

"It just so happens," he said, "my brother is a partner in an accounting firm."

We set up a meeting. Then I started thinking.

How was I going to judge how good an accountant was when I didn't know anything about the subject? I knew I would have to follow my instincts and look for something I had relied on throughout my life in judging people—clues.

I put an ad in the *Detroit Free Press* for a certified public accountant. Within a week I was sifting through about forty résumés. I picked ten and set up meetings in addition to the one I had scheduled with Sidney Noveck, Harold's brother.

The first thing I *had* to find out was if they were honest. Then I wanted to know if they could do the job.

Looking through the financial section, I put together a list of ten questions I would have each applicant answer in writing, having no idea myself what the answers were.

When the applicants finished their questionnaires, I interviewed each of them individually. They all started out talking about accounting but I managed to bring the subject around to other things *I* knew about. When one of them mentioned something about boxing I said, "Oh, that's wonderful. I'm sure you're familiar with Sandy Saddler."

"Oh, yes, I know Sandy Saddler!" the man exclaimed. "How could any fight fan not know him?"

"Great welterweight wasn't he?"

"The best!" the man echoed.

He had failed my bullshit test. Anyone who knew anything about boxing would have known Sandy Saddler wasn't a welterweight at all but a champion featherweight. That applicant was off my list.

With some of the others I might bring up Charlie Parker and call him "the greatest tenor sax player in the world," when in fact I knew he played alto. Other times, I'd use a riddle or an old adage to see how a person's reasoning worked. I might say, "A bird in the hand is worth two in the bush. What does that mean to you?" I wanted to make sure that they spoke a language that was common to me.

171

Not always accurate, most of the applicants seemed to know a little something about everything I mentioned.

Sidney Noveck, on the other hand, said he knew so little about those things he'd rather not comment.

A short, unobtrusive little guy, he had no apparent talents for selling himself. And when I looked at his questionnaire I saw he'd only answered six of the ten questions. He was the only applicant who hadn't completed them all.

"What about the other four?" I asked.

"I'm not sure," he said. "I'd like to check them out and get back to you."

Hmm, not the brightest.

"Oh," I said, "maybe you ought to take up accounting."

"I did."

No sense of humor either.

He looked puzzled but continued, "I don't want to give you answers that may not be correct."

"I understand," I said, bidding him good-bye, never expecting or wanting to see this man again. I looked at the other questionnaires and through my own process of elimination came up with one applicant I really liked.

The next day I was about to notify the man I had chosen when Sidney called. "Mr. Gordy, I have the answers to those other questions."

I wanted to say, "No shit," but he was a sweet little man. So I just said, "Okay, what are they?"

"Question five applies to a tax case that was recently heard. The law had been changed. And on question eight, I had to check the record to be absolutely correct." He then gave me the two other answers he hadn't been sure of.

I had no idea what any of it meant, but in him I saw the character I was looking for. I hired him and his firm that day on the phone.

Eventually Sidney Noveck became the person I relied on to set up all my financial policies. He was simple, honest and determined to do things right in spite of anything and anybody.

He would sometimes drive me crazy. His books *had* to balance. He would spend endless hours and thousands of dollars trying to find a penny! But those countless hours to find a penny later saved me millions.

After working with Sidney a short time I found I did need the services of a tax attorney and I knew exactly who I wanted—his brother, Harold. Together Harold and Sidney would keep watch on the company's financial operation, keeping it clean, solid.

Whenever there were challenges from anyone, our clean financial records backed up our claims. Later, when there would be tax problems or complaints that artists weren't paid properly, the IRS or other auditors would swarm into our offices like vultures. And after looking at our books they would usually leave meekly, and in some cases even apologize. Throughout the years whoever ran my in-house Finance Department was subject to Sidney's and Harold's rules, regulations and policies.

I'd never dreamed as a kid that I'd be able to buy the Graystone Ballroom, where black people were only allowed in on Monday nights. But by Christmas of 1962, I owned it and we began holding our annual Christmas parties there. My brother Robert dressed up as Santa Claus and went around handing out our first bonuses to employees. We also presented a "Motown Spirit Award" to the person who most exemplified what Motown was about. Everybody in the company voted and there was always little doubt as to who would get it—either Smokey Robinson or Melvin Franklin. The first year it went to Smokey, the following year to Melvin. For five years, they were the only two people so honored.

Ever since that day in the boxing gym, years before, when I had seen the poster of the Battle of the Bands, an idea had stuck with me. Why not have a Battle of the Stars? And now that I had the Graystone, where people came to dance to all the latest records, I had the perfect place for it. On some nights, in between the dances, I would put on a special show.

These "Battles" were immediate hits—sellouts. I matched up everybody: the Supremes against the Velvelettes, Martha and the Vandellas against the Marvelettes, the Tempts against the Contours.

Everything went great until one night we pitted Marvin Gaye against Little Stevie Wonder. Going into the match, Marvin had a

173

string of hits, and Stevie only his first, a record that had come about when we were recording a live album at Chicago's Regal Theater.

One night after finishing "Fingertips"—a jazzy harmonica number—his producer, Clarence Paul, was escorting him off stage when Stevie broke away at the wings and ran back out on the stage. The bass player who was playing for Stevie, thinking the song was over, had left the stage and Mary Wells's bassist quickly moved in. When Stevie started singing the song again, the new bass player shouted out, "What key? What key?"

We're not sure why the record was such a big hit but leaving that mistake in didn't hurt. There are certain kinds of mistakes I love. They sometimes give things extra life and magic because of their raw, real quality. Not only was it our second #1 Pop single but it was the first live single to ever go to #1 in *Billboard* and the cornerstone hit of our first #1 Pop album.

Still, in my mind Marvin was the favorite for the upcoming battle at the Graystone. He was riding high on his third and biggest hit so far, "Pride And Joy." Both Stevie and Marvin were tough competitors, but Marvin, wanting to surprise the audience and ensure himself a victory, got himself a melodica, an oversized harmonica with a piano keyboard that you play with your fingers as you blow into it. He practiced on that thing like a maniac.

The big night arrived. They were ready. First round. Stevie came out singing and blowing like mad on his harmonica to "Workout Stevie, Workout." The crowd was dancing. They loved it.

Marvin was up. Like a prizefighter, he jumped on stage to one of his hottest songs, "Hitch Hike," dancing and shaking with everything he had. Then when he got to the third verse he whipped out the melodica. Surprise! Everybody went wild.

End of round one: Marvin slightly ahead.

Round two. Stevie came out with his bluesy "I Call It Pretty Music But The Old Folks Call It The Blues." Instead of Stevie ending the song, he segued right into *"Everybody say yeah . . . . . ."* Recognizing the intro to "Fingertips Pt. 2," the crowd screamed, *"Yeah!"* Stevie was back, working the crowd to a frenzy.

Now came round two for Marvin. He was confident, eager. The band struck up the intro to "Stubborn Kind Of Fellow" and Marvin skipped onto the stage, ready to take this thing on home. But instead of the big reception he expected there was some booing mixed in with the usual screams from the women. I was confused. And he was, too. Marvin ignored it and jumped into his song.

Then somebody shouted out, "Marvin, you should be shame o' yourself takin' advantage of a little blind kid!" A few others agreed.

Marvin continued on with even more gusto, determined to bring the audience back on his side. He finished that number with a smattering of applause and more boos. There was some hissing as well. He looked out at me as if to say "What do I do?" He was so embarrassed, but told the band to start his next number, "Pride And Joy." The smile on his face couldn't hide his pain.

I jumped on the stage, politely taking the mike from Marvin. "Thank you very much. The show's over," I said as I motioned to somebody to start playing records.

Marvin left the stage. I hurried after him and found him sitting backstage by himself with his head in his hands. I sat down next to him.

Putting my hand on his shoulder I said nothing. He said nothing. There was nothing to say.

Though I still felt competition bred champions, I could see that it also had a downside. And in this particular case of putting a grown man against a little blind boy I had blundered badly. That was the last Battle of the Stars at the Graystone.

Having long since outgrown the main Hitsville house on West Grand, we had purchased some of the other houses close by—making our working home a true neighborhood. Barney Ales joked that Hitsville was "the only high-rise that went sideways." My assembly-line dream was becoming a reality.

Not much could thrill me more than walking through the hallways of the various buildings and stopping in on the different creative stations. On a typical day I'd go from one end of the spectrum to the other—songwriting to corporate finance—problem-solving, encouraging, motivating, teaching, challenging, complaining. It might be giving the guys in the control room tips on balancing; or just being a fresh ear for someone who had sat too long at the mixing board. At whatever stage of the production I was jumping in on, I was in songwriter's heaven going from room to room telling those creative people—writers, producers, artists—how I thought they could make something better. In one little room there was Brian Holland banging out chord patterns on the piano, humming and singing a new song idea; in another, Robert Bateman singing melodies and matching chords to them on a piano. In a third room Smokey might be rehearsing with the Temptations or working with Mary Wells. And around the clock Mickey kept the studio in use, either cutting sessions himself or parceling time out to other producers.

Another busy spot was in the building across the street. Gwen and Anna had never stopped pushing for an Artist Development Department and when they had finally gotten me to say okay, they wasted no time in getting it started. They brought Harvey Fuqua over from Promotion to head the department. Drawing from his experiences at Chess Records and with his own group, Harvey and the Moonglows, he assembled a great team.

Gwen, a former model at Maxine Powell's Finishing School, and Anna, still the fashion plate of the family, helped select costumes for the artists while Maxine Powell herself came over to work with the female artists on everything. She taught them basic table manners, how to apply makeup, how to sit, and generally how to carry themselves—in public *and* at home.

"When you walk I want heads up, chest out, small ladylike steps," I heard her say many times. Smoking or drinking in public? "Ladies just don't do that sort of thing." She demanded respect—and got it.

To handle choreography, Harvey brought in Cholly Atkins, one half of the well-known dance team, Coles and Atkins. While Cholly worked with the artists individually or in classes, showing them everything from special dance steps to just basic exits and entrances, musical conductor and director Maurice King would be going over the on-stage productions, including band arrangements and teaching the artists harmonies.

Each department had its own weekly meetings. On Tuesdays it was Esther's ITMI meetings. In addition to protecting their money, working with booking agents and all the other things ITMI was

176

established to do, they helped plan an artist's career. My cousin, Evelyn Turk-Johnson, joined Esther and her chief of staff and artist manager, Taylor Cox, in ITMI administration. Also important to the work at ITMI were Esther's son, Robert Bullock, and her assistant, Emily Dunn. My sister Loucye not only continued to handle manufacturing, but since Ray had left for New York, she had taken over the publishing activities of Jobete.

On Thursdays, Barney Ales had his marketing meetings, where he, his top salesmen—Phil Jones, Al Klein, Irv Biegel and Mel Da Kroob and later Tom Noonan—and the rest of the growing sales staff would map out strategies for upcoming records and pinpoint areas of sales activity or recent releases.

When the Sales Department saw a record begin to take off, whether through sales orders or DJ and radio reports, they'd alert me. Switching hats from whatever else I was doing, I would call ITMI to get the artist into that area for a promotion if they weren't well known and a paid date if they were. We'd move our forces into that area promoting, advertising, passing the buzz from DJs to distributors to record stores, doing whatever we had to do to spread the record out from that area to the next, the next, and the next.

By the middle of '63 the Friday morning product evaluation meetings were much more intense. Whether people got to my office early to claim their favorite seats or dashed in just before the doors were locked at exactly five minutes after nine, there seemed to be a sense in the air, felt by everyone: "This day could change my life."

I remember one Friday morning. Mickey, Billie Jean and Smokey were early, as usual. Legal administrator Ralph Seltzer and his assistant, Bette Ocha, and Esther came in right afterward, followed by writers and producers Harvey Fuqua, Clarence Paul, Hank Cosby, Ivy Joe Hunter, Freddie Gorman, Norman Whitfield, Brian and Eddie Holland and Lamont Dozier. Around 9:04 and a half there was gridlock in the doorway as Barney, Phil Jones from Sales and Loucye and Fay Hale from Manufacturing were literally stuck there for a moment, trying to get in before the deadline.

Brian and Eddie Holland and Lamont Dozier were now the writing and producing team of Holland-Dozier-Holland. Shortly after teaming

177

up in March of '63, HDH had their first hit—Martha and the Vandellas' "Come And Get These Memories," which gave Martha her first hit, too. That morning they looked especially confident and cocky.

Ralph Seltzer found a seat next to Mickey Stevenson, who wasn't too thrilled because he was one of the creative people who didn't like Ralph and Bette sitting in judgment of his product. Ralph, who had a legal background, was now in charge of okaying all creative budgets. I liked his honesty and directness. He had begun with the company as coordinator of our out-of-town offices, keeping track of operations in New York and our newest outpost in Los Angeles.

Norman Whitfield, one of the new producers, was tall and broad-shouldered with a thick head of hair. He was quiet and shy—not someone you'd think would turn into the boldly innovative producer he later became. He had started at Hitsville like many others, doing everything: assisting Mickey in A&R, scheduling sessions, handling auditions on Saturdays, cleaning the studio, whatever.

His first collaboration of note was Marvin's "Pride And Joy"—along with Mickey and Marvin—but it would be a couple more years before I recognized what a talent he was.

Looking at the long list of productions we'd be hearing, I made my first announcement: "We have a lot of songs to get through today so any garbage will be eliminated quickly. Anyone submitting garbage try not to get upset." Amused, they started looking around at each other, trying to guess who had garbage. They knew what "garbage" meant. Garbage did not mean necessarily the worst record in the world—garbage, to me, was anything that we didn't think would reach the Top 40.

Billie Jean nudged me, pointing to the pile of acetates we had to listen to.

"Okay, let's get started," I said, turning to Smokey. "You got anything good on Mary Wells?"

"Good? Wait till you hear 'My Guy,' this new thing I'm writing. Number one—no question. I'll bet on this one, and I ain't even cut the track yet."

"I'll bet. I'll bet," five or six voices shouted. Mine was one of them. "Number one? How much?" I said.

"Well, I'm not gonna bet on number one, but I bet it'll be Top Ten."

"You said number one," I reminded him.

"Yeah, I know what I said, but that would be a stupid bet."

"Then you shouldn't have said it," I said. "But, okay, we'll let you off the hook this time, Smoke. 'My Guy' probably won't even make the charts, that is, if it gets released."

The first record we played that morning was on Marvin Gaye. A song called "Can I Get A Witness" written and produced by HDH, a record that got my attention right off with its Gospel uptempo feel and Marvin's passionate pleading.

Giving away none of my own reactions to it, I began our normal voting procedure.

"How many think it's not a hit?"

Four hands shot up.

"How many think it *is* a hit?"

Seven hands were raised.

Starting with Billie Jean, who had voted for it, I asked for comments. They ranged from her "It's different from other stuff out there," to Mickey's "The lyrics don't make no sense."

Many voting for it called it their favorite Marvin record, while Phil Jones piped up: "Number one all the way "

"What makes you think so?" I asked.

"I took it home last night and my kids could dance to it. White kids."

Ivy Joe Hunter said he knew it was a hit just because "it is."

I asked how they thought the record compared to Peter, Paul and Mary's "Blowin' In The Wind," which was high on the Pop charts.

"It's apples and oranges," they said. "How can you compare a folk song to a dance tune?"

"If you only had one dollar and could only buy one record," I said, " 'Blowin' In The Wind' or 'Can I Get A Witness'—which one would it be?"

They thought for a moment, then most picked Marvin's record.

"Now," I said, "if you were hungry and had only one dollar would you buy this record or a hot dog?"

Whenever I asked this, invariably they would pick the hot dog. But what I was looking for was how long it took them to make up their minds.

Here it took long enough to let me know that this record had solid support—including mine.

From the minute we heard the opening of the next HDH acetate—guitars leading the pace for the rhythm section—everybody's eyes lit up. As soon as Martha Reeves's voice let loose with *"Whenever I'm with him, somethin' inside starts to burnin' . . ."* I showed no expression but my toes were jumping.

When it was over, I asked in a flat tone, "How many think it's not a hit?" No hands. "How many think it is a hit?" Everyone's hands came up. There was nothing more to say about "(Love Is Like A) Heat Wave"—except "I love it" and "This has to go out as soon as possible. Next record?"

That night as I was leaving the studio on my way to the Graystone Ballroom I grabbed the "Heat Wave" acetate. I knew we had something and couldn't wait to see how the kids reacted to it at our weekly record hop. Whenever we put on a record that no one had ever heard before it would usually take them time to get used to it. I had prepared to play this one about four times. But the minute the needle touched down on the first few bars, the wood on the dance floor was nowhere to be found.

HDH didn't stop there. That same summer they hit again with "Mickey's Monkey," recorded on the Miracles. And in the fall, they achieved what had seemed impossible—a hit on the girls who had long been called the "no-hit" Supremes, breaking them into the Top 30 with "When The Lovelight Starts Shining Through His Eyes."

Just as Smokey had a lock on Mary Wells, HDH was now in the best position to do the same thing with the Supremes. Whoever got a hit on an artist automatically got the follow-up record. Unless, of course, someone else had produced a much better one on that same artist. It couldn't be a little better, it had to be a lot better.

By the fall of 1963 we had increased our visibility in Europe with the signing of an international foreign distribution deal with EMI.

Because the Tamla label was already so popular in Europe, when we introduced the Motown label, we used Tamla-Motown as our international label name. Also through George Schiffer, my copyright attorney and international adviser, we set up our own publishing operation throughout Europe.

Our international success proved to me once again that my theories were right—all people have so much in common. Our music conveyed basic feelings, cutting through cultural and language barriers. It's just a matter of communication. Communication breeds understanding and understanding breeds everything else. Words, our primary form of communication, often mean different things to different people. That's why I've always been more concerned about what people mean rather than what they say. Sometimes the most innocent words can lead to big trouble.

I made the horrible mistake one day of calling Marvin Gaye "boy." I'll never forget that day because it was the same day President Kennedy was killed.

Friday, November 22, 1963.

Not long after the last of the stragglers had left the Friday morning meeting Barney called.

"Berry, we got a little problem. Marvin just left here screaming about his record not being pushed. And you know we work our asses off promoting the hell out of his stuff."

"They're fucking with me, BG," I heard as I turned my chair around to see Marvin standing in front of my desk.

"He's here," I told Barney. "I gotta go." I looked up. "What do you mean?"

"I was down in the Sales Department, BG, and they're bullshittn', man. They were supposed to get my record more airplay but all they're pushing is Martha and the Vandellas' 'Quicksand' and the Miracles' 'Mickey's Monkey.' 'Can I Get A Witness' is just barely breaking into the Top thirty and it's been out over two months."

"Marvin," I said calmly, "I've told you, you can't be running into the Sales Department screaming at those guys. It's just not wise on your part. You're the artist. I want them to like you—not hate you. I told you before, you got a problem, come to me." I reminded him of everything that Sales was accomplishing for him—marketing his records and breaking him through to white audiences here and in the rest of the world.

Marvin didn't care.

"I don't like the way they talk to me," he said. "They told me they didn't have time. They fronted me off."

I set up a meeting for later that day for the two of us and included Harvey Fuqua, Marvin's close friend, and Phil Jones to represent the Sales Department.

Rebecca Nichols, my secretary, had brought in some correspondence for me to review and I had just started on it when somebody, I don't remember who, ran in and said the President had been shot!

We scrambled to the radio and it sounded like it might have been just a wound of some kind. But shortly after, the news came back that he was dead.

Stunned, I decided for the next hour or so to sit in my office quietly. Calls came in from family and friends to find out if I knew. No one was able to say much. Marvin called to see if I still wanted to have the meeting. I told him yes.

The meeting got off on a sad note but soon grew into a heated argument between Marvin and Phil. Explaining his side, Phil brought in the radio sheets and store reports, showing the great amount of effort that had been put behind the record, along with saying what a fan he was of Marvin's, and how much he liked him. But Phil added that the record just didn't have the legs to go to #1 as he had expected. And the reason it had stayed on the charts as long as it had, he said, was because of Sales making sure the stations kept it on their play lists and pushing the distributors for reorders as hard as they could.

"Bullshit," Marvin said, arguing a point we knew was a problem—the fact that black records weren't always charted like white records. Even though many black artists sold more records in the black stores, the people who tracked sales for the different Pop charts would usually call the white stores more than they did the black stores. Not surprisingly "Can I Get A Witness" did better on the R&B charts—peaking at #15, while it went no further than #22 Pop.

Marvin was not wrong in calling this practice unfair—except that he was blaming our Sales Department for it, the very people, especially Barney and Phil, who were working so hard to change it, developing close contacts with the top people at all three of the main charts—*Billboard, Cash Box* and *Record World*. (Long sympathetic to our cause, George Albert, the owner of *Cash Box*, was helpful to Motown throughout the years, including making sure his people accurately charted our records.)

Harvey, who besides having been our first promotion man, knew a lot about different facets of the record business, joined with me in trying to convince Marvin we were all on his side. Stubborn though he was, Marvin began to understand.

As the meeting was nearing the end, with everybody in better spirits, I tied things up by saying, "So once again, Marvin, I'm asking you. Don't run into the Sales Department cussing them out. Be a good boy, okay?"

"Boy!?" Marvin jumped to his feet, glaring at me from across my desk.

The mood of the meeting took a major turn.

"See! See, BG! That's a whole bunch of bullshit. You think I'm a boy just like the white man."

Silence. I stared at Marvin. He stared at me. I stood up. He stood up.

" 'Boy' is not a bad word. My father calls me 'boy.' I call my sons 'boy.' It is not what a person *says*, it's what they *mean*. If they mean something bad by it, then it's bad. If they don't, then it's not."

Marvin pounded my desk. "See, that's how you do it. You con everybody, BG. Talking to you, man, you try to switch shit around and stuff."

Before I even thought about it, I had backhanded the top of my desk, scattering everything in arm's reach to the floor. "What the fuck are you talking about, man?" I said, stalking over to stand face-to-face with him. "Don't you realize that the President was killed today? Don't you understand that I stayed here just for a meeting with you to solve a problem because I care about how you feel? How about how *I* feel?"

I stormed out of my office, hurried down the stairs and out into the street, not knowing where I was going. The last glimpse I got of Marvin I saw he had a look of understanding. He told me the next day he did understand.

I realized later it wasn't so bad I had lost my cool. I spent so much of the time smoothing other people's tempers in calm, logical ways that when I flipped out it was like shock therapy to Marvin—and probably to me, too.

I was deeply saddened by the death of John Kennedy. I believed him to be an honest man and a good man. I believed him to be a great President who had embraced and created hope for black people in a way that had not been felt in modern times. A feeling of loss and shock hung over everything in those months of late 1963 and early '64.

Then in March, came a joyful personal event when Margaret Norton and I had a son. I named him Kennedy William Gordy, in honor of President Kennedy and William "Smokey" Robinson.

BYE BYE BABY

HIT FEVER WAS CATCHING the spring of 1964. What we were hearing in those Friday morning meetings was so exciting, it was often standing room only in my office. One of the greatest songs to really explode off that turntable was an acetate of the first production we heard on the Four Tops. They had finally come back and signed a contract—two years later.

They said the reason they hadn't come back sooner was not because of the wording in the contracts but because they weren't sure a little black company like ours would be able to stay in business. They felt more confident when they saw so many of our artists getting hits and I felt great when they did come back. The instant I heard "Baby I Need Your Loving," with rhythm, horns and finger snaps, three Tops wailing away on the intro, and Levi going right for our hearts, I knew

184

it was a winner and my mind was buzzing with possibilities for their future before the song was even over. HDH had done it again. The Four Tops were on their way.

But the most talk was centering around Mary Wells, our biggest hitmaker, who had been going strong ever since "Bye Bye Baby." It had been Smokey with his poetic genius teamed with her unique talent that started a romp through the charts that grew stronger with each release, culminating with the record Smokey had boasted would go to #1 Pop—"My Guy"—which it did in May of '64. He was sorry he hadn't bet.

While the company was wild with celebration, I was badgering Smokey. "What do you have to follow this up with?" I had asked him the minute I heard it was going to be #1.

"I'm working on it."

"Working on it? The record's going to be #1 next week and you don't even have a follow-up!"

Smokey would always spend long hours trying to come up with something totally new and different. I told him it was hard for *anybody* to continue topping themselves. And there was nothing wrong with coming out with a record somewhat similar to the previous one so the people that bought the first one would get a feeling of familiarity. A similar kind of theme would take it further, faster, in a shorter amount of time—and make it a little easier to write.

Smokey didn't agree. He refused to make any attempt in any way to copy himself. He hated jumping on any bandwagons, not even his own. But due to a sudden turn of events, Smokey would not have to worry about the next Mary Wells record, so our discussions about it would turn out to be academic.

Later in the year, however, he did write a tune with a similar title—but different gender: "My Girl" for the Temptations. But to my amazement, it was brilliantly different in almost every other way. He went from—

Nothing you could say
could tear me away from My Guy.
Nothing you could do
'cause I'm stuck like glue to My Guy . . .

185

to—

I've got sunshine on a cloudy day.
When it's cold outside
I've got the month of May.
I guess you say
What can make me feel this way?
My girl . . .

My relationship with Mary had always been great. She worked directly with her producers and writers, but if she needed me Mary knew I was always accessible.

Mary was hot. All the producers wanted to record *anything* on her—they didn't give a damn what it was. Whether it was an A side, B side or just a tune in one of her albums, they knew they would make money.

But all of a sudden no one was able to get in touch with her. Finally, reluctantly, Mickey told me about the problem.

"I just don't know what's going on over there. I think this Herman Griffin cat is putting a lot of shit in her head. BG, I think you need to check her out."

That was the last thing I wanted to hear. Of all people to be having trouble with at this time it had to be my biggest star, the person responsible for selling the most records. When Mickey told me how long this had been going on, I hit the ceiling.

"Why in the hell didn't somebody tell me about this before it got out of control?"

"BG, with all your problems you shouldn't have to concern yourself with this kind of shit."

"I *got* to concern myself with it if you can't handle it. Who's going to handle it if I don't?"

"I can handle it all right, but I know how much she respects and looks up to you so I figured you could probably deal with it better."

"Okay, man, okay."

As soon as I got Mary on the phone, I noticed a difference in her voice. When I told her I wanted to meet with her she agreed, but added she could not leave the house. I told her I'd be over.

"Have a seat," Mary said when I arrived. Her strangely cool attitude was obvious as she led me into her living room. Saying little else, she left the room. The fact that she kept me waiting for half an hour was confirmation that things had already changed between us.

When she finally returned I said casually, "So, uh, Mary, what's happening?"

In her raspy yet sugary voice, she said, "Oh, I don't know. I'm just here trying to do some things." She seemed tense.

I asked her why she hadn't been to the studio lately. She told me she hadn't been feeling well. When I asked her what was wrong, she told me "nothing much."

"Well, Mary, it seems there's some kind of problem. Don't you think we should talk about it?"

Silence.

"I mean, if you're unhappy about something, just let me know what it is so I can do something about it."

Silence. She looked as though she almost felt sorry for me. Another bad sign.

I just sat awkwardly, trying to find something funny to say or hoping she might say something light and amusing to prove my thoughts wrong and brighten the mood. I must admit at this point, I probably would have laughed at anything she said.

"Mr. Gordy, I think you should talk to my lawyer."

I didn't laugh. I did smile, however, probably out of some natural instinct as a poker player.

"Lawyer? What do you mean, lawyer?"

"Well, I have a lawyer from New York. I think you should talk to him. His name is Lewis Harris and he'll be over to the office tomorrow."

That was definitely not good news. Still smiling, I said good-bye, telling her I'd be happy to meet with her lawyer. I lied.

When I got into my office the next morning there was another surprise. On my desk was a letter from Ray's attorney in New York, informing me that the Mexican divorce we had gotten two years before was not valid and I was still married.

Before I could even finish reading the letter, Rebecca buzzed me, telling me that Mary's attorney was here to see me.

He came into my office and got right to the point. He told me Mary had been twenty-one for a few months now and was disaffirming all her contracts with Motown. When I wanted to know why, he said she could get a better deal from another company.

"What else?" I asked him.

"That's about it," he said.

"There's much more value here than meets the eye," I told him, "and money is only part of it. Let me show you the whole picture."

First, I took him to the writers' and producers' rooms, then to the studio, the management operation, and the Promotion and Sales Departments. He said he was most impressed.

"But wait, there's more," I told him.

I then took him to Artist Development. This was one time I could really appreciate the importance of Gwen's and Anna's contributions.

Even before the tour was over Mr. Harris was full of praise.

"Mr. Gordy," he said, "I have never seen a company that does this much for any artist." He was convinced there was no place in the world for Mary but Motown, and assured me that he was going to tell her "just that."

He called me the next day and told me he had been fired. And then went on to give me a piece of advice.

"Mr. Gordy," he said, "you'd be better off spending half of the time *doing* what you do for the artists and the other half *telling* them what you're doing. Believe me, they'll never understand if you don't."

That was good advice. But I knew if I spent only half my time doing for them, they would only go half as far. And I would be only half as successful.

Mary then hired a Detroit lawyer, Herbert Eiges, and the legal battle began.

While this was going on, I got a call from Barney in New York with more bad news—bootlegging. Bootlegging, unauthorized duplication and sale of records, had become a real cancer for the record industry. Every time a cache of bootlegged records was found, Motown's were heavily among them.

This time, Barney told me, they were *all* Motown, and the bootleggers had been caught. "Guess who?" he said. He then told me it was not only somebody I knew, but the same somebody who was running my Jobete office in New York, my I-thought-we-were-divorced ex-wife, Ray.

This had to be a joke. Knowing that Barney and Ray had never gotten along that well, I laughed and waited for the punch line. There was none.

Ray called me from jail that same day.

She told me she needed money and thought bootlegging our records was the only way she could get it fast. I was furious but she was the mother of my son and had been too important in my life for me to press charges.

We redissolved our marriage and, once again, parted amicably. So amicably that after she later married Eddie Singleton I loaned them money to start their own record label in Washington, D.C. When that didn't work out, she came back to work at Motown in 1968. Ray would leave and return to Motown on and off throughout the years until the mid-eighties. As far as I was concerned, whether we were married or not, we would always care for each other.

Then in 1990 Ray wrote a book.

This was not the first book written that cast a negative light on me or Motown. Over the years there have been many books with inaccuracies and rumors printed as "facts." I generally ignored them, but with Ray's book it was different. It bothered me that she rehashed some inaccuracies but the accusation that most confounded me was her claim that I had removed her name from the original loan agreement I had received from my family. Not only did it not happen but it *couldn't* have since only family members were eligible to borrow money from Ber-Berry.

She had often told me that she felt her contributions to Motown had never been publicly acknowledged. When books came out they usually gave me all the credit for Motown's success. That was unfortunate, not only for her but for many of the other great unsung heroes who helped make Motown what it is today.

"But Ray," I said, when we were finally on speaking terms, "I haven't written *my* book yet."

Ray, like many others, was not able to make the long trip with me. But that in no way diminishes her incredible contribution to Motown. And because Ray knows how I've always felt about this, we have managed to overcome our differences. She did in fact later retract her statements at some public speaking engagements, after apologizing to me personally.

Today, we are closer than ever.

After many months of negotiation, Mary Wells's departure was finalized.

Because she had continued to work with us for a few months after her twenty-first birthday, it was hard for her and her people to prove she had disaffirmed her recording contract at the age of majority. In addition to whatever 20th Century-Fox Records offered her, they agreed to pay us a percentage of her record royalties for the three years remaining on her contract with us.

Over the next eighteen years, Mary would do more than twenty-six records at five different record companies—but it was Motown with whom she would forever be associated.

Mary had helped to write an exciting chapter in our history and would always be special to me for that. But at the time I was hurt. I had lost the female star I wanted so much to have.

Before the verdict had come in that she was gone for good, a significant article appeared in *Billboard* magazine. Dated July 18, 1964, it was from an interview with Barney:

> Ales stated that Berry Gordy, Jr., president of Motown was "surprised and hurt" when he learned that Miss Wells was "apparently receptive" to offers. Ales noted that Miss Wells has had the benefit of an intensive three year promotional and sales campaign by the organization, all of which is reflected in her present status as an artist. Ales, stating that he is aware that many offers are proffered to an artist who has had a top record, added that he would like to alert the industry to a group of young ladies called the Supremes, "who will have the next No. 1 record in the U.S.". . . .

Barney was a salesman, a marketing man. And luckily—a prophet.

PART THREE

I HEAR A SYMPHONY

I HEAR A SYMPHONY

You've given me a true love
And everyday I thank you love,
For a feeling that's so new, so inviting, so exciting.

Whenever you are near, I Hear A Symphony
A tender melody—pulling me closer, closer to your arms.
Then suddenly, your lips are touching mine.
A feeling so divine, 'til I leave the past behind.
I'm lost in a world made for you and me.

Whenever you are near, I Hear A Symphony
Play sweet and tenderly—
Every time your lips meet mine my baby,
Baby, baby, I feel a joy within
Don't let this feeling end,
Let it go on and on and on now baby.
Baby, baby those tears that fill my eyes
I cry not for myself
But for those who've never felt the joy we've felt.

Whenever you are near, I Hear A Symphony
Each time you speak to me—
I hear a tender rhapsody of love.
Baby, baby as you stand up holding me,
Whispering how much you care,
A thousand violins fill the air now.
Baby, baby don't let this moment end,
Keep standing close to me.
So close to me, baby, baby, I Hear A Symphony.

EDDIE HOLLAND, LAMONT DOZIER, AND BRIAN HOLLAND

Brother is it true?" Danny Bakewell, head of the Brotherhood Crusade, a community action group headquartered in South Central L.A., asked as the two of us sat down at my house. He was referring to a rumor that I was refusing to sell my company to black people.

Rumors like this were no stranger to me. They had been plaguing me for almost thirty years. Building an interracial organization at the time I started Motown was a natural for misconceptions. A black-owned organization with white employees—trying to capture the general market?

Everyone told me it couldn't be done, but I had remembered back in 1947 when Jackie Robinson broke the baseball color barrier and became the first black to play in the major leagues. His team, the Brooklyn Dodgers, went on to win the pennant that year. Aside from being proud of the way he carried himself in the face of intense bigotry, it made me see that any team that had the guts to hire the

193

best person for the job, no matter what their color, could win. I wanted to win.

That was my idea when I hired Barney Ales, an Italian, to promote records by black artists to the white Pop stations. I knew for anyone to want to buy my records they first had to *hear* them.

When Danny asked me if what he'd heard was true, I was so relieved that he was simply "asking" rather than "telling" or "attacking," I hugged him.

I could sense his surprise at my emotional display. Letting him go, I laughed and told him, "No, Danny, it's not true."

He told me he had a black buyer, and asked if I'd meet with him. "Of course."

A meeting was set up for a few days later. Aside from my staff, also scheduled to attend were California Speaker of the Assembly Willie Brown and Assemblywoman Maxine Waters, both of whom had expressed concern about the situation.

Except for Willie Brown, who was stuck on a flight somewhere, everyone showed up.

Within minutes of clearing up the misconception, everyone could see that the potential buyer present—Dick Griffey, who owned Solar Records—was in no position to buy Motown.

As much as we might have liked it to be otherwise, everybody quickly realized that only a big corporation with global distribution would be able to buy Motown, preserve its legacy, and position it properly to move into the twenty-first century. After that meeting I never heard anything more about it.

In the meantime, while MCA and I were close to a deal, there were many important conditions I still had to fight for. Money was a big one, but even more important were assurances I needed in trying to preserve Motown's black heritage.

While all this was going on Diana called. Just hearing her voice always made me feel good, no matter what she had to say. Having left the company several years before, she urged me not to sell. She said she was ready to come back to Motown. When I heard that I wanted to shout out, "Too late, you fool. I'm almost broke!" But as mad as I was at her that day, what she said, and the way she said it, made me think for a moment of not selling.

Diana meant more to me than she could ever imagine. It is absolutely true that at one time I was obsessed with her. In the heyday of the Supremes I saw the butterfly emerge from the cocoon and I was dazzled. She was magic and she was mine. Diana was willing to let me make her a star and I knew she had the talent, drive and stamina to go the distance. It was, in retrospect, a perfect arrangement and as long as we were a team we were invincible. We treated setbacks the same way we treated success. They were both opportunities.

I loved her because she gave everything to our mission. She had a willingness to discipline herself, to work like a maniac to get it right. All of a sudden I wasn't the only perfectionist. I had a wonderful counterpart and she wanted what I wanted and so we set off to get it . . . and we did.

And along with all of that getting we got each other. The good, the bad and finally, the big good-bye.

We did fall for each other in a way that is more complicated than most relationships. How did it happen? People are always asking me that.

8

THE *SUPREMES*
1964–1965

CALLING OUT AROUND THE WORLD

WITH MARY WELLS'S LEAVING, a sullen air had settled over Hitsville. We all took it hard, but Smokey took it the worst. I told him this was the normal reaction in any family when one of its members cuts the cord. "Nothing's changed," I said. "No big deal." I lied. A lot had changed. It would take time to shape a new image, match up new material, build a new star. Smokey had had a lock on Mary's productions. Now he would have to compete like everybody else to get a record out on other artists coming up.

It was a little after eleven o'clock in early June of '64. We had just finished our Friday morning product evaluation meeting where, as usual, a group of us had battled hard over which records would be the next releases. Everybody had left my office except Smokey and Mickey Stevenson. Smokey and I were continuing an argument we'd been having at the end of the meeting. Mickey had hung around, supposedly as a mediator between Smokey and me, but the only thing he really wanted to mediate was me changing my opinion about one of his productions, a Kim Weston song that had been turned down

196

for release. Both Smokey and I knew what he was up to, but didn't mind. We loved an audience.

"How can you listen to Billie Jean?" Smokey argued. "How can you take her opinion over mine? What has Billie Jean ever produced in her life? Nothing! And yet she can tell you whether my record is going to be a hit or not? Bullshit, man. That's totally ridiculous. How can you do that?"

"I'm not doing anything. Billie Jean is head of Quality Control and gives her opinion just like the others. Nobody else thought it was a hit either, including me."

"C'mon, BG. I know 'You've Changed Me' on Brenda Holloway is a smash!"

"Well, if you know it, then why didn't anybody else know it?"

Smokey was intense. "Because they don't know, man, that's why. They just don't know."

Edging his way into the conversation, Mickey slung in a fast opinion. "That's right, the same way they don't know my record on Kim is a number one record!"

Smokey and I frowned in Mickey's direction. Giving us a well-you-can't-blame-a-guy-for-tryin' smile, Mickey said, "Okay BG, but I do agree with Smokey about Billie Jean. She *is* ridiculous, always sittin' there whisperin' in your ear about something."

Just then my sister Esther rushed into my office. Seeing we were heavily involved she just stood there, anxiously waiting for an opening. Smokey never skipped a beat. "See, 'cause man, everybody is so political. You vote for mine, I'll vote for yours. That's bullshit, man."

Smokey took a breath.

Esther jumped in. "Dick Clark's office just called."

Silence.

Dick's name was magic. Our attention was glued on Esther's mouth.

"They want Brenda Holloway on the *Caravan of Stars*," she said so much faster and louder than her usual slow, soft-spoken way.

"Great," Smokey shouted.

We all knew how important *Caravan of Stars* was. Dick was a great promoter, taking the hottest acts on tour across the country, exposing them to Pop audiences. It was like the ultimate record hop. Dick and his TV show, *American Bandstand*, had been responsible for building many artists from nothing to superstardom.

Dick loved Brenda's record, "Every Little Bit Hurts," and *Bandstand* had been playing it heavily.

Hal Davis had produced the record with Marc Gordon out of our California office, and brought it into our Friday meeting. The song had a waltz tempo and everybody knew I didn't like to put out waltzes. Only a few of them ever became big hits. But from the minute the needle touched down on this one I was mesmerized like everybody else. Brenda's deep, full voice vibrated throughout the room. We all voted it a smash. And it was.

All of our artists were being booked and promoted throughout the country and on television. With acts like the Miracles, Martha and the Vandellas, the Temptations, the Marvelettes, Marvin Gaye and Little Stevie Wonder all having top hits on the charts, Esther and the other managers at ITMI had no trouble keeping them busy. Brenda Holloway was so hot that not only did Dick Clark want her on *Caravan of Stars* but she would later open for the Beatles on their North American tour. The one act who didn't have the hit power yet and who needed an extra push was the Supremes.

"What great timing," I said. "Can you get the Supremes on that same show? It would be great exposure for their new record."

"I'm way ahead of you," Esther responded. "They don't want 'em. They're not big enough. I just got off the phone with Roz Ross, Dick's assistant. I pushed all our available acts. They only wanted Brenda."

"No," I said, "you don't understand. Please listen to me. 'Where Did Our Love Go' could be an out-and-out smash. The R&B guys are wailing on it already. We need Dick Clark for the white people. I gotta have that tour, and you gotta get 'em on it."

"No way," Esther said. "I tried. Roz is tough. They're already way over budget."

"Budget! To hell with budget. I'll pay *them* if I have to," I screamed. "If we can get them on his show, he's got to play their record on *Bandstand*." I could see she was starting to get the point. "Roz may be tough," I said, "but so are you."

I knew Esther. I knew her pride. She was under pressure but loved it, because she knew if it worked she'd be a hero.

As Esther headed out the door, Smokey went right back to his point.

"See man, remember 'The Way You Do The Things You Do,' the Tempts' first smash, their breakthrough record? You didn't think that was a hit either."

"Smokey," I said, "please, not that story again. We've already heard it a thousand times, and that was over six months ago."

"A thousand times?" Mickey jumped in. "What story?"

He knew damn well what story, but Mickey was an instigator and always got a kick out of seeing me squirm.

"Okay," I said to Smokey, "we all know you went out and got people that had nothing to do with the meeting to come help us decide on the two records."

"Yeah man," Smokey interrupted, "and all ten of them picked my record over yours."

"No, Smokey, only nine. I voted too, remember."

Smokey laughed, resting his case.

"Yeah, but what about all them other times when I was right?" I defended.

"I'm not talkin' 'bout no other times. I'm talkin' 'bout *that* time."

Rebecca stuck her head in the door.

"Barney's on the line. He wants a meeting with you."

"What about?"

"He said it's personal."

I tensed up. It always bothered me when Barney Ales wanted a personal meeting. By now Barney had become so important to me that I could never casually dismiss his requests. Mickey and Smokey both noticed my change of mood.

"I'm gone, BG," Mickey said.

"Me, too," Smokey added as I reached for the phone.

"Smash, smash," Barney shouted. "Fantastic. Everything is great. Chicago came in for another five thousand on Brenda. The Tempts' 'I'll Be In Trouble'—fifty-one with a bullet. 'Where Did Our Love Go' is getting some action, too. And your record, 'Try It Baby,' on Marvin is cooking. We're hot, my man."

It was always good hearing this kind of news, but my response to Barney was measured, knowing he wanted to meet with me. I knew the more excited I got the more it would cost me.

"What do you want to meet about?" I asked.

"Oh, nothing. Just get together, go over some stuff, bring you up to date on what's happening."

"Isn't that what you're doing now?"

"Oh, yeah," Barney said, "but we got to look into each other's eyes, you know, face-to-face."

"Okay, Monday morning," I said, as I sat back in my seat contemplating the meeting. I knew once again our cat-and-mouse game was in play. I wondered what it would be this time.

Reappearing in the doorway, Esther interrupted my thoughts.

"It's done," she said.

"You mean you got 'em on?"

"Sure did. It's done."

"Great!"

Esther was a hero.

Monday came quickly, but I had a plan. While Barney was waiting for Rebecca to call him to my office, I showed up at his.

"What's happening, my man?" I cheerfully asked as I sat in the lower chair in front of his desk. I wanted to show I wasn't afraid to put myself in an inferior position.

He quickly ended a phone call. "I thought you wouldn't be ready for me for another hour or so," he said, as he hollered out for some sales figures.

"I couldn't keep someone as important as you waiting," I smiled. "What's up?"

"Like I told you, everything is great. Brenda's record is out there kickin' ass and it looks like—"

"What do you want to see me about?"

Grabbing a dart from his desk, he tossed it at the board across the room, missing it completely, hitting the wall. "You beat me the last time," he said. "Aren't you gonna give me a chance to get even?"

I had positioned myself well. Barney was off balance. I relaxed, slumping even lower into the chair. "Naw man, I think I'll just gloat a little longer. So, what's up?"

"Oh, well," he said. "I've been wondering just how important you thought I was around here."

I said nothing.

"Selling is the lifeblood of any organization," he continued, "but you're always talking about how our creative people are what makes Motown so different."

"And they are, but I'm always telling *them* how their records wouldn't be smashes without sales and promotion."

"Okay. Then don't you think I deserve a bonus?"

What! I sat straight up. "A month ago you asked for a bonus for your whole department and I gave it to you."

"I gave all that to the men."

"The men? You said it was for everybody, including *you.*"

"I know, but they're the best in the business and I have to keep 'em happy."

Now *I* was off balance. The pro had regained his footing. I realized what had happened; I had said yes too fast the last time and Barney thought he hadn't asked for enough.

"Berry, if you want to keep good people you do have to keep them happy, don't you think?"

"If you gave it all to your men and didn't keep any for yourself, whose problem is that?"

"I got a better idea," Barney said. "Forget the bonus. How about two percent of gross?"

"Gross! Gross profit? Are you telling me that you want to make money whether I do or not?"

"All I can say is other companies give gross participation to their top people. Gee whiz, Berry, two percent of everything that comes in is not the worst thing in the world."

"How much was that bonus you said you wanted?"

"I didn't, but let's put a pencil to it," he said.

I paid him the bonus that day, but I had a feeling I had not heard the last of that gross business.

* * *

When Esther got back to me with the details of the Supremes' deal, I realized she had taken me literally when I said I'd pay *them* if I had to. She agreed to a deal where Dick Clark would only pay the Supremes six hundred dollars a week. Diana's mother went along as chaperone, which meant that the money had to be split four ways.

When Diana, Mary and Florence left on that thirty-six-day tour with the *Caravan*, they were on the bottom of a bill of seventeen acts. Then "Where Did Our Love Go" began to move up the charts. They had no idea what was happening. All they knew was that each day they were getting more and more applause. By the end of the tour they were getting ovations. The Dick Clark people had to reprint the posters over and over again, moving the Supremes further up toward the top. At the end of July the girls came rolling back into town as stars—with their record on the way to #1.

By late summer of 1964, we were beginning to explode. Hitsville shook with excitement as more and more people's dreams were coming true. Shimmering Cadillacs lined West Grand Boulevard in front of our door. I couldn't wait to get to work in the morning and hated to leave at night. Inside, in every corner and cubbyhole, hits were being made.

That summer the song that seemed to tie everything together for me was Martha and the Vandellas' "Dancing In The Street." It was written by Mickey Stevenson, Marvin Gaye and Ivy Joe Hunter, and produced by Mickey.

Paul Riser, one of Motown's all-time great arrangers who was becoming known for his string and horn arrangements that merged classical traditions into Motown funk, was the one who created the brilliant horn and rhythm arrangements on "Dancing In The Street."

My goal to hook people in the first twenty seconds was never accomplished better. The intro was a hit before Martha even opened her mouth. And when she did it was devastating.

Calling out around the world
are you ready for a brand new beat?
Summer's here and the time is right
for dancin' in the street.

202

They're dancin' in Chicago,
down in New Orleans,
up in New York City;
all we need is music, sweet music,
there'll be music ev'rywhere
There'll be swinging and swaying,
and records playing,
they're dancin' in the street . . .

When I later asked Mickey how he got that tremendous backbeat, he looked at me and laughed. "Well, BG, there's some things I just got to keep for myself."

"Mickey, were there two drummers on that session?"

"BG, there's just some things—"

"Forget it, Mickey. Whatever you did, just keep on doing it."

While the Supremes were still out on the road, we had been gearing up for their return. I was only concerned about one thing—their next record. I couldn't wait to get them back in the studio. Neither could HDH. They had been writing and cutting tracks like mad. As soon as the girls returned, they went on to complete the *Where Did Our Love Go* album.

Their next single was going to be "Baby Love." I liked it but told Eddie it didn't have enough life and the opening wasn't catchy enough.

They took it back in the studio and recut it, giving me what I wanted and more. Speeding up the tempo just a bit gave it life and the seductive "Ooo-ooo-ooo . . ." they added was just the right gimmick to make the beginning ring out with its own identity. Brilliance. Releasing it in September, we didn't have to wait long to see it climb to #1 in America. By November of 1964 "Baby Love" had gone to #1 in the U.K. as well. We had had big hits internationally before, but this was the first to top the British charts.

As much as I preferred Creative to Business, with this level of success there were many times Business had to come first.

One day I got a call from a man in the London office of the Beatles' manager, Brian Epstein, telling me the Beatles wanted to record three of our songs for their next album entitled *The Beatles' Second Album*. The songs were "Money (That's What I Want)," "You've Really Got A Hold On Me" and "Please Mr. Postman."

I had met Epstein only a few months before, when he paid a visit to Hitsville and expressed his and the Beatles' excitement about the Motown Sound, telling us of the great influence it had had on them. Now, as the man from his office explained, they wanted a discount rate on the publishing royalty. Rather than pay us the standard two cents per song, they only wanted to pay one cent and a half.

I told the man how happy I was with the prospect of the Beatles doing our songs, but I didn't want to give a rate. He said that was customary in the business. I said no.

The very next morning the same man called again. He said they were sticking firm to their demand and I had until twelve o'clock noon that same day to wire them an answer.

I looked at the clock. It was 11:30. "Fine," I said, hanging up the phone.

I quickly called in anybody I could find to help me with this heavy decision—Smokey, my brother Robert, my sister Loucye, Billie Jean, Ralph Seltzer and Barney all came to my office. Once I told them the story, everybody had an opinion, all talking at the same time.

Billie Jean: "Don't do it."

Robert: "What if they're making up their minds at this very moment as to what is going on that album. You could lose a lot."

Barney: "Do it! It's done all the time."

Ralph: "Stick to your guns. We've got great songs."

Loucye: "Special rates aren't that unusual. Other publishers do it, especially if they do more than a couple of songs."

Barney: "We're talking big bucks. They might sell ten million."

Me: "Brian Epstein would never not use a great song just to save a half cent. No way. I'm holding out."

And I did—until about two minutes to twelve. I had lost the game of chicken. I rushed a wire off to England agreeing to their demand of the one-and-a-half-cent rate.

Everybody was jubilant that I had given in, including me—until about two o'clock that same day when we got the news. Capitol

Records had the albums in stock at their distributors and were, at that very moment, sending them out to radio stations and stores. The Beatles' new album with our three songs on it, had already been recorded, mixed, mastered, pressed and shipped.

!?#@!!?

Then again, I'd probably make that same decision today. I have learned you should never outnegotiate yourself. A part of something is always better than all of nothing.

Another lesson I learned around this time came when the Supremes' third single from their *Where Did Our Love Go* album, "Come See About Me," was on its way to #1. We were in San Francisco where they were to appear at a distributors' convention. I got a call at my hotel from a record store owner who wanted the Supremes to come by his shop to sign a few autographs. He told me how much he had been promoting their records and that he was a big fan of mine.

Not wanting to be rude and tell him flat out no, I said that because of our tight schedule, I didn't think the girls could do it.

He asked me if I would just think about it.

I told him I would but I was sure they couldn't make it.

The next day I heard ads on the air heavily promoting the Supremes' appearance at his record store.

I jumped on the phone to the guy. "What the hell are you doing? I didn't tell you they'd be there."

"Yeah," he said, "but you didn't say they wouldn't."

"What I said was I didn't think so."

"I know, but you said you'd think about it and you never called back. I've got five thousand fans out here waiting and if the Supremes don't show up, there's gonna be a riot."

"That's your problem," I said. "We are definitely not gonna be there."

"Well, then, I'm definitely gonna sue you," he said. "And the girls."

I slammed the phone down, knowing it was all my fault. I should have been clearer. I got the girls together and went to his store. I translated this lesson into another saying for myself that I called Three Ds, and not Four: Be Direct, Decisive, Deliberate, but not Dumb.

205

* * *

For the past two years the Motortown Revue had been so popular when we took it on the road we decided to bring it home and stage what would become an annual Christmas Show at Detroit's Fox Theatre, downtown. The first one started on Christmas Day, 1964, and ended in a gala New Year's Eve performance. This sold-out engagement with four shows a day was a chance for the local kids to see their hometown heroes in action. As usual, the lineup could change from show to show, depending on the audience reaction. It didn't matter who had hits or how popular you were—you had to be great on that stage. Driving the audience crazy was the only thing that counted. And you could never take your spot for granted. That was something the Supremes found out.

When the engagement opened, they were third from the prestigious closing spot, followed by Marvin Gaye and finally the Miracles—the stars of the show. Two days after the show opened, the Supremes had to fly off to New York where they made their debut on *The Ed Sullivan Show*. This was television's biggest entertainment hour. Viewed by millions—Sunday nights, eight o'clock—live. They sang "Come See About Me," their third consecutive #1 hit. Though they had won over Ed Sullivan and won the hearts of the whole country, when they got back home to do the show they had lost their spot to Stevie Wonder. He had become wildly popular with the audience.

By this time Smokey had become a master showman and the Miracles were so respected by the rest of the artists that no one ever complained about them closing the show. Their hits got great reaction, but what usually brought the house down was Smokey's closing number, "Mickey's Monkey."

Smokey would start lowering his body, bringing the song down with him as he'd tell the band "a little bit softer now, a little bit softer now"—until he was lying on the floor, whispering into the mike in the sexiest voice. His snapping fingers echoed through the theater as the audience sat hushed and spellbound. Then Smokey would begin rising slowly as he told the band "a little bit louder now, a little bit louder now." By the time he got to full volume with the other Miracles doing the monkey, the crowd was on their feet dancing right along with them.

A couple nights after the Supremes returned from the Sullivan show, Smokey came to me complaining about Diana. He said people were accusing him of stealing the Supremes' act, so he sat in the audience that day to find out what they were talking about. He was shocked to see Diana fall to her knees, singing "a little bit softer now."

"And," he said, "the crowd loved it. It's ridiculous. She's doing my whole bit. You gotta stop her."

"Smoke," I said, "the Supremes lost their spot and Diana's just trying to get it back."

"And mine, too."

That tickled me.

"But Smokey, you're the star. You'll just have to come up with something else. There's no way I'm gonna stop her."

"I know," he chuckled. "I didn't think you would. And then too, as fine as she is, I wouldn't stop her either."

I guess I loved her before I even knew it.

She was the inspiration for a song I'd written, "Try It Baby." As usual, my idea for this song had come from real life.

I imagined a girl like her with a guy like me who was building and guiding her career. I envisioned this guy investing all of his time and effort in this girl, while at the same time falling in love with her. What if she got so big, so popular, so caught up in fame and fortune that she no longer had time for him? I felt the Blues coming over me. I headed for the piano. I played and sang and played and sang. Finally, I had a song:

Now you're moving on up, pretty baby
You're leaving me behind
Ev'rybody seems to love you,
You're doing just fine, fine, fine.
But take away your good looks and all your fancy clothes
Why don't you just try it baby, try it baby, try it baby, try it baby
You'll see that nobody loves you but me

Now you tell me that you're so busy, pretty baby
You ain't got much time

Oh how well I remember
When all of your time was mine, mine, mine
Well move on back, 'cross the tracks where you came from
Why don't you just try it baby, try it baby, try it baby and
You'll see that nobody loves you but me

I really want to hold you pretty baby
In my arms again
But I can't get close to you
For all your loving friends, friends, friends
But take your name from the bright lights
And tell them that you're all through
Why don't you just try it baby, try it baby, try it baby, and
You'll see that nobody loves you but me . . .

I recorded it on Marvin Gaye, the artist I thought could express my feelings best. He did not let me down. Benny on drums, Jamerson on bass, Earl Van Dyke, piano, and the Temptations' phenomenal background vocals helped make it a hit.

I never told Diana she was the inspiration for that song. I found myself falling for her more and more, but I stayed cool, incredibly cool.

Meanwhile in the media, the Supremes were everywhere. The black press had gotten behind the girls early on. John H. Johnson's *Jet* and *Ebony* magazines were the first to give them covers. *Jet's* managing editor, Bob Johnson, took a special interest in all our acts. Then, the white magazines like *Look* and *Time* started jumping on the girls full force. It was a Supremes invasion.

I loved the way the Supremes could do standards and Broadway songs like "Make Someone Happy," "You're Nobody 'Til Somebody Loves You" and "Put On A Happy Face" in pure, three-part harmony without a band, a piano or anything. Snapping their fingers, enjoying themselves, they were incredible. I don't think they ever thought seriously about singing standards and show tunes, but I did. Even though our experience had taught us with Marvin on his standards albums that the public wanted only Top 40 hits from Motown artists, I knew those standards were the key to taking our people to the next level of show business—top nightclubs around the country. And I knew the Supremes could lead the way.

It was common knowledge that in order to be booked into the major clubs and showrooms, you first had to make it at the Copacabana in New York. Once you did, the other clubs would then book you. A #1 record meant nothing to the Copa, which was home to superstar entertainers like Frank Sinatra, Tony Bennett and Sammy Davis, Jr. You had to be a seasoned act with years of experience or the Copa was not interested.

My idea was that if I could get the Supremes to do a standard on national TV, millions of people would become believers like me. But every time I tried to get a TV producer to let them do one, they were not interested. Valuable TV time on old standards? No way. "Just their hits is all we want. Just the hits."

Finally, Gary Smith, the producer of *Hullabaloo*, agreed to let the Supremes do "You're Nobody 'Til Somebody Loves You" for a show they would be taping after we came back from Europe. After so many tries, I had finally come through. For the first time, millions of people would see them doing something that they were not known for, totally different from their hits. What a showcase for their other talents. Many shows might have done it had I pursued long enough, but it was Gary Smith who did. This opportunity was critical to me— a shot I couldn't afford to blow. Not only because it could take the Supremes to the next level, and higher, but if done right it could break down other stereotypical barriers in the world of national TV. I had visions of Motown songs on Broadway. Motown songs in movies, clubs, everywhere. Would we be ready? You're damn right we would.

The timing could not have been better as our first international Motortown Revue was about to kick off in London and proceed on a tour that would include performances and television bookings throughout Great Britain, Germany, Holland and France. Having earlier launched our international label, Tamla-Motown, the artists now would be getting international exposure, many for the first time. And it would give me the opportunity to work out the kinks with the Supremes on "You're Nobody 'Til Somebody Loves You."

In addition to the Supremes, the Revue lineup included the Tempts, the Miracles, Martha and the Vandellas, Stevie Wonder, the Earl Van Dyke Sextet and musical arranger, conductor and trumpet player Gil Askey. A gifted musician and a natural entertainer, Gil was indispensable both on and off stage. He not only wrote the Supremes' arrangements but was the glue that held their entire show together.

Besides a large entourage of chaperones, road managers and assistants, I also took along members of my family, my three oldest kids, Hazel, Berry and Terry, and Mother and Pop. They were happy to see me and my troops in action.

When we touched down at London's Heathrow Airport, we were greeted by cheering fans holding banners that read, "Welcome to the U.K." and "We Love Tamla-Motown!" Because we couldn't get our records on the government stations, our earliest airplay had come from *Radio Veronica* and *Radio Caroline*, "pirate ships" anchored a few miles off the coasts of England and Holland. Now we were being heard on the BBC, *Radio Free Europe* and *The Voice of America*, even in countries behind the Iron Curtain. Many not only loved the artists but followed the writers and producers as well. I had heard how popular we were outside America, but this was my first chance to really experience it.

London was a whirlwind—promotions, engagements, and taping the Rediffusion TV special *The Sound of Motown*, hosted by Dusty Springfield.

One day Pop, the kids and I stopped at the Pinewood movie studios where we met the Beatles—Paul, John, Ringo and George.

While taking photographs together, I told them how thrilled I was with the way they did our three songs in their second album. They told me what Motown music had meant to them and how much they loved Smokey's writing, James Jamerson's bass playing and the big drum sound of Benny Benjamin.

"We love all your artists," John said in his Liverpool accent, rattling off the names of most of the artists on our roster, including Marvin "Guy."

My kids could barely speak, but Pop pulled two of the Beatles aside telling one of his stories about how hard work always pays off. I tried to rescue them by telling Pop we had to go, but they said they wanted to hear more.

Our second stop after London was Manchester, where we were doing two shows a night. Now was the time to start working on "You're Nobody 'Til Somebody Loves You."

The theater where we were booked had about five hundred seats and I was disappointed that the first show played to a house that was only half full. Not wanting that to dim their spirits and wanting them to see how proud I was, I made a point of sitting right up in the front row.

I had seated Mother, Pop and the kids several rows back so I wouldn't be distracted. I sat down, ready with my pad and pencil as the Earl Van Dyke band hit the stage.

This night everybody gave their all, and the response from the audience was great. But as usual I had notes critiquing every act on something.

The Supremes were great on their first two numbers. Then they went into "You're Nobody 'Til Somebody Loves You." The crowd took a break. They didn't recognize or understand the song, much less Gil Askey's unique Jazz arrangement. The girls struggled to make it work. It didn't, but I was delighted. I had a plan and I could now see it was gonna work. The Supremes closed with "Baby Love" to rousing applause.

After the show I dashed backstage to tell everybody how great they were and give them my notes. They all seemed in high spirits, happy that they'd gotten through the first show. That is, all except Diana.

She was seething, biting out her words in a low whisper, "Can I see you alone?"

"Of course."

Once outside the dressing room she exploded. "I don't know what you are trying to do but I'm not gonna let you ruin my career! They hate the song, and so do I. I'm not doing it anymore."

I stood there, knowing how much she hated dying in front of any audience. She was a real star. But when she said she wasn't doing it, I was shocked. She had never said anything like that to me before.

"Look," I told her, "those are just a few people. I'm talking about TV and over forty million people. This song could open the door to everything we've wanted."

"I don't care. I'm not doing it. I'm not ruining my career for you or nobody."

"Okay," I said slowly and as calmly as I could, "let me explain what the situation is."

Stony-faced, she just stood there.

"Those people will see you tonight and maybe never again. I'm talking about your whole career."

"I'm not singing the song anymore. I'm just not gonna do it."

"I tell you what," I said, "just make up your mind who you want to satisfy. It's either me or them. It's your decision." I turned and left.

As I walked to my seat my heart was sinking into my stomach. I had given her an ultimatum. And now *I* was locked into it. Insane! This might just be my last show with the Supremes!

Inside me there was a power struggle between the effect Diana had on me and my need to win. I knew if I backed down now I would never be able to direct the group properly in the future. *Why did I have to give her an ultimatum? Maybe I overreacted.*

In the past when lesser disagreements had faced us, Diana had always come around. I was hoping.

I slumped into the seat, waiting for the second show to begin.

When the Supremes finally came out with their usual opening number, I was a knotted ball of tension. When they came to the part of the show where they were supposed to do "You're Nobody 'Til Somebody Loves You" they skipped it. My heart sank to my knees.

I began to think of my life without the Supremes. What would I do? Retract the ultimatum? No, never. Leave the tour and go back to Detroit? Concentrate on someone else? Quit the business? Nothing made any sense.

Each time the Supremes came to a new song I was praying for a miracle. But nothing. When it got near the end, knowing that Gil and she prearranged which songs they would do, so that he could prepare the music beforehand, I gave up. My heart lay busted on the floor. I was numb.

Then I heard the band playing the next intro. Was I dreaming? Was it wishful thinking? Yes, it was the intro to "You're Nobody."

And when she started to sing the words it almost brought tears to my eyes. I wanted to jump for joy. My heart was soaring. But my stomach—that took time to settle.

I had gambled once again and won, not only for myself but for the Supremes, who I wanted to be the biggest female singing group in the history of the world.

When I saw Diana after the show, I told her how happy I was she had done the song.

"What song?" She smiled. "I still don't like it, but," she paused, glancing at me, "I did it for you." And then walked away.

WHAT A LITTLE MOONLIGHT CAN DO

AFTER MANCHESTER, the Supremes sang "You're Nobody 'Til Somebody Loves You" at each performance, and as audiences began to like it more and more they gained confidence. Margaret and I had broken up several months earlier, and now, each time I thought about Manchester I realized how much Diana meant to me. I was madly in love. I think she knew it.

The tour ended in Paris. Diana and I were walking down the street when she said, "Black . . ."

Ever since that experience with Marvin, when I called him "boy" that day, I had been taking so-called negative words and using them in positive ways.

Long before black was "beautiful" I began to call Diana that as an affectionate nickname. She started calling me Black as well. A word can mean anything you want it to mean. And in Diana's and my case, Black meant pride, love and affection.

". . . why don't we stay a couple days after the others leave?"

When she said that I was rocketed off my feet. April in Paris. Alone? Phenomenal!

"Sounds great, Black," I said nonchalantly.

It was two days before the scheduled flight back to Detroit and I kept panicking that she was going to get an emergency phone call or something forcing her home. Those two days seemed like two years. But finally, in front of our hotel when Mother, Pop and the kids, the last of the group, were leaving, I was in such an excited daze that it was hard to concentrate on our good-byes.

So there we were on a beautiful April evening in Paris. We strolled back into the hotel and waited side by side for the elevator to take us up to her suite.

I took her hand and we entered a magnificent room decorated in rich golden colors. With the curtains and windows opened wide, we could hear, see and smell Paris coming alive at night. We held sparkling crystal glasses of champagne high in the air. We toasted success; we toasted the moonlight shining in our window, the tall stone monuments of important French heroes that stood just outside the hotel. We toasted everything.

I was shy, giddy, but happy. So happy. Happy because on her face was a smile that could have lit up the world—the most peaceful, joyous, beautiful smile I could have imagined.

After some drinks, talk, things got quiet. The awkward stage.

What do I do now?

She relaxed out in front of me. Laying her head back on the pillows, her eyes pulled me closer, like a magnet, bewitching me.

Slowly we began to kiss and to touch. Tentatively at first, as pure pleasure and love and desire blended into one. For what seemed like an hour we caressed, my excitement mounting with every minute. Now that I saw her desire, too, that the hopes of all these months were finally going to be fulfilled, I began to remove her clothes tenderly, but with a pace that quickened until I was ripping off my own. Within seconds one of my greatest desires would be fulfilled. *This is it!!!*

But what if she doesn't like it? What if I can't perform? Oh shit!

Everything stopped working.

The more I tried the less able I became. I never felt more panicked, more embarrassed, more useless. I rolled over, plopping my face down into the pillows with thoughts of smothering myself.

Here I was—this "big man" who could make other people's dreams come true but when it came to my own, I'd knocked myself out in the first round.

"I think it would be better if we just stayed friends," she said softly. "No, no," I screamed to myself. That was the last thing I wanted to hear. I said nothing.

She took me in her arms, hugging me softly. I had to get out of there.

I went back to my room, feeling as dejected as I could ever remember.

All I could think of was that I only had one more day.

The next day everything was cool. Just good friends wanting to have a good time, Diana and I jetted over to some island on a speedboat.

As we plunged through the breaking waves I must have shot a thousand pictures of her with my little Leicaflex 35mm camera.

I was constantly trying to preserve every subtle shade of Diana's moods. She had long developed a love-hate relationship for that Leicaflex—and me using it. When I later directed *Mahogany*, ideas for Anthony Perkins's role of the crazed photographer and the failed sex scene were enhanced by my experiences with Diana.

That evening I took her to some clubs in Paris where I arranged for her to sit in with different musicians. I loved to see the electrifying effect it had on people when they recognized she was Diana Ross of the Supremes.

That night, she serenaded me in club after club as I was sipping wine. We were having great fun. Feeling a little tipsy I knew it was time to go back to the hotel and try again.

From the minute I closed the door behind us, I knew my mind would not get in the way this time. I think the wine helped keep it in check, allowing what took place next to unfold like a great piece of soaring music. We fit perfectly, like a carefully choreographed dance. Ecstasy to the tenth power! And after that night it only got better.

But as strong as our romantic involvement became we vowed not to let it or anything else take the focus off her career and my vision.

FOR LOUCYE

AFTER THE SUPREMES performed "You're Nobody 'Til Somebody Loves You" on *Hullabaloo* things changed. The big TV shows wanted them to do at least one standard. They were reaching audiences they'd never reached before. Then came another big break—that special club booking that had been eluding us for so long—the Copa.

Nearing the summer of '65—when club business was slow—General Artists Corporation, the New York talent agency that was booking the Supremes, convinced the Copa's powerful owner, Jules Podell, to give the girls a shot.

That was just about all that he was willing to give. Knowing what a major launching pad his club was, Jules made us pay for everything. Nobody got breaks at the Copa. No discounts on food or drinks; you paid full price no matter who you were—manager, husband, musician or star.

On top of that we had to sign what many considered a "slave contract" for three years. We would appear for two- or three-week periods, seven days a week, two shows a night for less than $3,000 a week. The second year (if he wanted us back) it would go to $10,000, and the third $15,000. *His* option.

But I was always willing to lose money if it meant building stars.

Never before had we planned such a costly show. I amassed all our forces. Everybody in the company got behind this event. The Artist Development crew—Gil Askey, Harvey Fuqua, Cholly Atkins, Maxine Powell, Maurice King, Gwen, Anna and others—worked around the clock handling staging, choreography, costumes, patter and musical arrangements. I oversaw it all. Esther and Taylor Cox and everybody else at ITMI, Al Abrams in Publicity, Loucye and Barney Ales used all their contacts to make sure that the top press, distributors, DJs and all the other record industry people would be in attendance.

Following the example of Broadway producers who took their plays to smaller out-of-town theaters to try them out, we set up camp in Wildwood, New Jersey, where we could break the show in at a local club called the Rip-Tide.

Rehearsing by day, performing at night, we created, shaped, improved and enhanced every possible detail of the show. We were ready. As July 29 approached, we prepared to make the move from Wildwood to the biggest opening of our lives—the Copacabana in New York City.

Suddenly I received a phone call that my sister Loucye was seriously ill in the hospital and I would have to fly back to Detroit.

At the hospital, my family told me that she had had a cerebral hemorrhage and needed surgery. When I went in to see her she said she wanted me to be the one to make her medical decisions.

As soon as Loucye put me in charge I got a funny feeling. Of course I was so proud that she thought enough of me, and enough of my decision-making ability and all the respect that goes with that, to put me in charge of her life. But I was a realist. I hadn't been there when she had taken ill. Everyone else had worked hard to coordinate with the doctor and all the other people to get her to the hospital, to make all the prior arrangements. They had a plan and a program. Why she put me in charge of all that, having no prior facts of what had gone before, I wasn't sure. The discussion that followed with the family soon showed me why.

The family was happy I had come in and not unhappy that she had decided to put me in charge. They loved Loucye as much as I did. They knew it was a critical situation. They knew I was good at making decisions in a crisis. So they were happy to let me run the show. But when I said I wanted a second opinion, that was a problem. She had great faith in her doctor and he had come up with a specialist to operate. It was too late, they said, for me to bring in a brand-new outsider, plus I was told her doctor would be insulted. He was doing all he could and he had gone out of his way to bring in a top specialist.

The pressure was on. I considered everything everybody said. But still I wanted a second opinion. I knew it was the right thing to do in something as serious as this. The doctor agreed and arranged for another specialist to come in and consult. One day before the scheduled operation the new specialist was called out of town on an emergency. So I was told. I was torn. I thought about canceling the operation. I was assured by her doctor that everything would be fine. His specialist was one of the best in the business and to postpone it at this time would cause a much more serious threat. I gave my permission to go ahead.

In the waiting room I couldn't get out of my mind how much I owed Loucye. How she had taken me into her home during the early days. How she had sacrificed to help me make Motown a success. How much she trusted me.

Loucye had been such an important person in helping us get through the years of struggle. She had to witness the fruits of her labor. She had to come with us to that next stage. She had to.

After long, agonizing hours the doctor came in to address the family. He told us the operation was a success—but the patient died. Just like that.

I sat alone for a long time thinking about what that meant. It meant that the doctor, reputation intact, would go on to other patients, living his own life with a clear conscience. I would, however, go on living mine without Loucye—and with guilt, all because I had not followed my own instincts.

"Everything always happens for the best," people said, trying to console me.

Bullshit! Everything doesn't always happen for the best; but you should make the best out of everything that happens. I had to make this count for something. I would never put myself in the position to feel this kind of guilt again. Maybe sadness, disappointment or even anger—but never guilt. I would never again let anybody talk me out of what I felt was right.

Loucye's funeral was held the same day as the opening at the Copa. After the burial service most of my family flew to New York for the show. We dedicated the performance, and later an album, to the loving memory of Loucye Gordy Wakefield.

That night when I got to the Copa, I spent a few minutes sitting by myself.

It's so strange how life can hand you some of your saddest and most triumphant moments at the same time. I thought about "Somewhere," which the Supremes would be doing in the show, and I felt my sister was somewhere close by and could hear me when I said silently, "Thank you, Loucye, thank you."

9

THE EXPLOSION
1965–1968

HITS IS OUR BUSINESS

VERY FEW THINGS IN LIFE are as exciting as an opening night. You never know what to expect. Everything that can go wrong usually does. It's the first look everyone has at the show, including the reviewers, who can make or break you.

Our opening at New York's Copacabana was a madhouse. I was running all over the place trying to make sure everything was perfect.

Normally the fire marshal would have shut down a place that packed, but this legendary room was owned by Jules Podell, a cigar-smoking, gravel-voiced, no-nonsense wheeler-dealer, whose reputation hinted at underworld ties. Even Jules was not prepared for this: a black Rock 'n' Roll group he'd hardly heard of, selling out his joint—off season!

That night he took charge, shouting orders to his staff, sending in new tables, trying to cram in enough chairs to make room for all his friends and regular customers.

I saw our people, who thought they had front tables, now pushed two or three rows back as Jules added more tables ringside. Barney was getting crazy because some of the people important to us—

220

distributors, DJs and press, were being shuffled around. But Jules Podell was one person Barney could not mess with.

Gil Askey took his place in front of the band and raised his baton. It was show time. With a downward thrust of his arms the overture began. An orchestrated medley of the Supremes' Rock 'n' Roll hits arranged in a unique classical style sent an already excited crowd into a frenzy.

I stayed in the back of the room so I could see and hear everything better—the girls, the lighting, the sound and the overall crowd reaction.

So much was riding on what was about to happen. If the Supremes flopped they could set our music back ten years. If they did well, it could open doors for other Motown acts.

"And now, ladies and gentlemen," the announcer's voice echoed through the room, "Jules Podell proudly presents the Supremes." The lights came on and there they were—my babies, playing the Copa.

Fast, crisp finger snaps and an upright bass started pumping through the room. It was our opening number. Gil had done a Jazz arrangement on a Cole Porter song I had heard sung by Diahann Carroll and really liked. That walking bass fiddle and the Supremes' finger snaps set a dramatic, uptempo feel for about five seconds, then Diana's voice rang out, laying right into that fast-paced groove: *"From this moment on—you for me, dear, only two for tea, dear. From this moment on . . ."*

Diana was cooking. Starting the next verse, it reached an even higher peak when the girls added their trio power in unison. Gil brought the band in with sharp staccato licks in all the right places. After that they went into "Put On A Happy Face." Another surprise. This was Broadway.

I looked over and saw Jules sitting with Sammy Davis, Jr., and Ed Sullivan, smiling from ear to ear, probably thinking he had really gotten me on this deal. And maybe he had, but what he didn't know was I would have done this one for no money at all.

They ended the song with their arms stretched high to thunderous applause and a standing ovation. Without losing a beat they moved quickly into the intro to their third number. Again in powerful unison: "Now here's a little song that you made popular, and we hope you like it now." Diana jumped in with that most familiar sound that so many people identify only with the Supremes. *"Ooo-oo-ooo, Baby Love, My Baby Love . . ."* Pandemonium broke out and this was just the beginning of the show. I couldn't wait to see the audience's reaction to what was coming later.

After the girls did two more of their hits, "Come See About Me" and "Stop! In The Name Of Love," they broke into "Rock-A-Bye Your Baby With A Dixie Melody," twirling straw hats and canes and dancing up a storm.

Awesome entertainers that night, the Supremes did everything from a comedic "Queen of the House," written to the tune of Roger Miller's "King Of The Road," to a moving rendition of "Somewhere" from *West Side Story.*

We ended the show with the song that had made it all possible, "You're Nobody 'Til Somebody Loves You."

As I stood there filled with pride, I was watching what the reviewers would later say was one of the most dramatic openings the Copa had ever seen.

My eyes fell upon my family. Seeing their proud faces I felt a strong bond between us, of victory, sadness and love.

Shortly after the Copa the most exclusive clubs in the country started booking the Supremes. The Flamingo Hotel in Las Vegas signed them a year in advance—sight unseen!

When I look back at these years from 1965 to 1968 it seems we could do no wrong. The stream of hits was endless. The whole world was fast becoming aware of our overall success—our artists, our songs, our sound. I was being called the star maker, the magic man.

During that time, at Hitsville, a battle for another kind of supremacy continued. For our first five years the strongest thread in our musical tapestry had been sewn by Smokey with his clever, poetic lines pushing the Miracles, Mary Wells and the Tempts to the top. Now the texture was being dominated by the Holland-Dozier-Holland hooky, simple—yet deep, driving, melodic overtures. But the competition to stay on top was no small matter for HDH. When they gave Marvin another hit with "How Sweet It Is (To Be Loved By You)"

Smokey answered with "My Girl" on the Temptations, their first #1 record. HDH then hit again on Martha and the Vandellas with "Nowhere To Run." Smokey came back with one of the sexiest records of his career, "Ooo Baby Baby," on the Miracles.

There was no stopping HDH, whose #1 "I Hear A Symphony" on the Supremes became one of my favorites of that era. HDH seemed to hit as easily on newer artists like the Isley Brothers' "This Old Heart Of Mine (Is Weak For You)," Shorty Long's "Function At The Junction" and the Elgins' "Heaven Must Have Sent You."

HDH benefited from my policy that, if two records under consideration were equally strong, the release would be given to the producer who had the last hit. In addition to the monster hits on the Supremes, in the next couple years they would give the Four Tops five smashes: "I Can't Help Myself (Sugar Pie, Honey Bunch)," "It's The Same Old Song," "Reach Out I'll Be There," "Standing In The Shadows Of Love" and "Bernadette." I loved them all but for me "Bernadette" would epitomize the Holland-Dozier-Holland genius for capturing a listener's ear and not letting it go. It also helped fuel my belief that Levi Stubbs of the Four Tops could interpret and deliver the meaning of a song better than anybody. He made Bernadette live. I wanted to meet her myself.

What was equally remarkable was that though Smokey was on the road most of the time he continued to compete, often writing or producing with fellow Miracles Ronnie White, Pete Moore and Bobby Rogers, as well as longtime friend, Marv Tarplin, the group's guitar player. These different collaborators produced hits on the Miracles like "Going To A Go-Go," "The Tracks Of My Tears," "I Second That Emotion" and "More Love," and on other artists like the Marvelettes with "Don't Mess With Bill" and Marvin Gaye with "I'll Be Doggone" and "Ain't That Peculiar."

"Tracks Of My Tears" brought out something about Marv Tarplin and Smokey working together that always touched a dramatic chord with me. It became my favorite song of theirs. I began calling it a masterpiece.

Smokey was now more confident than ever. It looked like he couldn't lose. Then, after he had kept almost a complete hold on the Tempts for about three years, he did "Get Ready" in early 1966. It went to #1 on the R&B charts but couldn't get past #29 Pop. A crack in Smokey's armor. That was all Norman Whitfield needed.

At the Friday meeting Norman sat confidently as we listened to his new production on the Tempts—"Ain't Too Proud To Beg." The reactions were mixed, from "I hate it" to "It's a big hit."

I was the last one to give my opinion. "I love the feel—it's street," I said. "But it doesn't have enough meat. I gotta hear more story."

The next week Norman was back with an improved "Ain't Too Proud To Beg." It got more votes, but was again rejected. Norman looked crushed when the group went along with my "Not quite there."

But the following week he was back—and taking no prisoners. David Ruffin's voice came jumping off that record begging like I'd never heard before—

I know you wonna leave me,
but I refuse to let you go.
If I have to beg, plead for your sympathy,
I don't mind 'cause you mean that much to me.
Ain't too proud to beg . . .

Just as HDH had a lock on the Supremes and Tops, so began Norman's on the Temptations. He had snatched them right out of Smokey's pocket.

Norman had such passion. He was relentless. When a song wasn't a hit on one artist he'd produce it over and over again on other artists. After "Ain't Too Proud To Beg," he continued with hits like "Beauty Is Only Skin Deep," "(I Know) I'm Losing You," "You're My Everything" and "I Wish It Would Rain." Each song was different, but there was always something undeniably Whitfield about Norman's productions. He was versatile, unique and getting stronger and cockier with every hit.

I told him he had fire deep in his soul and a little would come out each time he produced a record.

Though I was finding less and less time to get into the studio, early in '65 I, too, jumped into the mix, co-producing a record with engineer Lawrence Horn. It was a tune called "Shotgun," written by Jr. Walker for himself and his group the All Stars.

Junior was incredible. His saxophone sound was like nobody else's. The down-home feeling he and his band got when he sang and played his horn made it easy to produce him. All we had to do was get a good sound balance in the studio and just wait. He could put together some of the damnedest lyrics you'd ever heard—and come out with a smash:

Shotgun, shoot 'em fore he run now
Do the jerk baby, do the jerk now
Put on your high heel shoes
We're goin' down here now and listen to 'em play the Blues
We're gonna dig potatoes
We're gonna pick tomatoes . . .

He broke every rule in the book, but I still loved it.

New people were coming all the time and from everywhere. When I think of the two young songwriters who came to us from New York around this time one word comes to mind—TALENTED! Nickolas Ashford and Valerie Simpson had joined our growing writing staff at Jobete after an earlier hit they'd written for Ray Charles, "Let's Go Get Stoned." When I first saw them they both seemed warm and quiet. While that held true, I later found out Valerie was a pint-sized ball of dynamite, especially when working in the studio.

One day Harvey Fuqua, in his quest for material for a new duo he had put together—Marvin Gaye and Tammi Terrell—listened to a demo of their songs. Liking what he heard, he and Johnny Bristol produced "Ain't No Mountain High Enough" and "Your Precious Love." Both songs became big hits.

Sooner or later just about every songwriter, and some performers, want to produce their own records. But talent in one area doesn't always mean you have it in another. With Nick and Val it did. The success of their songs earned them a chance to produce some of their own material.

Their production of Nick's lyrics with Valerie's melodies and arrangements added a new sophisticated and dramatic element to our overall sound. When their first production on Marvin and Tammi was brought into the Friday meeting, there was no debate. "Ain't Nothing Like The Real Thing" was voted a smash and it was. When their next record on the same duo, "You're All I Need To Get By," was played, it sounded so great to me I didn't bother to take a vote. No one complained. It is still one of my all-time favorites.

I was excited that hits were coming fast on a lot of our artists, but I was worried about Stevie Wonder. He hadn't had a hit since "Fingertips" almost three years before.

We had opened doors with his #1 single and album and hadn't taken advantage of it. That was a no-no for our company. As far as I was concerned that was a sin. As hard as it is to establish an act, once you do, once you open that door, you just have to march right in. With Stevie we hadn't and now it seemed we couldn't.

He was an adolescent and his voice was beginning to change. We were trying to get a hit on him before that happened. Too late!

But, as it turned out, his voice changed for the better. That young, undeveloped, high-pitched sound that I hadn't loved when I first met him turned into a controlled, powerful, versatile instrument. Stevie's confidence soared, which led to the emergence of another of his great talents—songwriting. In late '65 he was back on the charts with "Uptight (Everything's Alright)," which he wrote with Hank Cosby and Sylvia Moy.

Writing "Shoo-Be-Doo-Be-Doo-Da-Day" he scored again with the same team, and on "I Was Made To Love Her," his mother, Lula Hardaway, joined them as a co-writer.

"Uptight," produced by Hank and Mickey, had come as a major breakthrough for Stevie, containing many of the elements I was always looking for in hit records—simplicity, cleverness, a different kind of feel, and one that was irresistible.

Another guy I found different but clever was Ron Miller.

"Mr. Gordy, I don't want to write that Blues shit," he said when he first came to Motown. Ron was a white songwriter from Chicago

Mickey Stevenson came across when Ron delivered a pizza to Mickey's hotel room.

When I heard the kind of show tunes he was writing, I could see he was talented. But very opinionated. He made it clear he felt his musical taste was above ours and wanted a written guarantee that we wouldn't try to force him to write Rock 'n' Roll or Blues.

I told him that wouldn't be necessary. Nobody was gonna make him do anything he didn't want to do. We released some of his songs on Marvin Gaye and they weren't hits. Ron argued that was because of the poor taste of the public.

"You can bullshit yourself if you want to, and worship your own stuff in your basement for the rest of your life," I told him, "or you can try to write something a million people can relate to."

The broker he got, the more he got the point. He started writing songs that sounded like a combination of show tunes and Blues. They felt like old standards and I wanted people to think they were. Now I had a problem. If I put them in my publishing company, Jobete, people would know they were new songs, since Jobete had only been around for a few years and was known for publishing the Motown hits. I had to come up with a new company and name that would make the songs seem like they had been around for ages.

I went through the telephone book, looking for names. Two separate names caught my eye. "Stein" and "Van Stock." I put them together. Stein and Van Stock. It sounded old line, classy—and Jewish.

Now I had two publishing companies. Jobete for my Motown-type songs, and Stein and Van Stock for my standard-type songs.

My favorite of Ron's songs, "For Once In My Life," was one he wrote with Orlando Murden. Ron hustled it all over Detroit, getting every singer in local bars and clubs to include it in their acts. Within a year most everybody in town knew it.

Finally he got Tony Bennett to record the song for Columbia Records. When it was released and I read a review in Billboard calling it a great revival of an old classic from Stein and Van Stock Publishing, I was thrilled. An old classic! An old classic.

After Tony's record was a hit, we recorded a hipper, faster version on Stevie Wonder that went straight to the top of the charts.

227

Everyone started recording and performing it, from Jackie Wilson to Jim Nabors to Frank Sinatra. "For Once In My Life" became a genuine standard.

Ron was primarily a lyricist. As hard as he worked to find singers to sing his songs he seemed to work just as hard to find writers to collaborate with. They were as numerous as the hits he would eventually have. He wrote "A Place In The Sun" and "Yester-Me, Yester-You, Yesterday" with Bryan Wells for Stevie and "Touch Me In The Morning" with Michael Masser for Diana.

Shelly Berger, the new head of our West Coast office, was amused when he received the latest memo I had issued.

"We will release nothing less than Top Ten product on any artist. And because the Supremes' world-wide acceptance is greater than the other artists, on them we will release only #1 records."

"Is he kidding?" Shelly laughed to others. "What does he think this is? The Ford Motor Company? 'We will only manufacture red cars!' "

I first met Shelly on the Fourth of July 1966, when I was coming out of the Harlan House Motel, near Hitsville, where I'd just finished a meeting. My ex-wife, Thelma, pulled up in her car with Hazel, Berry and Terry in the back seat. As I leaned in the window, hearing "Hi, Daddy!" in unison, it was hard to miss the grinning white man in the front seat with Thelma. "Berry," she said, "this is Shelly Berger. He runs your California office."

"Oh, Mr. Gordy, this is great! I was beginning to think you didn't exist," he said, extending his hand. "Why don't you come with us to the company picnic? We could play some ball. Y'know, L.A. versus Detroit."

His hand still extended, I shook it reluctantly. "Nice to meet you." All I could see was some fast-talking Hollywood white guy who had come to Detroit, hit on the first woman he saw, who just happened to be my ex-wife, sitting in a car with my kids, and inviting me to my own picnic.

Since our L.A. office was getting busier all the time, Shelly had been hired by Ralph Seltzer to find TV and movie tie-ins for our artists and music. After hearing what a great job he was doing, I

228

thought it would be a good idea to meet him in person, and had arranged for him to fly in to Detroit.

And now, here he was.

Word must have traveled fast about my less than jubilant meeting with Shelly, because at the picnic people treated Shelly like the plague. Even Rebecca, who had made the arrangements for his trip here and had picked him up at the airport, all of a sudden was acting like she had never seen him before.

A creative, witty ex-actor, Shelly had a clear vision of where our artists could be and great ideas on how to get them there. He had helped set up a Dick Clark show called *Where the Action Is*, to be taped the following week in Detroit at a local club, the Roostertail, using all Motown acts. By the time Shelly and I had our next meeting, I recognized he was definitely the right person for the job.

At that meeting, I did, however, work my way around to asking him how he knew my ex-wife.

"I don't really," he said. "I was just a new guy in town and Rebecca asked Mrs. Gordy if she would give me a ride back to my hotel. Royal treatment, I thought. Who knew that by riding with that nice lady and those three little kids, my whole future would be hanging by a thread."

Many times we'd laugh about our strange beginning—and about how wrong first impressions can be.

When Shelly first came to the company, it was at a time when we were having a slowdown on the charts. The Supremes' last two releases had broken their string of #1 hits.

I had been on the warpath when I circulated that memo about only releasing #1 records on the Supremes. I was shooting for the top, realizing that if we missed it we'd still be up there somewhere. I had no idea we'd actually do it.

"You Can't Hurry Love," "You Keep Me Hangin' On," "Love Is Here And Now You're Gone" and "The Happening"—they all made it!

"We dangerous," I remember saying to Brian Holland one day.

We *were* dangerous. Sometimes even to ourselves. These were the days of the killer poker parties. When our royalty checks came we— Mickey Stevenson, Harvey Fuqua, Johnny Bristol, Eddie and Brian

Holland, Ron Miller, myself and a few others—might get together for a game at one of our homes, which for most of us were new purchases. What a sight! The table was piled high with thousands, and everyone concentrating, holding their cards close to their chests.

We hard-core players could have written a book on the art of bluffing. Me, I played it very deadpan, strategic, subtly trying to give the wrong clues. Eddie and Brian were masters of the poker face, whereas the suave Harvey kept on a gentlemanly smile the whole time. Johnny, Ron and especially Mickey were a lot more dramatic—no matter what their cards were, they took on the attitude of sharks circling.

And then there was Smokey. He always did the wrong thing at the wrong time. He loved poker, but poker didn't love him. I had to bar him from the game many times.

But sometimes when he'd show up and hang around, begging to get in, it was hard to say no. Smokey was a favorite at these poker parties. Everybody knew how big his royalty checks were.

One night he pulled out a fat roll of hundred dollar bills—the kind Norman Whitfield would flash around when he was trying to hustle somebody into a pool game.

"Have a seat, Smoke," Mickey said, rubbing his hands together.

"Smokey's barred." I smiled. "You know he's a patsy."

I meant that to be funny. Smokey didn't think so.

Mickey laughed. "BG called you a patsy, Smoke. I know you ain't gon' let him get away with that."

A serious Smokey said, "That's ridiculous, man. It's my own money! If I wanna play, I can play."

The others chimed in their support for Smokey.

"You're the one that's ridiculous," I said, "but you're right, it's your money."

Smokey happily pulled up a chair, as Harvey called five card stud—and dealt the first card face down.

During that very first hand Smokey decided to show us all how well he could play. On the fourth card there was a thousand dollars on the table. Smokey was animated.

"I bet the size of the pot," he said confidently. "One thousand dollars!"

It was clear he was bluffing. Remaining cool, everybody called. "Deal the last card," Mickey said.

Harvey dealt the fifth. Everybody checked until it got to Smokey. "Oh no," he said, "there won't be no checkin' here. Five thousand dollars!"

He sat back in his chair, looking from face to face. Everybody was shocked. We could see he was trying to scare us, but nobody wanted to chance $5,000 to make sure. That is, nobody except Mickey, who looked right back into Smokey's eyes.

Smokey was smiling, staring Mickey down, as little beads of sweat began forming on his forehead.

"I call," Mickey said, slowly counting out $5,000 in hundred dollar bills.

Smokey looked at Mickey in disbelief.

"You're such a fool, man. You've lost," Smokey said, as if Mickey was going to pick his money back up. Smokey waited for a moment, then turned over his hole card. Nothing! He didn't even have a pair. Mickey won it with only ace high. Smokey was devastated. I looked at him in disgust. He never looked my way. I felt worse than he did.

A few hands later Smokey started looking more dejected than ever. We knew he had something. Sadly shaking his head, "Five hundred," he said, throwing it in the pot.

Johnny: "I'm out."

Ron: "I'm out."

Brian: "I'm out."

Eddie: "I'm out."

Harvey: "I'm out."

Mickey: "I'm out."

"I'm sorry, Smokey, but I'm out, too," I said.

Smokey turned over his hole card. No one was surprised. He had aces back to back. He sat there with his winning hand, the sorriest sight I'd ever seen.

Regardless of his begging I never let him play again after that.

Out of the blue came a familiar voice singing over the telephone: "Hey, man. This is Billy, Billy Davis!"

"Billy! My man, what's happening?" I screamed.

"You are, baby, you are! I been hearing about you down here in Birmingham and you' hot man. You' famous!" he said with wild enthusiasm.

Hearing his voice I realized how much I had really missed the guy. I hadn't heard from him since my 3D Record Mart days when he decided to spend his military severance pay on clothes rather than going into business with me. Later he'd moved down South to work in a private nightclub.

"I've got to get out of this place," he said. "I wanna come and help you. I know you need help with all the stuff you're doin'."

"Your sudden concern for my well-being overwhelms me. All these years I been working my ass off. Where was you then?"

"Then, you was po'," he laughed.

That made me laugh, too. "But Billy, what makes you think I need help? I'm fine."

"Come on, man, I *know* I can help you. Take care of your clothes and shit, keep you clean. You never did know how to dress. You be wearing blue socks, black shoes with a brown suit."

I looked down at what I was wearing and he wasn't that far off.

"You wanna come back 'cause you think I got money."

"I *know* you got money and I'm happy for you. But you know me. I don't want to be no millionaire. I just wanna live like one! I tell you what, man, I'll just come up and visit for a few days. After all, I ain't seen you for about ten years."

"When would you wanna come? In a couple of months or so?"

"No, no, man. I'll be there Friday. All you got to do is put me up someplace. I can take care of myself."

"Wait a minute, I have to get with Rebecca to work out some arrangements, get a budget and come up with a memo."

"Memo? Man, fuck memo! Just do it. You' in charge, ain't ya?"

I called Rebecca and told her to make arrangements for the ridiculous little character.

Those few days turned into twenty-one years. Billy, somehow, knew about the finer things in life and was determined to show me what they were. He immediately became my valet and when buying my suits, ties, shoes or whatever kept us both "sharper than a dog."

Billy had such a positive attitude about life. He had a unique style for lifting people's spirits, helping them, telling them what they needed to hear, whether good or bad, and they loved it. His enjoyment of things was contagious. He really loved to see the artists perform and they all wanted him to come to their shows, especially Diana. Always with a large group, Billy and his friends would sit right up front, cheering the artists on. His snaps and claps were so loud and had such personality they'd get everyone going.

Billy loved to have fun. A party never felt like it was really a party until Billy got there. When we walked into a room of strangers in a group I was usually overlooked. He was exactly what many thought Berry Gordy would be.

Billy became a part of my traveling entourage with the Supremes and shared most of my adventures. An important link between me and those he befriended on my behalf—family, friends, business associates, celebrities, politicians, royalty, heads of state—Billy became a Motown institution.

To many he was as much a star as Diana, Mary and Flo. Whenever I'd meet people, no matter where they came from, no matter how removed from the entertainment business—once even an ambassador from Uganda—they'd often surprise me with, "How's Billy?"

The fall of 1966 brought the Supremes' most hectic schedule ever. We joked there were times when we'd have to check the itinerary to know what continent we were on. One day, touring Japan, we'd have a private audience with a future prime minister, entertaining him with an a capella three-part harmony rendition of "Put On A Happy Face." Another day we'd be doing a sound check at the Flamingo Hotel, nervously preparing for our Vegas debut. Then off again—Europe, the Far East and finally home.

We were swept up in the most glamorous lifestyle imaginable, but the bottom line was still hard, very hard, work. The girls seldom got a chance to socialize. That was something Mary Wilson brought to my attention in a hotel lobby one night in London.

"Flo and me," she said, "we like to have fun at night. Don't make us go to bed just because you're jealous of Diana meeting somebody else."

I laughed. "That's got to be the dumbest thing I've ever heard in my life."

"She's the one who needs to save her voice and get sleep, not us. She leads. All we do is 'doobee-doobee-doo.' " Mary looked squarely in my eyes. She had always been direct, smart and calculating, but I had always managed to stay a step ahead. This time she had put me on the defensive and she knew it.

Though we were discreet, it was common knowledge that Diana and I were going together.

She said it again. "If you're jealous of her that's your problem, but don't make us suffer."

"That has to be the dumbest thing I ever heard," I stupidly repeated. I stared her down for a moment but, feeling uncomfortable, I smiled. "Mary, you'd say anything to get out at night."

She smiled knowingly.

"Let me think about it," I said as I left her standing there all dressed up in that hotel lobby, waiting for me to give her the green light.

I went to Diana's room, resigned to let them all go out, and told her about Mary's comments.

It amused her that I might be jealous. "Black," she said, "I have no desire to go out anywhere. I need all the sleep I can get. I've gotta protect my voice." Her instincts were incredible.

I told Mary they were free to go out, but still within reasonable restrictions.

I never knew whether Diana really wanted to go out or not. But the fact that she was willing to make sacrifices thrilled me. Jealousy or whatever it was, I had found another reason to go 110 percent for her—she was going 110 percent for herself.

Diana's happiness or sadness always affected me. And that was not just one-sided. Twice she threw me a surprise birthday party. Probably the greatest surprise I ever gave her reads like a little vignette that I'll call "Just for a Smile."

The story began at the El San Juan Hotel in San Juan, Puerto Rico, where the Supremes were performing. I was thinking about what I could do to thrill her.

Over the past many months, Diana had been talking nonstop

about how desperately she missed her nine-year-old brother, Chico. Wherever we were, he was always on her mind. Boston, Philadelphia, Europe, anywhere. "Black," she said at every opportunity, "you know, I really miss Chico."

So many times, spotting a kid on the street, pointing, she'd remark, "That boy sure looks like Chico, don't you think?"

Suddenly, sitting in the El San Juan Hotel, a perfect idea came to me. For the next two days I made all the arrangements, enlisting everybody else in the entourage to play a part in this major operation. Just anticipating Diana's reaction, I was filled with joy.

Finally everything was ready.

Diana and I were sitting in the grand, spacious, tropically decorated hotel lobby. Overhead fans whirled. Palm trees and other greenery surrounded the many clusters of chairs and sofas. Hotel guests milled about.

Two sofas away sat the real Chico Ross with his back to us. My plan had worked perfectly up to this point.

As Diana glanced around the lobby her eyes focused on the back of his head.

"Here I go again," she said. "See that kid right there? Boy, I'm telling you, he really looks just like Chico."

"You're right. There you go again."

"I just don't know anymore, but I swear the back of his head is identical to Chico's."

"Whose head?"

Diana pointed. "That boy. That boy right there."

I looked where she was pointing. "Now that you mention it, he kinda does."

As if to wake herself up, she blinked her eyes a couple of times, shaking her head.

"Why don't we see what he looks like from the front?" I suggested.

Diana got up from the seat and walked around to his front side. I stood off to the side and saw THE MOST MARVELOUS DOUBLE TAKE OF THE CENTURY. Diana, not believing her eyes, blinked several times. Chico played it to the hilt, dragging out his recognition of her. Finally he cracked a smile.

"Chico?" Diana asked tentatively.

He nodded. "Yeah, it's me."

Diana gasped in disbelief, jumped up and down, grabbed Chico, hugged and kissed him all over his face. She was crying. We all were.

After the Supremes' big smash at the Copa, nightclubs all around the country had not only opened up for them but for other Motown acts as well. Esther and her ITMI staff did an incredible job assigning managers to the various artists. They took great pride in moving very fast toward any booking opportunity that would benefit our acts. There was action all the time. Martha Reeves and the Vandellas had a sensational run at the Copa, where the Temptations had also been a hit. The Four Tops were standing room only at the Latin Casino and Stevie was getting standing ovations at the Eden Roc.

Every artist had their own notion of how to reach the top. Marvin Gaye was one who always wanted to prove he could do things his way. Knowing how much that meant to him I always tried to give him some space.

We made a deal for Marvin to play a week at Bimbo's, San Francisco's most prominent nightclub. Marvin was in Heaven. This was his dream. I reminded him not to get carried away by this fancy nightclub but to play to his audience, the people who would come from miles around to see him, especially the women. That was one of the few times he agreed with me completely.

Marvin was a sex symbol from the start. That gave me the idea to encourage the writers to create "You" type songs where he could sing directly to the women. "*YOU're a wonderful one . . .*" "*YOU are my pride and joy.*" "*How sweet it is to be loved by YOU.*" "*Little darlin' I need YOU . . .*" He even recorded a song just called "You."

Marvin's secret, he said, was that he sang every song to his wife, Anna, in tribute to the love they shared. Other women seemed to feel he was singing only to them.

When I offered to help him prepare for Bimbo's he said no. He had a great plan and would rather work it out himself.

Jumping into heavy rehearsals with the Artist Development crew—Harvey Fuqua, the show coordinator, Maurice King, band leader and vocal coach, and Cholly Atkins, choreographer—he convinced me he really meant business.

Well, the night finally came and Bimbo's was jammed. Settling proudly into my seat, I became a fan myself, getting caught up in the anticipation.

"And now, ladies and gentlemen," the announcer's voice boomed from off stage, "the man who brought you 'Stubborn Kind Of Fellow' and 'Hitch Hike' . . ."

Applause.

"The man you've all been waiting for is here, baby . . ."

Cheers, whistles and more applause!

"The man who brought you 'How Sweet It Is' and 'I'll Be Doggone' . . ."

Louder!

" 'Wonderful One' and 'Ain't That Peculiar,' baby . . ."

A deafening roar.

"Bimbo's is proud to present your 'Pride And Joy.' Maaarvin Gaye!!!"

Insanity.

The stage was black as the band struck the downbeat to a Broadway-type intro. With one pin light spilling down to show Marvin dressed in a tuxedo, top hat and cane, swooning females were letting out strange, high-pitched sounds as he stood there posing.

Finally the band built to a crescendo and bang! The band stopped. Quiet! Marvin, snapping his fingers, started singing in a slow calm voice:

"Me . . . and my shadow . . . strolling down the avenue."

What?! I thought I was dreaming. *Hoped* I was dreaming. But as he continued through the whole first verse I knew I wasn't. He then made a sharp turn, tipped his hat, flipped his cane and tapped it on the floor.

He was Fred Astaire! Where was "Pride And Joy"? Where was "Wonderful One"? Where was *Marvin Gaye?*

For his next number he slid right into "Blue Moon." There was. Fred Astaire again. The crowd was becoming more and more subdued, but continued with polite applause.

After four or five numbers like that, finally he said, "Ladies and gentlemen, there comes a time in everybody's life when they have to do things like make a living. I've put together a little medley of some of my hit songs I hope you like."

His fans came back to life with screaming applause.

He then proceeded to do almost every one of his hits in a medley that took no more than five minutes. Sitting there in a state of shock, my anger swelled as I watched my top male star apologizing for singing some of the greatest songs of the time.

When he finished the medley he sighed, "Now that that's over let's get into some real music," and went into "The Shadow Of Your Smile."

I was numb for the rest of the show, every now and then getting mad at the audience, who were probably as disappointed as I was but still applauding whatever he did.

I kicked myself for letting Marvin talk me out of seeing any rehearsals.

"BG, I just want to see you there opening night. This is going to knock you out," he had told me. Well, it did.

Knowing he never could have pulled it off without Harvey, Cholly and Maurice, the minute the show was over I dashed backstage to attack *them*. I don't know what was funnier that night—the dumbfounded look on my face watching the show or the three of them knocking into each other like bowling pins trying to get out of my way.

Marvin smiled when he saw me being pushed and pulled through the crowded doorway into his dressing room, which was blocked by a crowd of admirers. He was so excited that I had seen his show he stopped the man who was toweling off the sweat from his bare upper body to hug me. "Whatcha think, BG?"

"Marvin," I said, "what the hell were you doing out there?"

"You didn't like it?" he said with an expression that told me he thought he had done the greatest show of his life. I could see how much it meant to him to surprise me in what he thought was a wonderful way. Everybody in the dressing room knew it hadn't worked, but they weren't about to tell him. And, after realizing how hurt he'd be, neither was I.

"Oh, I liked it all right, but don't you think you should've given your hits a little more respect? I mean, most of those people came to hear *them*."

Marvin's entourage of yes men seemed paralyzed. Marvin was puzzled. He had only been hearing how great everything was. Now no one was talking.

I was still seething inside, but this was not the time for me to go crazy. Marvin was very sensitive and knew me well, and I could see he was beginning to feel something.

"I must admit, though, you really did look phenomenal in that top hat and cane. Where did you learn those steps?"

"Cholly put me through hell. Did you like 'em?"

"Oh yeah. I liked them," I said. "You were really good, but I just think you could have balanced out the show with a few more of your hit songs."

"I think BG's got a point," Harvey said. "We probably should change the show for the weekend and do more hits."

"You think so?" Marvin said.

They all chimed in, "Yeah," hoping they could get off the hook with me.

They never did. I still remind them of that today.

Marvin was full of surprises. Once he called me in the middle of the night. "BG, I've got this incredible idea for a new career."

"For who?"

"Me."

I held my breath. "What is it, Marvin?"

He paused for a moment and then came out with it. "Boxing. I want to be a boxer!"

Once before it was football. He actually tried out for the Detroit Lions and came back telling me how depressed he was when they told him he was too old. One great thing about Marvin was, even in his pain he could always find something to laugh about.

"BG, I guess I roar better than I rush," he chuckled.

Marvin had a wonderful sense of humor. His jokes were not always funny but the way he told them always made me laugh.

One day at the Rancho Park Golf Course in L.A. Marvin and I sat waiting at the seventh tee in a golf cart.

"BG, did I ever tell you the story about the proper English woman, M'lady, and her butler?"

"Only about a hundred times but I'd love to hear it again. Nobody can tell it like you," I said.

"Well," he began, in what he thought was an aristocratic English accent, "this woman comes home one night, tells her butler to follow her and she goes directly to her bedroom. Then, she says, 'James, take off me dress.' James says, 'Me-Lye-dy!' 'That's all right, James, just take it off.' He does. Then the woman says, 'James, take off me stockings,' and he says, 'But me-Lye-dy!' She insists, so he does. 'Now James, take off me brassiere.' 'Oh, but me-Lyyye-dy!' and she says, 'Take it off, I say.' And he takes it off."

The people behind us drove up in their golf cart, irritated that we were still there talking rather than playing. I jumped out of the cart and grabbed my driver. Taking a swing, I hit the ball about two hundred yards, much further than I would have if I'd stood there and taken a hundred practice swings, like I usually did. Marvin got out and hit his ball fast, too, but he wasn't so lucky, hooking it into the trees.

"Shit, BG," he said, "You know I don't like being rushed." We jumped into our cart, riding first to Marvin's ball. He got out, walked to his ball, took a couple of practice swings and started laughing. Came back over to me sitting in the cart.

" 'Now, James,' " he said, " 'take off me panties.' "

"What are you doing? Come on, Marvin, we're already holding people up."

"Oh no way, BG, you gotta hear this punch line." His voice got even more dramatic with the butler's response: " 'But me Lyyye-dy.' 'Come on, James, take them off, I say.' " Then Marvin looked at me sternly, shaking his finger, delivering his punch line: " 'And James, don't you ever, *ever* wear me clothes again."

Marvin got a bigger kick out of it than I did, but I must admit I laughed hard, not so much at the joke but at the way he told it.

There was another person in the company who we called our resident practical joker. His name was Stevie Wonder.

39. U.K. welcomes first wave of the Motown invasion.

40. The Beatles, with Pop, Terry, Berry IV and Hazel.

41. Marvin's secret weapon on the golf course was to tell me jokes.

42. The Supremes won so many gold records that it must have knocked me off my feet. *From left:* Barney Ales, Mary Wilson and Florence Ballard get a good laugh while Diana Ross and George Albert, owner of *Cash Box Magazine*, give me a helping hand.

43. I was a fanatic with all the acts, but especially with the Supremes, coaching them even while they were on stage.

44. Having fun with the Supremes during a photo session.

45. Sweethearts in Las Vegas.

46. Norman Whitfield along with Barrett Strong *(at the piano)* remind Barney Ales that he's marketing, not creative.

47. In 1963, presenting Dr. Martin Luther King, Jr., with Motown's recording of his speeches as Lena Horne and jazz musician Billy Taylor look on.

48. Two months after Dr. King's assassination, I joined Sidney Poitier, Nancy Wilson and Sammy Davis, Jr., in the Poor People's March to Freedom.

49. Sharing a joke with Pop before his big event.

50. Mother and Pop sprint down the steps of the Bethel A.M.E. Church where they celebrated their 50th anniversary by renewing their vows before their children, family and friends.

51. Diana helped present the Jackson 5 to the music industry during a party we hosted at a Beverly Hills disco, The Daisy, in 1969.

52. My son Kerry gets in on the action during a baseball game with Michael and the other Jacksons.

53. My young creative assistant, Suzanne de Passe, was always passionate about what she believed in.

54. The Corporation *(standing from left to right)*: Deke Richards, me, Freddie Perren and Fonce Mizell were responsible for the first three hits on the Jackson 5: Tito, Jackie, Michael, Marlon and Jermaine posing with their platinum records.

55. Director Sidney Furie bringing out magic in *Lady Sings the Blues*.

56. During the shooting of *Lady Sings the Blues*, talking to Diana, Shelly Berger and Richard Pryor at Malibu beach.

57. Marvin Gaye at his 40th birthday party, waiting for his turn to talk.

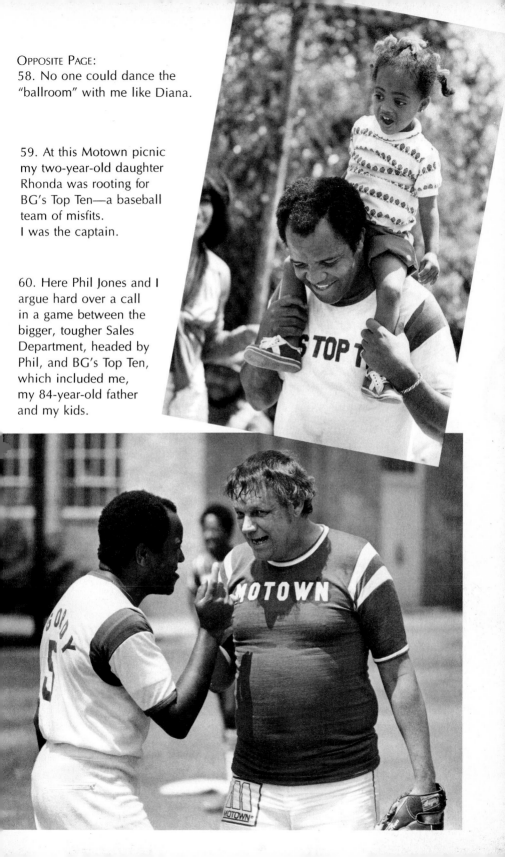

OPPOSITE PAGE:
58. No one could dance the "ballroom" with me like Diana.

59. At this Motown picnic my two-year-old daughter Rhonda was rooting for BG's Top Ten—a baseball team of misfits. I was the captain.

60. Here Phil Jones and I argue hard over a call in a game between the bigger, tougher Sales Department, headed by Phil, and BG's Top Ten, which included me, my 84-year-old father and my kids.

61. In Rome directing Anthony Perkins
and Diana Ross in a scene from *Mahogany*.

62. In Chicago, shooting the final scene of *Mahogany* with Billy Dee Williams
and a cast of hundreds.

I was heading to the studio one day when I heard somebody say: "I like that suit, Mr. Gordy."

I looked around and saw a young Stevie Wonder smiling at me. "And that's a great tie. Green, isn't it? Where'd you get it?"

I figured it was one of his pranks. Somebody had tipped him off about what I was wearing, so I decided to fool him.

"I'm not wearing a tie," I responded. "I took it off just before I came into the studio."

"Well, if you *are* wearing a tie, can I have it?"

"Okay, Stevie, who told you?"

"What? Am I blind?"

Stevie was delightful. His wit, I was told, was inherited from his mother, Lula. I always had a special fondness for her. She had helped shape Stevie's perspective on life by not allowing him or his five siblings to focus on his blindness. Ted Hull, the private tutor we hired to tour with him, though legally blind, was another very positive influence.

Stevie's sensitivity, intelligence and the way he compensated with his other senses impressed everyone. There were even some things he did that a lot of us envied—like when he was being introduced to someone. With his highly developed sense of touch, it was normal for Stevie when meeting anybody to reach out and feel their face or shoulders. After that, he would automatically recognize the person. Sometimes when it was an attractive girl, reaching for her face, his hands would "accidentally" find their way to the breast area.

Embarrassed, Stevie would quickly apologize to the girl for his "mistake." Then he'd smile in our direction as if to say, "Eat your heart out, fellas."

That was the atmosphere at Hitsville. Always a new comedy. Always a new crisis. Always a behind-the-scenes soap opera unfolding. People were still hanging out on the front lawn—some trying to catch a glimpse of one of their favorite stars, others hoping to meet somebody to get them through the front door for an audition. They came from everywhere.

Hal Davis, from our California office, had told me he was sending out a girl he wanted me to audition. Hal was hot, known in L.A. as "Mr. Motown." Remembering he had sent Brenda Holloway, I was not about to ignore him.

Chris Clark was an avid Motown fan. This opportunity meant everything to her.

The story of her audition became something she and our reception-ist, Juana Royster, loved to tell.

Seeing Chris waiting nervously downstairs, Juana sent her up to my office saying, "Don't worry. Mr. Gordy is a very nice man. Just be yourself."

While on the phone I looked up and saw a tall, earthy-looking girl with straight blond hair and blue eyes, casually dressed in sandals, coming into my office.

I smiled and motioned for her to hand me her demo record and have a seat. Getting off the phone, I played the demo she had brought. I didn't like the songs but I loved her voice. "How about doing something live," I asked.

"I hadn't planned on that."

"I know. That's why I want you to do it. For all I know you could've worked on that demo for two years."

"Do you have a piano?"

"No, I'd like to see what you can do with no help."

She took a deep breath and started belting out a soulful rendition of Etta James's "All I Could Do Was Cry"—a song co-written by me. Smart move.

"Where'd you get so much soul?" I asked.

"I spent years traveling on the road with Jazz musicians and I picked up a *lot* of things. Not the least of which was soul."

She had a kind of wit I found appealing. I also liked her voice and later found out she could write songs.

When I told her we would sign her, she was so happy. Rushing downstairs, she was stopped by Juana, who asked, "So, how'd it go?"

"Oh, I was so nervous at first," Chris confided, "just sitting there waiting, with that big black ape staring right at me."

Shocked, Juana copped an attitude.

"Oh no," Chris said. "I mean, that ceramic ape sitting on his desk."

242

Juana was relieved. "Oh, that one."

Chris had to take her shot. "Oh, I definitely wasn't talkin' 'bout that *other* one."

They both laughed and so did the whole company when they heard the story.

Over the years Chris and I became close. Very close. I loved her companionship and found with her a different kind of security, a mental security. Her mind was quicker than mine. Some people didn't know what to make of Chris's razor-sharp but extremely subtle wit or her rapid-fire jumps from one subject to the next.

We wrote many songs together, including one I produced on her called "I Want To Go Back There Again." It didn't get too big, but it is a song that meant a lot to me. Even today, it's something I love playing and singing whenever I sit down at the piano. She helped me with many creative projects for other artists. She would later be nominated for an Academy Award as a screen writer of *Lady Sings the Blues*.

It was Chris, more than anyone else, who made me realize that there were many facets to a relationship. There were definitely different levels to the one she and I had. The mental and verbal side was always there; over time the physical developed—but was never the most important part of the relationship. Since Chris had been the first white woman I had been involved with, I learned a lot from my experience with her about how the world looks at mixed couples. Color was never an issue between us but we knew it was for many others, both black and white.

The tasks of running the company had grown as explosively as the company itself. I was wearing more hats than I could count. One I did not have to wear was the day-to-day running of the A&R Department.

Except for that problem with Mary Wells, Mickey kept everything running smoothly. I did, however, get a complaint now and then when he wanted a larger percentage of a song than he was entitled to.

Mickey was a street cat, a wheeler-dealer, but I knew it was that same hustling quality that made him the superstar A&R man he was.

He could match up any kind of team—writers, producers, artists—
any combination.

He himself many times came up with a key idea, word or phrase on
somebody else's production that helped make it a smash. A motivator,
Mickey inspired greatness. He was tough but took care of his people.
They loved him and so did I.

But the time came when Mickey wanted to run his own show.
That day he called to see me I could hear something was up in his
voice. Heavy confidence was attached to his lower tones. But when
he came into my office he was a little more humble, as he told me
about a major offer he had received from MGM to set up and run a
record division for them on the West Coast.

"I think it's a big shot for me, BG. What do you think?"

What could I say? He was only asking my permission out of deep
respect. I knew we'd miss him but I wished him luck.

I would always remember Mickey Stevenson for his loyalty and
dedication. He was one of the greatest creative forces during our
formative years.

When Mickey left I decided to put Eddie Holland in as the head
of A&R. And when Billie Jean Brown took a year and a half leave
of absence to go to Spain with her husband, I appointed Brian Holland
to her position as head of Quality Control. Both moves further increased the power of HDH. Both were moves I would come to regret.

With all the action in our A&R Department there was just as
much growth and change over in our Sales Department.

As the Motown Machine was becoming more and more finely
tuned, I again decided to try something new—integrating our sales
force. With the promotion aspect of sales this had never been a
problem.

Our in-house black promotion men were vital to our growth by
getting airplay with the all-important black radio stations.

Harvey Fuqua had been our first, followed by others like Sonny
Woods, an old friend of mine who'd sung with the Midnighters, and
Weldon McDougall III, who promoted records while accompanying
artists on promo tours. We were fortunate when we were able to
get two great veterans of the business, DJ Jockey Jack Gibson from

Cincinnati and the legendary Larry Maxwell. Jack Gibson understood the mentality of the DJs better than anybody and Larry Maxwell, I felt, was absolutely the tops at promotion.

But when selling records to the mainstream market I had learned long before that you had to deal with people's prejudices.

I had not forgotten the hurt I felt when my brother's record, "Everyone Was There," had died when the public realized that this white-sounding record was performed by a black artist.

That was why we released some of our early albums without showing the artists' faces on them. The Marvelettes' album *Please Mr. Postman* had a picture of a mailbox on it; *Bye Bye Baby* by Mary Wells, a love letter. We put a cartoon of an ape on the cover of *The Miracles' Doin' Mickey's Monkey*; and an Isley Brothers album had two white lovers at the beach on its cover.

This practice became less necessary as our music's popularity started overcoming the prejudices.

But there were so many other color barriers to overcome. I remember one day sitting in Barney's office in a sales meeting when I noticed I was the only black person in the room. My own company!

After the meeting I talked to Barney and Phil. "How come there's nothing but white folks in the Sales Department?"

"You just now noticed?" Barney asked.

I smiled. "I guess I never saw black and white, I only saw record sales."

Of course I knew the Sales Department was all white. Barney had built it with experienced people he knew in the business. They were a powerful team. With their know-how, they not only dealt successfully with the distributors but with one-stops and a new sector of the market known as rackjobbers—the guys who sold records in large quantities to supermarkets and drugstores.

"You always told me you wanted a general market company, and that's what we got here," Barney said. "We want to sell our records across the board and when I put my team together, there were no black salesmen I knew out there that had ever done that or that could do it the way we needed done."

"Have you tried to find any?"

"Well, no."

"Well I think you should. If black promotion men can get white stations to play a record, why can't black salesmen get white distributors to buy them as well?"

I could see Barney was surprised because he had never known me to challenge him on the basis of race. I felt a little strange myself.

"Getting radio play is one thing, but selling records is another. The distributors are going to give you a lot more resistance than any DJ," he said. "It would be really tough—especially in the South."

"That may be. But I think we're so strong now we can change things. It's time."

"He's right," Phil jumped in. "I think we can." It was rare for any of Barney's people to side with me—in front of him.

But Barney was all for it. "Let's get on it," he told Phil.

"But we can't hire just any black guy," Phil said. "He's got to be real special, strong."

They were lucky. They found Miller London. He was shortish and thinnish, with a pleasant face and a great smile that he used a lot. My first impression was that he might be too fragile. I was wrong.

Soon he was joined by other black sales and promotion men—Chuck Young, Eddie Gilreath, Ralph Thompson and Skip Miller.

Phil enjoyed telling about one of the first incidents when he sent Miller London on a trip to the South.

As soon as Miller arrived for his first appointment at one of our major Southern distributors, Phil got a hysterical call.

"Phil," the distributor screamed, "you sent a nigger down here to sell white Pop accounts? Are you fuckin' nuts?"

"How much money do you make a year off Motown?" Phil responded.

"Oh, I don't know. Quite a bit I guess."

"Well, if you want to keep making that 'quite a bit,' you better get used to looking in that nigger's face."

Miller had been waiting in an outer office. As soon as the distributor got off the phone he rushed out smiling: "Miller, nice to see you, come on in, my friend."

Miller was in. But it took about a year of insults, threats and narrow escapes before he could breathe easily.

Mother loved coming to the company. One of her favorite places was the Sales Department.

The salesmen all loved her and developed a little routine for the times she'd bring her friends over for a tour of the company.

She'd always ask Phil Jones: "Please tell my friends who you are and what you do here."

Phil would stand up and say, "My name is Phil Jones and I sell LPs, the big records with the small holes," and sit back down. Then Irv Biegel would stand up and say, "I'm Irv Biegel and I sell 45s, the small records with the big holes." She'd go through the whole department and each would oblige her, reciting their particular duties. Then Mother would thank them and continue the tour.

As she was leaving she was sometimes heard to say, "And my son owns it all."

GROWING PAINS, BUT THE BAND PLAYS ON

MEANWHILE, AGAINST THE LARGER BACKDROP of the world around us, anger and confusion were the dominant moods of the day. In addition to the racial strife, the fighting and bloodshed of the Vietnam War had continued to mount. So too had antiwar protests and demonstrations. Polarization within the country increased.

But in all the camps there seemed to be one constant—Motown music. They were all listening to it. Black and white. Militant and nonviolent. Antiwar demonstrators and the pro-war establishment.

When I heard that kids were burning their draft cards or becoming conscientious objectors, I thought how much had changed since I was in the army. Now outspoken activists were voicing the same questions I had asked myself privately about the Korean War. What are we fighting for? What are we dying for?

The Watts riots of 1965 had been a definite sign that the simmering anger from decades of oppression could no longer be suppressed. In its wake, challenges were sent out to topple the message of nonviolence with militancy; advocates of a new creed—Black Power—were on the upswing.

In the summer of 1967 the hurricane of rage came to Detroit in what was being called the worst race riot in the nation's history.

Curfews were imposed as armored tanks patrolled the streets and National Guardsmen armed with assault rifles were stationed on the roofs of buildings, their weapons aimed down at the uneasy streets below. Hitsville was near the center of the hardest hit area. The Motown Sound gave way to sirens and bursts of gunfire as nervous producers scurried between buildings, protecting master tapes.

I ordered the offices closed but people came to work anyway.

"Keeping busy takes my mind off it."

"It's no safer at home."

"This is my home."

We continued business as usual but outside were constant reminders of the turbulence surrounding us: flames jumping, broken glass and debris from shattered windows and looted stores. Despite martial law, the rioters were still out there, running up and down the streets with stuff—toasters, sofas, stereos, TVs, everything they could carry.

During this period the civil rights movement was finally center stage in the nation's consciousness. Because of Motown's prominence, I was deluged with requests for benefit performances, contributions and endorsements from a multitude of groups. The requests were as varied as their ideologies: from "Support our peaceful sit-ins in the South," to "Stand up and be counted brotha," to "We need a positive black symbol like you to help us drive the blue-eyed devil off the face of the earth."

While I didn't agree with some of their ideologies I respected all people who were fighting against bigotry and oppression. I knew there were many roads to freedom. And just because someone wasn't on the same one as me did not mean they should be silenced.

We created the Black Forum label so that different voices could express their views. Primarily a spoken word series, it featured the speeches of Dr. Martin Luther King, Jr., Stokely Carmichael, Ossie Davis, Wallace Terry, Elaine Brown, poets Langston Hughes and Margaret Danner, and Leroi Jones—using the name Imamu Amiri Baraka.

Many years earlier, even before the great Thurgood Marshall was their counsel, the NAACP was in the forefront of the fight for civil rights. As a kid I remembered them always taking up some unpopular fight for freedom and justice. Now some thought the National Association for the Advancement of Colored People had done too little. I often said if it hadn't been for them we would never have come this far.

In 1963, on the Gordy label, I released two albums of Dr. King's most inspiring speeches ever, "Great March to Freedom" and "Great March to Washington." Not since Pop and the Reverend William H. Peck, had any man's words aroused such deep feelings within me.

Dr. King spoke of how no good could come from hatred or violence. He told me we were all victims. I was a victim and he was a victim, but white people were victims, too, when they allowed their hatred to propel them to act in the ways that some did. He understood it was coming from ignorance, fear and insecurity so he didn't hate them.

I saw Motown much like the world Dr. King was fighting for—with people of different races and religions, working together harmoniously for a common goal. While I was never too thrilled about that turn-the-other-cheek business, Dr. King showed me the wisdom of nonviolence.

He also showed me in other ways why he was such a great man.

One such incident was in Detroit when we were discussing arrangements for his speeches, which we were releasing on record. He wanted to give all the royalties to the Southern Christian Leadership Conference. My suggestion was that since it was his artistry and his performance, it was only fair that half the royalties go to him and his family. Dr. King said, "Absolutely not." He told me, "There is enough confusion out there right now, as it is. I cannot allow the perception of personal gain, right or wrong, to confuse the message of the cause."

249

I understood, admiring his vision. He made it clear—it was not only important to stand up and fight for what you believe in, but also to make sure not to confuse others.

Then in April of 1968, I heard the news. Dr. King had been assassinated in Memphis.

The very man who had fought with the weapon of nonviolence, violently shot down. He who had refused to hate when all around him were hating, now ironically snuffed out by hate. A man I so loved and admired. A man who was my friend. He was thirty-nine years old, a year older than me.

I couldn't contain my anger. I wanted to fight. But who? I knew I couldn't make it a personal fight—I had to be a part of some kind of organized response.

The first person I thought of was Ewart Abner. Ab, as we called him, was the same man who had impressed me so much at the NARA convention in Chicago back in the early sixties.

A person of high integrity, rich vocabulary and a strong sense of black pride, he had asked me for a job when his company, Vee Jay, went out of business. I jumped at the chance and hired him in May of 1967 as director of ITMI to ease the load Esther was carrying.

The other person I needed to respond to this crisis was Junius Griffin. A journalist and Pulitzer Prize candidate, Junius had been an assistant to Dr. King for two years in the mid-sixties. In the spring of 1967, I had hired him as my director of publicity. I knew he was passionate, deeply committed to the civil rights movement.

Junius was our link to the black community and theirs to us. He kept us in touch with our roots. And during personal tragedies to come, he would be the one I would turn to to handle difficult logistics. Junius and Ab became fast friends along with George Schiffer, my copyright attorney and legal adviser. George was a white Jewish liberal who'd been with me from almost the beginning. The three were the most outspoken at Motown when it came to social causes.

Junius and Ab accompanied me to meetings in Atlanta, where I had been summoned by calls from Coretta King and Harry Belafonte, to put on a benefit concert using Motown artists to launch the Poor People's March to Freedom held shortly after Dr. King's funeral. I brought Diana and the Supremes, Stevie Wonder, Gladys Knight and the Pips and the Temptations to perform. After the concert we all joined in to start the march from Atlanta that would end in Washington. I was not only proud of all the artists that came to donate their time but I felt good marching alongside Sidney Poitier, Sammy Davis, Jr., Nancy Wilson and so many other great people. As I was walking the words to a song I had written five years earlier came to my mind. "May What He Lived For Live" was a song that was very special to me for several reasons. First because the message in it was as relevant about Dr. King as it had been about President Kennedy. Second, it was recorded by one of the greatest singers I had ever worked with, a girl named Liz Lands with a four-octave range. (Ironically, Dr. King himself had introduced me to Liz at a SCLC gathering in Detroit.) And third, because I had co-written it with my sister Esther and with a gentleman who called himself W. A. Bisson. W. A. Bisson was the actor known as Stepin Fetchit, who had been the epitome of black embarrassment in the movies. It was so funny how bad he made me feel as a kid. Yet I was excited to meet him as a man. I guess I realized that he had done what he did the best way he could. And he had been a screen star bigger than life. He had been a working black actor when it was not easy for them to get roles—more power to him—and his roles had nothing to do with the smart and fine person I found him to be.

Two months later came the killing of Robert Kennedy. And so the hope of the sixties—once at an all-time high—was shattered. Things were crazy now. The bad guys were killing off our dreams one by one.

MAY WHAT HE LIVED FOR LIVE

May what he lived for live
May what he lived for live
May what he strived for
May what he died for live

251

May what he stood for stand
May what he stood for stand
Freedom for every man
And peace in every land

Enemies he made, trying all to save
Let it be now that he's gone
Dreams he had for men have no dying end
May what they tried to kill live on,
Live on, live on, live on, live on

May what he strived for
May what he died for live.

Against this backdrop of craziness and uncertainty, Motown continued to create and grow. The only thing that hadn't grown was our office space. While we continued to record at our Hitsville studio on West Grand Boulevard, we had to move our administrative offices downtown to the Donovan building, a ten-story high-rise on Woodward Avenue. But along with that growth came problems—more bills, more conflicts, more taxes, more egos.

Growing pains—we all felt them. They were part of the Cycle of Success, no different from the one that had started with me when I had my first Jackie Wilson hit. Since that time, less than ten years before, I had gone from borrowing eight hundred dollars from my family to having a company that was being embraced by the world, influencing culture. Things were moving so fast, I couldn't conceive of what it all meant.

Now many around me, most of them kids who had gone from relative poverty to wealth and fame, were getting caught into their own Cycles.

Aside from the normal problems and pitfalls facing the artists as individuals, the groups had an added one. I saw over and over again the natural process that pulled the lead singer into the spotlight. It was supply and demand. Vicious. No matter how vital the whole group, the public usually pays to see that person up front.

Unlike most other groups, in the Temptations *everybody* was a lead singer—but not like David Ruffin. He was a natural star, electrifying.

252

You knew it the minute he walked into a room. Talented he was, humble he wasn't. The more successful the Temptations became, the more the public singled him out and the more he began to isolate himself. He traveled in his own mink-lined limousine with his name on it. I was told he wanted the group's name changed to David Ruffin and the Temptations.

This was a tough, dangerous request. The Tempts' essential quality was that they were a tight, precise, perfectly synchronized unit. The five moved as one body. David was threatening that unity. It was not just their problem, it was ours, too. The seriousness of it became clear in one of our Friday meetings. The Temptations' new single was overdue.

"So, Mr. Whitfield, where are we?" I wanted to know.

"I got the tracks and the tunes, but not all the Tempts. Everybody showed up but David. This is crazy and," Norman continued, "it happens all the time. I'm tired of it and the guys are fed up."

Reports from the road were not good; tempers were out of control. I sent Shelly Berger. Whenever there was a problem with an artist who related more personally to me and I couldn't be there I knew I could count on Shelly to deal with it.

He called from Cleveland to say the group had decided to replace David. "They can't stand it anymore. They want to put him out now!"

"Wait a minute. Tell them not to be too hasty."

"I did, but they all voted. Unanimous."

David was out.

They lost no time in getting Dennis Edwards, an ex-Contour, whose soulful, gritty voice and strong presence made him a perfect replacement in the lineup.

David refused to accept it. He kept showing up at dates, trying to go on. They had trouble getting him off stage, especially since the public wanted him on.

All that stopped once we released records on him as a solo artist, something he had wanted all along. His first record, "My Whole World Ended (The Moment You Left Me)," was a hit right out of the box.

This was not the last time the Temptations' lineup would change. Years later Eddie Kendricks decided to follow a solo career, staying with the company. Working with producers Frank Wilson and Leonard Caston, he conquered the seventies disco market with hits like "Keep On Truckin' " and "Boogie Down."

Paul Williams, who I always considered the heart of the group with his emotional baritone voice, soul, rhythm and style, had sung one of the most heart-wrenching versions of "For Once In My Life" that I had ever heard. He left the group in 1971 because of ill health and died a few years later. He had been replaced by Richard Street who remained with the group until the early nineties.

Despite many personnel changes in the Temptations over the years, it was original members Otis Williams and Melvin Franklin who kept their incredible legacy alive and their group sound and style consistent. Because of them, the Temptations survived the negative pull of that vicious Cycle of Success.

While the Supremes spiraled through their own Cycle, they stayed great friends for a long time before their trouble started. From the beginning, though, there was always that subtle internal battle between Diana and Mary.

Mary didn't have the advantage of the unique voice that Diana had, but she was always in there pushing with her personality, sex appeal, acting ability and her own voice—which was good. Anytime she led a song or had a solo she attacked it with everything she had. But the more she pushed, the harder Diana worked. Diana always had to stay on her toes because she knew Mary was right there breathing down her neck.

Flo was Flo and everyone loved her. She was a unique character whose wit, sarcasm and deadpan comments kept us laughing. At times she was outgoing, fun-loving and even challenging. At other times, withdrawn and depressed. In a sense, she controlled us all. When she was happy we all were. When she wasn't it could be a nightmare. Flo was caught in the middle. The harder Diana and Mary worked at trying to outdo each other, it seemed the less motivated she became.

Traveling together there were many times of fun and closeness before the Cycle tightened its noose and a major cold war developed among the girls.

One day in London when we were doing a BBC radio show, I got together with Mary and Flo privately.

"We have a major problem," I told them. "We have a lead singer who is miserable because she is being isolated from her friends."

"We're the ones being isolated," Mary snapped. "She gets out there on the stage and acts like we're not even there."

"Yeah," Florence added, "she ain't nothin' but a show-off."

"I agree with you," I said, "but let's take a look at it. Nothing has changed. Remember when I first met you all? She was a show-off then, too. In fact one of the reasons we're here doing this show today is *because* she's a show-off. We should all be happy about that. But that's not the real issue." I went on to tell them that they were the Supremes, the top female group in the world, and reminded them that they all shared equally, that even though Diana was the lead, she didn't make any more money than they did, and didn't want to. All she wanted was the way it used to be—friends. "One thing I know for sure is that she loves both of you. It seems to me you all should be able to work it out."

"You're right," Mary agreed.

"We'll try," Flo nodded sincerely.

Back in Detroit running the company, I had much less contact with them over the next few months, but based on what I was hearing from the chaperones and road managers, nothing had really changed with the girls. Plus, they told me, there was another problem—Flo's drinking. She was showing up late for shows and interviews, skipping rehearsals, putting on too much weight.

Diana and Mary confirmed this and told me how hard it had been on them. Their keeping it from me had actually brought them closer together.

Everybody knew how I felt about drinking and drugs. They had heard me say many times: "It's easier to stay out than to get out."

It seemed the harsher the warning, the more flagrant Flo's behavior became. It finally got to a point where we had to bring in Cindy Birdsong, formerly of Patti LaBelle and the Blue Belles, to be on standby and go on when Flo didn't show up. Cindy was good. She had a great voice, a sweet disposition. She learned the routines quickly, and, most of all, she was reliable.

Florence became less and less so. Finally, in July of 1967, we all knew she had to be replaced.

At the time we decided not to publicly disclose the reasons for Flo's dismissal. In the sixties alcoholism was not dealt with the way it is today. It was something to be kept secret.

Although we decided to record and release records on Florence as a solo artist, before we could do so she got an offer from ABC Records and severed her relationship with Motown.

A lot has been written and said about the tragedy that surrounded Flo's life after she left Motown—the stint at ABC that didn't work out, the legal action she brought against a lawyer whom she accused of misappropriating her funds. She was caught in a downward spiral that took a terrible toll on her life. Her death nine years later was very sad to all of us who knew her in happier times.

I will never forget Flo, Tammi Terrell, Paul Williams, Shorty Long and those other unique and talented people who made outstanding contributions to Motown and died too young.

The same summer Cindy came in, the name change to "Diana Ross and the Supremes" was made.

Shelly Berger made a deal for them to do a guest appearance on an episode of the *Tarzan* series.

Tarzan was shot on location in Mexico. James Earl Jones co-starred with Diana, Mary and Cindy, who were playing nuns. Because this was their first dramatic acting opportunity, I was frantic to make it work. At this point I was unfamiliar with this part of the business so there was not a lot for me to do. I just sort of hung out, taking in this whole exciting process.

I noticed Diana and James Earl Jones off to the side, working on something. I went over and heard them rehearsing the words to a duet.

Songs, singing? Great! There *was* something I could do to help—make this duet the greatest ever.

During spare moments I got Diana and James together under the trees to work on the song. James was excited and could not have been more cooperative. He, with that deep, beautiful voice, and

Diana, soft, seductive, blending with the authentic jungle noises. I loved what I was hearing.

Just as I reached my highest point of enthusiasm, the director came over and politely but emphatically kicked me off the set.

Embarrassing. Especially in front of Diana.

Besides, I was the Supremes' manager and deserved more respect. I knew how bad the show wanted the girls.

Should I threaten to take them off? No, much too dramatic. Plus if they called my bluff I'd be in worse trouble.

I tried another approach. On location with us was Mike Roshkind, the aggressive head of our Public Relations Division. I wanted him to find the person who owned the show.

"Ask and you shall receive, my friend," he said.

Mike could do anything. The only problem was he would never tell anybody how he did it. (He did confide in me once, though, when I was amazed that he was able to find an out-of-town heart specialist in an emergency, that he had gotten the doctor's number from the yellow pages.)

Anyway, Mike found out who owned the show. It turned out to be a guy in Los Angeles named Sy Weintraub. When I called him, he was very warm.

He knew of me and my music and thought my ideas for that episode were great, but told me there was nothing he could do. He never got involved with the shows.

I understood.

It was clear to me I had to make peace with the director.

So the next morning before going on the set I prepared my personality for an extensive exercise.

Walking on the set I saw he was busy and was about to turn away when he caught me in his view and started walking my way.

Oh shit, more trouble, more embarrassment. But my well-trained personality kicked into gear and was ready for action.

"Mr. Gordy," he called. "I'm glad you're here." He reached out to shake my hand. "How are you today?"

"Uh, fine, fine. How are you?"

"Y'know that idea you had about having them sing it freely and natural without the music was *wonderful*. I love your help on this stuff and any more ideas you get *please* feel free to just come and let me know."

I don't know what Sy did, but whatever it was, it was very effective. Sy and I later met in California and became the best of friends. He told me that the airing of that show brought the highest rating of any *Tarzan* episode.

That show had given me my first real feeling of the movies.

Toward the end of '67, in New York City, I first met Suzanne de Passe. The girls were making one of their frequent appearances on *The Ed Sullivan Show* when Cindy Birdsong introduced me to her friend.

I could see Suzanne was young, bright and pretty. I soon found out she was also brash. When I saw her again a few months later in Miami with the Supremes, she didn't hesitate to tell me what was on her mind.

"Mr. Gordy, I love your company but I don't think it's being run right."

"Excuse me?"

"They're not taking care of business and I just thought you should know."

She then told me of the troubles she had been having trying to book Motown acts for a New York theater owner. "No one at your company returns calls. For the last month I've been trying to get the Miracles. If they don't want them to do the show, that's one thing. But to not even return a call is just rude—*and* bad business."

The more we talked, the more impressed I became. I liked the way she got right to the point, didn't waste my time. I could use somebody like that.

"You think maybe you could help run the company better?"

"Who me? Well I'd love to try."

I liked her. I had no idea what her job would be, but two weeks later I flew her to Detroit. I put her on the payroll, telling her to return to New York and I would get back to her later.

After a few weeks of not hearing from me, she called my office in

Detroit. "Mr. Gordy, have you forgotten me? You're paying me and I'm not doing anything."

"I know. When I have something for you to do, I'll let you know. Don't you think you're worth waiting for?"

"Oh, yes sir, Mr. Gordy, sir. How stupid of me! How crazy we mortals become on lack of sleep . . ."

"Can I go now?"

"Of course, Mr. Gordy, sir. I'll be right here."

When I announced I was bringing in a new girl from New York everybody was puzzled.

"To do what?" Ralph Seltzer asked.

"I don't know," I said, "but I know she's great and should be here. Probably my creative assistant. She knows about music and artists."

Ralph's face showed that familiar expression of frustration that my executives had whenever I made up my mind to do something they thought impractical.

In my first talk with Suzanne about the best way to work together, I gave her my ground rules: "As long as you're honest with me, everything will be fine. If I ask for an opinion, don't hesitate to be critical—even of me. Never say something just because you think that's what I want to hear. Be yourself. I pay people for *their* ideas not mine."

She took me at my word—and her first day on the job was almost her last.

My sister Esther was also in charge of the Art Department at the time and had some new album covers she wanted me to approve. Esther was very dedicated to anything she did. From the time she pioneered our first bookkeeping office at Motown to now, she had always fought for the very best for me, the company and the artists. I loved her devotion but I didn't like her taste in album covers— which was a small point of controversy between us. She had heard me say many times, "The real boss around here is not me, it's *logic*," so she was "logically" trying to show me why those album covers were good. I couldn't always put my finger on what it was I didn't like; all I knew was they didn't knock me out.

I got the bright idea that if I brought in a fresh, objective opinion more connected to what was going on out there, we might both learn something. I think we did.

I took Suzanne up to Esther's office, spread the new album covers out and asked what she thought.

Suzanne, being new, didn't know anything about Esther's power or prestige or that she was responsible for the covers, or that I was sort of setting her up. All she knew was to be honest.

After studying them for a few minutes, Suzanne pointed to the Temptations' cover. "Outdated. Nobody's got processed hair any-more. They've been into naturals for some time now. These must be old photos. And that Four Tops' cover looks very stiff. Levi looks like he's smelling something."

Then picking one up, she said, "Smokey, my favorite artist. Where did they get those clothes?" She continued, spotting something wrong with most every cover. Turning to me with a shrug, she said, "Basi-cally, Mr. Gordy, I guess you could say they don't really work for me."

She knew she had done exactly what I had told her to do and exhaled with pride, looking at me for acknowledgment of a job well done. I gave her a smiling nod while knowing she was in big trouble with Esther. But she was not the only one. I had proven my point and won the battle, but now the war was about to start.

Esther was silent. There was a growing tension in the room. I told Suzanne to go wait in my office.

Esther still hadn't said anything as the two of us stood there alone, avoiding each other's eyes. I had wanted to prove a point to Esther and now that I had I felt bad. I tried to think of something to say that would make everything all right. "So what do you think of the new girl," I said half jokingly.

"Either she goes or I go," Esther said and walked out.

Soft-spoken, easygoing Esther had just given me an ultimatum! I hated ultimatums. But I was a realist and I knew losing Esther would be a lot more damaging than losing a newcomer.

On the other hand, how could I, in good conscience, fire someone for honesty, for doing exactly what I had told her to do? For a few days Esther avoided talking to me. Finally, I went into her office and I tried to explain my position, practically begging her to understand that it wasn't Suzanne's fault and that she was only doing what I had told her to do. How could I fire her for that? "It's a matter of principle."

As mad as she was with me, she understood that.

Esther didn't leave, but she did check out Suzanne's comments with some other people, and soon after revamped the Art Department and brought in a new director.

Adherence to principle was always an important recurring theme for me. Earlier, Diana had come to me about something that was really bothering her—the terms of the "slave contract" at the Copa. We were about a year away from fulfilling the three-year deal I'd originially made with Jules Podell. Even though the girls were stars now, they wanted to know why they were still only earning $15,000 a week at the Copa, when they could be making $50,000 for one-nighters.

"When we signed the contract it was worth it then and now we've got to honor it," I explained. "Sure, you could be getting $50,000 a night now. And you know why? Partly because of the Copa. Without the Copa, you wouldn't have gotten the Cocoanut Grove, or Vegas, and all the other big nightclubs. When I signed that 'slave contract' we needed them. Now, we have to be honorable." Though we lost money every time they played the Copa, it had been more than well worth it.

When the three years were up Jules offered a much better deal. But his best deal was nowhere near the Waldorf-Astoria's and that's the one I took, moving Diana Ross and the Supremes on to greener pastures. Insiders to the club scene were stunned. "You're going to have real trouble with Jules Podell," they warned, suggesting that I ought to fear for my life.

I never gave it a second thought. I knew we did right by him and he wouldn't forget it. Much to the surprise of many—I lived.

There was never any rest, never any letup. I got used to putting out little fires that ignited every day. But I was about to have an inferno on my hands—a real disaster. HDH was leaving.

Signs of trouble had sparked several months before when their productions began to drop on the charts. After their Supremes' "Reflections" went to #2 in September of 1967, the next release, "In And Out Of Love," only made it to #9. Then I was told HDH had stopped recording and were on some sort of strike.

Eddie Holland, Brian Holland and Lamont Dozier were nowhere to be found.

By February of '68, having no new product for the Supremes, we were forced to go back to the can, releasing "Forever Came Today"— cut a year before. That record stopped at a dismal #28.

As creative people they might not have been able to come up with any new ideas, but how could Eddie, my head of A&R, and Brian, my head of Quality Control, be on strike? And why?

I thought back to around the time of their first hit, Martha and the Vandellas' "Come And Get These Memories," when Eddie had come and told me he would be representing the group.

"For what?" I asked.

"Business. I'll negotiate for all three of us."

"You all have long-term writers' and producers' contracts. What's there to negotiate now?"

"Oh, I don't know," he said. "Brian and Lamont aren't money-minded. I have to keep them motivated."

It was true—Eddie was much more money-minded.

"Does Brian know about this?" I asked.

"Yes."

Brian had been with me even before there was a Hitsville. Most of the time he slept on a couch or on the floor, always watching, assisting, learning. He was sensitive, sharp and had a pure heart. I cared about him and we'd always had great communication.

When Eddie told me about this I went to one of the piano rooms to talk to Brian. I could see he felt awkward and was having as much trouble as I was with the situation.

"I hope you understand and have no hard feelings," he said. "But that's my brother and you know how it is . . ."

I knew how much Brian loved his brother and I understood. I was apprehensive about it, but I understood.

True to my apprehensions, Eddie's constant requests for added incentives had mounted through the years. They were great as a team and I knew I had to pay an additional cost to keep them happy. It was a part of doing business.

After a series of generous readjustments to his compensation package, which I had agreed to, there had been that last "request" Eddie had made for a personal, interest-free loan. I had said no. I felt this so-called strike might have had something to do with that.

"They are negotiating now with Capitol Records," I was being told by everybody. This was really bad news.

Not only had they become one of the most prolific writing and producing hit teams of that time, but had risen to such power positions in the company that their leaving could mean disaster in many ways.

Though I could not calculate what losing them would cost, I sued them for $4 million for breach of contract. I wanted them back and I figured it was only a matter of time before they would come to their senses.

Everyone in the company rallied around me. When Smokey got the news, he came into my office burning. "Berry, how can they do that? After all you've done for them, for all of us. But don't worry man, we'll keep it going. Me and Whit and the others will get plenty of smashes. We can handle it. You'll see."

I appreciated Smokey but I didn't think he was aware of the extent of the problem. Aside from our losing their creative genius, the departments they headed were already in chaos—masters needed Brian's approval and the studio scheduling and other duties that Eddie was in charge of were not being handled.

Although I had some serious fears about the situation, my ego would not permit me to think that I couldn't do it without them. After all, I had taught them, given them opportunities and driven them not just to be good but to be the best.

When they didn't come back to work after I filed the lawsuit, I knew I had to move forward without them. As much as everyone else wanted to help me, I knew the company's survival was all on my shoulders. If what I did worked, I'd be a hero; if it didn't, a bum.

I let my legal people worry about the lawsuit, and appointed Ralph Seltzer to head A&R, now referred to as our Creative Division. Billie Jean Brown, back from her leave of absence in Spain, took over

Quality Control. I took my battle into the studio where my mission was clear—to come up with a record on the Supremes that sounded so much like HDH that nobody would know the difference.

I wanted the song to be a little deeper than the typical Supremes songs, but I had no idea what that would be.

First I had to assemble a group to work with me. I looked around for people who were really talented and wanted to prove themselves. I came up with three relative newcomers—Deke Richards, Frank Wilson and R. Dean Taylor. In Deke, who had a soulful feel on the guitar, I saw great potential as a writer and producer and made him my assistant in charge of the project.

I thought Frank Wilson, from the West Coast, also had tremendous potential as a writer/producer. R. Dean Taylor was an artist and writer/producer from Canada who I felt was very clever with lyrics. Then, to keep everything together, I brought in the more experienced Hank Cosby from the A&R Department.

I called our new production unit "The Clan."

"Klan?" they asked. "Like the Ku Klux Klan?"

I told them it was a matter of semantics. Once again I wanted to take a so-called negative word, and use it positively. I was using Clan with a C for its meaning as a group of friends linked by a common purpose. Our purpose was to get a #1 record on the Supremes.

I didn't want to use individual names because I wanted to keep egos at a minimum. "We're a team and we'll stay together and produce many more songs."

I took them down to Detroit's Pontchartrain Hotel where I told them we'd lock ourselves in until we came out with the right product. We worked around the clock, everyone grabbing a few hours' sleep here and there.

On about the second day of coffee and frustration, throwing ideas out in the air that nobody particularly liked, I started playing what felt like Holland-Dozier-Holland type chords—to get in the mood for what I was looking for.

In the key of A minor I started playing with a sad, soulful feel. Soon everyone in the room was throwing out lyrics and melodies to match my chords.

After what seemed like a mountain of mediocre ideas, Pam Sawyer

264

came up with a concept I liked. Pam was an offbeat English writer signed to Jobete who I'd called in to help with the writing.

"What about a baby born out of wedlock?" she said. " 'Love Child.' "

" 'Love Child?' " somebody muttered. "A song about a baby with no daddy for Diana Ross and the Supremes?"

"No," somebody else said, "not the Supremes. They're America's sweethearts. It's too heavy for the Supremes."

"I like it," I said. "I want an idea that's heavy. It fits, it really does. 'Love Child'—I love it."

That's how the song began. After that, I asked Pam to expand on what the story might be. As she told it, coming up with a lot of the lyrics at the same time, we all added and changed, added and changed, refining and adapting as we continued to work. Ultimately, we arrived at a really touching story about a girl who herself was born out of wedlock and is telling her boyfriend that she doesn't want to go the wrong way with him and bring another love child into the world. We had managed to take a negative image and turn it around in a positive way. Now it was perfect for the Supremes.

From there it was a matter of Deke and me working out the rest of the chord structure as we all polished lyrics, melody, and began getting the production ideas lined up. We left the Pontchartrain and went immediately to the studio to cut the track.

When the Supremes recorded the song the depth in the storyline I had been looking for came through:

You think that I don't feel love,
What I feel for you is real love,
In other's eyes I see reflected a hurt, scorned, rejected.
Love Child, never meant to be,
Love Child, born in poverty,
Love Child, never meant to be,
Love Child, take a look at me.
I started my life in an old, cold, rundown tenement slum
My father left, he never even married Mom.
I shared the guilt my mama knew,
So afraid that others knew I had no name.

This love we're contemplating, is worth the pain of waiting.
We'll only end up hating the child we may be creating.
Love Child . . .

When we released the record, everyone assumed it was HDH. We felt it was a #1 record and we were right. But we were surprised when it got there so fast and when it outsold every Supremes record before it.

Shortly before the release of "Love Child," we had made a deal to do three television specials in partnership with the producers of *Laugh-In*, George Schlatter and Ed Friendly. I had heard that there was nobody better at comedy or variety shows than George Schlatter, so I was looking forward to working with him. Then we started rehearsals for the first one—*TCB—Takin' Care of Business*, starring Diana Ross and the Supremes and the Temptations.

My system of getting right to the point and saying what was wrong and then doing it again and again until it was right was demanding, I admit, but it had always worked with Diana. She thrived under that kind of pressure. That was all she knew. Then along came George.

George was someone who had his own style, and it was different than mine. Though I used charm and humor sometimes to get things done, it was not like George's.

"Diana," he'd say, tickling her ribs, "did you know you have a funny box in you?"

"I do?"

"Yes you do, and whenever you turn it on, something funny will come out."

One day he said cheerfully after a run-through of "I'm Gonna Make You Love Me" with both groups, "I loved what you did, that little skip you added when you came down the ramp, and your nod to Mary and Cindy, and the way you smiled at Melvin, and taking the mike from Dennis and handing it back . . ." He continued, going over everything he loved and then with Diana beaming he said, "Just a couple things . . ." Then he went into problems at least twice as long as mine would have been. The problem for me was when he got through Diana was still beaming.

266

At first I thought that was a waste of time, but when she started coming off funnier, I started paying more attention.

I could see Diana wished I could be more like him. At times, I did, too.

He not only did that with Diana, he did it with everybody—including me. I loved working with the man. He could be so outrageous. The atmosphere on the set was always an up one. When he wanted one of our acts for his shows that he couldn't get through the agencies or our other people, he would hunt me down. One time he was doing a show with Lucille Ball and Dinah Shore called *Like Hep* and he needed Diana to complete the threesome. Having been turned down by everyone, he sent me a telegram from a ship somewhere in the Atlantic telling me how good this would be for Diana, and if I said no he was canceling his trip and coming back to burn crosses on my front lawn. I could never refuse George—but it all paid off.

Some years later Diana brought over the tape of a TV show she'd done on her own that needed major help. The air date was a few days away. I needed George. When I called him, he told me he and his wife, Jolene, were leaving for China with Frank Sinatra. After hearing of my predicament, he said he would let the boat sail without him and join them later. George and I went into the studio to reedit the show. He was the only man I knew who could get technical people to actually have fun working with us nonstop for something like forty-eight hours straight to get it done.

TCB, our first special together, aired in December of 1968 on NBC. It received rave reviews and a huge audience. The show's soundtrack album went to #1. This had all been exciting for us. But I, meanwhile, was dealing with a devastating situation. A month before I had gotten a call from Harold Noveck.

"You're being countersued by HDH for $22 million."

"They're suing *me*?? For what?"

"For everything."

"Like what?"

"Like everything. I'll have the complaint over to you tomorrow."

It wasn't necessary for me to read the complaint, because in the next few days it was all over the newspapers. *Jet* magazine's headline said: "PRIZEWINNING SONGSMITHS SUE MOTOWN CORP. FOR $22 MILLION." The *Michigan Chronicle*, the black newspaper that I had grown up with, blasted the headline: "SONGWRITERS CLAIM: MOTOWN SUIT NOT VINDICTIVE MOVE." The *Detroit Free Press* proclaimed: "SONGWRITERS SUING 'DADDY' GORDY FOR $22 MILLION: THE STORY BEHIND THE SOUR NOTES AT MOTOWN."

It was clear to me that instead of defending themselves against my lawsuit, they were throwing up a smokescreen with this absurd counterattack, attacking me on everything I stood for in business and as a person.

Nobody ever said HDH were not creative. They and their attorneys had charged me with every allegation in the book: cheating, conspiracy, fraud, deceit, portraying themselves and all the Motown artists as exploited victims held prisoners by this Svengali monster.

Seeing these allegations in print really bothered me. It hurt to think many in the public would believe them.

Most at Hitsville were dumbfounded. Some were outraged. Smokey was one of them. He took it upon himself to issue his own press release, writing:

> Motown was started on the idea of whatever money a person has coming—give it to them. Whether it's a penny or a million dollars—if they've earned it—pay them. "Honesty is our only policy." So it gets me angry to hear people who have been a part of our love and family feeling—telling people that Motown has not paid them every penny they had coming.
>
> Each year Motown pays out many millions of dollars to its creative people who keep coming up with the product. I've seen royalty checks for people from ninety-eight cents to hundreds of thousands of dollars. I know Motown pays. I've even forgotten some of my royalty checks and been called two weeks after royalty date and asked to please come pick up the check. This makes it hard for me to understand how guys like the three well-known writers and producers, who to my knowledge, never had jobs before being made

popular at Motown, could ever leave. They were paid millions in royalties and had key positions in the organization. What more could a young man ask for?

Summing up, Smokey recommended that anyone in doubt ought to stop by our management offices and check out just what was being done for the artists on a twenty-four-hour basis:

> Even our not so popular artists are receiving free artists development training courses so that they can still work on dates and earn some money. There are many beneficial things happening and going on at Motown on behalf of our artists, producers, and writers, which are not even considered at other companies. No brag—just fact.

Though I had always ignored rumors before, this had me so emotionally charged I wanted to go straight to the press and tell everybody how totally ridiculous this was. But after thinking about it more I realized that that would not necessarily make it better and it might even make it worse. So I restrained myself, deciding to continue letting the legal people handle it.

Few successful institutions or people escape rumors, because they're usually more exciting than the truth. We were no exception. One of those had sprung up a couple of years before: Motown was controlled by the Mafia.

That rumor started when a mysterious little article appeared in a small neighborhood news sheet. Without any specifics it alleged that Motown was being taken over by the Mafia. Because that paper had such insignificant distribution, we paid no attention. In fact, we laughed at it.

Well, that little article turned out not to be so funny when larger papers picked it up.

The mere fact that Barney Ales, an Italian, was running our powerful Sales Department was enough to perpetuate such a rumor. There was no substantiation whatsoever, but through time it picked up steam and plagued me for many years.

The FBI even called me into their offices because of the rumor.

269

No one is ever so innocent that getting called down to the FBI is fun.

When I got to their offices that morning they assured me it was just routine. I was taken to a room by two agents who said they had information on every mob connection in the country. They knew everyone who was controlled by the mob, and either there was a mob guy they didn't know about—which was unlikely—or I was not connected to the mob. That was the end of it, except for a personal request of me: "By the way, can we have your autograph?"

But even after that FBI clean rating, somehow the Motown-Mafia story kept resurfacing. *They gotta be crooks!* How could one of the most successful independent record companies in the world be owned and operated by a black man without being crooked?

Barney did not mind his newfound celebrity. He had fun with it. Occasionally someone would ask him about it.

"Mr. Ales, this Mafia connection, is it true . . . ?"

"Well, *I am* Italian and *I am* from Detroit," he'd say with a deadpan expression—and then lean right into their face. "You godda problem wid dat?"

The one good thing about it was sometimes it was a little easier to collect our money.

But over the years no rumor was as painful to me as the one that accused Motown of cheating its artists. The HDH allegations had helped to make it worse.

People were looking for reasons why Motown was so successful. Because of the reputation of some independent companies ripping off their artists, some people assumed that Motown must be doing that, too. Ironically, the very reason that artists and writers were stampeding to our door was because they found out that we *were* paying. I was a creative person just like they were and knew the value of paying creative people for what they already loved to do. The reason this accusation bothered me so much was I had made every effort to ensure that people would be paid everything due them. Not only was it the right thing to do, it was good business.

What was due them was clearly defined in our contracts. When our royalty rates were questioned, I checked it out and reconfirmed that Esther had originally patterned our contracts after United Artists'. So we knew they were on par with the industry, and in some cases, even better than other labels.

The systems set up by the Novecks, who were exact to the penny, made sure that every cent of an artist's earnings was paid to them and that all expenses charged to them—like sessions costs—were authorized and correct. A fanatic for checks and balances, I insisted they create safeguards to prevent overcharging expenses or undercrediting earnings. For example, after the Royalty Department generated the royalty statement they would meet with heads of Management and A&R, questioning each and every charge to make sure there were no errors in processing the information.

The issue of cheating bothered me also because I felt we were unique in keeping artists who weren't necessarily getting hits under contract for year after year. We treated them just like the artists who *were* getting hits—spending money on recording and promoting them, paying many different types of bills for them, and giving them cash advances. All of our creative people were always asking for advances, and I, being a creative person, usually gave it to them.

When you're a star or just living like one you tend to forget about those advances through the year that let you live that way. But at royalty time when you see the money you already spent reflected in the size of the check, it's understandably disappointing. But no one's been cheated.

Still, anytime complaints were brought to my attention or if an artist thought he had something more coming, I would jump on it immediately and get to the bottom of it. Because it was such a personal thing with me, I did everything I could to find out what it was and correct it if there was a problem. I would have artists and their representatives come in and check our books until they were satisfied.

In spite of over thirty years of audits that have confirmed accurate accounting and proper payment over and over again, the rumors have persisted. Probably the biggest reason they did is because I did not defend against them at the time. My policy was never to comment publicly on the bad or good. Maybe I should have set this record straight a lot sooner. Then again, if I hadn't stayed focused on my mission, there may not have been a Motown to have rumors about.

The HDH lawsuit dragged on for around four years. As time went on I felt more and more that this was becoming a personal vendetta on Eddie's part, benefiting none of us.

Disagreement or not, the fact was these guys had once shared my vision and helped me make history. I did not want war to be our legacy.

On January 3, 1972, we settled. I don't know how many hundreds of thousands of dollars it cost all of us, but the only financial winners were the lawyers.

Despite the victory with "Love Child," HDH's leaving in 1968 adversely affected us in many ways. As hard as we tried, we never were able to find writers and producers who could deliver with the same consistency for groups like the Four Tops and Martha and the Vandellas.

One person HDH's departure did not hurt was Norman Whitfield—who was now on the rise. Even back in '67, before HDH left, Norman had started coming on stronger than ever.

It was at that time that he started writing regularly with Barrett Strong, the artist who had sung "Money," one of my first hits. Their collaborations would yield almost five years of continuous hits as they led the Tempts in a whole new direction toward uptempo, driving rhythms with lyrics that reflected a growing social consciousness. And the very first Whitfield and Strong collaboration was about to become a major hit on two different artists.

At the Friday meeting when we first heard "I Heard It Through The Grapevine," Billie Jean Brown was seated next to me, tightly clutching the master references that she had decided would be voted on that day. Near her, as usual, were two turntables upon which the competing songs would be played. In the case of a close vote she would switch back and forth between the two to give everyone in the meeting a chance to better compare.

Billie Jean was feared by almost every producer in the room because they knew she "had my ear." She had as keen a sense for what was a hit as anyone I knew. And she knew it. That's why she sat there like a diva in the last act waiting for her solo. She was expressionless; nothing moving except her squinting eyes, which darted back and forth from one hopeful producer to the other as if to say, "Yes, I hold your fate in my hands." She knew, like we all did, that the moment of truth had arrived again.

For Norman it was his production of "I Heard It Through The Grapevine" on Marvin Gaye, up against the HDH production also on Marvin called "Your Unchanging Love."

When the majority of the votes were for "Grapevine," Norman was encouraged, but he knew he still had to overcome a major obstacle—me. Most of the time I gave in to a majority vote, but this time I announced I was overriding the group and going with "Your Unchanging Love." I personally liked "Grapevine" better, but I felt the other record was more in the romantic vein of what Marvin needed.

Norman sprang to his feet to make his case. "This is a smash, a number one record and I know it. I got those chills I get when I know I got a hit! And you know my chills don't lie!"

"Norman," I told him, "I love innovation, but I'm going with HDH. That's it."

Though Norman was devastated, he knew in our game "a winner wins and a loser keeps on trying." He became even more persistent. For the next few months, everywhere I went it seemed he would be there mentioning "Grapevine." One day he followed me to the 20 Grand, came over to my table and said, "Uh, excuse me, sir. Since it can't go out on Marvin, can I cut it on another artist?"

I stared at him in disbelief. I'll never forget the look on his face. He was begging for something he really believed in. At that moment he probably could have gotten anything from me.

"Norman, do whatever you want to do with it. I don't care. Just stay out of my face till it's done."

"Thank you," he said, rushing off.

The next time I heard the song it was a totally different production. Gladys Knight and the Pips' version, with its uptempo Gospel feel, bore little resemblance to the version Norman had cut on Marvin. It zoomed through the Friday meeting and right to the top of the charts.

When I had first seen Gladys Knight and the Pips perform at the Apollo in 1966, I knew right away how sensational they were. Gladys was smart. She could talk to an audience and articulate what she wanted to say with just the right words. And those Pips—her brother

273

Merald and cousins Edward Patten and William Guest. Smooth. Sharp. They were dynamite backup for Gladys, complementing her on every turn. I was impressed with their class, artistry and stage presence. And on top of that, Gladys could "sang." What a voice! From Atlanta, she had warm Southern charm and a hint of Country soul, mixed in with an infectious Gospel feel.

There was also a family feeling about them that made me feel close to them from the beginning. Unlike many of our main acts who had been through our artist development process, Gladys and the Pips were already seasoned before coming to Motown. That meant I would not have to spend as much time in a hands-on capacity with this group. They had actually worked with some of our key Artist Development people earlier in their career. When they were starting out Gladys's mother had written to Maurice King at the Flame Show Bar and asked him to work with them. And Cholly Atkins, our choreographer, had been responsible for their stage routines I liked so much. Larry Maxwell, the great promotion man I had hired, was also their manager.

I was thrilled when Norman gave them their first big hit.

About a year later, he was campaigning to release Marvin's record of "Grapevine" as a single, reminding me of the great vote it had gotten at that Friday meeting—and also reminding me that the HDH record that I did release hadn't done well.

I told him he was right, but now it was too late. It would be crazy to release the same song on Marvin so soon after it had gone to #1 on Gladys and the Pips.

"Yeah, I know," he said, "but they're two totally different arrangements."

"So what? They're still the same song. Forget it, Norman."

When it came time to release another Marvin Gaye album, Norman was right back in my face. This time in front of Hitsville as I was going in. "Mr. Gordy, I know you told me not to bug you about this song no more," he said cautiously.

"Yes, I did."

"But sir, you always told us that name value songs help albums sell better."

"Yeah."

"Well, 'I Heard It Through The Grapevine' has name value now. So can I put it on Marvin's album?"

"What did Billie Jean say?"

"She said it's too late. The songs have already been picked and sequenced in the album."

Realizing I'm talking to a man with a #1 record now, I was a little more respectful. "All right, Norman, you got it. I'll have Billie Jean change the lineup and stick 'Grapevine' in."

He was so happy he looked like he wanted to hug me.

The DJs played it so much off the album that we had to release it as a single. Almost a year to the day after Gladys Knight and the Pips' version had reached the top, Marvin Gaye's version of "I Heard It Through The Grapevine" was at #1. It was Marvin's first #1 Pop single and the song became the biggest seller in Motown's history at that time, remaining at #1 for seven consecutive weeks.

Very soon after I had given the go-ahead to release the single on Marvin, there Norman was again outside Hitsville—waving an acetate in my face. "Mr. Gordy, you've got to hear this new record I just cut on the Tempts. It's great. I can't wait for the meeting, you've got to hear this now."

I knew now that whenever Norman Whitfield was this excited he usually had something. I couldn't wait for the meeting either. We went into my office to play it:

Childhood part of my life, it wasn't very pretty.
You see, I was born and raised in the slums of the city.
It was a one room shack that slept ten other children besides me.
We hardly had enough food or room to sleep.
It was hard times,
Needed something to ease my troubled mind.
Listen!
My father didn't know the meaning of work.
He disrespected Mama and treated us like dirt.
I left home seekin' a job that I never did find,
Depressed and down-hearted, I took to Cloud Nine

* * *

I'm doing fine up here on Cloud Nine . . .
Let me tell you about Cloud Nine.
(Cloud Nine) you can be what you wanna be,
(Cloud Nine) you ain't got no responsibility,
And ev'ry man, ev'ry man is free,
(Cloud Nine) and you're a million miles from reality.
I wanna say I love the life I live,
And I'm gonna live the life I love up here on Cloud Nine
I'm riding high—On Cloud Nine . . .

As soon as I heard the intro, I loved the song. The rhythm, melody, vocal arrangements were unlike anything he had done before. It was another of Norman's innovations, another example of his refusal to stay in one place creatively. The performance of the group, especially Dennis Edwards's lead, was great. But I had a problem with the lyrics. The first verse was fine about growing up poor in the ghetto. I could relate to that. But what were they talking about—*"I'm doing fine up here on Cloud Nine . . . a million miles from reality . . . riding high"*?

When the song was over I said, "Great, Norman—it was really great. But the words, you gotta change them. They just won't work. We can't put this record out. Not because it isn't a good song but because it sounds like you're promoting drugs."

"No," Norman protested, "it's not drug-related. It's art."

"Norman," I said, reminding him how people saw Motown as a clean, straight institution, "we have a responsibility not to send out a message that could be interpreted the wrong way."

"Artistic freedom of expression!" he argued. "Ain't that s'pose to be what Motown is about?"

I smiled. He did have a point.

Norman continued. "Besides, this is nothin' compared to the type of stuff other labels put out."

"I don't care what other labels put out. I don't care if it has some commercial shock value. There's nothing wrong with a shock technique, it works. But to use it where it sounds like you're talking about using dope is taking artistic freedom a little too far."

Even during this fight, I couldn't help feeling proud of the distance Norman had come. He was a lot different from the kid who used to hide from me in the halls. Now he was definitely somebody to be reckoned with.

"Cloud Nine" was brought into the Friday meeting battlefield.

This time, though I could have used my veto power, my objections were overruled and I went with the majority decision. They were right; the public loved "Cloud Nine." In cases like this, I didn't mind being proved wrong. I didn't mind either when the following spring it won a Grammy—Motown's first.

Christmas of 1968 brought headlines blazing throughout the music industry. In the week ending December 28, Motown had five records out of the Top 10 on *Billboard*'s Hot 100:

#1 Marvin Gaye's "I Heard It Through The Grapevine"
#2 Stevie Wonder's "For Once In My Life"
#3 Diana Ross and the Supremes' "Love Child"
#7 Diana Ross and the Supremes' and the Temptations'
    "I'm Gonna Make You Love Me"
#10 The Temptations' "Cloud Nine"

But even more important than that, we captured and held the #1, #2 and #3 positions for one solid month, an unprecedented feat that to my knowledge has not been done since.

1968 had wound up an incredible year.

Five out of ten! The not-quite-grown-up kid who had once depended on lucky rolls of the dice and who had watched and studied the numbers guys on the streets computing the odds in their heads, had 50 percent of all the ten top-selling records in the country. Impossible! And, we'd done it without HDH. The verdict was in: We would survive.

10

CHANGES IN THE GROOVES
1968–1971

THE JACKSON 5

WHEN I FIRST BOUGHT a house in California in the fall of 1968 I had no concrete plans to one day move my whole operation to the West Coast. I wasn't looking down the road that far. Our California office was getting busier and busier and I had been spending so much time in Los Angeles with our various television projects, living there made sense.

As a kid, I had been there twice—once in my boxing days and another time to visit my sister Anna, who had moved there. I loved the weather and how it somehow felt like the end of the earth to me. And I loved the fact that movies were made there.

As I look back on those days I can see how unaware I was of realities of time and space. People I worked with often had to move mountains or create miracles to meet the challenges I presented. One example was when I made up my mind to move to L.A. I contacted my assistant, Dick Scott.

It was just before Labor Day in Detroit when I told him, "By the way, Dick, I got to have Hazel, Berry and Terry in a new school on Tuesday."

Dick had been with me for a little more than two years. Ambitious, full of energy, he loved a challenge. "No problem," he said hastily. "I got four days."

"In Los Angeles."

"What? That's three thousand miles away."

"I know."

The following Tuesday, Hazel, Berry IV and Terry—ages fourteen, almost thirteen and twelve—were enrolled in school in Los Angeles and living with me and my staff at the Beverly Comstock Hotel. With the help of Warren Cowan of the international public relations firm Rogers & Cowan and his wife, actress Barbara Rush, who took a personal interest in helping to get the kids and me settled in, we felt at home right away. The kids took over the hotel, treating it like a big house. There was a pool in the back and sunshine every day and they could have room service just by picking up the telephone.

In October, we moved into a house in the Hollywood Hills I had purchased from Tommy Smothers. A short time later, we found a house down the hill on the same street for Diana to rent. We were closer than ever in those days. And the move to California was exciting for both Diana and me.

What stands out most dramatically about those first years on the West Coast was the launching of a new young group we had auditioned in Detroit the summer before I moved to L.A.

In Detroit, riding up the elevator at the Motown office building on Woodward Avenue, Suzanne said, "You gotta hear these kids."

She told me she had first heard about them from Bobby Taylor. He and his group, the Vancouvers (which included Tommy Chong of the future Cheech & Chong), had performed on the same bill as this group of youngsters.

"I know you're gonna love 'em," she said.

"I hate kids groups, minors, chaperones, the courts, tutors . . ."

"Oh, no you don't. Not if they're great."

She knew me too well.

A few days later several of us gathered in a room on the eighth floor. I had told Dick Scott to bring along my new video camera. I had seen how efficiency could be enhanced by technology and was always trying new things. Recording this audition worked out very well because that now famous footage has been seen on television around the world.

When I look at it today I can still remember the intensity we all felt standing there that July morning watching those five young boys from Gary, Indiana, perform. Nine-year-old Michael, eleven-year-old Marlon, fourteen-year-old Jermaine, and fifteen- and seventeen-year-old Tito and Jackie meant business. All of them moved, sang and played their instruments like winners.

They tore into the Temptations' "Ain't Too Proud To Beg"—all moving together like little David Ruffins, but with a style all their own. When they sang "I Wish It Would Rain" and "Tobacco Road," they made the songs sound like they were written just for them. They wound up with little Michael doing James Brown's "I Got The Feelin'." His dazzling footwork would have certainly made the Godfather proud.

This little kid had an incredible knowingness about him that really made me take notice. He sang his songs with such feeling, inspiration and pain—like he had experienced everything he was singing about. In between songs he kept his eyes on me the whole time, as if he was studying me.

All the right clues were there—their professionalism, their discipline, their talent. And something else that Michael had, an unknown quality that I didn't completely understand but I knew was special. Somehow even at that first meeting he let me know of his hunger to learn, and how willing he was to work as hard as necessary to be great, to go to the top. He let me know he believed I was the person who could get him there.

After their performance, with applause still echoing in the small room, the boys looked in my direction, anxiously waiting for the verdict.

This was always the hard part for me. If the artist was horrible, it was hard to tell them. If they were brilliant it may have even been harder.

If they were horrible it was good-bye, but if they were great and you wanted to work with them, as I did, these kids would be a heavy responsibility and the beginning of a complex association. Managing any artist was a big responsibility. And these were minors. What I said at this moment could affect their lives in many ways forever. I knew it was just as important for them to grow as people as it was for them to grow as stars. They, just like everyone else, would have to make it through that vicious Cycle of Success. The public would come after them. The fame. The money. The girls. I had seen it with Jackie Wilson, Marv Johnson, Smokey Robinson and the rest.

All this was going through my mind as I walked over to them, trying not to smile too much.

The other boys seemed nervous, but not Michael. He knew I loved them.

"Obviously you've done a lot of hard work and it shows," I said. "The only thing that can stop you from success now, is *you*. Keep your humility and discipline, continue to work hard, and we'll do the rest."

"Uh, Mr. Gordy," Jermaine said, after a glance to his brothers, "does that mean you're gonna sign us?"

"Yes," I said. "Yes, it does."

The boys broke into cheers.

I wanted everybody in the company as enthusiastic as I was about the Jackson 5. I arranged a get-together to introduce the group to the Motown family at an old mansion on Boston Boulevard that I had bought and renovated. (We later called it the Gordy Manor.)

Three stories high, with frescoed ceilings and marble floors, it had an authentic English pub and an underground tunnel connecting the main house to the pool house, where there was an indoor Olympic-size swimming pool and a bowling alley. It was so grand, I didn't feel comfortable living there, but it was great for entertaining. Whether it was the formal charity balls my family hosted for the Loucye Gordy Wakefield Scholarship Fund that benefited inner-city students, or this very casual party for the Jackson 5, it worked well.

Except for the people who had been at the audition, no one was prepared for what they were about to see. As I watched them for the second time, performing in the pool house alongside the swimming pool, I could appreciate them even more, with their energetic, fast-paced routines.

Everyone started coming over to the bar where I was standing.

Abner, head of ITMI, pointed to some young girls, one of whom was my own daughter Hazel. "They love them and little girls all over the country will, too."

My brother George: "Little? The little girls'll have trouble getting out of the way of the big ones."

Barney Ales joked: "Gee whiz, Berry, you think we can sell 'em?"

While Barney was laughing at his own comment, Junius Griffin, publicity director and the pioneer of our Community Relations Department, boasted confidently: "There's nothing out there like them. They're wholesome, clean, cute and black. I can't wait to put together their press kit."

The head of our Public Relations Division, Mike Roshkind, hurried over, pulling me aside. "I'm about as creative as a doorknob," he said, "and even I can tell you they're gonna be big."

Suzanne de Passe just gave me an "I told you so" smile.

While I was thrilled with everyone's predictions of success, I knew nothing was going to really happen unless we got hit records on the group.

Within the next few days artist and management contracts were signed and we were ready to go. Then Ralph Seltzer got a call from an attorney in New York. The Jackson 5 already had a manager. This was distressing news. Their father, Joe Jackson, had said they were totally free and clear. I told Ralph we had made a deal in good faith and any deviation from our agreement was unacceptable.

After that I got a call from a guy who said his name was Richard Arons. "I'm Joe's partner," he told me. He said he didn't want to hold the boys up from doing well at Motown, but he had a prior deal with Joe and wanted me to intervene.

I told him that was between him and Joe and we would have to hold off until they got it straight.

It took them several months to resolve whatever it was but in March of 1969 the boys were free, we finalized our deal with them and I moved them out to California.

They were so energetic in Los Angeles they practiced all day and all night. After being kicked out of a number of places we leased for them and because they were spending so much time at my house anyway, I decided to move them in with me. They also spent a lot of time down the street at Diana's.

In some ways, the three-ring circus that took over my home that summer in the Hollywood Hills reminded me of the old days at Hitsville. Music vibrating throughout the house, writing sessions on the floor of the living room, pep talks in the kitchen while eating, rehearsals through the midnight hours, impromptu baseball games at the nearby park, swimming, shooting pool, basketball. Camaraderie, creativity and, of course, competition.

Even before the Jackson 5 got to California I was very clear on the musical direction I wanted them to take. Michael reminded me of a young Frankie Lymon, the lead singer of the late fifties group, Frankie Lymon and the Teenagers. And when I thought of their big hit, "Why Do Fools Fall In Love," I knew that was the kind of feeling I wanted in any song we would write for Michael and his brothers.

For days I walked around the house humming a bright, happy little tune with Michael in mind—"*Oh baby, da da da dee da . . .*"—trying to come up with a great melody that could translate into a hit record.

As with "Love Child," I decided to put together a creative commando team to write and produce it. I called in ex-Clan member Deke Richards, who brought in two new young writing talents, Freddie Perren and Fonce Mizell. Once again I was trying to have an anonymous, unified team where nobody's personal names or egos could get in the way. Deke suggested I call this group the Corporation. The Corporation it was. This group in my opinion would become the biggest single factor in the Jackson 5's success.

It almost always starts with the song. And in this case it was no different. I had the Corporation listen to my melody—"*Oh baby da da da dee da . . .*" Then Deke got together with the other guys and came up with the greatest little track. Perfect. As we came up with lyrics for the song, we used the J-5 as our demo singers, recording their voices right onto the master track. So by the time the demo was done, we practically had a finished record.

Within a short while "I Want You Back" was ready to be released. But before that we had to move forward with a strategic plan to launch the group. Knowing how great their act was, all we had to do now was to give them an image, dress them up and show them off properly.

I went to Diana and asked her if she would present them. She loved the idea. Everything was in place. Their very first album would be *Diana Ross Presents the Jackson 5.* Having her name associated with a group of unknowns really helped announce their arrival on the scene. When people started saying Diana had discovered the group—that didn't hurt, either. It was ironic that she was later accused of stealing credit for the Jackson 5 discovery when in reality she had done me and them a great favor.

August 11, 1969. The first significant event was scheduled to take place at the Daisy in Beverly Hills. That's where we met Bob Jones, Rogers & Cowan's first black executive and the publicist assigned to our account. Later, Bob came to work at Motown as our publicity director. He and Junius Griffin were a potent team, Junius with the black community and Bob with celebrities and the press. That night at the Daisy, together with Warren Cowan and Paul Bloch of the firm, he did an incredible job of getting industry people out.

Most of Hollywood was there to see Diana present "her kids," who did a short performance that quickly turned that clubful of stars and press into fans. "I have never seen anything like 'em!" was the most repeated comment that night.

August 16, 1969. Five days later. The Jackson 5 opened for Diana Ross and the Supremes at the Forum in Los Angeles. We could see then that the bigger the audience, the more sensational they became.

October 7, 1969. Less than two months later we released "I Want You Back." Our sales, marketing and promotion people moved into action.

October 18, 1969. Eleven days later. The boys made their TV debut on *The Hollywood Palace,* hosted that night by Diana Ross and the Supremes and Sammy Davis, Jr.

November 1969. The following month. We moved mother Katherine and the younger children, La Toya, Randy and Janet, to California to join the boys and Joe. The family was reunited in a house we leased for them on Queens Road in Hollywood.

December 14, 1969. A month later. "I Want You Back" was on its way to #1.

Now it was time for the world to meet the Jackson 5. We booked them on *The Ed Sullivan Show*. I sent Suzanne with the boys to New York to supervise the engagement. After nearly two years as my creative assistant I was sure she could handle it. It was always my concern when doing a live TV show that the song sound as much like the record as possible, so I sent producer Deke Richards along to help Suzanne.

Because of the three-hour tape delay, I had not yet seen it when Suzanne called me in California from New York.

"The show was great! They were a smash! You should have seen the look on Ed's face when they finished!" She could barely wait, she said, to hear my reaction.

"Great, I can't wait to see it."

"I'll call you back in three hours," she said.

Finally, glued to the TV set, a wide smile plastered itself over my face as I watched Ed announce them to sixty million people. Suzanne had dressed them in brightly colored outfits—bell-bottoms, hats on their short Afros, fringed vests, little platform boots—cute as can be. Terrific. But then, just as swiftly, my smile vanished as a feeling of nausea came over me. The tempo was off. I was devastated.

The minute it was over the phone rang. Suzanne asked happily, "Well, how did you like it, boss?"

"That tempo . . ." I said, sounding like a man who had been poisoned. "How did you let them do the tempo like that?"

"The tempo—what are you talking about?"

"It was too slow, too slow."

"Oh," she said somewhat defensively. "Well, that was Deke. He's a producer on the record, that's what he was here for, wasn't it?"

I don't remember specifically what I said next or how I said it but it was probably something to the effect that she was in charge, she was familiar with the record, so it had to be her fault.

"Why didn't Deke take the fucking record," I screamed, "play it and get the tempo off it and count the band off from that? I mean, it wouldn't have taken a genius to figure something out like that."

Suzanne was crying at this point.

Being a perfectionist has its downside. In retrospect I may have

285

been too hard on her, but she was in charge and that was the only way I knew.

The day after the Sullivan show all hell broke loose in the press. The Jackson 5 were proclaimed the new media darlings. The show was heralded as a phenomenon by everybody. The only person who probably noticed the slight tempo change was me. In fact, I couldn't imagine that the reception could have been any better, even if the tempo had been perfect.

Eventually, Suzanne understood my obsession with perfection. Eventually, she forgave me. I think.

January 31, 1970. "I Want You Back" was #1.

But long before that happened, I called a meeting of the Corporation. "One record's not going to do it," I told them. "The second record's as important as the first—maybe even more so," I said. "We've got to solidify the group, get back to work and get *them* back into the studio. Come up with a concept that's young and in the vein of the first song. And keep it simple." Deke understood perfectly what I wanted.

Shelly Berger's hands were full. In addition to managing the Temptations and Diana Ross and the Supremes, he was now managing the Jackson 5. Different venues were starting to show some interest in them and Shelly was getting offers in the range of $2,000 a night.

"Beege," he said one day in my office, "it looks like we've got a number one record. How many do you think you can get—back to back?"

"With this group, about five," I said.

"Well, all I need is three. If you can assure me of that then I can work my plan."

"You got it," I said with an attitude.

Shelly sent telegrams to the major promoters and arenas saying, "The Jackson 5 are available for $25,000 a night." The only responses he got were a few "Jackson whos" and laughter. As Shelly explained to their booking agents at William Morris, his plan was to take advantage of the fact that Motown could turn down offers that other managers, who lived on the commissions alone from their acts, could not.

Deke had taken me at my word. The concept he came back with for the Jackson 5's next record was simple, although while working on the lyrics we kept changing our minds from "1-2-3" to "A-B-C."

On February 24, 1970 "ABC" was released and by April it was #1, knocking the Beatles' "Let It Be" out of the top chart position. Shelly got calls offering $5,000 a night.

The third song, "The Love You Save," was filled with classic J-5 breaks and hit #1 in June.

Shelly was now getting offers for the boys at around $20,000. He was cockier than ever and held his ground.

"Guess what?" I said, getting the boys together one day. "You guys are doing the Forum!" Shelly had gotten the $25,000—plus a percentage.

"That's wonderful," Michael said. Then, pausing for a moment, curiously, "On whose show?"

"Yours."

"Yeah, but who's the star?"

"You all are. You're the stars."

Michael, Jermaine, Jackie, Tito and Marlon all looked at me and each other in disbelief.

Once they comprehended they were the stars, they *were* stars. They drew over eighteen thousand people, selling out the house. After that bookings started pouring in from all over the world.

But, as always, I was more concerned with the next record. The first three songs had been fast, upbeat. It was time for a change. Maybe a ballad.

After three consecutive #1 records I felt the Corporation, which included me, had become a little complacent. This was evidenced by the fact that our fourth record was not coming together well. It sounded too much like the other three, but not as good. While we continued working on it, Hal Davis and newcomer Willie Hutch, who were not in the Corporation, woke me up at five o'clock one morning and said they and another writer, Bob West, had the makings of a hit tune for the Jackson 5, but wanted my help. I told them, "It better be good."

When I first heard it I wasn't overly thrilled, but I liked the concept. It was a change of pace, a ballad. Perfect for the Jackson 5's fourth

287

release. All we had to do was make the story more relevant to the image I had for these young stars.

With Michael's sweet, serious voice promising *"I'll be there to protect you"* and trading off verses with Jermaine singing a soulful *"I'll be there with a love that's strong—I'll be your strength, I'll be holdin' on,"* and the simple background from the other Jacksons, the record, "I'll Be There," was pure gold.

With it, the Jackson 5 made Top 100 history as they became the first group ever to have their first four singles go to #1.

Those four records had happened within an eleven-month period. In that short time five brothers from Gary, Indiana, had gone from anonymity to a household name. Their hard work was unconditional and they were willing to sweat for perfection. They had such respect-ful, soft-spoken manners, that I never even heard a normal complaint of being tired. It seemed like the Motown machinery had been just waiting for the Jackson 5 to come along.

I didn't realize that the launching of the Jackson 5 would mark the end of something major for me. They would be the last stars I would develop with the same intensity and emotional investment as I had with the earlier Motown artists. They would be the last big stars to come rolling off my assembly line.

MERCY MERCY ME

BUT JUST AS THE JACKSON 5 were soaring, Diana Ross and the Su-premes were breaking up. Diana was going solo.

May 7, 1970. It was a boiling hot Las Vegas afternoon when Mike Roshkind slowly lowered the phone to its cradle in my hotel suite. Pale in his face, "Terrible news," he muttered.

Everything had been building to the night that lay ahead of us— the Las Vegas debut of Diana Ross—alone. Her new career was riding on that evening at the Frontier Hotel. The press was expected in full force. All she had to do now was deliver. And I knew she would.

The breakup of Diana Ross and the Supremes had taken its toll on everybody. For nearly a decade they were the symbol of the many triumphs of the Motown Machine. Their breakup represented the end of an era but it was inevitable. The growing tension between Diana and Mary was becoming obvious to everyone. The more the public clamored for Diana, the harder it became on the other two—and Diana herself. Cindy, however, being the newest member, was not affected as much.

I knew Mary. I knew how she felt. She knew me, and how I felt. She knew Diana was my baby. Everybody did. She also knew how much I loved and respected her and understood the pressure she was under. She was a fighter, always hanging in there. Now it had become too tough on all of them.

I spent a long time trying to figure out how to make Diana's leaving a positive. "Two-for-one stock split," is what Mike said when I told him I was determined to try and find the best replacement in the world for Diana.

We started a massive search, everybody looking everywhere. After a few months I found her, Jean Terrell, the sister of heavyweight boxer Ernie Terrell. I saw her at a club in Miami. She had class, style, looks and talent. If anyone could step into Diana's shoes, I felt she could.

Mike Roshkind, doing his normal PR thing, was telling everybody about our two-for-one stock split.

We'd have two great entities instead of one.

That was exactly how we approached it. Though I knew my time would be spent working with Diana, I made sure the new Supremes had strong support. I assigned talented producer Frank Wilson to work with them, Gil Askey as their musical conductor, and Shelly Berger as their manager.

We released the last single on Diana Ross and the Supremes, "Someday We'll Be Together." A rich, emotional production by Johnny Bristol, which he had co-written with Harvey Fuqua and Jackey Beavers, it became their twelfth and last #1. They took their final bows together on a high note.

Two of the first Frank produced on the new Supremes were big hits: "Up The Ladder To The Roof" and then "Stoned Love." They were off and running. Their bookings were strong and we were ecstatic.

Everyone knew the big business Diana Ross and the Supremes had done as a group, but as an unproven commodity, booking Diana by herself was very difficult. Because of the enormous success of the group's farewell engagement at the Frontier Hotel, they decided to give her the first shot as a Vegas star headliner. Together with Rogers & Cowan we mounted a major campaign, buying taxi cab ads, renting billboards, getting magazine covers, all of it.

When Mike told me that day in our hotel room that he had terrible news I thought it might have something to do with the show that night. "What could be so bad?" I asked.

"No reservations! Only about five hours to go to show time," he said, shaking his head. He had just gotten off the phone with the hotel management and out of approximately six hundred seats, only about thirty had been reserved for Diana's opening show. Disaster.

"Must be a joke," I said.

"No joke," Mike assured me.

"We're in such trouble."

"What do you mean we?"

We laughed but knew it was no laughing matter. "Okay, okay, let me think," I said. "First of all Diana must not know anything! If she walks out there and sees a handful of people in that big room, I'm dead. Her faith and confidence would be shattered in herself—and me. I want some people there. I don't care how we do it." I got up and started pacing.

Mike left the room to get some air. When he returned I had a plan.

"We'll tear twenty dollar bills in half and give one side to people on the street, promising if they come to Diana's show tonight, they'll get the other half."

"Strangest damn idea I ever heard, but you know me, the stranger the better."

"Okay," I said, "we ain't got much time."

290

"But wait. Let me call the Frontier people. We need to calm them down before they get some stupid thoughts of canceling the show." He grabbed the phone and told them that historically Diana got big walk-in-traffic, a last-minute audience.

They bought it. We then hit the streets talking to everybody, cab drivers, locals working in restaurants, tourists sunbathing at swimming pools.

"Ever heard of Diana Ross?" we'd say.

"Diana Ross! Sure, she's with them Supremes ain't she?" was a typical response.

"Well, not only can you come see her show at the Frontier but . . ." I'd give them half of a twenty, "you can get the other half of this when you get to the show!"

"Ain't this my lucky day," said one lady, clutching the money as if she'd just won big on the slots. Within a couple of hours, we had covered the strip.

Luckily, we got to the showroom early. People were already there wanting the other half of their twenties. It had worked! Our scheme had worked. We were in business. Right away we started trying to match the serial numbers on the twenties. Impossible. We couldn't find one number that was the same. Soon that little crowd had turned into a noisy mob.

"I need cash," I screamed out.

"I got a couple hundred," Mike shouted.

"That's not nearly enough. Plus I need it in twenties."

"Don't you have credit here?"

This was one time my old gambling habits paid off. I had good credit with the casino.

I rushed to the cashier's cage and ordered about $10,000 in twenties. We collected all the halves and gave the people crisp new $20 bills in exchange. We ended up with a happy audience and a big bagful of torn-up money.

Diana was normally on edge on any opening night, but she, like all of us, knew how important this night was. Though many things went wrong, it turned out to be an incredible opening night.

Despite light cues that were missed, the tempo too fast on some of the songs, a broken zipper on one of her quick-change gowns, Diana proved herself a star once again, smiling her way through the whole show, giving the performance of her life.

I had no idea she was seething inside until I rushed to the wings to congratulate her as she came off the stage.

"That was a horrible show," she said. "People paid to come see me and didn't get their money's worth!"

"Oh, Diana, I think they did."

If she only knew.

The reviews were great and for the rest of her Frontier engagement the audiences continued to build. And so did her solo career.

She was now at the threshold of becoming the superstar we had always dreamed she could be.

For the past five years she and I had been intensely involved both professionally and romantically. They were interchangeable. One fed off the other. We had had success after success together. I don't think there was a question in either of our minds that we would always be together. I felt certain that our dream was within reach. And I wanted to go for it all the way. So did she. But as in any long-term relationship the question of marriage had come up. Could our romantic relationship continue without it or would marriage destroy our dream, everything we'd worked for? We both knew that the conflict between our personal relationship as lovers and the roles we played professionally was taking its toll.

I was her mentor, her manager, her boss. She was my protégé, my artist, my star. We both recognized that my role had become too defined, too demanding and too unyielding to exist in a loving marriage. And in order to take the dream all the way my role would have to become even more intense. Emotionally, we were on a collision course. We ended our personal relationship sadly and by mutual agreement so we could focus completely on the professional one.

Nineteen seventy was not only a good year for Diana Ross, the Jackson 5 and the new Supremes but several of our other artists were hitting big.

Smokey Robinson and the Miracles had themselves a #1 with

"The Tears Of A Clown." A song written by Smokey, Stevie Wonder and Hank Cosby, it had been used as an album cut three years before, never intended for release as a single. But when it became a big hit in the U.K. we decided to release it as a single in the U.S.

Gladys Knight and the Pips had a big hit she almost didn't record during this time. When Gladys first heard "If I Were Your Woman," written by Pam Sawyer, Gloria Jones and Clay McMurray, she didn't think it fit her image. She later told me she wouldn't have cut the record had I not convinced her to do it.

As the new decade was beginning, the changes happening in society inspired changes in our music. Norman Whitfield and Barrett Strong's songs captured the spirit of this era:

People movin' out, people moving' in,
Why—because of the color of the skin,
Run, run, run, but you sho' can't hide.
An eye for an eye, A tooth for a tooth,
Vote for me and I'll set you free.
Rap on brother, rap on.

Well the only person talkin' 'bout love thy brother is the preacher.
And it seems nobody's interested in learning but the teacher.
Segregation, determination, demonstration, integration,
Aggravation, humiliation, obligation to our nation.
Ball of confusion—that's what the world is today . . .

The production of the Tempts' "Ball of Confusion (That's What The World Is Today)," with its electrifying, yet melodic tracks, was pure Norman.

Next, he and Barrett took on the Vietnam War in a record on Edwin Starr:

War—Uh! What is it good for?
Absolutely nothin'!

War, I despise
'Cause it means destruction of innocent lives
(say it again)

293

War means tears in thousands of mothers' eyes
When their sons go out to fight;
And lose their lives . . .

War! It's nothing but a heartbreaker
War! Friend only to the undertaker
Peace love and understanding, tell me, is there no place for them
today?
They say we must fight to keep our freedom, but Lord knows, it's
got to be a better way . . .

"War," with Edwin's thundering vocals and Norman's raging tracks, charged up to #1 and became almost an anthem of the times—voicing the deep antiwar feelings of a growing number of people.

Norman was like a madman. He continued to keep the Tempts on top with songs like "Runaway Child, Running Wild," "I Can't Get Next To You" and "Psychedelic Shack."

Norman's great versatility, his edgy, raw street energy always thrilled me. He ultimately amassed a body of work that I think makes him one of the most important producers of his time.

By now it was clear my life was in California and, bit by bit, the company and much of my family began to join me. Gwen and Anna had already been here for a few years. For Mother and Pop, the warm weather and beautiful scenery was a welcome change. They were still both very much a part of the company. Ever since I had bought Pop's contracting business, I had put him to work at the company in a variety of capacities—consulting on our different buildings and being a company liaison, providing an open ear for any concerns from artists and employees alike. I had come up with a policy years before that required two signatures on every check that was issued and Mother was one of the few signators.

In these matters, having family to depend on was critical to me. Fuller, the head of Administration, was another signator. Laid-back, yet detail-oriented and methodical, he had just the right personality and skills to handle the demands of being in charge of personnel, purchasing and company policy maintenance.

Esther and George chose to remain in Detroit, Esther to oversee company activities there, and George to take over a pressing plant we had bought in the area.

My brother Robert has always liked unique challenges and games that called for mental sharpness. He was good at a lot of things. In '65 when our sister Loucye died, Robert asked to take over Jobete. He didn't have much experience in the publishing area, but I knew he had the talent and ability to do it. Robert took on the challenge of Jobete and brilliantly ran it for the next twenty years.

Since we have been so close as a family, and we can often take family for granted, I probably never gave Robert, my little brother, the credit he deserved. So Robert, I'd like to thank you for moving Jobete from a holding company for our copyrights into a highly profitable, competitive international publishing company, keeping us #1 for many years. And also just for being my little brother.

We now had a Motown recording studio in L.A. The person most responsible for it, as well as other technical and creative areas, was Guy Costa. I met him when I first came to California. (He was the nephew of the great music arranger, Don Costa.) It seems I was always meeting these little creative geniuses. In the early days it had been Mike McLean, who built my studios at Hitsville when I first started. Now it was Guy Costa, who made sure our facility on Romaine Street in Los Angeles, not far from the company offices on Sunset, was state-of-the-art. Though we called it Mowest at first, it was later renamed Hitsville.

Engineers are often some of the most important yet overlooked factors in a record's success. From those early days when Lawrence Horn had to handle most of the recording and mixing, we had been fortunate to build one of the best engineering teams in the business that included Larry Miles, Calvin Harris, Art Stewart and Russ Terrana. Russ was the one I worked with most. He loved competing with me to see who could get the best mix. Though he was supposed to be just an engineer, doing what he was directed to do, he always wanted his own shot to beat out the producers. And many times he did. At the same time our engineers made the move to California, some of our musicians like James Jamerson and Robert White were migrating, while other local professionals were becoming regulars in the studio. But no matter where we were, the same feelings went into the music—the love, the honesty, the soul and the family way of doing things.

Some things, though, about my new life in California were different.

Unlike in Detroit where people usually recognized me on the street or in public places, here, I was just an ordinary citizen and I liked that.

I remember one night I went to a party in the Hollywood Hills. Because I'd had some wine with dinner I was driving slowly down the unfamiliar roads. I was stopped by the cops, who pulled me over, shining lights in my face. Now I was not just an ordinary citizen, but a black guy in the Hollywood Hills—driving a Rolls-Royce. After checking my license and registration they put me through their regular routine—asked me to walk a straight line, asked how many fingers they were holding up. No problem. They weren't quite satisfied. "Say your ABCs," one of them said.

He could not have asked a better question.

"Frontwards or backwards?"

They looked at each other, smirking. "Backwards," the other one said.

Mother was right again—whatever you learn is never wasted.

I did it—perfectly. Surprised, the first one said, "Get out of here—and don't drive so slow."

The Jackson 5 had become a real part of my family. On weekends we would have baseball games at a nearby local park where a neck-and-neck competition was ongoing: the Jacksons versus the Gordys. Since Michael was the smallest he was the catcher for his team. At this one particular game, I kept noticing that every time he missed the ball and started running off to get it, a little scrappy kid would appear from out of nowhere, beat him to it, scoop up the ball and throw it into the infield.

The kid was good—he was fast and accurate. His baseball hat turned sideways, he had spunk and a spirit I liked.

But after four or five times of this, I could see Michael's frustration had turned into embarrassment. My little star was being upstaged. That meant I had to diplomatically remove his competition. I walked over to the fence where the kid was standing.

"Hey, you're really good. I love the way you play," I said, "but this is a private game, a family affair. I'd like for you to just let him get his own balls. Okay?"

"Okay," he said, nodding as though he understood the situation. But I did notice that he slumped as he leaned back against the fence to watch the rest of the game.

When it was over, as I was walking away, I felt someone pulling on my shirt. It was this same little guy with the sideways baseball hat.

"Do you know Ray Singleton?"

"Sure I know Ray. She was my wife."

"Well, I'm her son, Kerry," he said.

I stood there for a moment, looking into his greenish eyes. I was stunned. Then I grabbed him and hugged him real tight, whispering, "You are my son, too."

"I know," he said, his voice muffled into my shoulder as he squeezed me even tighter.

Ray and I had barely spoken to each other in six years, since the bootlegging incident, and I hadn't seen Kerry, or even pictures of him, in that time.

Kerry helped mend the fence between Ray and me, so when she expressed an interest in working for the company again, I brought her back. Ten-year-old Kerry wanted to come live with me and Ray not only agreed, but was happy for us to get together.

Another child I was determined to have much more frequent contact with was my youngest, Kennedy, who was still living with his mother, Margaret, in Detroit.

Even though I was living in California and totally immersed in my work, she had done a fine job keeping me updated on everything concerning our son. An update is one thing, *being* with him another. It was time for me to bring them both to L.A.

It was very common for our management company to receive calls and letters from fans claiming to be celebrities or other famous people in the hopes of getting through to their idols. Fans are relentlessly aggressive—they will use any and all means. We were used to these impersonations. One day I got a call from Abner, head of ITMI, telling me that another one of those crazy letters had come in. This one was for Jermaine Jackson. And this time the writer was impersonating Hazel.

Usually it was one of the artists who were impersonated or sometimes even me, but Hazel? I was amused—my daughter was a celebrity and I couldn't wait to tell her so.

"Isn't this ridiculous?" I said. "You wouldn't believe some of the stuff this person wrote. 'I love you, Jermaine. You are my prince, my dream. I need you, Jermaine. I will love you forever.' I mean, isn't that funny?"

Hazel wasn't laughing. "Daddy, that's personal!"

"No, no, it's fan mail. You don't really believe that the artists are actually reading all these letters themselves?! They're on the road. They have no time for that. So we have to do it for them."

"But, Daddy, that's still personal. It's none of your business."

She had a funny look on her face, one I'd never seen before. Her eyes were beginning to well up.

It dawned on me. She had written the letter.

This was my fifteen-year-old daughter, my baby, my firstborn, madly in love with an image that I was responsible for creating. The last thing I wanted to see was my daughter involved with an entertainer. Even if he happened to be someone I worked with. Especially if he happened to be someone I worked with.

Hazel had always been such a quiet, pure and innocent child. But I could see that this so-called love was the most wonderful feeling she'd ever had in her life. I could see it was real for her but I also believed that time has a natural way of taking care of these kinds of things.

So I decided to bet on time. I told her, "A fan letter is not the way to go about it. If you want him, if you really love him as much as you think you do, take some time to think about it and after three months, if you feel the same, I will tell you the secret of how to get him."

"Oh Daddy! You will?"

"Wait, wait . . ."

I knew this was risky, but I was sure the crush would disappear.

I wanted to occupy her time with positive things. "In the meantime, I want you to be more concerned about your duties around the house."

"Yes, Daddy! Anything."

"Better in school."

"Daddy, I will get all As. Anything else you want?"

I told her I thought that would do it for now.

Hazel did everything I'd asked and then some.

As the next months rolled by, she fell more and more into her new program. As far as I knew she'd stopped thinking about Jermaine.

Then one evening she asked me if she could talk to me alone. We went up to her room. I sat down beside her on her bed. Hazel looked at me with a beautiful, expectant smile on her face.

"Three months are up," she said.

"Oh, yeah, so it is. Three months are up. Do you still like him?"

"Daddy, I love him. I love him more than anything else in the world."

I had a problem.

There's never been a time when I'd promised my kids anything that I didn't follow through on. And they knew that. They knew they had control over me. Whenever I committed to something, they knew I had to do it.

Unable to wait a second longer, she reached over and took my hands. "What is the secret?"

"Secret? Oh yeah, secret."

She was looking at me like I was about to give her that last breath she needed to live. I put my arm on her shoulder, saying nothing.

She waited.

I leaned over and whispered in her ear softly, "Be yourself."

"Yes, and?"

"That's it."

"That's what? What's the secret?"

"That's it. That is the secret."

"Daddy . . ." The tears began. "You fooled me."

"Sweetheart, that is one of the greatest secrets in the world, and also one of the most well kept."

She looked at me without understanding as I tried to explain, telling her about those days when I was a kid hiding who I really was whenever I was around the girls I liked.

"The problem with people in relationships the world over is when they want to get the person they love to love them, they think they have to be someone other than themselves. The secret to any relationship is just the opposite: being who you are. And you are a beautiful person. So just be you. I know you trust me. Now, I'm asking you to trust you."

I assured her that being herself—with her fine values—would make her stand out from any crowd. "You are like a rare painting, valuable because there is only one."

She believed me. She did it. It was tough at first. It took another two or three weeks for her to adjust to being her true self. But eventually, she and Jermaine were having conversations that turned into fourteen years of marriage and three beautiful kids.

She has always thanked me for passing on such a simple but universal secret. I always appreciated her trusting me enough to believe in herself.

It was now 1971. We hadn't gotten to the end of January when Suzanne had the unpleasant task of bringing me the news: Diana had married a man by the name of Bob Silberstein.

When she called me in my office that day I had all kinds of emotions. I was surprised and shocked, but at the same time I was relieved. The relief came because I knew this would bring to an end any romantic feelings that up to this point had refused to die. I could now focus completely on new areas of her career—TV, movies, stage.

In the beginning I had no clue she was pregnant but once she began to show I did have a few fleeting thoughts—*Could it possibly be . . . ? Nah.* Then I thought back to a night some months before, right before Christmas. Though we had broken up, I was over at her house when nature took the place of better judgment and we found ourselves intertwined and giving in to that "one last time" or maybe it was just "one for the road."

In August of 1971, Diana gave birth to a baby girl whom she named Rhonda. Watching her as she grew, it didn't take me long to realize I was her father.

Diana and I finally acknowledged to each other that it was so. She told her husband and would later tell Rhonda. During Rhonda's early years I spent a lot of fun times with her. She, and later her two sisters, grew up referring to me as Uncle BB. Diana brought them to my house frequently where we played practically every game in the book, mostly riddles and creative mental games.

I took Diana's marriage in stride. I convinced my concerned friends it was the best thing that could have happened. I was happy for her. I was happy for me. I was happy for everybody. I could fool myself but I could not fool Chris Clark. Hearing the news she came into my office. In her own witty, sarcastic way she comforted me. She knew I was hurting. She was my sounding board and collaborator on many of my creative projects. Mentally and emotionally we were close, so naturally she was quick with the comments. "You've got to give her credit. To catch you off guard is a pretty formidable thing, don't you think?" she said.

I felt like I had to get out of town. I took Chris to the Bahamas where I got a call from Smokey.

Smokey had refused to move to California. He was deathly afraid of earthquakes. "It's gonna fall into the ocean," he'd always tell me.

Smokey was out in L.A. playing a two-day engagement, calling me from his room on the Century Plaza Hotel's seventeenth floor.

"It's swaying like a dog!" he screamed. "What the hell am I doing here, and you live here and you're in the Bahamas? I'm here for two days an' there's a fuckin' earthquake!"

"Is it going on now?" I calmly asked.

"You're damn right it is. Aftershocks."

By this time we were laughing.

"Well Smoke, if you're gonna get caught in them anyway you might as well move there." (In 1972, after a farewell tour with the Miracles, introducing his talented replacement, Billy Griffin, Smokey settled in California and started his solo career.)

Smokey's call reminded me of another call I received the last trip I had made to the Bahamas. It was from Marvin Gaye. He wanted to do a protest album.

He had done nothing for the past year and all of a sudden he wants to do a protest album. "Protest about what?"

"Vietnam, police brutality, social conditions, a lot of stuff."

That scared me. "Marvin," I said, "don't be ridiculous. That's taking things too far."

"I'm not happy with the world. I'm angry. I have to sing about that, I have to protest."

Marvin was a good soul. I always admired the deep feelings he had about wanting to do something positive in the world. He wanted to do right, but many times he had gotten off track and I would try to get him back on. Not through force, but by logic, common sense. I tried again.

"Marvin, this is crazy. Stick to what you do. Stick to what's happening. Stick to what works!"

He chuckled, as he often did when he thought he had me one-upped. "Stick to what works? Come on, BG. You've never done that in your life. You've always done something different."

"But I am never different just for the sake of being different. It has to mean something positive. If you're gonna do something different at least make it commercial."

Marvin was silent.

I kept going. "Marvin, you've got this great, sexy image and you've got to protect it."

In his soft, almost melodic voice, he said, "I don't care about image, BG. I just gotta do it. You've got to let me do this. I want to awaken the minds of mankind."

I loved what he had said. There was no way I was going to try and hold him back.

"Marvin, we learn from everything. That's what life's all about. I don't think you're right, but if you really want to do it, do it. And if it doesn't work you'll learn something; and if it does I'll learn something." The album was called *What's Going On*. I learned something.

By April, the single went to #1 and a month later when the album came out it shot up the Pop chart. Marvin's first self-written, self-produced album was a major smash, with phenomenol arrangements by David Van dePitte.

The songs were laced together in fluid motion producing a sound quality on Marvin I'd never heard before. What an artist Marvin was! His voice on lead vocal, backed up with other colors and tones of himself on background, it was Marvin on top of Marvin on top of Marvin.

I was surprised to find out that even with this departure in subject matter, he came off just as sexy as when he sang his "You" songs directly to women.

As Marvin promised, he protested everything. He protested pollution and brought attention to the environment in "Mercy Mercy Me (The Ecology)"; he sang of the pain of ghetto life in "Inner City Blues (Make Me Wanna Holler)." He pleaded for the future with "Save The Children." He touched the spirit with "God Is Love" and "Wholy Holy." Inspired by his own brother, in "What's Happening Brother," he told of the frustration of a veteran returning from the Vietnam War.

Marvin's music is as relevant today as it was then.

I was glad I took Chris with me to the Bahamas. We had a great time and I had a chance to sort out some of my feelings and to be honestly happy for Diana. Long after Diana was married, Chris was still convinced that because of my love for Diana there would never be a solid place in my life for her. She was wrong, but I could never convince her otherwise. (She later married screenwriter Ernest Tidyman.)

In one way or another, many of the artists were growing up, gaining new levels of independence and autonomy—something I greeted with combined feelings of relief, pride, resentment and indigestion.

Stevie, who was turning twenty-one in May of 1971, was definitely coming into his own. Creatively and technically, the artist we once called the twelve-year-old genius was an adult. The year before, "Signed, Sealed, Delivered (I'm Yours)" had been the first single he produced by himself. He was now in the process of producing his own album, *Where I'm Coming From*—early evidence of what an innovator Stevie would become.

He was working with Syreeta Wright. I will always love Syreeta Wright—a great woman who co-wrote and sang on some of his records and whom he married in September of 1970. She is not only one of my favorite singers of all time, but favorite people as well.

Versatile, with a rich, interpretative voice, she was one of those artists who really should have made it but didn't. The timing and material didn't come together the right way to do her justice. Yet whenever her voice was on a record, even in the background, it could steal the show.

I'll never forget what fun we all had when I threw a twenty-first birthday dinner for Stevie at the Gordy Manor on Boston Boulevard in Detroit. As usual when Stevie and I got together we either joked around or we talked some heavy philosophy.

We all laughed and told stories as the party went on into the early hours of the morning.

The following day, tired but in great spirits, I flew back to L.A.

Waiting for me at the office was a letter from a lawyer I'd never heard of disaffirming every contract Stevie had with us—effective upon his turning twenty-one.

I couldn't believe it. I couldn't believe we could have been together the night before like we were and he not prepare me for something like this. That was not Stevie. But if it was, I was definitely going to tell him about it. I called his house and talked to his wife, Syreeta.

"Stevie's not home," she told me, "but I don't believe he knows about that." She went on to tell me how much fun they both had at the party. And again told me she didn't think Stevie knew anything.

She was right. Stevie called back shortly and was very upset. He said he had planned on renegotiating his contract, but not that way. He apologized and explained that his attorney, who was based in Omaha, Nebraska, had acted without his knowledge.

Stevie immediately fired the attorney, but then got another one who was probably ten times tougher—Johanan Vigoda.

Whenever an artist's contract is being renegotiated, especially an artist who is as close as Stevie was to me, it is a tense time for everyone. This one was no different but during the whole time Stevie made it clear that he was staying at Motown. He also made it clear he had his own ideas on what and how he wanted to create his music. He was ready to do his own thing and do it his way. Though I had some misgivings when he asked for total creative control, I thought of the progression he had made from an eleven-year-old high-pitched singer banging on bongos to a full-voiced vocalist, writer and now producer. I agreed to the creative control. Stevie was ready to fly. Several months later he turned in *Music of My Mind*, a beautiful, flowing concept album. It was only the beginning of what we'd hear from him throughout the seventies.

The artists were not the only ones changing. I, too, was going in a new direction—the movies. The crazy part was instead of me having to look for them, they came to me.

SUNDAY, JUNE 5, 1988—LATE AFTERNOON, SPAGO RESTAURANT,
LOS ANGELES

I was standing in the middle of a noisy party, a fund-raiser for Jesse Jackson's presidential campaign, my mind far, far away—caught up in details of the ongoing poker hand with MCA, wracking my brain for loose ends. So far so good on some major concessions—obtaining assurances that the Motown body of music be kept intact and that there be an established percentage of minority ownership. I also had some thoughts on what to do about the master recordings of Dr. King's speeches.

I knew people looked at Motown as something belonging to them, and at me as just the caretaker. That had always made me feel good in the past. But not now. How can I say to the world: I don't want to be the caretaker anymore—Let me let go.

Public perception had me locked in. "You—in financial trouble?" "You want to do what?"

"Berry Gordy . . ." I heard a voice and looked up to see Jesse

305

making his way toward me. "My office has been getting calls about you . . ." he began.

"No kiddin'," I said. Changing the subject, I asked him how the campaign was going, but he seemed much more interested in talking about the sale of my company.

Articulate as ever, Jesse hadn't changed much since the first time I met him back in the early sixties when I had squeezed him in for a fifteen-minute meeting that lasted three hours.

For the first two hours we discussed many things, but mostly he told me about how important I was to the black community, and the phenomenal impact we were having around the world. The next hour was spent asking me for money.

He wanted it for Dr. King and the Southern Christian Leadership Conference.

I asked questions. Exactly what was the money for? Exactly what were their plans? And exactly what did they stand for?

Jesse was irritated, but too smart to lose his cool. He not only answered all my questions, but gave me a history lesson on the whole civil rights movement.

"Not only am I goin' to give you the money," I told him, "but I'd like to do more." I went on to tell him I wanted to memorialize Dr. King's speeches on record for future generations.

"Wonderful," he said, "but how about the cash first?"

"Okay."

That was many years ago and now here I was at a different kind of fund-raiser—this same black man was running for President of the United States. Going through all parts of the country, including the South, with his Rainbow Coalition had moved Jesse out front in many of the primary polls.

"Selling Motown," he said, "would be a blow to black people all over the world."

"I know, but Jesse," I said, "allow me to use a Jesse-ism of my own. I have three choices—sell out, bail out or fall out. Which do you suggest I do?"

He laughed. I could see he loved my Jesse-ism. "Just think about it," he said, as someone was pulling him away to make a speech.

I stood there recalling other confusing times in my career. Back in 1971 I decided to have a Rock 'n' Roll singer, who had never acted in a movie before, star in the life story of Billie Holiday.

The word was out. "He's crazy. Berry Gordy has really screwed up this time."

II

NEW HORIZONS
1971–1975

LADY

THE STORY BEHIND THE MAKING of *Lady Sings the Blues* began many years ago. When I was a teenager my friends and I looked up to the cool, hip people, most of whom were Jazz enthusiasts, and Billie Holiday was their queen.

The songs she sang all seemed to be about life—her life. I felt her pain was greater than any I had known. She was involved in a way of life I had not experienced and she told us about it.

"Good Morning Heartache," "Don't Explain," "God Bless The Child," Billie had a song for every emotion. Through her songs I knew her and loved her. And then one night I met her.

It was at the Flame Show Bar. I was in my early twenties and had come to the club with my brother Robert and our friends, Cecil Alleyne and Mable John, to see the great Lady Day. We walked in. Lo and behold there SHE was on stage singing. Her tone, melody and feeling were so much like her records, yet so much more. I was mesmerized.

She was into the song, deep into herself. Expressions occasionally moved across her face, showing her serenity and sometimes her pain.

Other times, serenity within her pain. Her eyes were closed. It didn't seem like she was singing for us at all. It seemed as though she was singing for herself and we just happened to be around.

I appreciated her, felt sorry for her, and loved her all at the same time. I wanted to hold her, but I knew that was out of the question. I'd be lucky if I could just meet her.

Thanks to Gwen, I *was* lucky. She somehow arranged it. I will always hear Billie's voice when I asked her if she would take a picture with me.

Slurring, soft, she said, "Sure honey, I'd love to. Where would you like to do it?"

"Right here at the bar would be fine," I said. Everybody was pushing, trying to get to her and she was taking time out for a picture with *me*. I knew there was only time for one. "Would you mind if my brother and friends got in the picture?" I asked.

"Just anybody you want is okay with me," she said in the kindest way.

When she died just a few years later, even though I had just that one brief encounter with her, I felt like I had lost someone very precious to me. I went looking for that photograph. It was only then that I realized I had lost it—my only tangible connection to the great Lady Day.

That was the back story. The actual story began in early 1971 when Joe Schoenfeld, an agent at the William Morris Agency, told me about a project in the works at Cinema Center Films about the life of Billie Holiday.

Joe set up a meeting for me with Sidney Furie, the director, and Jay Weston, the producer. They told me how great they thought Diana was and how she would be perfect for the role. Sidney had seen our TV special, *Diana!* in which she had done some brilliant comedic sketches of Charlie Chaplin, W.C. Fields and Harpo Marx. With instincts like that, he said, he knew she could do drama. His every other word was, "Magic. She's magic."

He asked if Diana had ever acted before.

"Of course she has," I said. "She's been acting all her life—as most black people have to do just to survive."

We spent several exciting hours together, exchanging ideas and getting to know each other, and at the end of the day we shook hands. We had a deal. They flew out to New York that night and I sped over to Diana's to give her the triumphant news.

Three of my wishes were coming true: 1) To honor Billie Holiday; 2) To continue to move Diana Ross to unparalleled heights; and 3) To make movies.

Making movies had long been a dream. To me it was total artistic expression.

I had always wanted to see up on that screen what I knew to be true of the black experience and the real beauty of the people I grew up with—the tough, proud, nurturing mothers, the wisdom and wit of the old men I'd listened to in the barber shops, the glamorous, shapely ladies, the handsome, smooth-talking cats, the street hustlers and the Jazz musicians lost in their own world.

Three days after I told a thrilled Diana about our great luck, I got a call from Sidney.

"They don't want Diana Ross."

When he'd gotten back to the company in New York they scoffed at his choice of a "Rock 'n' Roll" singer with no acting experience. I was so disappointed but hid my feelings when I went back to Diana and told her she didn't have the part. "This will give us more time to prepare for the next opportunity," I told her.

She took it a lot better than I did.

About a week later I got another call from Sidney. The deal with Cinema Center Films had fallen through.

"We took the film to Paramount," he said, "and they *will* accept Diana Ross."

"Great!" I screamed.

"Wait a minute," he said, "there's just one thing."

"Oh?"

"You've got to guarantee the deficit financing."

"What does that mean?"

"It means," he said, "if it goes over two million dollars you have to pay the rest."

I called in Jim White, whom I had hired as vice president of Business Affairs for Motown Productions, and discussed the feasibility

310

of that budget. Jim came back with a reassuring "No problem." Based on the script, he told me we could do it.

That turned out to be one of the most well-intentioned miscalculations I ever heard. Jim, not having worked on a creative project with me before, had no idea what he or the budget were in for. Neither did I.

By the end of the summer the major players were all lined up: a Paramount Pictures film, a Motown-Weston-Furie Production, Jim White and Jay Weston, producers, Sidney Furie, director, Diana Ross the star. I was not only executive producer, but the on-screen opening credits were to read: *Berry Gordy Presents Diana Ross as Billie Holiday in Lady Sings the Blues.* The deal was on.

When word got out that Diana was going to play Billie Holiday, criticism came from everywhere. "That skinny little Rock 'n' Roll singer is going to do *what?*" "That role should go to an experienced actress, someone who's paid her dues, worked at her craft." "What makes her think she can relate to Billie Holiday?" The comments went on and on. And for good reason. Billie came up the hard way; Diana had not. Billie's singing came from pain and blues; Diana's did not. Billie's was a tortured, troubled life; Diana's was not. Billie Holiday was an addict; Diana Ross was not.

Bombarded with complaints all I could say was, "Well, this *is* called acting, isn't it?"

Sidney Furie never gave it a second thought. He just kept walking around saying, "She's magic."

Everything about this movie seemed to be magic. Then I started reading the script. Panicked, I called in Suzanne de Passe and Shelly Berger to get their opinion. They hated it, too.

We set up our first script meeting with an anxious Sidney, who wanted to hear what we thought. As he had written it with a writer named Terence McCloy I had to be very careful.

I started by telling him some general things I thought inappropriate—like, for instance, her robbing a drugstore with a gun, looking for pills. "I think that's a little overdramatic, stereotypical, don't you?"

He didn't look too happy. "Anything else?" he asked.

311

Suzanne and Shelly smiled, looking at me.

"Sidney, I think it could use more blackness," I said.

Sidney just stood there, slowly nodding his head. I could see doubts already forming in his mind about our relationship. I was hoping he would see the benefit of our working together. I was hoping he wouldn't call the whole thing off. "You're probably right," he said, "we probably could use more blackness."

Things warmed up as he said how happy he was with honesty and truth. As the meeting went on Suzanne and Shelly chimed in with a few more comments, holding back some we'd discussed before. The first thing we all agreed to do was get a black writer.

But by the end of the meeting, he was confident enough in us to turn over all the research so we could fix the script.

This "fixing" would ultimately turn into a major rewrite starting four months before production and continuing all the way to the last day of shooting.

We left that meeting all looking for that new writer. Then I realized I already had one—Suzanne. She had been my creative assistant for four years now and had proven herself on every other project I'd thrown her way. Why not this one?

"Me? I've never written a script before."

"So what? You're one of the smartest people I know. And you do know about black people—don't you?" With me, Suzanne always had trouble living down her middle-class upbringing.

Though I had now made her an official writer, everybody continued to work on it—the same unconventional team approach we had always used in music, TV and stage shows—that initiallly included me, Shelly and shortly afterward the sarcastically creative Chris Clark.

She, too, had never written a script. But I figured with her Jazz background and subtle wit, she would add something important to the mix. None of us had any idea that this white girl could come up with such great black dialogue. I made her an official writer along with Suzanne, while Shelly and I continued to give input.

Indispensable to the process was Billy Davis, who was forever reminding us what Billie Holiday had stood for in our lives. We'd be in the middle of writing a scene and in he'd come, singing one of

312

Lady Day's tunes. "Man," he'd say, "remember at the Flame—the lighting, that pin spot on her face, the gardenia in her hair. You gotta capture that same glow in the script."

There were aspects of the story that we took liberties with. We were not making a documentary but presenting one view of this beautiful woman's life. In real life, Billie's sidekick, we were told, had been the great Lester Young, my favorite tenor sax player. But for our storyline purposes, we created a character called "Piano Man" to be her confidant. When it came to focusing on a romantic interest, we chose her real-life husband, Louis McKay, who had been the most well known of the men in her life.

In the course of researching, Billie's estate had graciously sent us some of her things. One day while looking at a bunch of photographs spread out on the floor of our production office at Paramount I heard a giggle from Shelly Berger. "Beege, have you ever taken a picture with Billie Holiday?"

"Yeah, once," I said, "but I lost it a long time ago."

"Well, I found it." He handed me a copy of that same photograph taken at the Flame Show Bar many years before.

I was shocked, but so thrilled. Billie Holiday had had a copy made for herself. At her death she had only a few things left and this was one of them.

Now this movie was more meaningful to me than ever.

The production office at Paramount was jumping. Around me the team of writers toiled as assistants and secretaries ran in and out with pages of revisions, clippings and transcriptions. There was also that constant ringing of the phone from the Motown offices across town.

The casting room was jammed. People everywhere. Just watching the beautiful people coming in and out, auditioning for various parts, fascinated me. This was Hollywood.

Looking for an actor to play Piano Man, I brought a comedian I had managed many years before to Sidney's attention. I had signed him after I saw him perform at the Apollo Theater in the mid-sixties. His name was Richard Pryor.

Soon after he walked through the door for that first meeting, talking his shit, we knew he could provide comedy relief and the drama we wanted. Sidney and I looked at each other in amazement, saying at the same time, "Piano Man!"

Suzee Ikeda, who became my favorite all-around assistant in the studio, had been bugging me for weeks about some guy named Billy Dee Williams who had played in the TV movie *Brian's Song.* She said he was handsome, sexy, perfect for the role of Louis McKay.

Though there were many actors who read for the part of Louis McKay, Sidney and I both agreed on one thing: Billy Dee Williams had been the worst.

First of all, he came with an attitude. Pompous, a pretty boy.

"Read? Me read? I've been acting for twenty years. She's never had a role. You want *me* to read?"

Sidney assured him if he wanted to be considered for the part he had to read first.

Taking forever to start, he read with Diana, missing his lines constantly.

Clearly unprepared, he struggled through the scene, making jokes every time he messed up. The only person who found him amusing was Diana.

Sidney had already planned screen tests for callbacks and Billy Dee was not going to be one of them, had he not piped up and said, "I know I could do a lot better if I had my glasses." This told us he really wanted the part and was willing to go back and work on it.

We agreed to give him another chance. But as impossible as it may seem, his screen test turned out even worse than his reading—and this was *after* he had prepared.

That really should have been the end for Billy Dee, but something had gotten to me. Both times, regardless of his poor readings, I could see the interplay between Diana and him and I liked it. They had fun together. Great chemistry. I knew the part was his.

"Don't worry," I whispered in his ear as he finished the screen test, looking dejected, "you're Louis McKay, I just gotta convince the others."

At first Sidney disagreed, but eventually I was able to persuade him to take a chance, using a word he knew well: magic.

While the casting and other preproduction work were going on, Diana did her homework—poring over books, pictures, news clippings, studying the smallest details. She walked around all day and went to sleep at night with headphones on, listening to old live recordings of Billie's. Even before production I started calling her "Billie." She started becoming Billie.

When Sidney and I heard the recordings Gil Askey had made in the studio of Diana singing several Billie Holiday classics we actually thought we were listening to old recordings of Billie. Spooky.

I told Gil to pull her back a notch from Billie Holiday and leave a little Diana Ross in there because, "Her future's got to extend far beyond this picture." Gil went back and recorded the songs all over again, in addition to arranging and composing other pieces for the movie. After watching *Brian's Song* I fell in love with Michel Legrand's music and wanted just that same feeling for *Lady Sings the Blues*, so we hired him to compose the score.

Finally, on December 3, 1971, in the Los Feliz section of Los Angeles, which looked just like the Baltimore of Billie Holiday's youth—we rolled camera.

Much has been said about the making of *Lady Sings the Blues* and the fiery relationship between Sidney and me, some of it true, some of it not so true. Indeed it was fiery. My inexperience in making movies and his inexperience in working with somebody like me made that inevitable.

I was thrilled to be in this fresh, new business where I could put my natural abilities to work, once again dealing with a pure creative process, and on something I was so passionate about.

But I was being looked upon only as the money man—the angel—the backer. I resented that. There was no way I could sit around and watch *my star* in the role of her life and not get involved.

To me it was crazy, but then I didn't know the movie business. I had been under a major misconception—that a movie producer (like the producer of a record) would have some creative control.

Those next three months of production were tumultuous.

Despite the differences that developed between Sidney and me, we somehow made it through. That "somehow" came about because I began to see how my well-meaning opinions were making his job of directing impossible.

One day he just walked out of a rehearsal, leaving me to run the whole show. I was lost, wracking my brain for who could take his place.

Seven o'clock the next morning, to my great relief, he was at my house, telling me of his love for the project and how he could never abandon it.

"I want your ideas," Sidney said. "After all, you're the executive producer, you've worked with Diana for years and I respect that, plus you have great ideas. So I really want your help. It's just that I can't deal with it in the middle of trying to direct. We've got to have one boss on the set."

I agreed with that. I knew that was the right way. We made a pact. I told him that I would never interfere with anything he said or did on the floor. If I didn't like something I would tell him personally and in private.

I kept my promise. Sidney went beyond his. Not only did he work with me and listen to my ideas, he even encouraged me to try out some of them with the actors.

The first time was the scene at the plush Cafe Manhattan where Billie goes on a first date with Louis, and the dialogue had been sounding stiff and unnatural. Sidney was not satisfied. "I got to get more out of Diana and Billy," he said, "and the script is just not doing it."

"I got an idea," I said.

When I told him what it was, he said, "Try it—what have we got to lose?"

He told Diana and Billy I was coming over to talk to them about the scene. Getting right to the point I said, "What we're going to do is put our scripts down and ad-lib this one."

I told Diana, "Billie, you have a major crush on Louis McKay but you don't want to be no pushover. You want him to think you've been around." I looked at Billy Dee. "And Louis, you're gonna get her in the end but you've got to fight for it. You've got to charm her ass off."

Diana was ready. Billy Dee was hesitant. He told me he had an idea of his own he'd like to try. "After all," he said, "I've had twenty years' experience. You've had none."

"Right," I said, "but look at it this way. If I make a mistake I pay for it. If you make a mistake I pay for it. Get it?"

"Got it," he laughed.

Because it was an ad lib, Sidney had John Alonzo, our brilliant cinematographer, set up three cameras to catch all the angles—one hand-held that John himself worked. Then Billy and Diana did one of the cutest scenes I've ever seen—in one take.

Another scene Sidney asked for my ideas on happened to culminate in a kiss—the only kiss in the movie between Diana and Billy. During rehearsal, every time they got up to kiss, I yelled, "Cut!" and had them start again from the top. I wanted them to save the kiss so there would be more electricity when it happened.

The set was crowded—technical people, onlookers, the writers, other actors—everyone was watching. After a few rehearsals, we were ready to shoot.

"Action," I said, and we started the first take.

They got to the kiss and again I stopped them because the take wasn't right. When the same thing happened on the second take I heard some giggling from the set. I thought they were laughing at Billy Dee. Every time I would scream "Cut!" his movements were akin to a muscle spasm.

We rolled again, but this time when I did it there was a roar of laughter. I was laughing, too, but when I looked over at Shelly he gave me a knowing look. "Beege," he said.

Looking around, I realized that the joke wasn't on Billy Dee. It was on me. Everybody on the set could see my concern was not for the artistry of the scene. It had become obvious I didn't want them to kiss, at least not more than once. Now I knew I really had to shoot this sucker.

The next take would have to be it. "Take it from the top," I said. "Good, good. All the way down. Good. Good. This is it." I let it go. They kissed. A wonderful kiss. Tremendous. I waited for an appropriate amount of time. Not as long as I might have waited on another scene, I'll admit. "Cut," I said. They kept on kissing. "Cut, Goddamn it!"

I looked around for a fire hose. There was none. I rushed over,

317

pulling them apart. I could see Diana was struggling to free herself, but not nearly hard enough.

Sidney later told me it was a great scene but he got a bigger kick out of watching me wrestling with my mixed emotions.

Only in retrospect have I come to fully appreciate what a hero Sidney Furie was. I learned so much from him. A masterful director, he took on the most complicated emotional scenes and brought out the best in the actors. He not only gave his all to making the film, but he came to tolerate, understand and eventually love our working relationship. We had vowed early on not to let our egos get in the way of making a great film. We didn't.

In making any movie, there are days of major panic. My first one happened about halfway through shooting when Eddie Saeta, an assistant unit production manager, came to me saying, "Mr. Gordy, I know I'm going to get fired for this but you've got big problems. We're running out of money!"

Not having ever seen this man before I was surprised he had the nerve to come directly to me but I was grateful because I felt his concern was real.

When I talked to the auditors they confirmed that yes, we had used up 95 percent of the budget—and I was only halfway through the film.

I immediately made Eddie associate producer, putting him in charge of the money.

People in the business who knew about my predicament assured me it wasn't so bad. "All movies go overbudget." They told me this one was so great I would have no problem getting more money from Paramount. "It's done all the time."

Paramount Studios in those days was a hotbed of activity. In addition to *Lady, The Godfather* and *Save the Tiger* were in production. Enthusiastically making my way to Frank Yablans's office early in the morning, I passed many crews setting up for the day's shooting schedule. I waved to new faces like Bob Evans, the studio executive in charge of *The Godfather*, and Al Pacino, one of its new young stars.

Colorful as they come, Frank was a small, wiry, balding executive with a Napoleon complex who played the part of powerful studio head to a tee.

"How is it going, my friend?" he said.

"Fine, fine. Everything is great. We're doing Academy Award caliber stuff here but I just wanted you to know that we're going a little overbudget, and we should rework it."

Frank laughed out loud. "What are you talking about—rework the budget? You kidding?"

"No, I'm not. It happens all the time."

"Not with me, it don't."

"But this is a major work of art! Maybe you should come take a look at it."

"The biggest budget for other black films is $500,000 tops. We're giving you two million! You understand what that means, two million dollars for a black film? You should be happy."

"This is not a *black* film," I said. "This is a film with black stars."

"I guess you just don't get the point, do you," he said. "Let me see, you're from the ghetto, right? I'll put this in terms you can understand better. You went out and got yourself a case of the clap, and you infected me with it. And now you come back and expect me to pay you to get rid of yours! Does that make it any clearer?"

"Yes Frank, much."

"If you're out of money I suggest you end the film right where it's at."

"That's crazy. We're right in the middle of it! How could I do that?"

"Easy," he said. "Just fade to black and put letters on the screen that say T-H-E E-N-D."

(I told you he was colorful.)

"What are my alternatives?"

"Pay everything over two million and you'll get your money back after deferments, distribution fees, prints and ads and everything else. Or," he said with a smile, "just bring me a check for the two million and the film is yours to do whatever you want."

"Fine," I said, heading for the door. "I know my options."

The next day I handed a shocked Frank Yablans a check for $2 million. "The film is now mine to do with whatever I want."

Pausing, he slowly took the check. "Oh yes, but we have to distribute it."

"What do you mean? You said if I gave back the two million . . ."

"I know what I said, but you must have misunderstood me. We took the gamble, investing our money first. Under no circumstances would I have ever suggested that we wouldn't distribute the picture."

I didn't like his tactics but I had no choice. The studio kept control of the film, its ownership and distribution rights, even though I was the one on the hook for everything. That should have been a lot scarier than it was but I was passionate about the control and creative freedom that I was able to have from then on. Creative people many times do dumb things. Business people watch for the budget, creative people only for the magic.

After wrapping production, in early '72, we had only begun editing when I got a call from Frank. He was in New York meeting with Paramount's board of directors. They wanted to see what we had.

I told him it was nowhere near ready.

"Look, Berry," he said, "we have to know whether you've got a film or not."

"I can't bring the film to you now, Frank. We don't have the montages in there, we don't have music, we don't have a lot of stuff."

"Just grab the reels, put them under your arm, come to New York, and let us see them." When I protested further, he assured me, "Hey, we're movie people here—we know it's going to be rough. You can narrate the parts that are missing."

Against my better judgment, I hurried off to New York. By the time I got to the small private screening room to make the presentation, I was excited. And in watching the reels I had brought, even where we had spliced in "Scene to come" or "Music to come," I loved everything we had. I was sure everybody watching it felt the same way. But when the lights came on, I noticed a strange reaction— they were all sort of staring at the floor.

Frank said, "Can you meet me in my office?" and walked out without a smile.

I followed him into his office and sat down, feeling very confused. He looked at me sorrowfully and said, "The picture's in trouble but maybe I can help you. There's a couple of film doctors I know who can probably save it."

I was stunned. I couldn't understand how anybody couldn't see what I saw. I felt so stupid that I had let this man talk me into coming to New York to show them a film that was not completed.

In no uncertain terms I told Frank I was not interested in a film doctor, that all I wanted to do was take my film back to L.A. and finish it.

I had learned a big lesson about making movies. Not everyone is able to look at work in progress and see what it could be. They only see what it is.

Knowing Frank didn't like the film I took the opportunity to renegotiate the deal, getting better terms. I got a better deal in the foreign markets and lowered my distribution fee domestically. But they kept the negative and they wouldn't budge on the length of the movie. That meant cutting over four hours of film down to two.

I returned to Los Angeles with my reels, more determined than ever to make the movie that I envisioned.

"Get Barney Ales on the line," I told my secretary, Rebecca, talking on a phone in a small office near our editing room at Paramount. Though the bulk of the company was moving to Los Angeles by now, Barney wasn't. He was all over the place—busy in Europe, in Detroit and in Florida where he had bought a house, hoping to get me to move the business there. His resistance to moving out here was becoming more and more of a problem.

Because of his inaccessibility, I couldn't get any answers. Whenever I checked with his people I could feel they were under great strain not to tell me anything—from wanting to know where Barney was at the moment to what record was selling the most. They knew Barney would fire them or cut their bonuses and I wouldn't. Ours had always been a complex relationship. The situation was not unlike me being a president of a small nation, loved by all the folk, and him being the big general who controls the army.

Though it drove me crazy, that was part of the reason he was so strong.

Here was a man I valued not only for his marketing mastery and leadership, but someone who was my friend. We had gone toe-to-toe on many issues, but we were a solid team. Wherever we went—around the world putting our international machinery in place, making deals, turning the most boring of sales conventions into entertainment extravaganzas—Barney and I had fun.

I also realized that Barney was one of the few executives at Motown whose job I could not do. But now we were at odds. It was becoming harder and harder to control Barney. He wanted more autonomy than I wanted to give him. He refused to be subject to the controls I put in place. While I was off in Los Angeles making movies he refused to report to anyone else. He wanted to do things his way, not my way. I thought perhaps he wanted to go his own way. I made it easy. I told him he was fired. Once the words were said, it was kind of ironic; he seemed relieved and I felt sad.

I knew there would never be another Barney. He brought a style and way of leading and building that had been unique in the industry, that I probably would never see again.

I got Ewart Abner on the phone. I told him to take charge of Sales and Marketing temporarily so I could get on with my movie.

The main problem with editing the movie was simple. Too much film. We had shot everything, mistakes and all. After cutting hundreds of hours of great footage down to things we felt just *had* to be there, the film was still four and a half hours long. We had to get it down to around two hours so the studio could have more showings in theaters.

Sidney, editor Argyle Nelson, still photographer Larry Schiller (responsible for many of the great montages) and I—with the help of Chris, Suzanne and Shelly—studied and restudied areas that could be trimmed, changed or cut out altogether.

It was a painstaking process that ended with us eliminating many entire scenes. We finally got it down to about two hours and fifteen minutes. Something else had to go, but what?

The studio executives convinced us that we did not need to show the lowest part of Billie's life, which we called the degradation scene, where she has gone back to Dean & Dean's, the very first club she had worked, and hears her mother has died.

That was a real tough one for me, not only because it was a great scene but because my brother Robert played the role of Hawk, Billie's dope pusher, and had done a wonderful job, playing off of Diana and Richard Pryor, creating his own dialogue.

He had proven again to be a natural, this time in front of the camera, even though he had never acted before. Nevertheless we cut the scene from the movie.

We were on our way to Detroit for our first big preview of the film at the Americana Theater when it dawned on me that all of my family, and Robert's friends, were expecting to see him in the film, and his only scene was cut out. I got panicky. There was no way I could do this to my brother. I put that one scene back in just for the Detroit showing.

That brought the film back up to two hours and fifteen minutes. But after playing it for that first audience we all could see that Robert's performance was brilliant and that low point in Billie's career was exactly what was needed to make the higher points shine. We left the scene in.

Lady Sings the Blues opened in October of 1972 at New York's Loew's State 1, breaking the attendance record previously set by *Love Story*.

While there was some criticism for the movie's factual inaccuracies, the majority of the reviews were raves, not only for the film itself but for the acting debut of Diana Ross. Now the Motown machinery went to work. Promotional events were scheduled. Concert appearances. Magazine and TV interviews. International appearances, including a prestigious screening closing the Cannes Film Festival. "Good Morning Heartache," a single release from the film and soundtrack album, was climbing the charts. The soundtrack album had been assigned to Suzanne and my niece Iris, who edited and coordinated the album. With the help of Guy Costa they lived in the studio for about a week to make the release date.

Even though Phil Jones, our sales manager at the time, and his people had not been too enthused about the double album with expensive packaging, a higher price, "old-timey" tunes and dialogue from the movie, they worked on it like it was the greatest thing in the world.

With excitement for the picture building everywhere that double-record album shot up to #1 Pop.

In February of 1973 came five Academy Award nominations for *Lady Sings the Blues*. Diana's nomination for Best Actress put her up against four established actresses: Liv Ullmann for *The Emigrants*, Maggie Smith for *Travels with My Aunt*, Liza Minnelli for *Cabaret* and Cicely Tyson for *Sounder*. After winning the Golden Globe Award as Best Actress a month before, the talk around town was: Diana Ross is a shoe-in.

Diana had always said to me, "If you can think it, I can do it." And she really had.

Lady's four other nominations were: Best Art Direction (Carl Anderson art director, Reg Allen set decorator), Best Costume Design (Bob Mackie, Ray Aghayan, Norma Koch), Best Scoring: Adaptation and Original Song Score (Gil Askey). And a real personal victory was the nomination for Best Screenplay—Terence McCloy, Suzanne de Passe and Chris Clark.

By the time March 26 arrived, we were all crazy with anticipation. It was the night before the Academy Awards and Diana was throwing a pre-Oscar party to celebrate what was certain to be victory, as well as her twenty-ninth birthday.

Suzanne, Shelly and I were all too exhausted to really enjoy it. We spent most of the night collapsed on a sofa together—in a delirious, punchy state. Looking at Shelly, who was taking up a large portion of the couch, I was reminded of just how far beyond the call of duty he had gone. Besides making him responsible to Diana as her acting coach, I had also given him the impossible job of getting Diana to put on some weight. He had concocted this special fattening health drink, a disgusting-looking mixture of bananas, avocados and ice cream. The only way Shelly could get her to drink it was to have a glass himself. Diana's weight stayed the same but Shelly looked like he had gained over a hundred pounds.

In contrast to our quiet huddle, Diana zipped around that party in fitting glory. Nothing could have dimmed her spirits that night or the certainty everyone felt that the award was hers.

My only concern, I confided to Shelly, was that this was the first time in history two black women were up for Best Actress the *same* year. With Cicely Tyson's excellent performance in *Sounder*, there was a possibility of them canceling each other out.

Shelly whispered to me, "No way Diana can lose."

I smiled. "I know."

As confident as I was, it meant too much not to be nervous.

So when that moment came the next night at the Dorothy Chandler Pavilion when the Best Actress category was finally being announced and we heard, "And the winner is . . ." I must have lived ten lifetimes within that short pause.

When I heard "Li . . ." and not "Di . . ." shock waves went through my body. Then I heard ". . . za Minnelli for *Cabaret*." The seconds that followed were a blur. We were all heartsick, but later, when I watched it on tape, I was relieved to see that when the TV cameras panned to us we were smiling graciously. Not all of the best acting in Hollywood is done up on the screen.

Though none of our nominees had won, everyone tried to make the best of it. We put in our required appearances at the post-Oscar Governor's Ball, but then hurried along to the private party back at my house.

Just about everyone from the cast and crew was there—in a down mood. The songs from the movie were playing in the background, not sounding quite the same.

Sidney Furie and I consoled each other, talking about how happy we were just to have been nominated. That night I think we were both faking it, but later on I realized how fortunate I was. I had gotten five Academy Award nominations on my very first film.

MAHOGANY

A BIG SOUND HIT ME in the face as I walked through the control room door at our Hitsville studio in Hollywood. *"Let's get it on. Aw baby . . . Let's get it on."* It was Marvin Gaye's voice, low, full and sexy. Begging. Incredible! It engulfed me, giving me an emotional something that let me know it had to be a hit. A big hit.

After concentrating on making a movie for over a year and a half, I was relieved to move my focus back to the music business. One of the first things I did was to check out Marvin's session that night. And what luck!

Marvin had just finished his dub-in and the production group and engineers were in the control room listening to the playback. Not trying to mix it, they had left the faders at random levels set for listening purposes only. Everything raw and clear, it sounded perfect.

The minute Marvin saw me he jumped up and came over. We hugged. I told him he had never sounded so good.

"Think so?"

"I know so."

"If you love that just wait till it's finished."

"Finished? You're not going to mess with *that*? Are you?"

Looking at Ed Townsend, a veteran record producer who had co-written and produced this with him, Marvin laughed, "You ain't heard nothin' yet. We still got to put more strings, horns and other stuff on it. BG, this is gonna knock you out."

"I've heard that before, Marvin. Why don't you just run me a seven-and-a-half right off the board now?"

Marvin was suspicious. "What do you want with it? It's not even mixed yet."

"I know. I just want a tape of what I'm hearing right now."

"Aw, c'mon BG, this is too raw . . ."

"I love raw. People love raw." I could see Marvin turning from a friend to a foe. "Okay Marvin, you might be right, but so what? What have you got to lose? We'll compare them later and you can be the judge. Whatever you say we'll go with. Just run it off for me and I'll get outta your hair."

"Do it," he told the engineer.

Later, with the release date set, they brought me a finished master—polished, slick, with more strings, horns, all mixed and balanced as they'd planned. But when we compared the two versions it was shocking. His voice was fatter, fuller and sexier on the tape I had.

It didn't take Marvin long to make his choice. We released that little 7½ version and it became his biggest selling single.

Nineteen seventy-three was also looking like another good year for Norman and the Tempts. After picking up three Grammys for the previous year's "Papa Was A Rollin' Stone," by April they already had a major new hit with "Masterpiece." But I soon found out that there were deep problems in this creative marriage of group and producer.

With Norman's success, his ego had become gigantic. It was not uncommon to many in our Creative Division. In our competitive ranks if you didn't have a big one—forget it. Even so, Norman sometimes went overboard, with a real dictatorial style in the studio.

A frustrated Otis Williams came to me one day as spokeman for the Tempts. He told me they could no longer handle the pressure Norman put on them. "For one thing," he said, "we're supposed to be stars, but in the studio he treats us like some new artists."

A perfectionist and workhorse, Norman would push them for hours, often when they had just come off an exhausting schedule on the road. Otis told me that when they grumbled about that, he would just pat his bulging pockets and say "I got mine and if you want yours you better keep singing. *I'm not tired.*"

I agreed with Otis that Norman could be ridiculous, but I knew where he was coming from. He knew what he wanted and how to get it.

That was his style, I reminded Otis, and his style was getting them hit after hit after hit. "I really hope you guys can work it out."

"No way." Otis was adamant. "We've had it with Norman." He was nervous to the point of shaking.

If only I could convince Norman to show some humility I might have a chance to save this partnership. Just a word of appreciation for their hard work or an "I'm sorry" would do wonders.

But Norman, like Otis, was unbending. "Oh? They don't want to work with me? That's their problem."

"You may feel that way now," I told him, "but look at the bigger picture. You stop recording them, you're gonna lose, the group is

327

gonna lose, and the company is gonna lose—all because you insist on being ridiculous."

"They're ridiculous. I'm giving them hits, spending all my time writing the tunes and working on the tracks, getting ready for them to come off the road. What's ridiculous about that?"

"Patting your fuckin' pockets—that's what's ridiculous about that. I mean, how dare you sit in the studio and do that kinda shit?"

Norman smiled. "Maybe I am a little ridiculous at times but then so were you. You used to kick my ass all over the place. Did I complain? No. I just kept on learning. Besides, me and those cats are tight. They know me. They know I play a lot."

One thing I knew about Norman was his great sense of integrity and fairness.

"Put yourself in their place," I said. "You got writing royalties, producing royalties and other artists to write for and record. They, on the other hand, are out on the road, tired from busting their asses on all those one-nighters. They got all those expenses and on top of that they have to split their money five ways. And then they come home and have to deal with your ass."

"Look man, I fought too hard for too long to start lowering my standards now. I got to push those cats to get the perfection I know *you* want and *I* want. And I ain't changin' my style for nobody."

And so that was the end of the Norman Whitfield–Temptations era. The Tempts went on to work with other writers and producers— including me—but none of us could give them the super hit power Norman had.

In the meantime, it was the beginning of a whole new era for Stevie Wonder. After Stevie released his first concept album, *Music of My Mind* in early '72, I could see him developing a writing and producing style all his own. His lyrics were emotional, poetic and visual; his chord patterns intricate and different. His music covered many spectrums—Blues, Pop, Reggae, Classical, Jazz and Stevie him-self.

For the first time he began recording in studios other than ours, experimenting with synthesizers and other strange technological ap-paratus. That unique texture that was all his own broadened the base of the Motown Sound tremendously.

328

To give Stevie greater exposure we got him booked on a fifty-city tour opening for the Rolling Stones. When he came off that tour he had reached a whole new audience and his subsequent albums, which included *Talking Book* and *Innervisions*, went through the roof.

I'll never forget the night of August 6, 1973—just three days after *Innervisions* was released and orders were pouring in from distributors all over the country.

Whenever a record came in like this, it gave us the opportunity to collect the millions of dollars in receivables that our distributors owed us from past Motown hits. This was always a very sensitive dilemma: Do we ship the records and let them get further in debt to us? Or do we not ship and risk losing sales and chart action?

Several months before we had restructured the Motown Record Corporation and I became chairman of Motown Industries. This was a new umbrella company established to oversee all of our other companies—Motown Records, Jobete Music, MPI and our artist management company, ITMI. I promoted Abner, from his position as head of ITMI and vice president of Sales and Marketing, to president of Motown Records—the first time anyone except me had held that position.

Abner felt the best way to deal with this problem was to talk to each distributor individually. He and I would get together at seven in the morning and call them all personally. He was sure it would work. "The president and the chairman, they'll love it," he said.

This collection problem was a fact of life in the independent record business, but I knew this plan was going to be a winner. Thoughts of how we were going to handle this were swirling in my head as I tried to get some sleep.

As I was sleeping that night I kept dreaming of a ringing phone. Finally I realized the shrill sound I was hearing was real. I looked at the clock. It was three in the morning. I reached for the phone and heard a voice say something like, "Stevie—not expected to live." I was groggy, numb and hoping I was having a nightmare. I was, but I wasn't asleep. All of sudden nothing else was important.

The voice on the other end was Esther's. She told me she had been on the phone with a remote little hospital down South. "It's a madhouse down there," she said, "and I couldn't get many details except that Stevie was in a horrible accident. Berry, it doesn't look good."

Eleven years before I got this same kind of message when Beans Bowles and Eddie McFarland had been in an accident, and Eddie had died. I don't care how used to handling crises you think you are, when you hear something like this you are at a loss for exactly what to do. But you know one thing. You better do something fast and you better do it right. And the strongest person I had to help me do that at the time was Abner.

Within minutes, I had him on the phone, telling him what I knew and to cancel everything, including the morning meeting with me. "Don't worry," I said, "I can handle things here. Just get down there and keep me posted."

Ab quickly called the small roadside hospital in North Carolina where Stevie lay in a coma and found out what had happened from Stevie's brother, Calvin.

Stevie had been en route to Durham, where he was scheduled to give a benefit performance at Duke University, and the car he was riding in was following a trailer truck that was carrying a load of logs. When the truck slammed on its brakes, a log broke free, smashed through the windshield of the car and hit Stevie in the head. Though his driver, John Harris, had been injured, he was expected to recover. But there was little hope for Stevie.

Abner learned the hospital where Stevie was had no neurology department to deal with head injuries. He immediately made arrangements to move him to the closest hospital that did and caught the next plane to join him there.

After eight days Stevie regained consciousness, but was in and out of a conscious state for the next six days. It was a terrifying period for all of us. Ab stayed at his side, constantly reporting back to me.

When I heard he was playfully grabbing at nurses and entertaining the whole medical staff with his antics, I knew then he was well on his way to recovery. Ab eventually had him flown back to California for further treatment at UCLA.

I was standing with the whole group at the airport to welcome him home. I got such a kick seeing him come off the plane surrounded by stewardesses. He gave us that old eat-your-heart-out-fellas smile that we knew so well. He was in great spirits. That was such a relief. Such a miracle.

It didn't take long for Stevie to start pulling some of his classic pranks. Still good at imitating my voice, he called Edna Anderson, my executive secretary, one day.

Stevie: "Give Stevie a check for fifty thousand dollars right away."

Edna: "What?"

Stevie: "I said, give Stevie a check for fifty thousand dollars."

Edna: "I don't get it."

Stevie: "You don't have to get it. I worked out something with Stevie and just get it to him as soon as you can. I gotta go now. Bye."

I later got a call from Edna.

"Boss, fifty thousand dollars is way over my signing limit. You're gonna have to sign this check yourself."

"What check?"

"The check for Stevie."

It dawned on me what had happened, but before I could say anything, Edna said, "Oh shit, that damn Stevie. He got me again."

In March of 1974, seven months after the accident, I watched him walk out on stage at the Grammy Awards ceremony. The place went wild. He picked up a total of six Grammys that night, including Album of the Year for *Innervisions*. Each time he came up to collect another Grammy I kept thinking, *what a miracle.*

In these later days I continued to use my basic philosophies to run the business. One of the sayings I created that people tell me they remember most is, "There are three kinds of people—dumb, smart and super-smart. And you can't tell the super-smart from the dumb." My philosophy behind the saying has many applications, not only in business but life.

In a competitive, political working situation a thin-skinned person will always have a hard time making it. I call that person smart. The smart are easy to identify; they're defensive—their egos are bruised easily. They seek the credit for everything they do and need approval from others. If something is said that they understand to be insulting to them they take great offense. The other two kinds react differently. The super-smart don't care and the dumb don't know.

Suzanne was super-smart. Even though she was only in her twenties, I promoted her to head of the Creative Division.

One day she came to my beach house, crying.

Well, not actually crying at first but when I greeted her at the door I could see she was trying to push the ends of her lips upward. "You told me how to be a leader. You told me and I did it. And now look what's happened," she said as her voice started cracking.

"What?"

"You always told me if I brought in somebody stronger than I was, that things would work out better for me."

"That's absolutely correct. So what's your problem?"

"Well, I hired Herb Belkin to help me with Creative and now I don't have anything to do. In the last three months he has taken over everything. No one calls me anymore. I come in and just sit in my office all day. He's signing new artists. The department has never been more active, but I'm not really part of it. I'm not doing anything."

Her honesty was always so refreshing. I hugged her, laughing at the same time. "You're so great," I said.

"But I'm wasting your money."

"Are you crazy? Whatever I'm paying you is probably not enough. Do you know how many other executives would have the courage to bring in someone that might be stronger than themselves? None that I can think of. Do you know how valuable that makes you?" I told her what she was going through was simply growing pains. "If you're confident enough to bring somebody stronger under you, it just pushes you up."

I saw a little ray of sunshine trying to peek through that clouded face. I knew she understood.

"Now," I said, wrapping up as I walked her out to her car, "no matter how good Herb is at handling the creative side, you should concentrate on bringing in somebody else just as strong to attack some of the administrative problems I'm hearing about—like getting production costs down and making release dates on time." And, I told her, if she had too many strong people and had nothing to do, that meant she'd be ready to move up to a new job.

That was a great day for both of us. She believed in me and what I said and that made my responsibility to guide her the right way even greater. No matter what happened I had to be there to back her up. We parted that day with a little more conviction about each other. I knew she believed in me and she knew I believed in her.

But Suzanne had not seen her last challenge or crisis as head of Creative. In the earlier years, this area had been the number one force in the company, but it was becoming more and more complicated to run.

Moving up in my company affected people differently. When I first tried to hire Edna Anderson, she resisted the promotion. Since Rebecca had her hands full with family and administrative matters, I needed a strong executive secretary.

I sent out word that I wanted to find a qualified person within the company.

That's when I heard Edna was available. A strong young black woman, she had been working downstairs in the Publicity Division. She was Junius Griffin's secretary, very much an activist like he was. Junius was leaving to open up his own public relations firm, and Bob Jones, who'd been second-in-command, was taking over the department. Bob already had a secretary and Edna wanted to stay at Motown.

But when I sent word for her to come up and interview, she refused.

"What? Run that by me again," I told Rebecca.

"She refused because she said black people can't make it to the top here."

I sent word back—"It's because of people like you that black people have a hard time making it anywhere. If you're not up here in fifteen minutes, you not only won't have this job, but no other one here."

She moseyed up, with an attitude, proceeding to interview *me*.

I wanted to kick her out so bad, but I could see she was strong. I liked her. We agreed to a three-month trial period that began in April of 1972. In what seems like the blink of an eye, twenty years passed. She became the most indispensable administrative assistant I ever had. Edna made sure she set people straight on the rumor that even she had believed, and she also was one who never stopped encouraging me to set the record straight on other rumors.

With the increasing challenges I was handling, her responsibilities grew from day one. But when I later offered to promote her to vice president she wouldn't accept it. She said that without a fancy title she would still have the same power—but not the headaches.

Being an entrepreneur the way I was—having a hand in everything at my company—had always worked for me. But looking back, I can see it was around this time, the mid-seventies, that it started working against me.

The executive chain of command was fuzzy since everybody knew only one real boss—me. And their boss had a major preoccupation—making his second movie, *Mahogany*.

In many ways *Mahogany* was one of the most exciting projects that I'd ever done. I ultimately became the director. The chain of events that led to that end was bizarre.

Rob Cohen, the imaginative young producer I had hired to run Motown Productions, had had the toughest time finding the right movie project for Diana. Over the next four years Rob was responsible for building up our film credits with such projects as *The Bingo Long Traveling All-Stars and Motor Kings*, *Scott Joplin* and *The Wiz*, but it was this first film with me where he really was put to the test.

Though Diana's nomination for an Academy Award meant that we were swamped with scripts, none worked for me. Rob brought me some music-related projects that were okay, but the concept I wanted was something where she didn't sing—a role to solidify her ability as a dramatic actress. Also I had hoped to team her up with Billy Dee again. With the two as a romantic leading couple, I felt we could have a franchise—like Astaire and Rogers and Tracy and Hepburn.

But nothing seemed right for Diana until one day Rob and a writer named Bob Merrill joined Shelly Berger and me for lunch at my house. After we ate, Rob trotted us upstairs to my music room with a bunch of pictures that looked like comic books under his arm, as well as some easels and other props. Using the pictures on a storyboard, the way he presented *Mahogany* was a no-brainer. It didn't take much time either.

Quickly flipping the pages he told the story of a young woman from the inner-city ghettos of Chicago who dreams of being a big fashion designer and who eventually makes it to the top. At the height of her career in Europe, she realizes that the happiness she really seeks in life has always been back home in her own neighborhood.

The theme echoed my own feelings that happiness is within you; and the real fun and real love are usually in the valley where we start out rather than at the mountaintop where we hope to end up. Aware of Diana's love for fashion design, I knew she'd be thrilled to act out one of her dreams.

There was an ideal part of a love interest for Billy Dee, and in the role of the crazed photographer we cast Anthony Perkins—an actor I had admired since *Psycho*.

The screenplay, written by Bob Merrill, based on a story called "Such a Good Sport" by Toni Amber, was then rewritten by John Byrum.

Unlike *Lady*, where I put up all the money, in this deal with Paramount, I had only to put up half to get the control I needed to do the film my way—I thought.

Rob brought in Tony Richardson, the well-known British director who had directed the successful movie *Tom Jones*. I liked him personally, especially when he told me how much fun it would be working with me on the movie. I took that to mean we would function somewhat as a team.

Then shooting began. Two weeks into production, in December of 1974, we were on location in one of the roughest neighborhoods on Chicago's Southside, at the corner of 41st and Ellis.

Just a few blocks away from the set there was a housing project called the "Bucket of Blood." And for good reason. We heard that every weekend several people there were killed. The location was a great choice visually, but we were in a potentially explosive situation. And Mother was there. She had come to Chicago to spend a few days with me. Tony Greene, a longtime friend of the family who was also her personal assistant and companion, had brought her to the set. Even though Tony looked like an ex-linebacker and was very protective of Mother, I was still worried about her being in the area at that time.

Tony Richardson, an Englishman in a long furry coat, was barking orders at the black residents. If they were in the shot, he'd order them off their own porches. The locals were baffled and so were we. What really surprised us was that they did what he said. But we all wondered for how long?

From the time I had been coming to the set, I'd noticed that Tony seemed to be avoiding me. But since he had said how much he looked forward to working with me, I just assumed he was too busy concentrating on making a great movie.

However, when I told Rob I wanted to talk to Tony and warn him about the dangers we might be facing, I found out otherwise. That was when Rob first told me, "He doesn't want to talk to you. In fact, he doesn't want anything to do with you." Then he confided, "Or me either."

Rob reminded me how the movie business worked: Tony was the director and had the most power. Rob, the producer, had just a little. And me, the executive producer, the guy who put up the money, had none.

I was shocked. Not only my money was on the line but everything else, so I had to be careful not to do anything to jeopardize this project. I knew there could only be one boss on the set and wasn't about to challenge his authority. "All I want to do," I said to Rob, "is help any way I can. I will stay out of his way if that's how he feels. Whatever he wants."

"I'm sure I can work it out soon," Rob told me, "but for now it's best for the picture." When Diana and Billy started coming to me in private about problems they were having, I told them Tony was the boss and all I could do was encourage them to work with him.

Then I saw the dailies. They were coming out lifeless. That was more of a problem. The film was missing the point and I could see my money going down the drain.

Rob agreed and was getting nervous. Still, he told me I should stay away from Tony and just keep working on the script. "After all," he said, "you're great with words and timing and you know just what to write for Diana and Billy to make that magic."

"If I'm so great," I said, "why do I have to stay in the closet?" Anything I came up with, Rob had to present to Tony as someone else's idea. This bugged the hell out of me.

Each night after seeing the dailies I became more and more upset. I couldn't contain my frustration anymore. It all came out of me one night about two in the morning up in a suite at the Astor Towers, where we were staying. I was stalking around, Rob following me from room to room.

"He's ruining my movie. I can't go on like this. He's missing the drama—the feeling—the point. This is just another movie for him but this is my life."

Rob understood but warned, "If you're thinking about firing the director, don't. Do you know the ramifications of doing that once a picture starts shooting?"

"Not really."

He told me we'd lose the crew and have to shut down production. Paramount would then consider it a problem picture and lose confidence. The cost of starting all over again with a new crew would be astronomical. The picture would never get made.

Rob promised he would talk to Tony and again try to make things better.

The following day Rob got his own set of bad news. His father had died.

Before leaving to be with his family he gave me a last warning: "Just be cool with Tony for a few days and I'll be back. And remember, above all don't be stupid and fire him."

"One thing's for sure," I said, "stupid I am not. I won't even go near him."

The next day Diana frantically called me from the set: "Black, we got a real problem down here. I need you to come right away. I don't want to get into a fight with Tony." Her words spilling out, she told me that Tony had been rehearsing this big guy for the rapist scene who couldn't act at all and was throwing her off. But there was another actor, a little guy, rehearsing for the part—who was terrific. The problem was that Tony didn't think the little guy looked enough like a rapist.

When I got there Tony was not that unhappy to see me. He thought maybe I could help him explain to Diana why the big guy was better suited for the role. My solution was for both actors to read the scene. Afterward, Tony was quick to agree that the little guy was ten times better than the big one, and he would go with him.

The scene was being shot that same night out on the street—full lighting, full crew and everything. Breezing in about an hour after they had started, I saw Diana motioning for me to come over. As I drew close, she leaned up to my ear and whispered, "He's back! The big guy is back. Tony got rid of the little guy. We've already taken four takes. He's horrible."

No. Tony had given me his word. Now this? I didn't understand. Confused and angry, I rushed over to Tony. "I thought we agreed on the smaller guy."

"We did," he said, "but I changed my mind."

"Okay, we got a problem. We got a big problem. I want the little guy back." Though Tony had sent him home, I turned to one of my assistants, Andrew Davis, a former St. Louis policeman, and said, "Find the little guy! I don't care where he is."

Luckily Andrew got to him before he left the area and had him back on the set in no time, prompting Tony to say, "Oh, so he's back I see. But I am not going to use him at-tall."

At this point I was beside myself. "I'm telling you, Tony, I want this guy in the scene. You've already agreed to it."

"No," he said flatly.

"Okay, Tony, I'm begging you," I said softly, making sure Diana didn't hear me, "to please put the man back in as you promised."

He shook his head no.

"Okay, then I'm telling you precisely, put the man back in."

"And I'm telling you precisely. No!"

"You're fired!"

That was probably the first time I really got his attention.

He turned to his technical staff of other Englishmen and said, "I've just been fired. Berry Gordy fired me." He turned back to me. "Okay, it's all yours," he said and walked away.

I just stood there. In shock. What do I do now?

Shelly rushed up to me, "Don't worry, I'm with you. We can do it."

"We can do what? Have you ever directed a movie?"

"No."

"Well, neither have I. So what the hell you talking 'bout?" I really did appreciate his gesture of support, but here we were in the middle of the street, these big gigantic lamps lighting up the night, rows of shadowy figures everywhere and Tony's crew staring at me.

I can never be completely sure, but I think Tony wanted to be fired. It's possible that the whole argument over the casting of the rapist was his way of getting out of a project he felt was wrong for him. In any case, as soon as I agreed to pay off his contract in full he cooperated completely with me, persuading his crew to remain on the picture. I was happy with that.

I will never forget my first take as a director that very same night— the rapist scene with the little guy. The first assistant cameraman called, "This is a take! Quiet on the set!" The sound man hollered "Speed," the cameraman "Rolling," and a production assistant with a clapboard clapped loudly in front of the camera lens. This was exciting, yet scary. All of a sudden I realized the whole film was in my hands. I felt strange.

I called "Action!" From stillness to movement, everything swung into gear: Extras started walking. I cued Diana to start walking. She hurried along, turning back to notice this wiry little guy following behind her. The whole street had come to life just because I said "Action." What a thrill!

Even more so when I heard the lines of dialogue I had rewritten. No longer was I in the closet.

When it was over I started applauding and others joined in. Euphoric, I was hugging and complimenting the actors when Shelly came over to me. "That was great," he said, whispering in my ear, "but I think it might be nice if you said 'cut.'"

I looked around—shocked to see the cameraman still shooting, his eye glued to the camera's eyepiece. The sound and lighting people too were in motion, covering everything, paying no attention to what was going on on the set.

Oh. "Cut!" I shouted. Everything stopped. Quiet. The camera, the sound, recorders, the lights and everything just cut off. What power! I had felt it before, but never like this. Never this precise.

When it was time to do the next scene, the first assistant asked sarcastically, "Okay, Mr. Director, what do you have in mind for the next setup?"

Setup?

The dolly shot we had just done had been set up by Tony—who loved doing all kinds of moving shots I knew nothing about.

"Let me see," I said, going back to the only basics I knew. "I want three setups. A wide shot, a medium shot and a close-up."

"Okay, wonderful," he said, glancing at the others with a smirk.

I went over to Diana and Billy Dee. "They're not going to do anything to help us so it's all up to you. I'm just going to turn the cameras on. And you have to make the scene come to life without fancy dolly shots."

I saw new inspiration and excitement in Billy Dee and Diana. They did not let me down.

I left that night feeling secure. But the next morning I woke up with a shuddering realization—I had to call Barry Diller in New York.

Diller and I had been buddies for ages. He was the new chairman of the board at Paramount Pictures and *Mahogany* was one of the first movies under his regime. He was very confident because we had Tony Richardson, a director he respected.

This was a hard call to make.

When I got him on the phone I told him something had happened on the set that I wanted to bring to his attention.

"What?" he asked.

"I fired the director."

Silence. "You fired *Tony Richardson?*"

"Yeah, but I had cause."

More silence. "Well, who's going to direct the picture?"

"I am."

"Oh. Great! Then we have no problem. I know whatever you do will be right."

When I hung up the phone it was easy to see why Diller was such a winner with creative people. I laughed to myself thinking that he was probably panicking all over the place. But with a few words, he had pushed my button all the way in and had locked it there for the rest of production. I knew I had to deliver.

The power of somebody believing in you or convincing you they believe in you works wonders. Just as I had done that with others, Diller did it with me.

When Rob Cohen came back he was shocked but somewhat relieved that with me as director the tension was gone and he could now assume his full role as producer.

By the time we finished shooting in Chicago and were on our way to Rome, the cast, the crew, especially cinematographer David Watkin, and I were all in love with each other—and the movie.

When we got to Rome the production continued to go well but tension was growing between Diana and me. In the past, she and I had had our little fights but now they were beginning to be more cutting than before.

Diana was under more and more strain. My decision to let her actually design the gowns in the movie—something that I knew would mean a lot to her—had come back to haunt me.

Diana was attacking the project with a vengeance, staying up all hours working on the clothes. Always exhausted and irritable, her acting suffered. Clues that the problem was out of hand had come long before the shooting of a sweatshop scene where her character is about to have a nervous breakdown. In that scene, Diana didn't have to act.

She was becoming bone thin, but the more I talked to her about anything, the more irritated she got.

However it wasn't just her. It was me, too. I was pushing hard like I had done throughout her career. But now it seemed to bother her a lot more. I could feel a growing resentment.

By late January, we were falling further behind schedule when I got the news that my mother had suffered a cerebral hemorrhage and was not expected to live. Not again. It was similar to what had happened to Loucye ten years before. I had to be there. I left Shelly in the director's chair and hurried back to Los Angeles.

I knew Mother would want "the Chairman of the Board," as she always proudly introduced me, to be by her side with Pop and all of her children.

When I got there she was still breathing, but only with the help of a machine. In reality, she had passed away. But being with her in those last moments meant the world to me.

As was my family's way, we celebrated her life and her memory, thankful in the knowledge that she had lived a full and vital life. Her teaching, the value she placed on education and in always striving to better ourselves left us a great legacy.

I had always known what a great scholar and role model Mother was but I discovered she had been a brilliant writer as well. Looking through Mother's belongings, I found papers written by her fifty years before, tackling many subjects, including family, business, racism and religion. Strong, articulate and skillful, her writing was just incredible. I only wish she could have been here to help me with this book.

During the services for Mother, I remembered the pain I felt about a year before when I thought Pop was going to die.

Pop had been a very healthy man all his life. He was his own doctor and always had his special methods of keeping himself well. Whenever he had a cold he would clean himself out by drinking buckets of water. As kids he made us take castor oil. He never told us why, but he was such a great example of health that we figured he knew what he was doing.

But even Pop's home remedies couldn't stop the natural aging process. Finally his health took a bad turn. He collapsed and was taken to Century City Hospital in Los Angeles. When I got there Pop was lying in intensive care and his doctor had given up on him.

"After all," the doctor said, "at eighty-five he's like an old car whose batteries have just run down. He's really had a great life."

Had! "I want a second opinion," I said.

"That would be silly. We've done everything that can be done. He's had enough poking and jabbing. That would kill him sooner."

Was he kidding? Me, not get a second opinion? After Loucye's death and the guilt I carried throughout the years? No way.

I changed doctors immediately and moved him to UCLA, under the care of Dr. Bill Hewitt, where he was nurtured back to health. Though his left leg had to be amputated above the knee, he was better with one leg than most two-legged men half his age and his life was extended by several years.

After the services for Mother, I flew back to Rome.

Within weeks after Mother's death, Tony Greene, who now worked with Pop, brought him and Esther to Rome. I decided to use them in one of *Mahogany*'s most exciting scenes. It was Diana's big fashion show, which culminated with the audience leaping to their feet with thunderous applause.

I had planted Esther and Pop in a luxury box in the theater's balcony. Directing the standing ovation, I had the camera pan the audience and when it got to Esther and Pop, as I thrust my arms upward, they jumped to their feet.

We did many takes before it dawned on me that Pop was standing straight up on each take just like everybody else—but with only one leg.

Whenever I watch *Mahogany* today I get chills when I see how he was able to just stand there. I don't know where he got the strength.

I guess as he saw me pull my arms high motioning to everyone all he could think of was, "That's my son, the director, and he wants me up."

There were many great moments on *Mahogany* and then there were some not so great. One night a couple of weeks before the end of shooting, with Mother's death, the friction with Diana, my not being happy with all the takes, our being behind schedule, *and* Rob constantly rushing me, reminding me we were behind, my patience snapped.

We were in the middle of a difficult scene when I saw him pushing his way through the crowd with a doomsday glint in his eyes, to give me another one of his lectures. True to form, he blurted out, "Look, Berry, you've got to just speed it up."

"Hey!" I said, "you direct it your damn self. I'm leaving." I started walking off the set.

Rob's stern expression changed into one of panic. "Oh no, wait a minute." He called, "Berry, wait, Berry . . ." as he flew to my side and began to pamper me. Exactly what I had done for so many years with other stars. Yes, me, I was now a star! Me—Mr. Calm, Mr. Logic, always the one saying "Let's just be cool and talk it out. Let's break the problem down and solve it."

These were the words that I was now hearing from Rob Cohen. The shoe was on the other foot and I liked it. Why not play it out? I knew the script: "Forget it, I don't want to be bothered. I've had it."

Neil Hartley, the associate producer, ran up and tried to coax me back to work, saying he could understand my frustration but knew we could work it out.

When I saw Shelly off to the side, I thought—how strange—my right-hand man was the only one not pampering me. But then he came closer. With the smuggest expression on his face he sauntered over, turned me away from the others and whispered, "Who in the fuck are you kidding? You're not some director working for somebody else who's going to suffer if you walk off and have to kiss your ass to keep you on the film. This is *your* film, *your* money! You're not going anywhere, so why don't you go on up there and get your shit together and finish the movie?"

"Fuck you," I said, as I walked back to my director's chair to rehearse the next take.

It was no mystery to me what made Shelly so good at dealing with creative egos. One of the best artist managers I have known, in the early eighties he left Motown and started his own management company, which today includes the Tempts, who are busier than ever. Shelly certainly managed me well that day on the set.

I knew all along that Rob really wasn't the cause of my frustration. It was Diana. She was irritated with me and I was irritated with her. When I look back at what happened next, I realize I should have seen it coming.

By the end of February 1975 we were almost finished shooting. All we had left to do were some pickup shots—pieces of scenes needed to provide continuity.

When Diana came to the set her nerves were on edge. Everything I said to her, good or bad, was met with cool. We had just finished shooting one of the pickup scenes when I told Diana we had to do another take.

Turning to me with steely eyes, she said, "No we're not. I'm going home!"

"What?"

Everyone on the set stopped what they were doing.

"What do you mean you're going home? I want another take."

Then she did something. I don't know for sure what it was, a slap, a shove, something. Whatever it was it sent my glasses flying across the room as I turned to see her storm off to her trailer.

EMBARRASSING. I stood there looking down but glancing at the people who were just sort of staring at me with stunned looks on their faces. I hurried after her, still in a daze.

She couldn't possibly be going home—just a threat made in a heated moment.

But when I walked into her trailer and saw her throwing her things together as fast as she could I knew she was serious.

"Wait a minute, you can't do this."

"Don't tell me what I can't do, I'm leaving!"

"Please, Diana, you can't walk out now—I've got one more day of shooting. It's just not right. We've still got these pickups to do with your hands and arms. I need one more day."

She said nothing.

"Diana, listen," I said, "it's about principle, too. You don't walk out on any film but especially this one. My money is in it. I put it up for you. If you walk out now, you know that I can never ever do another movie with you where I put up money."

Too late. Never looking at me, she picked up her bag and left the trailer.

The hands and arms of my secretary, Edna Anderson, doubled for Diana's in the pickup shots. The movie was not hurt by Diana's leaving, but I was.

Which was the best shot? The best angle? Watching Diana's face over and over during the editing process put me at a major disadvantage. It was impossible for me to hold on to the anger I had felt after

345

she walked off the set in Rome. Looking at image after image, it did not surprise me that I quickly fell in love with what she could do all over again.

During much of the shooting of Mahogany, the new companion in my personal life was a woman named Nancy Leiviska, whom I had been with for the last year or so. Sweet, supportive, bright and outgoing, Nancy was pregnant with my eighth child, Stefan, who was born in September of 1975.

In my life I was not only lucky when it came to my business, but also when it came to some very special women. The thing that always made me feel good was that with my relationships, no matter how they ended, we would usually remain the best of friends. That was the case with Nancy. By the time I had begun editing Mahogany, our relationship had changed and we split up, but our friendship grew even stronger. She become good at video production, and went on to oversee the videotaping of many Motown projects and personal events throughout the years.

In the spring of '75 I was giving a graduation luncheon at the Bistro in Beverly Hills for my son Terry, who had just graduated from Beverly Hills High School. My third oldest kid, Terry was a natural at many things, not unlike my brother Robert. Quiet, thoughtful, easygoing, he was an academic star. As he was heading off for San Diego State University in the fall, this was a real celebration. I was called to the phone.

It was Jermaine Jackson, who had become my son-in-law when he and Hazel were married nearly two years earlier. Jermaine told me his brothers had just signed a contract with CBS. They were leaving Motown.

What? I knew we still had at least a year to go on their contract. "How can they do that?"

"I don't know, but they just did."

He told me his father had said Motown was having promotion problems and that was why their records hadn't been going to #1.

"What about you?"

"He wanted me to sign but I didn't," he said in a voice that let me know how tough the decision must have been.

"What did you tell him?"

"I told him Motown made us who we are today and if there's a problem, I want to stay and help them work it out."

I told him I appreciated him for standing up for what he thought was right.

Earlier around 1973, after four years of the group's success and Michael taking off with four solo hits, including "Ben," which he performed on the 1973 Academy Awards show, their father, Joe, went from being quietly behind the scenes to having many complaints and demands. It was everything from wanting a say in how they were produced, what songs they did or didn't do, to how they were being promoted and booked.

And now I had heard CBS had made a deal for the boys with Joe being a big part of it.

CBS had signed them a year before our term was up. We sued both CBS and the Jackson 5 for breach of contract. The Jacksons countersued, claiming they were due additional royalties. In the end, we owed them nothing and we were paid a settlement of $100,000. We'd won the battle but lost the war—the Jackson 5 were gone.

At that time, I didn't know the full extent of what losing an act like the J-5 would be. I also did not know that in the industry it was hunting season and Motown was the biggest game in town.

But, as always, I had to continue to forge ahead on my other projects and right now that meant completing Mahogany. By October, it was ready to go.

In the past I seldom took what critics said personally, but the advance reviews on Mahogany were so bad they made the negative ones on Lady Sings the Blues sound like love letters.

Sitting alone in my New York hotel room the night before that first showing at Loew's State Theater I was dejected—confused—but still confident, or continuing to convince myself I was.

Unable to touch my food on the tray that room service had just delivered, I was thinking how Mike Roshkind, my vice president in charge of public relations, had gone out on a limb prepromoting this film. He was saying what he always said when I came out with a major project of any kind, "If Berry Gordy says it's a smash, it's a

347

smash." So far I had been right. Why should this time be any different? My appetite came back. Right as I plunged a fork into my steak,
the phone rang.

It was Mike, telling me in a businesslike voice, "I just left the
screening room. They ran *Mahogany* for about ten or twelve people
from the industry, including some from Paramount and Loew's State."
Then he did his usual thing—silence, waiting for me to ask him the
inevitable question. Usually when this happened, it meant good
news. Not this time. "They didn't like it."

I came back fast. Defensive. "I don't give a damn about those
people. All I can tell you is the movie is a hit."

"Oh, I don't doubt that for a minute," he said in a nervous voice.
"I'll see you at the first show tomorrow."

Knowing my appetite was gone for good, I put the tray aside and
fell down on the bed, staring up at the ceiling. What if everybody's
right and I'm wrong? Didn't I know public taste after all these years?
For hours, my conscious and subconscious battled it out, the clock
moving past midnight, 1:00 A.M., 2:00, 3:00. My first directing job.
I had directed my ass off. Diana and Billy Dee were great and Anthony Perkins phenomenal. I went through the whole movie in my
head from beginning to end, scene after scene. I realized nothing
had changed. I still loved it. With that awareness, I was able to
get a few hours' sleep before it was time to get up and go to the
theater.

October 8, 1975. I don't know what I was expecting when I got
to Loew's State that morning. But I knew what I was not expecting.
I was not expecting to see *nobody*. And that's just what I saw: nobody.

The only people there were connected to the film or on my personal
staff and they were doing what I was doing—looking for paying
customers.

Everybody wanted to cheer me up but no one could think of
anything to say except for Roger Campbell, my chief of staff. He
walked over to me and said, "Sir, I think it's much too early to tell
anything, don't you?"

I stared at him in such a way that he knew it was time to disappear.
He did.

My body ached with sadness. Nothing added up. Was I on a

different planet? We had promoted the hell out of this film. We had a hit song from it, "Theme From Mahogany (Do You Know Where You're Going To)," already on its way to #1. People loved Diana. And she and Billy Dee were a team that people wanted to see. So where were the people?

About 9:25 A.M. a limo pulled up to the front of the theater. Rich paying customers! No doubt this was the beginning of the STAMPEDE!

The limousine door opened and out came my friends, Sy and Linda Weintraub. They had flown all the way from Japan to be with me opening day, the day I had told them would be one of the most exciting of their lives. Sy always smiling, Mr. Glad-to-be-Alive, Mr. Sunshine; Linda, his wife, even more so. The two of them could usually make a nightmare seem like a fairy tale. Sy had retired from producing movies and television shows, sold the rights to *Tarzan*, and was now exploring business opportunities around the world.

I appreciated their friendship so much that I tried not to show my deep disappointment and jumped right into their world, hugging and thanking them for being there for me. We went in.

A few more people were now appearing but my dream for anything near a full house had long vanished. All I wanted to do now was just get in and get out. In spite of this major disaster, Sy and Linda were oozing with compliments on my having directed a picture in the first place. They were saying all of the nauseating things good people say in circumstances like this. Every time my name came up on the credits, their heavy applause reverberated through the scarcely populated theater.

I personally loved the film but was glad when it was over. I didn't see Mike Roshkind anywhere, but couldn't blame him for hiding from me. I began thinking that I needed to reevaluate myself, my life, my choices.

Sy and Linda accompanied me back to my hotel suite. After an uncomfortably quiet period, they were about to leave when the phone rang.

Mike's voice came blasting over the wire. "It's a smash!"

"What do you mean smash? I was there. The house was practically empty."

"Yeah I know," Mike said, "but . . ." Then he went on to tell me he had been in the theater office the whole time, talking to the management. We had a third of a house—twice the number of people that *The Godfather* drew the first day at the same 10:00 A.M. show. The earliest shows never did much, they told him. They were predicting sell-outs starting with the 5:00 P.M. show with lines around the block.

"They can tell that fast?" I questioned.

"They can tell that fast."

Mike was right, not only for the five o'clock, but for the eight and twelve o'clock shows as well. Soon they were running ads letting crowds know they were open all night, adding a 5:00 A.M. show.

Three days later, the picture was still breaking records. We then opened it at Loew's Orpheum on 34th Street. Two theaters with record crowds for *Mahogany*! New York was my town—now for sure.

Despite that major triumph, *Mahogany* was a personal disaster in that things would never be the same between Diana and me. My favorite line from the movie, "Success is nothing without someone you love to share it with," had become painfully relevant. Memories of that slap that last day, followed by her walking out after I had begged her to stay, reverberated in my mind, signaling the beginning of the end of a great symphony.

PART FOUR

ALL IN LOVE IS FAIR

ALL IN LOVE IS FAIR

All is fair in love.
Love's a crazy game.
Two people vow to stay
in love, as one, they say.

But all is changed with time.
The future none can see.
The road you leave behind,
ahead lies mystery.

But all is fair in love.
I had to go away.
A writer takes his pen
to write the words again
that all in love is fair.

All of fate's a chance.
It's either good or bad.
I tossed my coin to say
in love with me you'd stay.

But all in war is so cold.
You either win or lose.
When all is put away,
the losing side I'll play.

But all is fair in love.
I should have never left your side.
A writer takes his pen to write the words again
that all in love is fair.
A writer takes his pen to write the words again
that all in love is fair.

© 1973 Jobete Music Co., Inc. and Black Bull Music, Inc.
Stevie Wonder

12

TROUBLES AND TRIBUTES

1975–1983

TIGHTROPE

Novomber 28, 1979. I was sitting alone in the big round Jacuzzi in the middle of the spacious living room of my suite at Caesars Palace in Las Vegas. It was my birthday. Every year I made a practice of disappearing around that time. I didn't want people bringing me gifts just because it was my birthday. I was much more concerned about how people treated me the other 364 days of the year.

I had come to Caesars Palace with my friends Billy Davis and Mira Waters. Mira was someone he had introduced to me many years before. She was a petite, pretty, black actress. She was hip, smart, confident, and funny.

Mira was downstairs playing baccarat. She was having a ball. Billy was partying with friends somewhere. He was having a ball. I was depressed. I had a lot on my mind. I had to analyze what was going on in my company.

Our popularity, like our overhead, was growing, while our revenues, like our roster of stars, was shrinking. Making movies had boosted our prestige but not our profits. I loved making them but

353

had a lot to learn about how to make money at it. In the meantime I had slipped in the business I *did* know something about—records.

I had to laugh when I thought back to 1968 and how we were all gloating over having five records out of the Top 10 in one week. We had no idea at the time that the seeds of our undoing were being planted. Across the country in offices of the major record companies skeptics who never thought there was a market for black talent went on the offensive to grab the kind of music they had always thought would stay "over there." That was the beginning of a whole new ball game.

Some companies started developing their own black artists, while others were coming after Motowners—not only the artists, but the writers and producers as well. This was not easy for them to do, since most of our successful artists, producers and writers were happy and dedicated. But the more big business it became, the tougher it was for us to maintain our growth and protect against the subtle and not so subtle rush to capture our people.

In these changing times, the value of a proven artist was skyrocketing into the multimillions. And when a label decided to acquire someone else's artist, one who was already under contract, something once frowned on as unethical, it was now tolerated. I had a problem with that. I had a problem anteing up more every time an artist we had developed got a better offer. To me it became values versus value. I began to realize there was a major conflict within me between my *values* and the artists' *value*. Perhaps stubbornly, I would not always pay what it would take to get them to stay. That might have been a mistake.

While we were continuing to sign and launch new artists, some of our top acts from the sixties were leaving: Gladys Knight and the Pips, the Marvelettes, Martha and the Vandellas. Other groups left and later returned, like the Four Tops and the Temptations. Some did well, others didn't. Some were signed by companies that had no idea what to do with them.

The problem was that many Motown artists were used to a record company that provided a creative environment, relationships, a team, the ability to launch careers of longevity. I always believed this was the record company's obligation to the artist. That worked well when I could keep costs down, but those times were gone.

Our move to California hadn't helped. In Los Angeles we were one of many record companies, while in Detroit we had been *the* record company. The seventies had seen the departures of some of our key producers and writers from the old days: Harvey Fuqua and Johnny Bristol, Ashford and Simpson, Norman Whitfield. In California, our in-house way of producing was being replaced by a different, much more expensive way of making records. We would more and more have to look to independent producers, arrangers and musicians. Developing a perfect match between them and our artists was now much more complicated.

I was beginning to wonder if I was the right person to be running this company. Over the years I noticed that many successful entrepreneurs are driven, self-taught people who have a great desire to be loved and respected. Sometimes they create institutions that outgrow their personal style. I think I fit into that category.

Whatever my goals were at any given time, my strongest inclination was that of a teacher. Not just about singing, dancing and music but about winning and losing in life.

It never mattered who I was working with, that person's growth inevitably became more important than the project we were working on. One project was just another project to me. But I knew if I strengthened that person in some way, even at the expense of that one project, they could go on to do hundreds of successful projects.

I was a fanatic about—not just teaching—but making them really learn. I, no doubt, went a little overboard at times.

There's an old saying I believe in: Give a man a fish and he'll eat for a day. But give him a pole and he can eat for the rest of his life. Pop had been doing that with us for years, so I guess I came by it naturally.

When it came to managing a complex operation growing at the rate Motown was, I could see my personal methods weren't geared for that. So I tried to set up a management hierarchy to do it for me—like other big companies. I brought in an outside consulting firm to do a thorough analysis.

After getting their reports I hired some of these same people who had given me answers to all of my problems to be my new executives.

This isolated me from the insider loyalists who had grown up with the company and had learned my style the hard way. They weren't about to let these new "wonder boys" with their new ideas come in and change things in ways that went against the principles that were the foundation of Motown. They wouldn't openly defy the people I had brought in, but they would sit back and watch these "corporate experts" self-destruct. And in some cases, help them. Many took bets on how long the "wonder boys" would last.

The man who most had to deal with these consultants was the president of my record company, Ewart Abner, who already had his hands full just running the operation day to day. For the past couple of years he had done a good job, but by 1975 I was no longer happy with his performance. Productivity was down and I held him responsible.

In retrospect, I realized the situation was more complicated than that. Suzanne was running the Creative Division, which was the key to our company's success and survival, and whenever Ab disagreed with her and tried to override her decisions, she knew she could come directly to me.

To further complicate matters, I had become somewhat of an absentee landlord.

It didn't stop with Creative. We had problems all over the place— bickering by middle-management people, confusion brought on by my new corporate "experts," and a president without a lot of authority, a situation made tougher by financial worries and the loss of the Jackson 5.

I wanted to revive the old days. I wanted a czarlike character—a screaming, scheming, get-things-done, calculating, demanding kind—to run the company. I wanted Barney Ales back. Lucky for me he wanted to be back. I made a three-year consulting arrangement with Ab and asked him to step aside.

Helped by some things Abner had already set up, Barney came in with a bang, using all kinds of unique marketing schemes. One of his most effective campaigns was on the Stevie Wonder album, *Songs in the Key of Life.*

Stevie had been a major force in getting us through the early seventies with his three genius albums—*Talking Book, Innervisions* and *Fulfillingness' First Finale*. But then I heard his contract was coming up for renewal. And other companies were wooing him like mad. *No! Not again! Not Stevie.*

Our negotiation with him became the most grueling and nerve-wracking we had ever had, mainly because Stevie was still represented by our old friend, Johanan Vigoda. But, as before, at no time was it ever even implied that he might leave Motown. I appreciated that.

In April of 1976, we made a $13 million deal with Stevie that, I was told, was unprecedented for the time. I yielded to a unique clause that in the event I sold the company, he had to approve the buyer. That particular clause didn't bother me at that time because selling Motown was about as out of the question as my going back to work on the Lincoln-Mercury assembly line, singing "Mary Had A Little Lamb."

Five months later, Stevie's next album was ready for release, *Songs in the Key of Life*. When Barney and I first heard it we knew it was a double-album masterpiece. Barney rushed to do his thing. He and his staff prepromoted it every way they could, including setting up phone calls at a convention in Chicago between me and all the distributors so they could personally feel my excitement. *Songs in the Key of Life* entered the Pop charts its very first week at #1, making Stevie the first American artist to do that.

In 1977 Stevie was back at the Grammys, taking home another five awards, the same number he had won two years before for *Fulfillingness' First Finale*. This made him the only artist ever to win Album of the Year for three consecutive albums.

Another act coming on strong by the mid-seventies was the Commodores, whom we had signed back in 1971. "Piggy-backing" this brand-new group on tour to open for the Jackson 5, we gave them some great exposure even before they had a hit. The story about their first record success began in the least likely of all places—on the island of St. Maarten, where I had gone to play in a backgammon tournament and to sneak a long overdue vacation. In my party was Suzanne de Passe, who wasted no time in promoting the new group.

As soon as we arrived at the hotel, she came to my room with a tape she said I just had to hear.

"You intentionally came here to ruin my vacation. It's a plot."

"Absolutely not," she protested. "One song, that's all." She then proceeded to play something she told me was called "The Ram."

It was full of interesting, fast-darting, staccato sounds. "I love the track," I told her, "but I'd rather you bring it to me when you have the vocals dubbed in, when it's finished."

"It is finished," Suzanne said. "It's an instrumental."

I couldn't even remember the last time we'd released an instrumental, but there was something about this one I liked.

"Okay," I said, "but it doesn't sound like a ram to me. Those darting sounds remind me of gunshots. Why not call it 'Machine Gun'?"

"Of course. What a great name!" (She would've agreed to anything to get the record out.)

Being musicians and songwriters in addition to vocalists, the Commodores were a self-contained group. Lionel Richie, who sang most of their leads, played saxophone; Milan Williams was on keyboards; Thomas McClary on guitar; Ronald LaPread played bass; William King—trumpet; and Walter "Clyde" Orange—drums. In early '76, "Sweet Love" broke them into the Top 10. Working with longtime arranger and producer James Carmichael, the group had major hits in the next three years that spanned everything from the Country-Pop-flavored "Easy" to the funky "Brick House." Their "Three Times A Lady" in 1978 became an explosive first #1 for the group. With hits like "Still" and "Sail On" in 1979 the Commodores were ready to sail on into the eighties.

But the company wasn't. In 1978 "Three Times A Lady" was the only Motown single to break the Top 10 for the whole year. We had become dangerously dependent on a handful of our superstars—like the Commodores, Marvin, Smokey, Diana and Stevie. When we got a new album from one of them it meant an influx of millions; when we didn't—it meant trouble. And without developing successful new acts, it meant even bigger trouble.

As head of the Creative Division of the record company, Suzanne was struggling too hard with the producers, writers and artists. Her talents were not being utilized properly.

She had worked closely with me on TV and movie projects and had shown great instincts, dramatic imagination and a real feel for the visual world. I moved her over to head our movie production company, MPI.

With the phenomenal Motown specials she would be responsible for, some very successful Movies-of-the-Week, and an award-winning miniseries, that would turn out to be a great move.

But the Creative Division of the record company—so vital to our strength—was still without that perfect executive. In my attempts to find such a person we would go on to have eleven different heads of that division while in California alone. But the problem wasn't just creative.

Barney and I knew we could never revive those old days. The circumstances weren't the same anymore. The business had changed and so had the excitement of the old days. And Barney's big motivation, that thing that inspired him to perform miracles in marketing, was money. I didn't have very much and he kept asking for more. In January of '79, once again, we parted ways. Once again I was back to running the company myself—and looking for a new czar.

By now it had been three years since Stevie's last album. We were waiting frantically for his new one. He was forever telling us, "Next month." We would gear up, gear down, gear up, gear down.

Finally, it was ready—a double-album soundtrack from a movie documentary—Journey Through the Secret Life of Plants. When I first heard it, I got a sinking feeling it might not be the smash we so desperately needed from Stevie. But because he was such an innovator, influencing a generation of music makers, I was hopeful. I wanted to be wrong real bad.

Before it was released, Fay Hale, vice president in charge of Manufacturing and devoted Motown employee, rushed in to see me, screaming that her office was ordered by Sales to press up two million copies for shipment.

"I have no ear as you always remind me," she said, "and I may be missing something, but a record about plant life with elephants stepping on glass? Do you know how expensive these double-album covers are? They've got special embossing, special die-cutting—and Braille!"

I hurried over to Sales where everybody was already celebrating what was to be the new Stevie Wonder smash of the decade. Stevie's past successes had made them big heroes, so they were adamant about going with the two million advance pressings. But I was more adamant that we cut the order in half, to one million. I won. And still that turned out to be around nine hundred thousand too many.

Now here I was, a month later, on my birthday, sitting in a hot tub in Las Vegas, depressed, trying to get it together. This wasn't just any old birthday, this was my fiftieth. All I could think about was overhead: sales people, promotion people, production, advertising, publicity, purchasing, administration, personnel, a legal department and all that other stuff.

Mira Waters came back to the suite and saw me still in the Jacuzzi. "Get yo' ass out of that hot water before you turn into a prune. Come on down to the casino. We need some of that Gordy luck."

"Yeah," Billy said, sticking his head in behind her, "and some of that Gordy money, too."

Those two always made me feel better. *Maybe the tables would lift my spirits.*

I lost $10,000.

Even so, on the plane ride home I was already cheering myself up. *Stevie will get a better album, Diana's there, Smokey's there, Marvin's there, the Commodores. I'm going to be fine.* By Monday morning I was optimistic.

"Hi, guys," I said cheerfully to the not-too-cheerful-looking Novecks, who were waiting in my office.

Still living in Detroit, they had flown out to L.A. for a meeting with me.

"Distressing news," Harold said.

"Like what?"

"Well," Sidney said in his Southern, Jewish accent, "you're insolvent!"

"Insolvent? What do you mean?"

"Bankrupt," Harold said. "You've got more liabilities than assets."

"But how could that be?"

"I've been telling you all along," Sidney said, "over and over again, Mr. Gordy, you're spending too much."

He was right. He had told me. Sidneygrams I called them. About once every few months—like the kid who cried wolf—he would send me a note complaining or warning me about something. I had gotten numb to them.

"But you're my auditors. There should be better checks and balances to prevent this kind of thing from happening." Even as I said it, I knew the responsibility was mine—I hadn't been paying attention.

About this same time, Jerry Moss, the head of A&M Records, came to see me at my beach house. Jerry and his partner, Herb Alpert, had also built their company from the ground up and we were looking for a way to survive. We had been grappling with a problem in the industry—the decline of the independent distributors. More and more, record labels like ours had been forced to switch their distribution over to the majors—the big record companies who had money and clout and their own branch distribution.

A few years before, Jerry and I had joined forces to set up our own distributorship, which we called "Together." We were hoping that by this alliance Motown and A&M could stay independent through ownership of our own distribution in some key areas. But now, they had decided to stop bucking the tide.

So Jerry told me A&M was making a deal with RCA for national distribution. In order to do that I had to release him from our five-year deal, which still had six months to go.

Jerry was a friend and had always been honorable in all our dealings. "No problem," I said.

He appreciated that but was concerned about me. I told him I wasn't ready to give up my independence. I wanted to stick it out a little longer.

One thing was certain: I had to drastically cut my costs. Coming up with a cost-cutting program was rough, very rough. We all knew we were too fat—way overstaffed. But many were like my family. Some were my family.

At the time, Alan Salke, my personal business adviser, had an answer. He wanted to save the company. And if I was really serious and really wanted to cut costs, I would have to "be dramatic." He suggested I get rid of half the employees by listing them in alphabetical order and firing every other name on the list—regardless.

"Great," I said, "but what if my name falls in the wrong place?" "Too bad," he said. "Just do it!"

Instead, I put through a 15 percent cut for all of the executive salaries and outside consultants.

Alan Salke's next recommendation was to sell Jobete, the highest offer being $27 million. Seeing no alternative, I seriously considered it. But because of contractual complications one thing led to another, so I decided, instead, for the first time in my life to get a business loan from the bank.

The bank. That's a place where you should only borrow money when you don't need it. Because then, they will give it to you on the best terms and with the best attitude. But when you do need it, like I did, everything is just the opposite. They even required that the money we got from our distributors go directly to a locked box at the bank where they would pay themselves first, then us. I had no option but to go for it.

And so, as a new decade began, I finalized the details of the loan and I teetered on a tightrope into the eighties.

Smokey had always wanted to come through with a big hit when the company needed it most. And with the release of "Cruisin' " from his hit album *Where There's Smoke*, he did.

More help came from Diana with her album entitled *Diana*, which had two hit singles, "Upside Down" and "I'm Coming Out."

Less than a year after the disappointing *Plants* album, Stevie redeemed himself with the sizzling *Hotter Than July*, which included "Happy Birthday," the song he had written in honor of Dr. Martin Luther King. Stevie, totally dedicated to the fight for human rights, was one of the main activists behind the campaign to establish Dr. King's birthday as a national holiday. That made us all proud.

After a year, I was able to pay off the bank loan.

By this time, I had hired Jay Lasker as president of the record company. A veteran in the business, he was known for his marketing genius, tough leadership ability and dogmatic, hard-hitting personality.

I had been looking for a czar to run Motown and Jay was just that—a strong, cigar-smoking powerhouse. At his first meeting as president he brought all the department heads together. "If anybody disagrees with me and goes to Berry Gordy and he agrees with you, that's fine," he told them, "but if he doesn't, you're fired."

Some of the employees couldn't get out of the meeting fast enough to tell me what he had said. They thought this would bother me, but it didn't. Jay was just the kind of guy I was looking for.

While Jay was outspoken and direct, he proved to be someone I respected and valued highly. He was forthright and honest and a great packager, taking many of our biggest hits from over the years and re-releasing them in new "best of" compilations.

Not only were we getting hits from some of our established artists and revenue from Jay's marketing techniques, we were also starting to break some new acts.

Lionel Richie, who by then had left the Commodores, became very hot in the eighties. His first album, *Lionel Richie*, was a smash—as was its #1 single, "Truly."

Another new act who struck gold with their second album, *All This Love*, was DeBarge, a family of youngsters led by a gifted singing and writing talent, El DeBarge. And then there was outrageous Rick James, taking our music in a totally new direction, coining phrases I had never heard before. Cocky and wild, he was considered the King of Punk Funk, coming out with smash hits like "You And I" and "Super Freak." His live shows were so daring they shocked me.

Rick did it all—singer, musician, writer, arranger, producer. Watching him work in the studio was amazing. He was innovative and could come up with some of the greatest rhythms and vocal arrangements in his head, on the spot. Aside from producing himself, he produced the Tempts, the Mary Jane Girls—whom he brought in—and a discovery of mine, Teena Marie, a young, white, talented singer who became a brilliant writer and producer in her own right.

As good as everything was it wasn't enough, but I knew we were on the right track.

Then the unthinkable happened.

In December of '80, shortly after Diana (no longer married to Bob Silberstein) started dating Gene Simmons of Kiss, a heavyset stranger came to see me. He said he was the group's merchandising man. He walked into my office, announced himself as a representative of Diana, and got right down to business. He told me I had the "inside track." He was giving me the first option to match a $20 million offer if I wanted to keep her.

My mind was reeling. "Very interesting," I said.

After *Mahogany*, I knew things were bound to change somewhat between us, but never in my wildest dreams did I see her leaving the company. I had taken her for granted. I somehow thought the careers of Diana Ross and Berry Gordy were linked forever.

Only a few months before she'd had the biggest album of her career, *Diana*, and her current single, "It's My Turn," was reaching the Top 10.

It was the title song from a movie, ironically, about a woman going off on her own.

I told the man, "I can't comment any further until I talk to Diana."

A few weeks later he returned with Diana and she assured me that he was representing her.

After a long discussion in which I went over the benefits of her staying with the company that knew her and knew how best to work with her, she gave me the hopeful feeling that she would come back and work things out.

She did come back, for a meeting at my house between the two of us. But when I met her at the door, the firm set of her jaw and the sharp click of her high heels on the wooden floor told me that working something out was probably not what she had in mind. I was calm, but not happy.

The two of us sat down in my library. Eyes not connecting. Cups clinking against saucers. Clothes being smoothed that were already smooth.

Looking at her face I saw many emotions: a mixture of respect, defiance, nervousness and yes, love, though it was impossible to know what she was really thinking. When she called me "Berry," instead of "Black," the affectionate nickname we had used for each other all these years, I knew she was leaving.

"This isn't easy for either of us," I thought she may have said, but what I heard more clearly was a young Diana laughing playfully as she jumped up on my lap while I sat mixing in the Hitsville studio control room. That skinny kid had blossomed into a magnificent creature who romanced the entire world. Images were going off in my brain like flashbulbs—Diana victorious on stage, raising her hands in triumph; me protecting her as we dashed through mobs of screaming fans; her face in close-up—serene, sexy, beautiful, sad and bluesy. She, dancing around me, soft and sensuous, and now, for the first time, moving away. Going for the big money, money I could not match.

"Money is only a part of value," I said softly. "Value is everything you have—your team, people who know you—love you." I wanted to remind her of what we'd accomplished together and what we could do in the future, but I knew it was too late. "If RCA is willing to pay you that kind of money, I guess you should take it."

In May of 1981, she signed a deal with RCA. I could understand logically and rationally why she did it, but it killed me. After twenty-one years, all of a sudden, she was gone.

MOTOWN 25

A LITTLE OVER A YEAR and a half later.

"Gotta run, boss," Suzanne de Passe said as she stood up from the chair in front of my oak wood desk. "I'm meeting Richard Pryor for lunch."

Great, I've got crises coming out of my ears and one of my top executives has to cut short a meeting with me to go and hobnob with celebrities.

"Lunch? Again?"

In our ongoing mentor-mentee relationship, Suzanne and I had mastered communication with each other to a seamless art, so when I said, "Lunch? Again?" she knew I was making a dig about her upwardly mobile lifestyle and the frequency of her "doing" lunch with entertainment notables. From the moment that Motown had made its move to California, Suzanne had set her sights on becoming an important player in Hollywood. And now, as the head of Motown Productions, she was.

"But didn't you hear what I said? I'm meeting Richard Pryor for lunch."

"I heard you."

"Want me to cancel?"

"Oh, no, no. You made a date," I said, "you keep it. Far be it for me to stop you from your social affairs."

Ignoring my sarcasm, she told me this was far from being a social affair. She was going to ask Richard to emcee a TV special she was trying to put together in honor of me.

"First of all, I don't want to be honored," I said. "And secondly, you're wasting time that could be used to help me with what I want to be helped with."

She told me the artists loved and respected me and this was a chance for them to show it.

"If they want to show it," I said, "why do they forget to mention me when they're on TV?"

"It's not that they forget mentioning you," she said, "they avoid it. And it's all your fault."

"Oh?"

"Competition!" She told me the very thing I had done to make them strong was now coming back to haunt me. "Some may have left, but none ever stopped competing. They compete with each other, the outside world, themselves, but mostly with you—the big guy, the father figure, the giant who once controlled their lives. Nothing they did was ever quite good enough for you."

She was right. I had never stopped pushing. Suzanne said she knew how they felt because she was one of them. She had gone through rougher times with me than most and had become a star in her own right. However, she explained, "Just because I understood the greater purpose didn't make it any less painful." Just before she headed out the door, she said, "You've created a great desire in all of us. It's called 'Beat the Teacher.' "

"Say hello to Richard for me," I said.

Four months later, Motown 25 was about to happen. I found myself getting excited. With the date for the taping less than three weeks away, Suzanne, the executive producer of the event, swept into my office and told me she was thrilled by how much the artists wanted to do it for me. "But," she added, "I want to fill you in on a few details."

"Okay."

"First," she said, "Lionel Richie won't be able to attend, but will do a video." He would sing a song to the little poster girl for sickle-cell anemia—which the TV special was a benefit for.

"Wonderful. And?"

"Stevie thought it was a great idea. He'll definitely do it. That is, if he can postpone his trip to Africa."

I knew Suzanne was building to something so I wasn't surprised when she said, "Oh, there's a little problem I need your help with. Two holdouts."

"Yeah?"

"Marvin and Michael."

"Oh, I thought it was gonna be someone important."

She laughed nervously.

"They don't want to do it, huh?"

"Oh no," she said, "they want to do it all right but I think Marvin wants you to ask him personally. And Michael said he was overexposed on TV but would definitely sit in the audience to support you." She said she was sure I could get them to do it if I would just talk to them.

"You want me to ask them to honor me. Are you crazy? There is no way I would ever do that."

March 25, 1983, I was comfortably seated in the balcony at the Pasadena Civic Auditorium waiting for the show to start—our twenty-fifth anniversary celebration.

More than just about anything, the night of Motown 25 has been the hardest for me to write about.

How do you clearly remember a night when so much of it was spent remembering? A night when you have the most complicated series of emotions you ever felt—images of the past and present constantly colliding.

Earlier, backstage, artists whom I hadn't had contact with for years were hugging and kissing each other and me. Old-home week. Because of so many of them in one place, there were nowhere near enough dressing rooms, enough makeup people, enough anything. Like those old Motortown Revues—everybody packed like sardines. No one cared. They loved it. That was a sure sign that these stars, no matter where they were in their careers now, were still Motowners all the way.

It was awkward sitting next to Diana for the first part of the show. We hadn't seen each other since she had left the company about two years before and neither of us could think of much to say. But then there were other feelings of having her at my side again for that night—sentimental, affectionate, warm.

Nostalgia came over me as the show began with some old film clips and I saw the caption "Detroit 1958" and that HITSVILLE USA sign on our little building at 2648 West Grand Boulevard. With some dramatic music in the background, I heard an announcer's voice: "Hitsville. It started here twenty-five years ago, the sound that rocked the world . . ."

Yep, I guess we did.

Smokey was the first Motown artist to appear on stage. He had been with me from even before there was a Motown, more than twenty-five years ago. *Where had all the years gone?*

When Smokey introduced Richard Pryor and said, "Once a Motowner always a Motowner," it brought back memories of how I had become Richard's manager back in 1965 after seeing him at the Apollo Theater on an amateur show. Seven years later I had hunted him down in California to play Piano Man in *Lady Sings the Blues.* And now he had been the first to commit to doing the show.

As crazy as I knew he could be, he took that whole night very

63. Two hams, Kennedy and his father, kick it up.

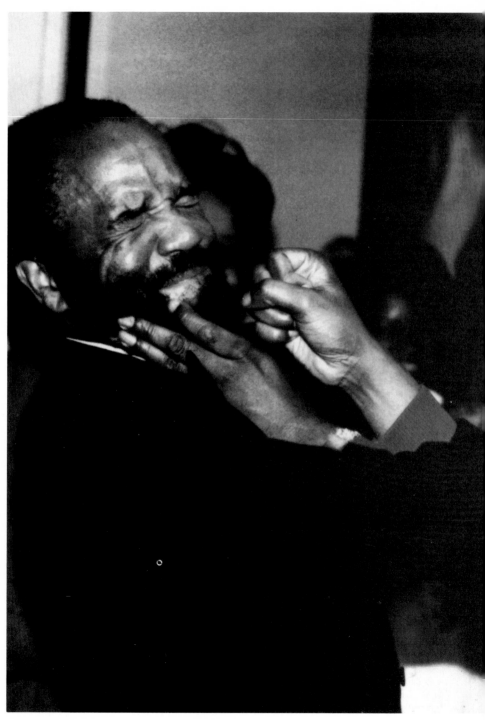

64. Stevie Wonder graciously accepts my congratulations after he received the Oscar for his song "I Just Called to Say I Love You," from *The Woman in Red* soundtrack.

65. At *Motown 25*, I was surrounded by the love of Stevie Wonder, Michael Jackson, Claudette Robinson, Smokey Robinson, Diana Ross, Richard Pryor and Marvin Gaye.

66. The boys have always been the clowns in the family. I wonder where we got it from? *Left to right:* Terry, Kerry, Berry IV, me, Kennedy and Pop.

67. Getting ready to do battle. The Four Tops with HDH in one corner,
the Tempts with Norman Whitfield in the other.

68. My youngest child, Stefan, on his 10th birthday.

69. Nineteen ninety-one Sibling Summit at Gwen's ranch. *Left to right:* Fuller, Gwen, me, Esther, Robert, Anna and George.

70. Harold and Sidney Noveck, my financial guardians for over 30 years.

71. My three beautiful daughters, Sherry, Hazel Joy and Rhonda.

OPPOSITE PAGE:
72. Proud of my protégé.

73. In 1993 I met Doris Day, who inspired one of my earliest songs.

74. Admiring my childhood hero, Joe Louis, with his wife, Martha.

75. With my idol Sugar Ray Robinson and my oldest son, Berry IV.

76. Smokey, a special kind of hero.

77. Pop, my biggest hero.

seriously. Richard is a funny man in his soul who cannot *not* be funny. I got such a kick out of him as I watched him brilliantly and sensitively deliver his rendition of *The Motown Story* . . . *A Fairy Tale:*

"Once upon a time in a kingdom known as Detroit there lived a young warrior named Berry.

And as a youth he fought in arenas with padded gauntlets for small sums of money.

He got his brains beat out.

So Berry took employment at a local chariot factory called Ford and learned skills of the assembly line.

But his heart, alas, was not in his work. No, no, no.

He took on the ways of the minstrel then and he began to write songs for others to sing.

And a local celebrity, Sir Jackie of Wilson, heard some of the songs and put them on circular platters called discs.

The townspeople liked the sounds that emanated from the pressed discs and turned them into something called hits.

But Berry realized something was astray—a bit awry here. Oh yes.

You see the great wealth he had anticipated never materialized.

He was busted.

So Berry went out on a great quest and he found Miracles and Wonders and Marvelettes.

And he brought the discoveries to a secret place called Hitsville and there he taught them wondrous things.

There was young Smokey of Robinson, and Mary of Wells and Martha of the Vandellas, Marvin of Gaye and Tammi of Terrell, and there were Pips and Knights named Gladys, and Temptations and Tops, Contours, Spinners.

And before anyone realized what was happening, it happened.

Hitsville became like its name—a house from which . . ."

Richard had lost his place on the TelePrompTer and quickly came out with something sounding like, "Loshfloshkosk," looking at the audience smiling, "but you know what I mean." They knew what he meant and they knew what had just happened and they loved it. Richard continued as though it was all planned:

> "And Berry said to himself once more, 'Self, this is a lot better than being punched in the head by padded gauntlets.'
> And all was going well at Hitsville when our young hero met three fair maidens from the projects of Brewster.
> He groomed them, he gowned them, he nursed them, rehearsed them, then gave out the news: that Motown gave birth to the Supremes.
> It was like something out of a fairy tale.
> And the family grew and everything they touched turned to gold—and bulging pockets.
> And Berry he had climbed the beanstalk to face the great giant and captured the goose that laid the golden records.
> And after five and twenty years, there's a chance—and everyone wants it—that it will happen to them and all will live happily ever after."

"We love you Berry, very much."

That show was one thrill after another. When Dick Clark said he was pleased to have been "in some small way" a part of the Motown story, it humbled me.

Some small way! Is he kidding?

When he talked about the revolution Motown had created in the world of music, I thought about the revolution he had made in my life on that day back at Loucye's house when I first heard Jackie Wilson singing "Reet Petite" on his show. And what a part he had played in the Supremes' history, when they went out on his *Caravan of Stars* as nobodies and came back as stars.

Before I could recall all the times that Dick was there for us, the show had moved on and Motown artists were singing their way through great moments of my life.

One minute it was Smokey and the Miracles—who had not per-formed together for over a decade—with "Shop Around" and "Tears Of A Clown." This moment was especially exciting to me because Claudette was there. One of the original members, along with Pete Moore, Ronnie White and Bobby Rogers, she was the real first lady of Motown.

Then Smokey moved me up to another era, when he later came back with Linda Ronstadt singing "Ooo Baby Baby" and "Tracks Of My Tears." It was strange for me sitting there watching the present but quickly falling back into the past—Detroit of the sixties. There was Martha Reeves, strong and soulful, with "Heat Wave." Her performance knocked me out that night as it always had. Next Mary Wells sang "My Guy" and Jr. Walker growled out "Shotgun." Those memories blended into recent California years with some of the newer faces—like the Commodores, who had captured the feeling of the past few years with "Brick House."

It was another special moment for me when the Four Tops and the Temptations came out. They were epitomizing something I had set up many years before—the Battle of the Stars. They had been challenging each other all over the country. I had just seen them a short time before at the Universal Amphitheater in Los Angeles. That night, after an opening segment with both groups singing about what they were going to do to the other, the Tempts left the stage.

There were the Four Tops. Four guys who had never changed any members—together even before Motown started, not only going strong but displaying practically a lost art. They were a combination of some of the greatest entertainers I had seen throughout my life—the Mills Brothers, the Treniers, the Ink Spots, the Will Mastin Trio and many others. They were not only one of the hottest groups of the sixties but great showmen.

Levi Stubbs, out front, had kept the audience in the palm of his hand with his soulful interpretations of great songs, while Duke Fakir and Lawrence Payton backed him up with the class and artistry of real pros. Obie Benson's face told it all. Bright, happy, having the time of his life as he bounced around with his bass notes and talking to the audience with his expressions and moves. After a few numbers, mesmerizing the audience, it was now time for the Tempts to do their thing. I wondered what they could possibly do to top the Tops. I was worried for them.

Once the Tempts hit the stage, moving through a medley of their hits in that familiar tight Tempts formation, I was worried no more.

Now, at *Motown 25*, because the show was so long, they could only do a compilation of both groups' hits. The Tops started with "Reach Out, I'll Be There" as the Tempts answered with "Get Ready." The Tops topped that with "It's The Same Old Song." The Tempts upped them with "Ain't Too Proud To Beg." The Tops were undaunted as they soared even higher with "Baby I Need Your Loving." Richard Street of the Tempts tapped Levi on the shoulder as if to say, "Watch this," as the audience started screaming over the intro to "My Girl." Jumping right in, Levi joined Richard on lead with that one, until the Tempts' Dennis Edwards broke off into "I Can't Get Next To You." This time Levi tapped Dennis on the shoulder as the Tops roared into "I Can't Help Myself (Sugar Pie Honey Bunch)" which pushed the crowd to a peak. The Tempts kept it right there as Dennis launched into "(I Know) I'm Losing You." The two groups were trading off lines, burning up with classic Temptations and Four Tops moves, dancing the finale. Once it was all over, like the ending of a twelve-round championship bout, they hugged and hugged and hugged.

After the intermission Stevie Wonder came on, singing a medley of his hits. Another time flash—from that little kid banging on those drums in the studio, making all that noise, to this exceptional man making incredible music.

Stevie was originally supposed to close the first half of the show, but he arrived late. That was not unusual for him. I could never get too mad at Stevie because his heart was always so much in the right place. He was often out front fighting for the humanitarian causes he believed in. And when it came to me and my family—birthdays, funerals, anything personal—he was always there, on time.

A few years before, when the company was facing bankruptcy, I decided the best of my bad options was to sell Jobete. But for Stevie's songs to be part of the deal I had to get his okay. He was coming to the end of a world tour for his *Hotter Than July* album when I caught

372

up with him in Paris. He was going to be there for three nights of concerts.

Sitting in the audience that first night, I was listening to "Signed, Sealed, Delivered (I'm Yours)," "Superstition," "Sir Duke" and "Higher Ground"—songs I had come to tell him I wanted to sell. Then he sang "Happy Birthday," the song he had written to honor Dr. King. I was thrilled to see how positively the French reacted to it. Afterward at dinner, we talked about his fight to establish Dr. King's birthday as a national holiday. We could both see how much power music had. I decided it would not be the best idea to talk to him about selling Jobete that night.

The second day, another show, another dinner. But the timing was never right. There were too many people around or we were distracted by something. Another day, another show, another dinner. On the fourth day there were no more shows but another dinner. By the end of that dinner it was me and him—just the two of us alone.

"Stevie," I said, "I need you to understand something. I am in serious trouble and I'm thinking about selling Jobete."

"What do you mean? Sell the publishing company? How can you sell the publishing?"

"I know it's a shocking thought," I said, "and I don't want to do it, but I think the time has come when I'd better be a little more realistic about the economics of the business."

Our talk quickly moved from banter to bickering with me finally grumbling, "It probably wouldn't have gotten so bad if I could have depended on you to deliver me albums when you were supposed to."

Stevie shot back, "Yeah, that might be true, but when I do give you albums you know they're gonna be good!"

I didn't elaborate then on all the financial troubles the company was in and Stevie did not give his okay. When I presented it to the buyers without Stevie they wanted to drop the price. I said no. The deal fell through.

Thank God for Stevie.

When Marvin sat down at the piano and began improvising some melancholy, jazzy chords it was déjà vu. That was what he was doing twenty-three years before, when my sister Gwen had pointed him out through the studio window at the Hitsville Christmas party and said, "That guy is really good!"

So much had happened since then.

Watching him sitting there filled me with incredible memories of a beautiful but troubled life. He was always in conflict with something, always rebelling. He didn't want to pay taxes; he got into drugs, he got out of drugs; he fought anyone who told him what or what not to do, including himself.

In the mid-seventies, Marvin's marriage to my sister Anna hit the rocks.

I had made it a point never to get involved in their affairs, but when these things were in the family, unfortunately, I was always somewhere in the middle because both parties sought me out to one degree or another. I was still Anna's brother and still Marvin's friend, sometimes father figure and confidant.

I was more concerned for Marvin. I knew Anna would be fine. She was strong, protective and had played every role with him— wife, friend, sister, sometimes mother. And it was obvious how much he depended on her.

They could not come to a settlement agreement, and Marvin did not want this to get messy. Neither did I. I presented him with an idea on the golf course one day that he loved. I would get all our best producers who knew his style to produce tracks for him. Then, I told him, "All you'd have to do is come off the road and spend two weeks of your time putting your voice on them. And whatever the album made would fulfill your responsibility for alimony and child support forever. If the album did not make enough, it would be my responsibility to take care of Anna and Marvin III. You would have no more responsibility. Two weeks of about six hours a day in full settlement after a seventeen-year marriage has got to be a good deal for anybody. It's a win-win situation," I said. "The only one that can lose is me."

Marvin thought this was the greatest idea he had ever heard— only two weeks of his time and he would never again have to worry about paying alimony and child support. But a few weeks later, when he came back off of a tour, he had changed his mind.

"I don't know, BG. What if it sells millions? I want a cap on it."

"Yeah, Marvin, but what if it sells nothing? You're off the hook and I'm on. Marvin, two weeks of your time?"

"Naw, BG, I don't think so."

Two years later, behind on his payments, he went before a judge who ordered him to produce such an album himself and if it didn't sell he had to pay additional monies. Marvin hated it.

He started out trying to make the worst album he could, but his true artistry took over. He proceeded to make a documentary-type album—charting the course of the relationship on record. He had to sing about what he was going through in this breakup—hurt, anger, love, longing, regret, resentment. The feelings were so raw. It was as pure Marvin as you could ever get. Knowing he had to hand it over to Anna, he gave it an appropriate title, *Here, My Dear*. Even the inside cover of the album, showing a Monopoly board with the words "Judgement" on it, the marriage partners as adversaries and their possessions as game pieces, was a masterpiece of symbolism.

Marvin remarried and when that marriage got into trouble, he became even more despondent and left the country—becoming a recluse. While overseas, he signed a deal with Columbia Records, who had been courting him.

It didn't surprise me—Marvin was always searching and when the time came I had mixed feelings. I was losing a major source of income, one of the powerhouses. But I also knew I was losing the pressure of dealing with Marvin's problems. And we would still be friends, go out to the golf course together, have fun.

When he came back to the States after his big hit, "Sexual Healing" (which won him his first and only Grammy), he called me for advice on a new song he was writing. He wanted to know what I thought of the title—"Sanctified Pussy." He was dead serious.

My first thought was what a relief—I don't have to deal with this one. "Well, Marvin," I said, "sounds great to me, but you might have a little trouble convincing Columbia." (Obviously he did, because it was later released as "Sanctified Lady.")

As Marvin got up from the piano bench and began to sing, I thought back to how after telling Suzanne there was no way I was gonna ask anybody to honor me, I had changed my mind and invited Marvin over for lunch.

When he arrived that day at my house, it was the first time I had seen him in almost two years. He was in great spirits. He loved the thought of my having to ask him to do something for me. But just knowing I was willing was enough; he never even made me do it.

"I was gonna do the show all the time," he said, "but you know me, BG. I just wanted to feel a little special."

"You *are* special, man."

Marvin smiled. He noticed a chipping iron lying next to a golf bag as we walked out to the patio where lunch had been served. "Still playing, huh?" he said, picking up the club, swinging it across the grass, hitting an imaginary ball.

"Gotta keep in shape," I said. "Never know when you'll come back trying to take my money again."

"That was fun, BG."

"Yeah, for you maybe."

Marvin smiled, still swinging the club. "I was pretty good if I must say so myself," he said, then reminded me of the day he sank a forty-foot putt on me for $2,000.

After lunch, I had him follow me into the house and up the stairs to a converted attic area, a meditation-type room with overstuffed pillows and Persian rugs, a hideaway I called the "Raj Mahal" after Roger Campbell, who had it done for me as a surprise when I was out of town.

We took our seats cross-legged on big brocaded cushions on the floor.

"Hey Marvin, what was that joke you used to tell about Ma' Laady?"

Marvin chuckled softly, "Y'know, BG, that's one of my favorites." Growing animated and bubbly, he started in.

Nobody could tell it like Marvin. He loved imitating English accents. Feeling comfortable, Marvin reached into his pocket and pulled out a joint.

"Hey, man, that's not cool," I said. "You still doin' that shit?"

"But BG, this is like . . ." His words trailed off as he made a gesture around the room, then telling me this was a special moment, a special meeting of the minds, and he wanted to celebrate it with a little grass.

Sensing what this meant to him I said, "Okay man, it's cool."

376

"Good shit, man," he said, holding his breath with tight lips after taking a deep hissing drag on the joint. Smoke curled out of his mouth as he extended the joint to me.

"No, no man, not me. It gets me much too paranoid. My mind's already active enough. I tried it when I was about fifteen and hated it."

But then looking hurt, he said, "Aw, BG, come on. This is you and me, man. You and me."

So I took a couple of puffs and as I did, I saw in his eyes a peace, a contentment. "Yeah," he said, "pass the peace pipe."

"Yeah," I echoed, "the peace pipe, man."

That's what it was.

We talked about all sorts of stuff. Marvin told me of the trials and tribulations in his love life. But not like someone crying on my shoulder. It was just Marvin being Marvin, honest; a man who could make his worst heartbreaks into the funniest stories.

Our conversation turned to the old days, which Marvin seemed to be missing. He told me he had thoughts of getting back with Anna and even returning to Motown.

A few days later he told me that that time together had meant the world to him. It was about two old friends, two everyday, anyday cats talking about the foibles of living and loving, and admitting to having done some stupid shit.

At *Motown 25*, as Marvin sang "What's Going On" I was caught up in his magic, his aura.

Mother, mother, there's too many of you crying,
Brother, brother, brother, there's far too many of you dying . . .

I had no idea that this would be the last time I'd ever see him do his thing. A year later, on April 1, 1984, April Fools' Day, a day before his forty-fifth birthday, he was shot and killed by his father.

Watching him that night, he reminded me more than ever of Billie Holiday—singing through his pain, smiling through his sorrow, crying through his joy. Marvin—such a star, such a character, the truest artist I have ever known.

For my emotional height, there was nothing that could have topped what I got from Marvin that night. But in terms of pure entertainment it was the other holdout, Michael Jackson, who stopped the show.

When he and his brothers came out on stage for a historic Jackson 5 reunion electricity shot through the whole place.

I thought back to my talk with Michael about appearing on the show, once again doing what I had told Suzanne I would never do. I caught up with him over at our Hitsville recording studio in Hollywood. Guy Costa, our technological pioneer, had built a state-of-the-art video facility there that many outside artists used. That day Michael was there overdubbing a video with producer Quincy Jones. When Michael saw me come in, he smiled, stopping to greet me. We hugged, then headed downstairs to talk privately.

He told me of his concern about being overexposed on TV.

"This is not TV," I quickly told him, "this is *Motown 25*." I pointed out that he and his brothers hadn't been together for eight years and what a reunion this could be. "Sure, this is going to help me and Motown, but if you think you're big now, you do this thing right and you can really go into orbit."

It began with an exciting buildup of various clips of a young Jackson 5—from their 1968 audition in Detroit to *The Ed Sullivan Show*. Then the boys, all grown up, hit the stage, bringing the crowd to their feet.

With the drama and precision of their early days, Michael led the group through one spectacularly choreographed song after the other in a medley of their Motown hits.

He then moved center stage for a solo spot with his latest hit, "Billie Jean." It was the most incredible performance I'd ever seen. He had touches of many of the greats in that one performance—Sammy Davis, Jr., Fred Astaire, Jackie Wilson, Marcel Marceau and James Brown. But it was his own *Moonwalk* that blew everybody away. When the special aired two months later Michael did indeed go into orbit.

As the night drew to a close there were film clips of the Supremes, each identifying a place in time where we were all together, the girls and me—Diana, Mary and Florence and later Cindy.

There was the Sullivan show, *To Tell the Truth*, a trip to China,

Japan, London. Each clip brought back a special feeling as I recalled how the Supremes had for so long led the way for Motown. They had become the standard by which girl groups were measured and had made their mark on history that would always be there. I thought of what a fighter and a survivor Mary Wilson was. She may not have been the lead singer, but in a sense she was the heart and soul of the Supremes. She had been the glue that kept the group and their legacy alive.

Then I heard Diana's voice coming from the back of the auditorium as she made her entrance singing, "Ain't No Mountain High Enough," moving down the aisle and up to the stage.

I felt a kind of a pain creeping in. Tonight there was nothing but glory but tomorrow, back at the office, there would be nothing but problems.

All night long everything had been going too fast, but now everything began to move in slow motion. Diana had been the love of my life, the person who had given me the most thrills.

But for the past few years things had not been right between us and tonight Diana would try to address that for the first time.

Looking squarely up at me in the balcony, she said, "There's a strange thing, but Berry has always felt that he's never been really appreciated."

A little voice in my head shot back—*No shit.*

She continued, her eyes still locked in on mine, but her voice cracking slightly and her stance wavering. "It's a strange thing, I feel a little emotional. But it's not about the people that leave Motown that's important. It's about the people who come back. And tonight everybody came back."

That little voice again—*No Diana, that doesn't cut it, that doesn't make it okay.* I knew that she meant what she was saying, that she sincerely wanted to smooth over the rough edges she knew I must be feeling.

Then Diana raised her fist in the power sign to me.

My automatic response was to give it back to her, raising both of my fists up and signaling—*Yeah, I'm with you, like always.* But just as automatic were my hands changing their mind. They opened up,

379

let go. I had given up. Not our love. I knew that would always be. What I had given up was my fight for her understanding of me and what I was really about.

I thought about a line from one of Stevie's songs: *"All is fair in love."* While she hadn't given me what I thought I needed, she had given me a dream come true. Long ago she had promised me, "If you can think it, I can do it." And she had. She was my star and will always be my leading lady.

Far off in the distance I heard Mary Wilson and Cindy Birdsong joining Diana on the chorus of "Someday We'll Be Together." Meanwhile, other Motown stars were slowly making their way onto the stage, singing along.

Still looking at me, Diana said, "Well, how long will it take you to get down here, Black? Ladies and gentlemen, Berry Gordy."

I was surprised. This had not been planned. With the overwhelming applause that had come once everybody—and me—realized that Diana was summoning me to the stage, I felt myself melting.

Walking down that aisle amidst a sea of people, a swarm of cheering, I couldn't contain my burning pride. In front of me was a dreamlike mural—the great cast of characters from my life—waiting anxiously on stage to hug and kiss me.

When I reached the stage it was as if nothing had ever changed. In these very real minutes I felt that whatever misunderstandings we might have had with each other meant nothing. Beyond rivalries, beyond misunderstandings, no matter what, they loved me and I them. And there was nothing anybody could do about it.

The topper to *Motown 25* came a few months later in the fall of 1983, when the show was nominated for nine Emmy Awards.

At home, I was lying in bed watching the broadcast on TV when the category for Outstanding Variety, Music, or Comedy Program was announced. I was tense. We had lost the other eight. This was the most prestigious award of all and our last chance to win.

When I heard those beautiful words, "And the winner is . . . *Motown 25: Yesterday, Today, Forever,*" a relieved excitement came over me as I watched an emotional Suzanne de Passe jump out of her seat, leading the way up to the stage, followed by director Don

Mischer, producer and writer Buz Kohan, and producer Suzanne Coston.

Suzanne picked up her Emmy and headed for the podium where she began her acceptance speech.

I was not prepared for my reaction when she ended the speech, looking straight into the camera with tear-filled eyes:

> ". . . a man who changed my life so extraordinarily and so dramatically that I just want to tell him, Berry Gordy, I love you . . .

And holding up the award she continued—

"and this one's for you!"

It was hard to hold back the tears. I had been thanked in front of millions of people by someone who really understood me and who really wanted to do it.

That was a big night for me. *Motown 25* closed one chapter on the building of my company and opened another one on the selling of it.

13

MOTOWN FOREVER
1983–1988

I WAS HOLDING OUR LATEST quarterly statement as I made my way down the corridor to Jay Lasker's office. The figures made it clear—our collection problems had gotten worse.

From the strong smell of his Cuban cigar wafting down the hall I knew Jay was in and I was not surprised to hear him screaming at one of our distributors.

"Don't give me that fuckin' 'the check is in the mail' shit. If I don't receive that fuckin' check by tomorrow, I'm pulling the fuckin' line."

I walked in just as he slammed down the phone. It made me feel so much better knowing that Jay was madder than I was.

"Just like the old days, huh Jay?"

"Worse. In the old days," he said, "at least you had something to look forward to. The independent distributors were getting stronger then. Now it's just the opposite."

For the past few months Jay and I had been discussing the possibility of going with a major. It had been over three years since Jerry Moss and A&M had made that move and we'd been sticking it out with the independents since that time. "We can't do it anymore," I told Jay. He agreed.

That day in May of 1983, we made the big decision to go with

MCA for national distribution. Irving Azoff, the new head of MCA's record division, had immediately come after Motown for distribution. Up until that time, the black division at MCA was virtually nonexistent.

By distributing us, Azoff knew that MCA could get a major foothold in the black record business. And for us, instead of fifteen to twenty different distributors, we could now look to one company for one check—that we knew would be there on time.

Within a few months after making the deal, Lionel Richie busted wide open with his *Can't Slow Down* album. True to its name, it never did. It went on and on, selling over ten million. Our distribution marriage was off to a great start.

Then along came "Somebody's Watching Me"—a big hit by an artist named Rockwell, half singing and half talking in a British accent. Few at the company knew that this artist, the writer and co-producer on the single and the hit album of the same name, was my son Kennedy. "Somebody's Watching Me" went straight to the top of the charts. In the past, whenever he tried to get me to take one of his songs to any of my established stars, I had rejected the material. In addition to not being up to my standards, I explained to him that it would be a conflict of interest, since I had turned down much better songs that the artists wanted to do.

But Nancy Leiviska, the mother of my youngest son, Stefan, really went to bat for Kennedy. When she played me some of his new songs, I realized what a talent he had become and okayed a budget to produce an album on him.

My son had become a star. Kennedy was on top of the world—until word leaked out that he was my son. He hated that. It took away from his legitimacy as an artist. He had really wanted to do something on his own and be recognized for it. He started resenting my getting credit for his success, and for good reason; I didn't deserve it. Though he enjoyed his stardom, he went through many moments of anger as more and more interviewers were implying I was the reason for his success.

"I know how you feel," I told him one day. "It's unfair for people to say that you didn't do this on your own. But rather than take it out on me or hold it in and be miserable, on your next interview, just tell them the truth. Tell them you made it in spite of your father, not *because* of him."

"Are you serious? I can do that?"

"Of course. Just tell 'em the story, tell 'em the truth."

The very next time he was interviewed, he told the story, but added his own ending. "My father never had time to work with me. He told me he had to work with Diana Ross, Stevie Wonder, Marvin Gaye, Smokey Robinson . . ." He stopped and then said, laughing, "Come to think of it, if I were him, I wouldn't have worked with me either!"

Kennedy felt a lot better toward me but not enough to let me be his manager when I offered to work with him. I understood. He needed to continue independently, doing things his own way, learning his own lessons.

While everything was seemingly going well at Motown again, I became involved in an outside creative project.

At the time, Gary Hendler had just become the president of a new company, Tri-Star Pictures. A Hollywood lawyer who had represented many top stars, Gary and I had become close friends in a very short period of time. We had come from different worlds—his Jewish, mine black. He, highly educated; me, a high school dropout. Despite our differences, we had the same backyard—a term I used when people shared the same values in life. Differences—race, religion, education, political views and even ideas—don't really matter if you have shared values, if the principles by which you live your lives are similar.

When Gary came to my house one Saturday for our weekly tennis game, he was very excited. "I'm really anxious to hear about the script I gave you," he said on the way to the court.

I had not been looking forward to that question. This was one of his company's first projects—a kung fu movie. I knew how important it was to him. But I had to tell him straight. "I don't like it at all." I was hoping the discussion would end there. But Gary wanted to hear more.

"Kung fu movies are big business," he said, "and this one's with black kids."

"That might make it different but that in itself is not enough. The story's got to be more human, funnier, romantic."

"Okay, so you're not crazy about it."

I told him there was a philosophy in there that needed bringing out. "Everything should be built around the concept that the Master he is seeking is in himself all along. That might not only make it a hit, but could be a positive message for kids."

"Berry, you've *got* to make this movie."

Within a few months I was off to New York shooting *Berry Gordy's The Last Dragon* for Tri-Star Pictures.

I worked with a fine young black director named Michael Schultz, who put together a wonderful crew. Together we came up with a tremendous cast, starring two newcomers, Taimak, as the martial arts star, and the beautiful Vanity as the female lead. Julius Carry III was sensational as Sho'Nuff, the outrageous gang leader. And Faith Prince, who did such a wonderful job as the redheaded "dumb blonde," was a delight to work with. I was extremely proud of the way *Last Dragon* turned out.

That movie was also significant to me in another way. While we were shooting in New York Suzanne de Passe had arranged for Rhonda Silberstein, her goddaughter, now almost thirteen, to be an extra in one of the dance scenes. I remember while shooting that scene I heard a buzz on the soundstage—"Diana Ross is here, Diana Ross is here. Over there."

Our eyes met for the first time since *Motown 25*. Diana had come to the set with her daughter, Rhonda. Diana walked over to me. We didn't hug. "She knows," Diana said. "I told Rhonda you were her father." We hugged.

"What did she say?" I asked softly.

"Not much. She was surprised and shocked, but she handled it like the champion she is." It was a soul-relieving hug and it continued for a while. When it started becoming awkward we pulled away.

"So what do you think?" I said.

"I think she'll be fine. I'm not sure whether she was sad or happy, she took it so well. After all, she's known you as Uncle BB her whole life. That made it easier, I guess."

I looked over to Rhonda, who was rehearsing. She was looking our way, smiling.

I couldn't wait to hug my daughter. I had done that many times before. But this time it would be a little different.

When the scene broke she came over. We hugged as we had before, and it *was* different. Diana stood there, beaming. Rhonda and I said nothing. There was too much to say.

Rhonda and I had lunch the next day, just the two of us. She was poised and well versed in so many things, I could see what a wonderful job her mother had done. We talked for hours. Now she was watching me as I had watched her for years, looking for similarities. Every now and then I saw what I thought was a smile of her recognition of some of me in her. We didn't talk about it as such, but I believe that day resolved some questions she may have asked herself over the years.

The atmosphere was jovial as we gathered in my dining room for a family meeting.

Our family never changed. We still settled disputes by bringing everyone together. At the company where many worked for me, I was the chairman—the boss. But at meetings with my sisters and brothers, I was just one of seven. Personally I did not like these meetings. That one-man-one-vote stuff was not something I looked forward to. Even so, it was I who had called this one.

The subject was to be Gwen and her house in Beverly Hills. Because her publishing company was doing so well with "Sweet Love," a big hit by Anita Baker, and her house had gone way up in value, she was spending money like it was water. Everybody hung out there. Day and night it was party time all the time.

This was not good for her health or her pocketbook. Since she loved horses, I had been trying for the longest time to convince her to move to the healthier environment of a farm somewhere.

She wasn't buying it, she was happy where she was.

I lobbied the family, who were as concerned as I was and had agreed to help me get her to move. Esther and George came out from Detroit.

386

As had happened many times before when the family met, the minute we sat down at the dining room table that day, I lost all authority—I was "Junior" again.

Though things started off fine, somehow Gwen's situation took a back seat and the meeting turned into an opportunity for everyone to bring up any insensitivities they thought I had shown them over the years. Though the others brought up theirs half jokingly, when Esther jumped in with hers, she was dead serious. I had no idea what she was talking about. It was something about me siding with Ralph Seltzer against her over a legal matter.

I told her I didn't remember any of it. "Are you sure?" I said.

"Oh yes, it was twenty-one years ago, in Ralph's office, on a Tuesday morning at ten o'clock . . ."

She knew the exact time it had happened!

Esther, now the family matriarch, one of my staunchest supporters, understood me and my business motives better than anybody. It seemed so out of character for her that I was sure the others would be just as shocked.

But when I turned from Esther to look around the table for support, scanning from face to face, there was none. There was Fuller, regularly so laid-back and easygoing, frowning at me. George, always fun-loving and joking, stared at his hands folded on the table. Robert, who had looked up to me all these years, was nodding his head in Esther's favor. Anna, always caring and bubbling over with warmth, was saying little. And Gwen, knowing why the meeting had been called in the first place, was pleased that the focus was no longer on her.

I was devastated. Had it come to this? After all I had achieved, had I lost my family in the process? I wondered. We adjourned without resolving anything about Gwen.

That night, late, overcome by sadness, I found myself in one of those moods where normally I would head straight for the piano. But this night it was the computer. I sat there trying to express my feelings in a poem to Esther. I decided to call it "I Wonder."

How have I hurt thee through the years . . . I wonder.
Your subjective recollection right or wrong on

closer inspection
The hurt was there and lingers on . . . the
realization of a forgotten fact, a decisive act
that may have changed the course of history.
Right or wrong, who's right, who's wrong, what's
right, what's wrong.
Do you love me . . . do you think you love me.
Or are you hoping for the day when you can say "if
you had only done it my way". . . I wonder.
Buried hurt carried through the years surfacing now
and then, takes its toll . . .
Remember when you said you wished me dead? I
never said . . . O yes you did!
On a Tuesday afternoon around three o'clock.
Behind the barn I took your bike I still hear you
screaming as if it were yesterday . . .
Wait a minute! What am I trying to say?
If I ever hurt you I swear I never meant to.
I believed whatever I did was right at the time . . .
I wonder.
I love you,
Berry

When Esther received it, she called to tell me how much she loved the poem and me, and told me I didn't have to wonder anymore, that she really understood. She insisted I send it to every member of the family.

A short time later Gwen bought a wonderful ranch where she could raise horses and start a new lifestyle.

Not long after this, in early 1985, Robert let me know we had a chance to get Lester Sill, the granddaddy of music publishing, for Jobete. We had been looking for someone to take it to higher international levels.

I had tried to get Lester Sill many times before and had given up.

"I think the time is right," Robert said. "We should try again." He was right. This time Lester agreed to come aboard.

Once hired he immediately started making plans to take advantage of previously untapped worldwide opportunities for our songs, significantly increasing Jobete's revenues.

Over at Motown Productions, where Suzanne was running the show, deals were being made for Motown-related TV specials like the Emmy Award–winning *Motown Returns to the Apollo, The Motown Revue* starring Smokey Robinson, a weekly summer TV show, and *Motown on Showtime*, a series of specials featuring Smokey, the Four Tops and the Tempts, Michael Jackson and Marvin Gaye.

Again, this was good for our image but did not help our bottom line enough.

The record scene was even worse. We had both creative and marketing problems. We still did not have enough quality front-line product, and what records we did have, we had trouble promoting properly. Marketing costs had skyrocketed. Now it was a minimum of $100,000 to promote a single record. And that didn't mean you were guaranteed heavy airplay.

Music videos were the marketing tools of the day, but Jay didn't believe in them. He was from the old school, didn't believe in spending a buck if he couldn't see two coming back in. He considered my money his money, and was furious about every expense incurred by the company, whether it was in his area or not.

It was not only that we were losing money. I had lost interest. From ever since I could remember my work was the thing that brought me the most pleasure. Music was never work. It was like my hobby. But now, after thirty years, it was work—real work. I thought that building a company was tough, but I now discovered that saving a company was much tougher.

Jay came to me one day and said that MCA wanted to buy Motown, something that had once been unthinkable. Not anymore. I now understood better what I did not know when I had gone into the distribution deal with MCA—whenever you give up the control of your distribution, you give up the control of your destiny. Our distribution agreement with MCA had been a necessary survival move for me. It had gone well for a couple years, but now Jay had to fight every day with them for better marketing of our product—better in-store position, all sorts of things. It was a natural conflict when a major record company takes over your smaller record label for distribution. They really want to sell *their* records, not *your* records. And the only way to make *your* records *their* records is for them to buy you out.

Even though I understood this, and knew how much trouble we were in, it was still a hard, hard decision to make. I didn't want to let people down. Aside from the employees, who depended on me for their livelihood, I knew there were so many others who looked to me to preserve Motown's legacy and its black heritage, and I had always planned on keeping the company in my own family, passing it on to my kids.

During this same time, I had my lifelong sidekick Billy Davis move in with me. He had AIDS.

As bad as he was feeling, he never stopped trying to run everything, nor trying to tell me what to do. We talked about his condition openly. I looked for whatever I could find to do or say that would make him feel better. Today there is still a great deal of misinformation about the disease, but back then there was practically no information at all. I studied everything I could find to learn about it. And so did Billy. "Don't worry. Somebody will come up with a miracle pill any day," he'd say, and with a confident wave of his hand and a snap of his fingers he would add, "I'll be fine, baby, I'll be fine. Don't worry 'bout me."

One night, Billy, a great pinochle player, was doing his regular thing of slamming a card down heavy on the table whenever he played one he thought was a winner. When the topic of his condition came up and how people with the disease were being treated, I quickly said, "I've been reading everything I can get my hands on. I'm practically an authority on it. People are definitely overreacting. You can't get it by casual contact, touching, saliva and all that stuff. So all these people that are so frightened about getting it that way are ridiculous."

In a serious, hushed voice, Billy asked, "You really believe that, man?"

"Of course I do."

He leaned over, got right in my face, and said, "Well then kiss me motherfucker!"

Billy exploded with laughter as he saw me jump out of my chair.

I fell down laughing. In fact, we all belly-laughed for the longest time.

That was Billy, a character in the truest sense of the word. Even when his condition had gotten worse, he was more concerned about me than himself. One night, lying in his bed at my house, he said, "You're tired, man. You better enjoy your life. Live. Look at me, man, I have lived. Traveled around the world, had a ball. I told you I didn't want to be no millionaire, I just wanted to live like one. Well, I did—and you paid for it. I've done everything in life but died. But you—you better get a grip. You got too much shit on your head. You've done it, man. You've done it. Move on. Look at our heroes—Joe Louis, Sugar Ray Robinson—one fight too many. Look at those other cats who didn't know when to stop. You could be just another nigger who made it to the top and died broke."

By the fall of 1986, I was immersed in looking at the different options I had. I sat at my computer for hours into the night, evaluating pros and cons. I weighed many scenarios: selling off personal assets, going public, merging with other companies. I even thought about auctioning off the rights to some of my master recordings at Sotheby's. None of these seemed to be the answer. The only way to keep the company intact and to protect the legacy was to sell—with some specific stipulations.

In November, Motown attorneys Harold Noveck and Lee Young, Jr., Jay Lasker and I met at my home for lunch with MCA's Lew Wasserman, Sid Sheinberg and Irv Azoff. Since the foundation of the deal had already been worked out, the meeting wasn't so much about the details, but about how much they wanted me in the MCA family and how great this was going to be for both companies. I felt good about that meeting and I had always felt good about the MCA organization and didn't mind being a part of it. But when the lawyers got together, and started hammering out the details, the tension really began to mount.

Stevie, meanwhile, still had a clause in his contract that said I couldn't sell the company unless it was to an approved buyer. Remembering what I had been through in Paris when I had tried to sell Jobete, I was worried. It was one more piece of pressure, one more item to juggle.

On Christmas Eve, the busiest day in the year, Edna went shopping with him that afternoon to make sure he got to my house for a six o'clock meeting with me.

At 11:00 P.M., an exhausted Edna arrived with Stevie, five hours late. The minute he got there he wanted to play me a few songs—six or seven.

As much as I needed to get the business of that clause settled I found myself getting caught up in the old habit of comments and critiques. Before long we were eating, listening to songs, laughing and having our usual fun, but I never forgot what we were there for. Neither did he. The minute I brought up the prospect of selling he started talking like he had in Paris about what Motown meant to him.

"As long as you own it I feel secure," he said. "In the hands of strangers it might change drastically."

This time I explained to him the grim reality of my situation. He understood this was a different time, a different place, and a different company.

"I'll do everything I can to protect our history," I assured him.

This time he gave me his okay and I was able to get back to negotiating the deal itself.

The main problem with the deal was how they were valuing Motown—not by its real worth, but by its current financial statements.

And there were other important things I had to fight for, not yet in the deal, like the Dr. King masters to give to his wife, Coretta, and assurances that a certain portion of the company would be held for minority ownership.

Then there were some boilerplate clauses I didn't like, restricting me from doing a lot of things. Some of these I understood had to be there, but others—no way. One I could not live with was not being able to use my own name in the business for five years.

Though the contract had gone back to the MCA lawyers several times for revisions, each time they would return it, it seemed never to reflect exactly what we had agreed upon. That, I think, bothered me the most. But time was against me. If I didn't make the deal by the 31st of December, I would lose a major tax break. They knew that, and I suspected that they were pushing me to the last moment, figuring I would drop some of the unresolved points.

Late at night, twenty-four hours before the deadline, I called Harold. "I've got a bad feeling about this. Call it off."

"Call it off?"

"I'm not going through with the sale."

"Have you thought it out?" Harold asked.

"Not as much as I perhaps should have, but I just don't want to do it."

"What about the tax break?"

"Forget it. I want to call it off."

Though Harold had gone through months of painstaking negotiations, he didn't argue with me. "Berry, if that's what you want, okay. We'll take care of it."

When the news hit the street, telegrams and calls of congratulations poured in from everywhere. But for the insiders the reactions were mixed, from the fear of "what if he had sold," to the joy that I hadn't, to the question of "would he ever?"

The week after I walked away from the deal Billy Davis died. As I had promised him, we held a celebration of his life that he, himself, had planned. "I know you got a budget for everything, but when it comes to my funeral I don't want no damn half-steppin'."

People came from all around the world to be there. Smokey, Stevie, Syreeta and Billy Preston paid tribute to him in words and song. A video was played of different moments with Billy that was set to one of his favorite songs, Diana's "Remember Me."

He had nothing to give anybody but himself, yet Billy was more loved than anybody I have ever known. He was quick with his many sayings like: "I may have had bad times, baby, but never bad taste." Even toward the end when he could barely talk, he had his own special way of saying good-bye: "I'm gonna do something for you the devil never did—I'm gonna leave yo' ass."

I went back to work, trying to save the company. My adrenaline was flowing. I was back in business and going for it.

After six months of restrategizing and focusing on every area of the company, I could see that Jay Lasker and I had different ideas of what the future of Motown should be.

I remember the bad feeling I got when I walked into a record store one day and first saw two great Marvin Gaye albums—*What's Going On* and *Let's Get It On*—together on a CD, selling for the price of one. They were in a back bin along with other Motown albums packaged together, like schlock merchandise, while the regular-priced CDs were up in front.

Jay Lasker was one of the great marketing men of all time and he had given me that forceful, trustworthy leadership I had needed for the past seven years. I knew he was doing his job and doing it well, but I didn't like giving away our music.

"These two-for-ones are keeping us in business," Jay said.

"But for how long? We're selling off our cream."

Jay was a marketing man and he brought in money any way he could.

I loved him for it, but at the same time, I couldn't stand it.

"This is depreciating our catalogue. If people start viewing Motown as back bin stuff it will change their perception of our music. There's got to be a better way."

He assured me there wasn't. Jay was as adamant about these two-for-ones as he was about not doing any costly videos. These and other differences continued. In the summer of 1987 he left the company.

After that, I decided to promote from within and brought Skip Miller over from his position as head of the Promotion Department. I paired him with Legal head Lee Young, Jr., and made them co-presidents of the company. As the new head of my Creative Division, I brought in Al Bell, an old friend of mine who had been the president of Stax Records. It was a good team.

We all knew we needed a miracle, not just one hit record but many—immediately. I knew that all new administrations need time to put their plans into action. And time was the one thing I did not have.

Hard decisions had to be made. I put through a series of new cost-cutting measures, scaling back further on personnel, cutting salaries. For many this was the shock of their lives. As far as they were concerned, Motown was forever—infallible. The general feeling around the company was, "We've had troubles before, so what? We'll get out of them. We always do!"

One afternoon in early '88, Smokey ambled into my office, plopped into a chair and gave me a knowing look. As always, when I was really in trouble he was right there, somehow understanding everything without being told. "Man," he said, "I want to get a smash right now more than ever."

I smiled. Smokey hadn't changed. He wanted to come through for me. The year before it was Smokey who had the only two singles to make the Top 10—"Just To See Her," a record that was about to win him his first Grammy, and "One Heartbeat."

I told him I needed a whole lot more than a couple of smashes. The only way I could save the company now was to sell it.

I will always remember that look on Smokey's face. His eyes were like saucers. I felt so bad. Motown was his life. He had named his son, Berry, after me and his daughter, Tamla, after our first record label.

As he sat there stunned I multiplied his reaction by millions of other people.

"I'm tired, Smoke," I said.

"I know you are. I know you are," he said as he nodded his approval.

FRIDAY, JUNE 25, 1988, LOS ANGELES

Up since dawn, I was sitting at my computer, trying to come up with a first draft of a press release. It was time to explain to the public the reasons behind my decision to sell.

Pecking slowly at the keys, I began:

After two years of intense contemplation, careful study, examination upon re-examination and after meeting with a variety of potential purchasers . . .

I stopped, leaned back in my chair for a moment, thinking of how crazy the past few months had been. Now that everything with the sale had come down to the wire, more than ever my nerves were like frayed electric cords.

Entertaining offers from other suitors besides MCA had helped my bargaining position, but my time had run out. I had to make a deal with somebody soon. Playing my cards close to the chest I could not show my eagerness, nor could I allow for any appearance of company weakness.

That meant keeping all our engines running, whatever the cost. I could not dismantle my expensive marketing operation, which was costing a fortune. During this period I came very close to making a deal with Virgin Records. They made me an offer I liked, until MCA, whom we knew better and who knew us better, matched it. This time, once we began serious talks with MCA, though they were still very tough, the negotiating atmosphere was much more favorable.

MCA had partnered with Boston Ventures, a financial investment group who seemed to have a better understanding of the true value of Motown. They put up 80 percent of the money, and met most of my demands. For the most part, a lot of restrictive legal clauses— the "thou shalts" and "thou shalt nots"—were gone and the deal was straightforward.

For an asking price more than 50 percent higher than before, what was being sold was the Motown name and record catalogue, the masters, and the artists' recording contracts. I wasn't selling Jobete Music Company, Inc., which owned the publishing rights to most of the Motown songs, or my film and television company.

The deal was so close to being done that my pent-up emotions were at their breaking point. I wanted this deal *over*.

I started back on my press release:

I have decided to sell Motown Records to MCA, Inc. . . .

The phone rang. It was Esther, calling from Detroit.

The media was having a field day—and she, like everybody else, had been following the stories. The *Los Angeles Times* had read "THE

END OF AN ERA—EXPECTED SALE OF THE LEGENDARY MOTOWN LABEL STIRS SOME BITTERSWEET EMOTIONS." The *Detroit News* had called it "MOTOWN SALE IS FINAL VERSE OF SWAN SONG." The European *Wall Street Journal*, which had distribution in every major European city, reported "THAT MO-TOWN SOUND MAY SOON BELONG TO SOMEONE NEW," while the Alabama paper The *Birmingham News* said "THE LEGACY OF MOTOWN IS ON THE AUCTION BLOCK."

"I've gotten a thousand calls about the sale," Esther said. "What do we tell them—is anything final yet?"

"No, nothing final. I'm just sitting here waiting."

"Listen, I've been thinking and maybe we should stick it out. It's been in the family all this time . . ." she said, breaking off midthought.

I reminded her how many times I had saddled her with major responsibility, not wanting to hear any excuses or blame if something didn't work. *"If you make it you're a hero, if you don't you're a bum,"* I had preached to her and others year in and year out. "Now it's my turn," I said. "Hero or bum is my fate. If Motown goes down the drain, it doesn't matter who, what or why, I'm responsible."

Esther was silent for a moment as I thought about how wonderful she was. Here she was, the same person who had been the most reluctant to give me the loan at that Ber-Berry meeting, who then put in thirty years helping me with my dream, doing everything I asked her to do and more. The same person who, when I moved to California, stayed in Detroit, pulled together all the stuff I left behind and started a museum with it at Hitsville.

The Motown Museum was now emerging as the one institution whose purpose and responsibility was to protect and preserve the Motown legacy.

"But Berry," Esther said, "what about you?"

"What about me?"

"Motown is your creation," she said. "It's been your life for most of your life—are you really sure you can let go? Are you sure you won't have seller's remorse? Are you ready to wake up and know it doesn't belong to you anymore?"

"Yes, yes and yes." Just saying that made me feel good. I said goodbye, telling her, "It's not over yet. Anything can happen. All we can do now is wait and see."

Within an hour, I was finishing up my press release:

> I have decided to sell Motown Records to MCA, Inc. Two years ago I considered selling Motown to MCA but did not, I was not ready then. I had not completely realized what Motown had become—an American institution. . . . It is the nature of institutions to take on their own life and to outgrow the individuals who create them. I am proud that this African-American heritage has been embraced by the world and has become permanently woven into the fabric of popular culture.

On Tuesday, June 29, 1988, the waiting was over. The headlines blasted the news: I had sold Motown Records to MCA for $61 million.

From eight hundred dollars to sixty-one million. I had done it. I had won the poker hand.

14

FULL CIRCLE

BUT . . . SURE I HAD WON the poker hand, from eight hundred dollars to sixty-one million. That was money. Still only a part of value. It was about much more than that. The total value was not only the money, but saving the company and keeping the legacy intact. These weren't just records. This was a body of work that in itself was an institution. I had to put it into the right hands under the right conditions at a time when I was losing a fortune. That was the real poker hand.

Four months later, standing at the large-paned window of my suite at the Omni Hotel, I was absorbing the sights of the vast terrain of the Detroit metropolitan area. It was in the heart of what is now known as the Renaissance Center, a cultural and retail district by the Detroit River.

Dusk. The city lights, some yellow, some white, slowly creeping on, bringing into focus a magical glow. I had moved to California over twenty years before. Now I was looking back over the city where I grew up, where my roots were. Where once my vision could only take in a couple of blocks of the inner city, now I was looking over all of Detroit and beyond. I had come full circle. I had come home.

I got a sad feeling when I thought about the old hangouts that were no longer there. The 20 Grand, the Flame Show Bar, the Frolic, other clubs on John R Street in Paradise Valley—all gone.

But looking toward Woodward Avenue where the Fox Theatre was still going strong, I thought of the many joyous Motortown Revues we had held there every year at Christmastime where many artists literally learned about show business and real competition. Down that same street, where the Graystone Ballroom had been, were more memories—from the forties Big Band era to the sixties Motown Battle of the Stars.

I had returned with my protégé, the top superstar in the world, Michael Jackson, who had agreed to make a contribution to the Motown Museum. He said he very much wanted to put something back into the soil from which he came and would donate the proceeds from an upcoming concert in Detroit.

"The only stipulation," he said, when working out the details with Esther and Joanne Jackson, who was helping run the museum at that time, was that "Berry Gordy meets me there." He was joking at first, but when he and I talked, we knew it had to be. We would have dinner together at the Gordy Manor, which held many fond memories for both of us, the house where he and his brothers performed that first time, and also where they stayed whenever they came back to Detroit.

Remembering how he and his brothers used to run through the house in stockinged feet, slipping and sliding on those marble floors, he asked if the two of us could do it again. I happily agreed.

Michael remained a perpetual kid, yet he was brilliant enough to call most of the shots in his own career. That was part of his mystique. He also had what it took, the talent, the drive and the drama. And a discipline perhaps greater than any I had seen.

Despite the pouring rain, 2,500 fans had crowded out front of Hitsville to witness his presentation of a check for $125,000 to the Motown Museum. He also donated a hat, a rhinestone glove and a stage uniform from 1972.

During that ceremony, I thought about how hectic the past months had been.

That very next day after the sale, Edna had tossed an article from a Detroit newspaper on my desk. "Boss, have you heard that Stevie said he was going to run for mayor of Detroit?"

First thing I thought was *Damn, I'll never get that Stevie album now.* Then I caught myself. *Wait a minute.* I looked at Edna and smiled. "That is not my problem anymore."

We both laughed. She knew I felt good saying that.

Others were rushing in to tell me about more crises. My favorite saying for those next few days became: "It is not my problem anymore."

But in addition to the huge task of transferring all the property and documentation to the new company, there were many things that were still my problem. Among them was finalizing a fair bonus and severance pay structure for all the Motown employees.

Another was setting up the Gordy Company to oversee the surviving entities, Jobete, our publishing company; Motown Productions, our film and TV company; and ongoing development of new projects.

These included the production of *Lonesome Dove*, an eight-hour miniseries that would be seen the world over. As its executive producer, Suzanne had shown me that she had definitely come into her own.

Since it was approaching the time when we would no longer be allowed to use the name "Motown Productions," I changed the name of the company to Gordy-de Passe Productions, giving her more visibility. I later turned the whole company over to her.

I was still very much in business. Retaining my chairmanship, I put my son Berry IV in charge of the Gordy Company. An employee of Motown for years, he had worked his way up to executive vice president of Motown Industries.

I now had more time to pursue other things I enjoyed like horse racing. I had gotten hooked about eight years before when, in partnership with Bruce McNall, I had bought my first race horse, Argument, for $1.2 million.

When Argument won the Washington, D.C., International, our first race, we were offered $5 million on the spot. That day I became a fanatic about horse racing. The horse's value had quadrupled and I didn't have to worry about him coming back to renegotiate his deal.

My sister Gwen was hooked, too. She set up stables at her ranch. I get such a kick out of seeing how much she and Anna enjoy themselves at the track. Avid handicappers, decked out, sharp from head to toe—they always come dressed for the winner's circle.

Another way I used my gambling instincts to advantage was trading on the futures market. I found out I could make money by paying attention to world events and interest rates, and by following a few basic principles.

I had time to go see a special lady who had been the inspiration for writing my very first full-length song—Doris Day.

I presented her with a specially framed copy of the sheet music to "You Are You"—forty-three years later. Doris was as enchanting, pretty and sweet as she had seemed to me back then. Even more. And when she asked me to sing it, I was as nervous as I would have been back then. Trying to avoid the Donald Duck side of my natural register, I sang it with everything I had:

> You are you—
> That's all that matters to me.
>
> You are you—
> And only you can be the one I love and yearn for,
> the one that my heart burns for.
>
> Yes, you are you—
> And that makes you best of all. . . .

During the song, Doris began to cry and afterward when I hugged her, so did I. The thrill of singing it for her after all those years was worth the wait.

The biggest undertaking I have had since the sale is writing this book. It has been the hardest thing I've ever done, but also the most rewarding. It has given me the chance to relive and relearn the lessons of my life. Again and again I've seen how important family always was to me, whether it was the family I grew up with, the Motown family or my family today of eight children and ten grandchildren.

Not unlike the household in which I grew up, each of my children have their own unique talents and personalities. But as different as they are from one another, they have in common a deep intelligence, wit and goodness. At this writing, all of them are doing well. Thank goodness!

Hazel, still the strong, staunch, principled person, has never changed. She's still the policeman of the family and in raising her own three great kids she has proven that she's one of the greatest mothers ever. Berry IV, with his own strong management style, is running the Gordy Company. Terry, true to his childhood desire to be around money, is a successful banker at Bank of America. He also works with me on many aspects of international investment trading.

Kerry attacks every project with imagination, enthusiasm and strategy. He has the greatest attitude and most optimistic outlook on life I've ever seen. A real people person. While he has his own company, Kerry Gordy Entertainment, he continues to be one of my top consultants and is currently a vice president at Warner Brothers Records.

My daughter Sherry, down-to-earth and independent, is an aggressive go-getter who has done extensive work in real estate and is now an executive at Aames Financial Corporation.

Kennedy has continued to grow creatively since his Rockwell days, exploring his own entrepreneurial ideas. Being the most naturally creative of all my kids, he and I relate on still a different level than the others.

Rhonda, singer, actress and director, is a graduate of Brown University and a scholar in African-American history. The youngest, Stefan, is a writer and producer whose music is already appearing in feature films.

Teaching has been one of the most fun parts of being a dad. Making learning fun was a big priority. Whether sports, cards, math or history lessons, I made a game out of everything.

My teaching methods developed over the years. As the kids got older, the more challenging it became, like with my youngest son, Stefan. Though he liked music it was his tennis playing that really impressed me. As a teenager, he showed so much promise I decided to go back into the management business. I became his manager.

I told him that we had three relationships. One was as father and son, where he had to respect me as he normally did. A second was, whenever we're competing, as we often did, we were equals. "You can fight, say and do whatever you want and nothing will be held against you. Now," I said, "when I'm your manager, you have to do things only one way—my way." He loved that arrangement. For a while it worked beautifully. The fact that we could hang out as equals was unbelievable to him. He tested me a few times and I passed.

But the better he got at tennis the more resistant he became. Finally, he stopped listening to me. Finally, I stopped being his manager. Stefan took off with a tennis-playing buddy for Sweden to play there. (Not on the best of terms with me, I might add.) That turned into a great growing experience for him. Because it was so cold and he didn't go out much, he started writing and producing songs. His mother, Nancy, kept him well stocked with recording essentials—keyboards, microphones and a recorder.

When a tape arrived from him for my birthday, I had no idea what to expect. What I heard was a thrilling surprise. It was a rap song, produced remarkably well, about all the things he had learned from me over the years that I thought he had never heard—about tennis, about music, about life. He hadn't missed anything I'd said and now he was rapping about it. What a joy that was for me!

I'm proud of all my children for what they're doing, but the most important thing to me is that they are all simply fine human beings.

In my backyard along one side of my lawn is a tall wall with a mural, painted in 1973 by Carolyn Thompson, an artist from Detroit.

There are about twenty little vignettes of ghetto life depicting the old neighborhood in Detroit where I was raised. The images are also about family, surroundings and dreams of a better life. I see that kitchen with the potbellied stove; everyone gathered at the table with only one pot of food. Mother, hardworking, doing the wash on a scrub board, the ironing; three or four of us kids in one bed; protective parents checking on us while we sleep. There's a young boy sitting on the steps holding his head, thinking, contemplating. That's me, and a lot of others like me.

Many people ask me why this mural is there. I tell them because every time I look at it I'm reminded of where I came from. Others sometimes see me as a guy with all these great accomplishments. But I'm quick to say, "Those are only my accomplishments; they're not me. They're up there somewhere. Me, I'm down here on the ground looking up at them in awe and thankfulness."

I never stop thinking how blessed I've been to have crossed paths with some of the greatest people in the world.

People like Smokey Robinson.

From the time I first met him—this eager teenager always wanting to show me his latest song, and me always sending him away to make it better—I knew even then that what I loved about Smokey was much bigger than a song.

I've had many great tributes but probably the greatest one I have ever received was one that almost didn't happen. It came at the end of a program at which I was being honored by the Brotherhood Crusade—Danny Bakewell's organization.

Being the honoree that night, I was under pressure. Even though I wasn't involved with the planning of the event, I somehow felt responsible for it.

The evening started off great. Danny Bakewell had brought everyone out this night—Jesse Jackson, Sidney Poitier, Diahann Carroll, Muhammad Ali, George Schlatter, all my family and friends. Even Gary Hendler, who had been stricken with cancer, had come from his deathbed to be there with me. After a speech by Jesse, eloquent as ever, Sidney and Danny presented me with the Pioneer of Black Achievement Award. And following my acceptance speech, the entertainment began—Smokey.

It was already late when he began and I could feel a wave of restlessness in the room as he did a pantomine of a private memory between the two of us, that trip to the Owosso pressing plant to pick up my first record, "Come To Me."

I could see no one understood what Smokey was doing sitting in a chair pretending to be driving a car that had slid into a ditch— twice. It went on forever. People began to squirm. I began to squirm. I wanted Smokey to get on with what people did understand—his music.

At last he went into some songs and the audience came to life. By this time it was really late. He was so wrapped up in what he was doing, he seemed to have no concept of time. I thought because it was so late, he would only do a few numbers, but now he was doing his entire repertoire.

Finally I couldn't stand it anymore and I sent word over to Sonny Burke, his musical director, to have him cut his show. I watched as Sonny walked over to speak to Smokey. Smokey nodded—then went into the next song. And the next and the next.

I was getting more and more frantic. This was my night. My friends. He was ruining it for me. I knew he meant well, but I sent word again, this time by Suzanne and Roger Campbell, to make sure Smokey got the message. Sonny confirmed it: "I told him."

"Well, tell him again," Suzanne said.

Once more Sonny went over and whispered in Smokey's ear. Once more Smokey nodded but continued into another song.

Right as he got close to finishing that song, I leaned over and whispered to Rog, "Smokey's ridiculous. We may have to pull the plug." That would mean cutting off the electricity controlling the mike and instruments. The song ended and I heard Smokey say, "Berry, I have a new song I wrote for you. It's called 'Berry's Theme.'" His sincere face was looking right at me, his eyes full of warmth, loyalty and love. He started:

Did you know all the joy you'd be bringing?
Did you know you'd be the song the whole world is singing?
Did you know when you dreamed your dream that you
would make so many other dreams come true?

By the time he had sung the second line, I was overcome with emotion. Emotion that was triggered by how wonderful the song was, but also because of how bad I felt about thinking of stopping this man's show. I would not only have hurt Smokey but missed out on one of the greatest moments of my life.

Did you know way back when first we met?
You and I would be as close as true friends can get.
Though the road has been rough at times we made it through
and I'd live it all again just to be with you.

406

By this point, my tears were flowing uncontrollably. It was one of the most beautiful melodies I had ever heard. I would have sat there till four in the morning the next night and the night after that and the night after that to have felt that loved, that trusted, that blessed as Smokey ended with:

And I'm hoping that right now you know my friend, my
wonderful friend, I love you so . . .

Though he was my protégé, Smokey always inspired me to be the best that I could be. Others did that in different ways. Some were my childhood heroes.

Joe Louis was one—the first person who made me know what the word hero meant. His phenomenal feats had opened my imagination to the possibility of being somebody in this world. And by some stroke of magic I was able to spend time with him once our acts started playing Vegas. Living there, Joe had become the official greeter at Caesars Palace. Whenever I was in town, the two of us would head out to the golf course. Every now and then, I had the urge to just shout out right there on the green to whoever was passing by—Hey, people, this is Joe Louis! I'm playing golf with my hero!!

I also became the greatest of friends with my all-time idol—Sugar Ray Robinson. In person he was as princely as he was in the ring. He and Millie, his devoted wife, who took care of him like her dearest little baby, used to come to the house. When he and I would walk the grounds, play boxing, I had to hold myself back from calling to my neighbors—Hey, people, this is Sugar Ray Robinson! I'm boxing with my idol!!

When he died in 1989 Millie asked me to speak at the funeral. I had been praising him for so many years, I had no trouble finding words. To the many people who came I started simply with, "The greatest fighter that ever lived—Sugar Ray Robinson! Swift, clean, sensitive, smooth, sharp . . . and deadly . . ." He was my man.

But out of all those who changed my life, in looking back over the years, my biggest hero of all—in the end turned out to be my father, Pop. Not a day goes by that I don't appreciate what it means to have been his son. In my youth, I knew I couldn't be like him—

I was too lazy. But as it turned out I ended up working longer and harder than he did, which made me realize there are probably no really lazy people. Just uninspired ones.

When we celebrated his ninetieth birthday on July 10, 1978, my brother Robert played a tape of a song written by two Jobete songwriters, Marilyn McLeod and Pam Sawyer. They must have spent a lot of time with Pop because they really knew him well. The song was called "Pops We Love You":

Anyone who's had the pleasure of meeting you in this life time
would recognize the strength in you, the sense in you
and the wisdom like sun shining through.
Pops, we love you, yes, we do . . .

Anyone, young and old alike, would feel free for your advice
and know you'd understand,
you'd give a helping hand.
All your life you have fought for what's right.

You always say first love the Lord
and then it's easy to love thy neighbor.
And from what we've heard,
you've always been a man of your word.

Like the roots of the strongest tree,
you give strength to your friends and family.
And anyone who has the luck to meet you, when they're
down you can pick them right up-up.
Pops, we love you, yes we do . . .

Pop loved it and was thrilled when Stevie, Marvin, Diana, and Smokey decided to record it as a commercial release, produced by my niece Iris, who was running the Creative Division at that time. I was thrilled with what they did as well.

Up till the day Pop died, November 21, 1978, he remained the pillar of mental and physical strength.

Pop often used to say, "You can give without lovin' but you cain't love without givin'," and sure enough he loved and gave to me with a capacity I have never found in anyone else. When I'd talk to most people I knew, they'd usually want to talk about the big hits or how much money I was making, but whenever Pop saw me the first thing he would always say was something like, "How ya' feelin' son? Gettin' enough rest? Are ya' happy?"

He was the greatest man in the world, he loved me unconditionally, and in so many ways let me know I was his boy.

That day on the podium in Detroit, in the hard-driving rain, standing beside Michael Jackson, my sister Esther and the mayor of Detroit, Coleman Young, I thought about my parents, Mother and Pop. I wished they could have been there to feel what I was feeling— pride. It was the same kind of pride I had on the night of *Motown 25*. Not just in myself and in Michael, but in Detroit, my home, the place that had nurtured me. And the museum, which would be the messenger of our history for generations to come. Not just a history of singing and dancing and building entertainers, but much more— a history of a black entrepreneurship that gave all people an opportunity to reach their full potential. We had done that at Hitsville where young people had learned how to write, produce, think, make choices. The choices they made and the dreams they followed all contributed to the magic that was Motown.

For a moment I was that eight-year-old kid again, running out of the house after Joe Louis had knocked out Max Schmeling, thinking, "How could I ever do anything in my life that could make this many people happy?"

And in that one moment, I thought maybe I had come close.

FURTHER ACKNOWLEDGMENTS

In addition to those I acknowledged at the beginning of the book, there are others I would like to thank who in one way or another played a part in my life story:

Muhammad Ali, Napoleon "Snags" Allen, Richard "Pistol" Allen, Jack Andrews, Army Archerd, Jack Ashford, Clarence Avant, Bob Babbitt, Burt Bacharach, Tom Baird, Jack Ballard, Frank Banyai, Ernie Barnes, Terry Barnes, H. B. Barnum, Ben Barrett, Pierre Bass, Benny Benjamin, Bob Birndorf, Louis Blau, David Blumberg, Avrum Bluming, Milt Bogrow, Hamilton Bohannon, George Bohanon, Ashley Boone, Dick Boone, Jeffrey Bowen, Ruth Bowen, Booker Bradshaw, John Britton, Jack Brokensha, Earl Brooks, Eddie "Bongo" Brown, Jim Brown, Larry Brown, Ollie Brown, Sonny Burke, Jheryl Busby, G. C. Cameron, James Carmichael, Barbara Carrera, Diahann Carroll, Carol Caruso, Tommy Chapman, George Christy, Dave Clark, Jane Clark, Tom Clay, Jim Cleaver, Dennis Coffey, Hazel Coleman, Robert Coleman, Dino Conte, Don Cornelius, Hank Cosby, Suzanne Coston, John Coursey, Bob Cousar, Warren Cowan, Frankie Crocker, Greg Crockett, Jim Crook, Sandra Crouch, Tony D'Anna, Bobby Darin, Clive Davis, Sammy Davis, Jr., Lloyd Dayes, Al DiNoble, Mike Douglas, Charlene Duncan, John Dunn, Ken East, Glen Eaton, Tomiko Eaton, Billy Eckstine, Shirley Eder, Herb Eiseman, King Errisson, Ahmet Ertegun, Yvonne Fair, Wilton Felder,

410

Jose Feliciano, Pete Felleman, Lester Felton, Bill Fitelson, Lon Fontaine, Don Foster, George Fowler, Rev. C. L. Franklin, Fred Freed, Gordon Frewin, Jimmy Garrett, David Geffen, Gertrude Gibson, Gloria Gilbert, Lee Gladden, Vivianne Gladden, Richard Gold, Leonard Goldberg, Martin Goldfarb, Marc Gordon, all the Gordy nieces, nephews and in-laws, including those who worked at the company: Denise, Desiree, Gregory, Iris, Karen, Linda, Patrice, Robert, Jr., Rodney, Roxanna, Tommy, and Robert Bullock; Debra Gorney, Dick Grace, Cornelius Grant, Ed Greene, Booker Griffin, Merv Griffin, Rita Griffin, Johnny Griffith, Al Gross, Bernie Grundman, Peggi Hager, Alex Haley, Dave Hamilton, Barry Harris, Maggie Hathaway, Burl Hechtman, Lois Hicks, Karen Hodge, Doris Holland, Brenda Holloway, Patrice Holloway, Robert E. Holmes, Daryl Houston, Thelma Houston, Buddy Howe, Joe Hunter, Chuck Jackson, McKinley Jackson, James Jamerson, Dani Janssen, Tommie Johnson, Ardena Johnston, Gerrie Gooden-Jones, Gloria Jones, Ken Jones, Quincy Jones, Regina Jones, Tony Jones, Uriel Jones, Ron Kaplan, Casey Kasem, Mary Kelly, Leon Isaac Kennedy, Kum Sook Kim, Coretta Scott King, Al Klein, Charles Koppelman, Ed Landry, Bill Lane, John Laragh, Mel Larson, Floria Lasky, Abe Lastfogel, Ernie Leaner, Norman Lear, Johnny Lee, Archie Levingston, the Lewis Sisters, Jack Lorenz, Peter Love, Jay Lowy, Clyde A. Luck, Jr., Michael Lushka, Si Mael, Jerry Marcellino, Wade Marcus, Teena Marie, Rose Merie Marion, John Marshall, Diane Martin, Michael Masser, John Matousek, Candace Mayeron, George "Sye" McArthur, Ray McCann, Clarence McDonald, Carrie McDowell, Gerald McFarland, Nate McKalpain, John McKune, Clay McMurray, Larry McMurtry, Barbara McNair, Curtis McNair, Bruce McNall, Quinton McRae, Benny Medina, Sue Mengers, Joe Messina, Sidney Miller, Bernice Morrison, Marshall Murphy, Carol Needham, John O'Den, Nikki Oliver, Terry Ormsbee, Mike Ossman, Mo Ostin, Gene Page, Ray Parker, Jr., Gino Parks, Johnny Pate, Don Peake, Gene Pello, Barney Perkins, Vince Perrone, Ed Pollack, Doryce Postles, Gordon Prince, Peter Prince, John Ramsey, Jimmy Raskin, Russ Regan, Robert Richey, Jr., Berry Berope Robinson, Ruth Robinson, Robert Robitaille, John Rockwell, Gwendolyn Rooks, Rona Rose, Robert Rosenthal, Ernestine Ross, Fred Ross, Jr., Lenny Ross, Jr., Frank

Rothman, Jimmy Ruffin, Barbara Rush, Mark Saginor, Abdul "Chiefy" Salaam, Alan Salke, Joe Sample, Van Gordon Sauter, Carolyn Sautter, Joe Schaffner, Bobby Schiffman, Tom Schlesinger, Jerry Schoenith, Tom Schoenith, Jimmy Schwartz, Robin Seymour, Robert Shapiro, Simone Sheffield, Gene Shelby, Louis Shelton, Bunky Sheppard, Richard Sherman, Willie Shorter, Alfie Silas, Lester Sill, Joe Smith, Michael Smith, Ariane "Honey" Sorps, Aaron Spelling, Katharine Stalford, Gordon Staples and the Detroit Symphony Strings, John Staunton, Larry Stephens, Michael Stokes, Ron Strasner, Troy Stratos, Tony Suglia, Joe Summers, Marv Tarplin, Ed Tawil, LeBaron Taylor, Mike Terry, Norman Thrasher, Alex Tovar, Earl Van Dyke, Tata Vega, Stanley Vogel, Ronnie Wakefield, David T. Walker, Ken Walker, Dale Warren, "Wah Wah" Watson, David Watts, William Weatherspoon, Myrna Webb, Jerry Weintraub, Wayne Weisbart, Sam Weisbord, Norman Weiss, Jay Weston, Jerry Wexler, Robert White, Reggie Wiggins, Amos Wilder, Ernie Wilkins, Andre Williams, Blinky Williams, Eddie Willis, Leroy Willis, David Wolper, Sonny Woods, Benjamin F. Wright, Jr., Greg Wright, Syreeta Wright, Richard "Popcorn" Wylie, Henry Wynn, Bernard Yeszin, Lee Young, Jr., Lee Young, Sr., Margaret Zito.

RELEASED COMPOSITIONS
BY BERRY GORDY

WRITTEN WITH ROQUEL BILLY DAVIS (AKA TYRAN CARLO)

Actions Speak Louder Than Words
Father Dear
I'm Wanderin'
It's So Fine
The Magic Song
Oo Shucks
Reet Petite
She Don't Love You
So Good
Soda Pop
Vacation Time
Who Wouldn't Love A Man Like That

WRITTEN WITH GWEN GORDY AND ROQUEL BILLY DAVIS (AKA TYRAN CARLO)

All I Could Do Was Cry
Hit And Runaway Love

413

I'll Be Satisfied
Just For Your Love
Lonely Teardrops
Oops, I'm Sorry
That's Why (I Love You So)
To Be Loved
You
You Got What It Takes
You Made A Fool Out Of Me

WRITTEN WITH WILLIAM "SMOKEY" ROBINSON

Ain't It Baby
All I Want Is You
Bad Girl
Broken Hearted
Custer's Last Man
Don't Say Bye Bye
Dynamite
Easier Said Than Done
The Feeling Is So Fine
Fire Fly
I Cry
I Love Your Baby
I Need A Change
I Need Some Money
I'm Gonna Cry
Insane
It
It's Me
It's Out Of The Question
Money
A New Girl
Oh I Apologize
The Old Miner
Shop Around

That Child Is Really Wild
That's The Way I Feel
Two Wrongs Don't Make A Right
Way Over There
Who's The Fool
Yes No, Maybe So
(You Can) Depend On Me
You Never Miss A Good Thing

WRITTEN WITH THE CORPORATION
(Alphonso Mizell, Freddie Perren, Deke Richards)

ABC
Bless You
Coming Home
Don't Let Your Baby Catch You
Goin' Back To Indiana
I Found That Girl
I Want You Back
I Will Find A Way
If I Have To Move A Mountain
I'm Gonna Get You
I'm So Happy
It's Great To Be Here
Live It Up
The Love You Save
Mama's Pearl
Maybe Tomorrow
My Little Baby
Nobody
One More Chance
Petals
She's Good
Sugar Daddy
To Know
We've Got A Good Thing Going

You Made Me What I Am
Your Love Makes It All Worthwhile

WRITTEN WITH ROBERT GORDY

Everyone Was There
Hang On Bill
  and George Gordy
Hold Me Tight
It Hurts To Be In Love
Moonlight On The Beach
Shock
You're Just Like You

WRITTEN WITH MARV JOHNSON

Ain't Gonna Be That Way
Baby Baby Baby
Come To Me
This Heart Of Mine
Whisper

WRITTEN WITH BARNEY ALES

Buttered Popcorn
Christmas Twist
Congo Twist
  and Loucye Gordy Wakefield, Ronald Wakefield
Flying Circle Twist
Mexican Twist
Old Folks Twist
Twist Ala BG
Twistin' Ales Style
Twisting The World Around

White House Twist
and Brian Holland

COMPOSITIONS WITH VARIOUS WRITERS

All The Love I've Got
Brian Holland, Janie Bradford
Angel
Charles Leverett, William Sanders, Robert Bateman
The Battle Song (I'm The One)
Willie Hutch
The Bingo Long Song (Steal On Home)
Ronald Miller, Berry Gordy IV
Blue Cinderella
Janie Bradford
Check Yourself
David English, Otis Williams, Al Bryant
Do I Owe
Alphonso Mizell, Freddie Perren, Deke Richards, Christine Yarian
Don't Leave Me
Robert Bateman, Brian Holland, William Sanders
Don't Let Him Shop Around
William Robinson, Loucye Gordy Wakefield, Ronald Wakefield
Everybody Knew It But Me
Gwen Gordy
Everything For Christmas
Teddy Randazzo
Get It Together
Hal Davis, Donald Fletcher, Mel Larson, Jerry Marcellino
Give Love On Christmas Day
Alphonso Mizell, Freddie Perren, Deke Richards, Christine Yarian
Glasshouse
Charlemagne (James Carmichael, Ronald Miller, Kathy Wakefield)
Going To The Hop
Charles Leverett

Got A Job
William Robinson, Tyran Carlo
Happy Days
Alma McKnight
Hello Detroit
Wille Hutch
I Call It Pretty Music, But The Old Folks Call It The Blues
Clarence Paul
I Don't Want To Take A Chance
William Stevenson
I Love The Way You Love
Mikaljon (Stanley MIKe Ossman, AL Abrams, JOhN Oden)
I Want A Guy
Brian Holland, Freddie Gorman
I Want To Go Back There Again
Chris Clark
If You Should Walk Away
Frank Wilson
I'll Be There
Hal Davis, Willie Hutch, Bob West
I'll Set You Free
Gwen Gordy, Ivy Joe Hunter, Renee Lee Tener
I'm Livin' In Shame
The Clan (Henry Cosby, R. Dean Taylor, Frank Wilson, Pam Sawyer)
I'm So Sorry
Earl Brooks, Lessie Brooks
Is It Him Or Me
Alphonso Mizell, Freddie Perren, Deke Richards, Christine Yarian
Isn't She Pretty
Eddie Kendricks, Otis Williams
Jim Dandy Got Married
Tyran Carlo, Alonzo Tucker, Lincoln Chase, Albert Green
The Joke's Not On Me
Gwen Gordy, Janie Bradford
Love Don't Want To Leave
Alphonso Mizell, Freddie Perren, Deke Richards, Christine Yarian

Love Song
Alphonso Mizell, Freddie Perren, Deke Richards, Christine Yarian
Lover
William Robinson, Brian Holland
Mama
William Robinson, Janie Bradford
Mama Done Told Me
William Robinson, Tyran Carlo
The Man With The Rock And Roll Banjo Band
Clarence Paul
May What He Lived For Live
Esther Gordy Edwards, W. A. Bisson
Midnight Johnny
Thelma Gordy, Richard Street
Money And Me
William Robinson, Freddie Gorman, Janie Bradford
Money (That's What I Want)
Janie Bradford
Motor City
Charles Leverett
Move Mr. Man
Rebecca Nichols
My Beloved
Brian Holland, Charles Leverett
No Matter What Sign You Are
Henry Cosby
Oh Lover
William Robinson, Brian Holland
Oh Mary
William Stevenson
Please Mr. Kennedy
Loucye Gordy Wakefield, Ronald Wakefield
Power
Angelo Bond, Jean Mayer
Reality
Wesley Henderson, Tom Baird

River Of Tears
  Gilbert Martin
Save Me A Star
  Gwen Gordy, Janie Bradford
Seven Day Fool
  Sonny Woods, Tyran Carlo
Someday Pretty Baby
  James Woodley
Sugar Daddy
  William Sanders, Charles Leverett
Sweet Man
  Angelo Bond, William Weatherspoon
Ten Miles Beyond
  Tom Baird
(They Call Me) Cupid
  Brian Holland, Norman Whitfield
Tonight's The Night
  Earl Van Dyke, William Stevenson
Up On The Housetop
  Alphonso Mizell, Freddie Perren, Deke Richards, Christine Yarian
Walk On Don't Look Back
  Alphonso Mizell, Freddie Perren, Deke Richards, Christine Yarian
What Goes Up Must Come Down
  Gwen Gordy
What Have We Got To Lose
  Willie Hutch
Wings Of My Love
  Alphonso Mizell, Freddie Perren, Deke Richards, Christine Yarian
Wrong Man, Right Touch
  Angelo Bond, William Weatherspoon, Iris Gordy, Barbara Mitchell
You've Made Me So Very Happy
  Brenda Holloway, Patrice Holloway, Frank Wilson

BERRY GORDY ALONE

Baby Don't Go
Baby Shake
Bam
Because I Love Her
The Beginning Of The End
Camel Walk
Come On Boy
Day By Day Or Never
Do Right Baby Do Right
Do You Love Me
Don't Be Too Long
Don't Let Her Be Your Baby
Don't Take It Away
Dream Come True
Everybody's Going
Everybody's Talkin' About My Baby
Farewell My Love
Have Yourself A Very Merry Christmas
Here You Come
He's Alright
Hot 'n' Tot
How Can We Tell Him
I Gotta Have Your Lovin'
(I Guess There's) No Love
I Need You
I'm Coming Home
I'm Gonna Stay
I'm Hooked
It Moves Me
It's Gonna Be Hard Times
(I've Got To) Cry Over You
Just Let Me Know
Keep Me
Let Me Go The Right Way
Let Me Love You

Let Your Conscience Be Your Guide
Looking For A Man
Magic Mirror
Merry-Go-Round
My Baby's Gone
My Daddy Knows Best
Never Again
Paradise
Part-Time Lover
Play A Sad Song
Please Forgive Me
Poor Sam Jones
Shake Sherrie
Show Me
Snake Walk
So Grateful
That's Where I Lost My Baby
That's Why I Love You So Much
Try It Baby
Was It Worth It
What Makes You Love Him
When Someone's Good To You
Why Do You Want To Let Me Go
Will You Love Me
You Ain't Gonna Find
You Better Get In Line
You Can Cry On My Shoulder
You Don't Want Me No More
You Knows What To Do
You Need Me
You'll Never Cherish A Love So True ('Til You Lose It)
You've Got To Move Two Mountains
Your Baby's Back
Your Love Is Wonderful
Your Wonderful Love

COPYRIGHT ACKNOWLEDGMENTS

423

COPYRIGHT ACKNOWLEDGMENTS

PHOTO CREDITS

PART I

#1	Esther Gordy Edwards
#2–6	The Esther Gordy Edwards Collection
#7	*Color Magazine*
#8	The Esther Gordy Edwards Collection
#9	*Color Magazine*
#10	The Berry Gordy Collection
#11	The Esther Gordy Edwards Collection
#12–14	The Berry Gordy Collection

PART II

#15–21	The Berry Gordy Collection
#22	Frank Dandridge
#23–24	The Berry Gordy Collection
#25	S. Melvin
#26–33	The Berry Gordy Collection
#34	Frank Dandridge
#35	The Berry Gordy Collection
#36	Pierre Bass
#37	Frank Dandridge
#38	The Berry Gordy Collection

PHOTO CREDITS

PART III

PART IV

INDEX

429

INDEX

INDEX

Ross, Ernestine, 156, 202
Ross, Roz, 198
Royster, Juana, 242–43
Ruffin, David, 94, 147–48, 224, 252–53
Rush, Barbara, 279

Saddler, Sandy, 171
Saeta, Eddie, 318
Salke, Alan, 361–62
Sanders, Sonny, 100, 162
Sawyer, Pam, 264–65, 293, 408
Schiffer, George, 181, 250
Schiffman, Frank, 117
Schiller, Larry, 322
Schlatter, George, 266–67, 405
Schlatter, Jolene, 267
Schmeling, Max, 8, 409
Schoenfeld, Joe, 309
Schultz, Michael, 385
Scott, Dick, 278–79
Seltzer, Ralph, 177, 178, 204, 228, 259, 263, 282, 387
Shearing, George, 60
Sheinberg, Sid, 82, 391
Sheppard, Bunky, 131
Shore, Dinah, 267
Shorter, Willie, 127
Silberstein, Bob, 300, 301, 364
Silberstein, Rhonda, 301, 385–86, 403
Sill, Lester, 388–89
Simmons, Gene, 364
Simpson, Valerie, 225–26, 355
Sims, Lloyd, 39–40
Sinatra, Frank, 159, 209, 228, 267
Singleton, Eddie, 189
Skouras, Daniel, 83
Smalls, Tommy (Dr. Jive), 134
Smith, Gary, 209
Smith, Harold, 43, 44–45
Smith, Maggie, 324
Smothers, Tommy, 279
Spencer, Crathman, 94
Springfield, Dusty, 210
Starr, Edwin, 293, 294
Starr, Ringo, 210
Steiner, Armin, 127
Stepin Fetchit, 10, 251
Stevenson, Mickey, 124, 126, 144, 147, 148, 150, 158–59, 160, 176, 177, 178, 179, 186, 196–97, 199, 202, 203, 226, 227, 229–31, 243–44
Stewart, Art, 295

Street, Richard, 254, 372
Strong, Barrett, 122, 123, 128, 144, 272, 293
Strong, Nolan, 100
Stubbs, Levi, 149, 184, 223, 260, 371, 372
Sullivan, Ed, 206, 221, 285
Syracuse, Joe, 93, 110, 113

Taimak, 385
Tarnopol, Nat, 87, 90, 97
Tarplin, Marv, 223
Taylor, Bobby, 279
Taylor, R. Dean, 264
Teena Marie, 363
Temple, Shirley, 10
Terrana, Russ, 295
Terrell, Ernie, 289
Terrell, Jean, 289
Terrell, Tammi, 225, 226, 256
Terry, Wallace, 249
Thompson, Carolyn, 404
Thompson, Ralph, 246
Tidyman, Ernest, 303
Till, Emmett, 166
Tillman, Georgeanna, 153, 160
Townsend, Ed, 326
Turk-Johnson, Evelyn, 86, 177
Tyson, Cicely, 324

Ullmann, Liv, 324

Van dePitte, David, 303
Van Dyke, Earl, 124, 208, 210, 211
Vanity, 385
Vaughan, Sarah, 73
Vigoda, Johanan, 304, 357

Wakefield, Ron, 160
Walker, Jack, 136
Walker, Junior, 160, 225, 371
Ward, Singin' Sammy, 94, 156
Washington, Booker T., 23
Washington, Dinah, 73
Wasserman, Lew, 82, 391
Waters, Maxine, 194
Waters, Mira, 353, 360
Waters, Muddy, 60
Watkin, David, 341
Weintraub, Linda, 349
Weintraub, Sy, 34, 257, 258
Weisenfeld, Sue, 170
Wells, Bryan, 228
Wells, Mary, 139–40, 141, 144, 150, 156, 158, 160, 164,

165, 176, 178, 180, 185, 186–88, 190, 196, 222, 243, 245, 371
West, Bob, 287
Weston, Jay, 309, 311
Weston, Kim, 160, 196
White, Granville (Granny), 131
White, Jim, 310–11
White, Robert, 124, 295
White, Ronnie, 91, 148, 223, 371
Whitfield, Norman, 177, 178, 224, 230, 253, 263, 272, 273, 274–77, 293–94, 327–28, 355
Williams, Andre, 100
Williams, Billy Dee, 314, 316–17, 334, 335, 336, 340, 348, 349
Williams, Milan, 358
Williams, Otis, 147–48, 254, 327
Williams, Paul, 147–48, 254, 256
Willis, Eddie, 124–25
Wilson, Frank, 254, 264, 289, 290
Wilson, Jackie, 74, 86–90, 91, 93–94, 96, 97, 106, 112, 127, 133, 140, 165, 170, 228, 252, 281, 370, 378
Wilson, Mary, 146–47, 202, 233–34, 254–55, 256, 266, 289, 378–79, 380
Wilson, Nancy, 251
Winehead Willie, 156
Wingate, Eddie, 160
Wonder, Stevie, 148–49, 150, 168, 173–75, 198, 206, 209, 226, 227, 228, 236, 240–41, 251, 293, 303–5, 328–29, 330–31, 356–57, 358, 359–60, 362, 367, 372–73, 391–92, 393, 400–401, 408
Woods, Georgie, 131, 132, 135
Woods, Sonny, 244
Wright, Syreeta, 304, 393

Yablans, Frank, 318–21
Young, Chuck, 246
Young, Coleman, 409
Young, Lee, Jr., 81–82, 391, 394
Young, Lester, 313
Young, Wanda, 153, 160

432